www.brookscole.com

www.brookscole.com is the World Wide Web site for Thomson Brooks/Cole and is your direct source to dozens of online resources.

At *www.brookscole.com* you can find out about supplements, demonstration software, and student resources. You can also send email to many of our authors and preview new publications and exciting new technologies.

www.brookscole.com
Changing the way the world learns®

CASE STUDIES

in

CHILD, ADOLESCENT,

and

FAMILY TREATMENT

Craig Winston LeCroy
Arizona State University

Janice M. Daley
Arizona State University

THOMSON

BROOKS/COLE

Australia • Canada • Mexico • Singapore • Spain
United Kingdom • United States

Executive Editor: Lisa Gebo
Assistant Editor: Alma Dea Michelena
Editorial Assistant: Sheila Walsh
Marketing Manager: Caroline Concilla
Marketing Assistant: Mary Ho
Advertising Project Manager: Tami Strang
Project Manager, Editorial Production: Candace Chen
Art Director: Vernon Boes
Print Buyer: Lisa Claudeanos
Permissions Editor: Joohee Lee

Production Service: Jamie Armstrong,
   G & S Book Services
Copy Editor: Laurie Baker
Illustrator: G & S Book Services
Cover Designer: Cheryl Carrington
Cover Image: Battered running shoes,
   © Tim Brown/Getty Images
Cover/Text Printer: Webcom
Compositor: G & S Book Services

Library of Congress Control Number: 2004102949

ISBN 0-534-52455-9

Thomson Brooks/Cole
10 Davis Drive
Belmont, CA 94002
USA

Asia
Thomson Learning
5 Shenton Way #01-01
UIC Building
Singapore 068808

Australia/New Zealand
Thomson Learning
102 Dodds Street
Southbank, Victoria 3006
Australia

Canada
Nelson
1120 Birchmount Road
Toronto, Ontario M1K 5G4
Canada

Europe/Middle East/Africa
Thomson Learning
High Holborn House
50/51 Bedford Row
London WC1R 4LR
United Kingdom

Latin America
Thomson Learning
Seneca, 53
Colonia Polanco
11560 Mexico D.F.
Mexico

Spain/Portugal
Paraninfo
Calle Magallanes, 25
28015 Madrid, Spain

Contents

SECTION III
Case Studies in Group Treatment   105

SECTION IV
Case Studies in School-Based Treatment   157

Preface

This book relies on a successful formula for teaching students about clinical practice—the case study method. Because of the success of an earlier effort that focused more generally on social work practice, *Case Studies in Social Work Practice,* we thought it would be equally valuable to create a case study book for students and practitioners working with children, adolescents, and their families. Also, we designed this book for *all* helping professions—counseling, psychology, social work, and family therapists—who work directly with children and adolescents. We invited noted practitioners and scholars from many diverse professions to make contributions to this edited volume.

Why Use This Book?

The motivation behind assembling a case studies book was to present to students material that is interesting, lively, action based, and pragmatic. We believe that case studies can help students learn the knowledge and skills needed to conduct clinical practice by actively engaging them in the material. Case studies are an action-oriented educational tool because they provide students with the opportunity to vicariously participate in the process of doing clinical work. Because of this participation in clinical work, there is a corresponding increase in interest and motivation for learning.

This book can be used in a wide number of classes and educational settings. Because it is a series of case studies, the material is flexible and can be used in many different ways. For example, because the book presents a diverse range of material, it could be used to teach students about the range and diversity of clinical work. Here the focus may be more about the fields of practice, organizational settings, and different roles that clinicians embrace. It could also be used as a primary or supplemental text for more advanced courses on clinical work with children and families. It would be an ideal text for a specific course on counseling with children and adolescents. Furthermore, this book may be of use in a field seminar course or as a guidebook for students in clinical internships. More ideas for organizing the case studies into units of learning are offered later in the section titled "How to Use This Book."

To the Student and Instructor

The purpose of this book is to help students learn to integrate theory and practice by studying how practitioners have applied clinical principles to particular case situations in the real world. In order to facilitate learning, each case study begins with a set of questions. These questions are designed to help the student engage with the material, to stimulate critical thinking, and to promote classroom discussion.

As students read these case studies, they can be encouraged to think about the cases as if they were the practitioners. How would you feel if confronted with this case? What stands out as important in this particular case and why? Do you agree with the approach taken by the practitioner? What alternative methods would you consider with this case? Classroom discussions can investigate the judgments made by the clinicians and what is considered good or bad about the approach taken in each case. Some suggestions about how these case studies can be used in the classroom include:

1. Have students think about what they might have done differently and why.
2. Have students write out treatment plans based on the case.
3. Have students describe and analyze policies, organizational factors, and ethical issues inherent in the case studies.
4. Have students gather theoretical and empirical studies that could have been useful to the practitioner in each case.
5. Conduct role-plays in which students act out the roles of the practitioners and clients in each case.

Our hope is that students and instructors can use these case studies to stimulate critical, analytical, and objective thinking about clinical practice. As a case is discussed, a number of perspectives are likely to emerge. Within this context, underlying assumptions about human behavior and clinical practice can be brought out in a discussion. Most importantly, the interaction and exchange of ideas can promote an atmosphere of critical discussion. Too often, clinical case presentations are accepted without critique and analysis—limiting the learning that can occur. We hope that as students and instructors move from case to case, they will begin to develop an accumulation of experience in thinking and reasoning as applied to the different case material presented, resulting in more effective clinical practice.

How This Book Is Organized

There are six sections to this book:

  I. Common Disorders of Childhood
 II. Individual and Family Treatment
III. Group Treatment
 IV. School-Based Treatment
  V. Child Welfare
 VI. Using Practice Evaluation

We have provided a brief overview at the beginning of each section to acquaint the reader with the topic area and to offer a thumbnail sketch of each case study included in the section. Each section includes four or five case studies. The alert reader will immediately notice that some of the case studies included in a particular section might be just as easily incorporated into another. For example, we have included Bogas's chapter on a child with ADHD in Section I, Common Disorders of Childhood, although it could fit just as snugly into Section IV, Family Treatment. Similarly, so much of the work with children and adolescents truly includes family involvement that we could have placed 70 percent of the case studies in the whole book in that section! That would not have helped our readers, however. In the end, we opted to group the case studies into these six categories because they seemed to represent useful frames of reference for students, instructors, and practitioners. We urge readers to peruse all of the case studies, but these broad section areas can guide reading selections for those with limited time.

As mentioned previously, each case study contains information that could apply to many aspects of clinical work. To make the case studies even more accessible, we have provided a "topic table" on the front and back covers of this book. The table contains at-a-glance information about each case study based on the following criteria:

- Case number
- Practice area
- Developmental issue
- Diversity
- Client group
- Values and ethics
- Social and economic justice
- Research and policy

By scanning this table, the reader may "create" a chapter or select a group of case studies to examine, based on any of these organizing topics. This book, for example, is rich in culturally diverse content. By scanning the column under "Diversity," it is possible to locate a case study on a depressed African American adolescent from Section I, an empowerment group for Mexican American girls in Section III, and treatment of a teenage Hmong boy in Section IV, just to name a few. We invite the reader to be creative. While we hope that our original organizing scheme is useful, the grid should make further fine tuning of lesson plans or areas of inquiry possible to achieve.

One last note on organization: Many case study books that we have seen in the past seem to include an exciting range of clinical experience, but in our estimation the structure imposed on the authors of each study seems overly restrictive. When we asked for contributions to this book, we asked the noted practitioners to *tell us the story of the case*. For example, we intentionally avoided asking authors to offer a DSM diagnosis for each case, justify it, and finish with conclusions about the accuracy of that diagnosis. We preferred to extract a more "organic" representation of the clinician's experience in the field. We asked them to tell us the story as it unfolded for them. We believe that this approach creates a more interesting, varied, and ultimately more realistic representation of the process of clinical work. We hope that you find the stories to be as interesting, moving, and instructional as we have found them to be.

Acknowledgments

This book would not exist without the many authors who graciously agreed to contribute a case study. We appreciate their efforts and their patience throughout the process. While many people helped to make this a successful project, we would particularly like to thank Alma Dea Michelena at Thomson Brooks/Cole for her constant encouragement and helpful suggestions.

We are also grateful to the following people who reviewed the book: Kathleen Jasook Bergquist, Illinois State University; Stephanie Craig, Keuka College; Gail Folaron, Indiana University, Purdue University Indianapolis; Raymond Lorion, University of Pennsylvania; Gordon MacNeil, University of Alabama; and James Herbert Williams, Washington University.

Contributors

JACK ARBUTHNOT, PH.D.
Professor Emeritus of Psychology
Ohio University
Athens, OH

SKYLAR ARBUTHNOT
Student
University of Washington
Seattle, WA

MARCIA BAAB, MA
Literacy Specialist
Clark County School District
Las Vegas, NV

MARY JO BARRETT
Associate Professor
School of Social Work
University of Chicago
Chicago, IL

LINDSAY BICKNELL-HENTGES, PH.D.
Associate Professor
Department of Psychology
Chicago State University
Chicago, IL

BETTY J. BLYTHE, PH.D.
Professor
School of Social Work
Boston College
Chestnut Hill, MA

SUSAN BOGAS, PH.D.
Private Practice
Princeton, NJ

PHYLLIS BOOTH, MA
Clinical Director
Theraplay Institute Chicago
Chicago, IL

HARRIET COBB, ED.D.
Professor
Department of Graduate Psychology
James Madison University
Harrisonburg, VA

JOANNE N. CORBIN, PH.D.
Associate Professor
Smith College for Social Work
Northampton, MA

JACQUELINE CORCORAN, PH.D.
Associate Professor of Social Work
Virginia Commonwealth University
Richmond, VA

KEVIN CORCORAN, PH.D., JD
Professor
Graduate School of Social Work
Portland State University
Portland, OR

JANICE DALEY, MSW
Prevention Program Director
Adjunct Faculty
Tucson Component
Arizona State University
Tucson, AZ

MANDY DAVIS, LCSW
Child Welfare Partnership
Graduate School of Social Work
Portland State University
Portland, OR

KELLY DRAKE, MA
Doctoral Candidate
Department of Psychology
University of Nevada
Las Vegas, NV

DANIEL J. FISCHER, MSW
Department of Psychiatry
University of Michigan Medical Center
Ann Arbor, MI

PETER FITTS, MSW, LCSW-C
Director
Progressive Life Center
Prince George's County, MD

CYNTHIA FRANKLIN, PH.D., LMSW, LMFT
Professor
School of Social Work
University of Texas
Austin, TX

JEWELLE TAYLOR GIBBS, PH.D.
Clinical Psychologist
Zellerbach Family Fund Professor Emerita
School of Social Welfare
University of California at Berkeley
Berkeley, CA

LYNETTE GILMARTIN, M.ED.
Teacher
Tucson Unified School District
Tucson, AZ

NANCY WELLS GLADOW, MA
Social Worker
King County Department of Public Health
Seattle, WA

NORA GUSTAVSSON
Associate Professor
School of Social Work
Arizona State University
Tempe, AZ

JUDY HENIZER, BA
Children and Family Advocate
Tuscon, AZ

JOSEPH A. HIMLE, PH.D.
Department of Psychiatry
University of Michigan Health System
Ann Arbor, MI

LORI K. HOLLERAN, PH.D.
Assistant Professor
School of Social Work
University of Texas
Austin, TX

DEBBIE HUNT, CISW
Supervisor, Child Welfare Training Unit
Arizona State University
Tucson, AZ

MARION HUXTABLE, MSW
School Social Worker
Tucson Unified School District
Tucson, AZ

CHRISTOPHER A. KEARNEY, PH.D.
Professor
Department of Psychology
University of Nevada
Las Vegas, NV

MELISSA C. KUHAJDA
Assistant Professor
Departments of Community and Rural Medicine
    and Psychiatry and Behavioral Medicine
University of Alabama
Tuscaloosa, AL

CRAIG LECROY, PH.D.
Professor
School of Social Work
Tucson Component
Arizona State University
Tucson, AZ

TAMMY LINSEISEN, ACSW, LCSW
Clinical Assistant Professor
School of Social Work
University of Texas
Austin, TX

JOHN E. LOCHMAN, PH.D., ABPP
Professor
Saxon Chairholder in Clinical Psychology
University of Alabama
Tuscaloosa, AL
Adjunct Professor
Department of Psychiatry and Behavioral Sciences
Duke University Medical Center
Durham, NC

JOHN LYNCH, PSY.D.
Associate Professor
Department of Psychology
Chicago State University
Chicago, IL

ANN MACEACHRON
Professor
School of Social Work
Arizona State University
Tempe, AZ

RANDY MAGEN, ACSW, PH.D.
Professor
School of Social Work
University of Alaska
Anchorage, AK

M. SEAN O'HALLORAN, PH.D.
Professor of Counseling Psychology
Psychological Services Clinic Director
Division of Professional Psychology
University of Northern Colorado
Greeley, CO

DEBORAH O'HARA
Parent
Glenview, IL

PETER J. PECORA, PH.D.
Senior Director of Research Services at Casey
    Family Programs
Professor
School of Social Work
University of Washington
Seattle, WA

FREDERICK B. PHILLIPS, PSY.D., MSW
President / CEO
Progressive Life Center
Washington, DC

KAREN L. SALEKIN, PH.D.
Assistant Professor
Clinical Psychology
University of Alabama
Tuscaloosa, AL

A. RENEE STATON, PH.D.
Associate Professor
Counseling Psychology
James Madison University
Harrisonburg, VA

BRUCE A. THYER, PH.D.
Professor
School of Social Work
Florida State University
Tallahassee, FL

TERRY S. TREPPER
Associate Professor
Department of Psychology
Purdue University Calumet
Hammond, IN

LILIANE CAMBRAIA WINDSOR, MSSW
Project Manager
NIDA Substance Abuse Research
    Development Program
School of Social Work
University of Texas
Austin, TX

I

Case Studies in Common Disorders of Childhood and Adolescence

When adults contemplate childhood, they often imagine an idyllic time of innocence and exploration. Unfortunately, for many children, life is fraught with stress. Biological and environmental factors contribute to the development of mental disorders in children, and many young people must struggle to achieve the developmental tasks that lead to a healthy adult life. It is crucial for mental health professionals from all disciplines to consider the common disorders affecting children.

According to Tuma (1989), between 15 and 19 percent of the children in the United States suffer from problems that warrant mental health treatment. The National Mental Health Association (2004) notes that anxiety is the most common type of mental health disorder in children, with up to 10 percent of young people affected. Attention deficit hyperactivity disorder (ADHD) is another one of the most common reasons that children are referred for mental health services, and it is estimated that as many as one in every 20 children is affected (U.S. Department of Health and Human Services, 1999). Depression becomes more and more of an issue as children grow to adolescence. According to the federal Center for Mental Health Services 2003, depression affects as many as one in every 33 children and one in eight adolescents. Eating disorders, while not as prevalent, affect an inordinate percentage of teenage girls. An estimated one percent of female adolescents have anorexia (National Institute of Mental Health, 2001), but upward of 80 percent of teen girls express negative emotions about body image (Desmond, Price, Gray, & O'Connell, 1986) and roughly the same percentage of early-adolescent girls are dieting at any given time (Berg, 1992).

The statistics clearly indicate that children in our society are not living the carefree existence that we would like to imagine. And yet few texts concentrate on treatment of children's mental disorders. When we treat children for physical ailments such as fever, we often use smaller amounts of the same medicine administered to adults. In children's mental health, however, there is no "downsizing" of doses. Instead, practitioners must approach treatment with a very different perspective. A child's unique physical, developmental, gender, social, and environmental factors must be considered carefully prior to and throughout the treatment process. It seems clear that all practitioners, whether they specialize in work with youth or with the broader population, must become acquainted with the common disorders of childhood and methods of helping young clients and their families.

There are four case studies in this section on common disorders of childhood. The first is a case study from Kearney and Drake that focuses on a girl who is experiencing an anxiety disorder. The authors share their insights on the processes of assessment and treatment and offer a detailed description of the predominantly cognitive intervention they employed to help their young client face the world. The second study, by Bogas, relates the tale of a young boy with ADHD. The author describes the important process of establishing rapport with the child, engaging and maintaining parental involvement in treatment, and the necessity of working as part of a treatment "team." The case study by Gibbs paints a picture of a depressed African American adolescent girl. Gibbs describes the importance of considering the client's developmental stage, environmental issues, and sociocultural issues from the very beginning of the case and shares her insights about exploring the client as a person rather than a problem. The chapter closes with a study by O'Halloran about an anorexic girl. The author offers an introspective description of her work with this client and her family through outpatient and inpatient treatment and describes her efforts to uncover the "function" of the client's eating disorder.

Each of these cases provides a window to the world of the practitioner and demonstrates the unique manifestations of common disorders of childhood. The emphasis on treating the individual child and the techniques that the practitioners employ to gain the trust and cooperation of their young clients merit special attention. These stories ring true because they are true (or composite) pictures of children's lives. Students and practicing professionals alike may profit from the glimpse into the treatment of these clients who experience some common disorders of childhood.

References

BERG, F. (1992, July/August). Harmful weight loss practices are widespread among adolescents. *Obesity and Health,* 69–72.

DESMOND, S., PRICE, J., GRAY, N., & O'CONNELL, K. (1986). The etiology of adolescents' perceptions of their weight. *Journal of Youth and Adolescence, 15,* 461–474.

NATIONAL INSTITUTE OF MENTAL HEALTH. (2001). *Eating disorders: Facts about eating disorders and the search for solutions.* Pub No. 01-4901. Retrieved February 2002 from http://www.nimh.nih.gov/publicat/eatingdisorder.cfm.

NATIONAL MENTAL HEALTH ASSOCIATION. (2004). *Anxiety disorders.* Retrieved January 2004 from http://www.nmha.org/infoctr/factsheets/index.cfm#anxiety.

TUMA, J. (1989). Mental health services for children: The state of the art. *American Psychologist, 44*(2), 188–199.

U.S. DEPARTMENT OF HEALTH AND HUMAN SERVICES. (1999). *Mental health: A report of the surgeon general.* Rockville, MD: U.S. Department of Health and Human Services.

Case Study 1-1

Questions for Discussion
1. Why are multiple sources of information important when collecting data about anxiety problems and school refusal behavior?
2. What kinds of behavioral problems do children with anxiety disorders display?
3. The practitioner interviews the child first, without the rest of the family present. What is the purpose of this?
4. How is cognitive therapy (a fairly complicated concept for a child) best presented to children with anxiety disorders?
5. What is the key goal of "exposure-based" therapy and how is it useful in treating children with anxiety disorders?

Case Study in Childhood Anxiety

Christopher A. Kearney and Kelly Drake

One of the most debilitating but least recognized problems among children and adolescents is anxiety. Anxiety disorders are common in youth but not always recognized or treated by laypersons or mental health professionals until a child deteriorates in key areas of functioning (e.g., academic, social, sleep, or eating). The most common anxiety disorders in children include separation anxiety disorder, social anxiety disorder, specific phobia, and generalized anxiety disorder. However, others, such as panic disorder, obsessive-compulsive disorder, and posttraumatic stress disorder, are also seen in youth. In many cases, children with anxiety disorders present with multiple symptoms of anxiety as well as comorbid problems such as depression and oppositional or manipulative behavior. In addition, many of these children present with school refusal behavior and test anxiety. In the following case, we discuss a youth with a range of anxiety problems and school refusal behavior. We discuss the symptoms, assessment, and treatment of this case.

Symptoms

Jessica M. was a 12-year-old multiracial (Hispanic and Caucasian) female who presented with severe problems attending school. She was referred by her parents and her school counselor for missing approximately 35 days of classes since the start of the school year (her assessment was in January, approximately the middle of the academic year). Her school counselor, Mrs. Zinnith, stated in an initial telephone conversation that Jessica began middle school in September with severe somatic complaints such as stomachaches, vomiting, nausea, and occasional headaches. These problems subsided a bit when Jessica was allowed to sit in the counselor's office during times when she felt most stressed. When this became untenable, however, because Jessica was missing many of her classes, she was told she could come to the counselor's office just once per day.

Following this restriction, Jessica missed a few days of school before returning with her mother, who met with Mrs. Zinnith and promised better attendance from her daughter. As a result, Jessica's school attendance throughout much of October and November was good, though spotty at times. In early December, however, students at the school were required to take standardized tests. These tests had no bearing on student grades but occupied 2 entire school days. The tests closely followed midterm examinations in many subjects, and Mrs. Zinnith noted that Jessica was suddenly coming to her office more often. Her nervousness about the tests had escalated and seemed to be interfering with her ability to complete her homework or even attend class. This was true despite Mrs. Zinnith's continued reassurances to Jessica that the standardized tests had nothing to do with her grades.

After Christmas break, Jessica attended school only sporadically. Mrs. Zinnith said that Jessica, when in school, would often cry in her office about the fact that school was too difficult and that no one seemed to like her there. She also made several comments indicating that she missed her family while in school and constantly worried that something bad might happen to them. Of particular concern to Mrs. Zinnith was Jessica's offhand comment that she would be "better off in another place." Mrs. Zinnith took this to be a possible reference to suicidal ideation or worse.

Toward the end of January, Jessica stopped coming to school altogether. A conference with Jessica's parents revealed that they were confused about their daughter's behavior and that she seemed tense and nervous. Both parents worked during the day, which complicated their ability to get Jessica to school. In addition, Mr. and Mrs. M. stated that Jessica was having trouble sleeping and was crying a bit more than usual. It was at this time that Mrs. Zinnith suggested that the family seek therapy from a psychologist who addressed youth with anxiety problems and school refusal behavior.

Assessment: General Procedures

The assessment of youth with anxiety problems and related school refusal behavior usually requires a comprehensive strategy that focuses on multiple sources of information and multiple means of collecting data about the presenting situation. Common sources of information include the child, parents, extended family members, siblings, teachers, guidance counselors, peers, dating partners, and school officials such as attendance officers and nurses. Common means of collecting data include structured diagnostic or unstructured interviews, child self-reports and parent/teacher ratings and questionnaires, behavioral observation, and, in some cases, formal testing.

Structured diagnostic interviews are often used in research-oriented or specialized settings to identify which anxiety disorder criteria are met (e.g., the Anxiety Disorders

Interview Schedule for Children). Most clinicians, however, use an unstructured interview that focuses on certain questions and themes. Questions during an interview with an anxious child often surround the three major response sets to anxiety: physiological, cognitive, and behavioral problems. For example, anxious children often display symptoms of high arousal such as accelerated heart rate, trouble breathing, dizziness, sweating, shaking, and hot flashes. However, some youth, especially those with more general anxiety problems, experience physiological problems such as muscle tension and sleep problems (this was the case for Jessica). It is important during the interview to fully document which physical symptoms are most prevalent during episodes of high anxiety and to have these symptoms medically evaluated later to rule out any organic problem (e.g., ulcer, urinary tract infection, or migraine).

Children with anxiety disorders also commonly display cognitive problems, or irrational thoughts that occur when they are near an anxiety-provoking situation (e.g., oral presentation or meeting someone new). For example, some youth will mistakenly assume that everyone will laugh at them in a given situation, that no one cares about them, that others are plotting against them, that they will necessarily fail a test, that their parents will be harmed, or that they will somehow get into trouble for some act. A common thread to all of these thoughts is an expectation that something "bad" will necessarily happen. For some anxious children, the "bad" event is something internal, such as a fear of losing control of oneself or going crazy. For others, the "bad" event is something external, such as never seeing one's parents again or being embarrassed before one's peers. During the interview, it is important to fully understand the exact thoughts the child is having when entering or experiencing an anxiety-provoking situation.

Children with anxiety disorders also display many behavioral problems, especially avoidance, escape from key situations, constant seeking of reassurance from others (e.g., repeated questions such as "Are you going to pick me up after school?"), and even disruptive behaviors (e.g., temper tantrums or refusal to move) to delay entry into an anxiety-provoking situation. Clinicians should identify which settings are most commonly avoided and which behaviors on the child's part are most disruptive to themselves and their family members. With respect to the latter, this often involves difficulties going to school, sleeping alone, separating from a parent, or attending social events.

Self-report measures are especially useful for this population because children are sometimes the best reporters of their internal mood states and secretive behavior. Therefore, measures of fear, general and social anxiety, depression, social withdrawal, and somatic complaints are often used. Parent and teacher questionnaires may also be used to identify more obvious signs of anxiety such as noncompliance, anxious verbalizations, and sudden changes in behavior. Looking for patterns of responses across all child, parent, and teacher reports is important given that different answers are sometimes given.

Behavioral observation of children with anxiety disorders is helpful as well. Of particular use are observations of the child in natural anxiety-provoking situations (e.g., those at school), although in-session observations can also be instructive. With respect to the latter, for example, a clinician could examine nonverbal behavior that indicates anxiety (e.g., fidgeting, crying, or refusal to separate from a parent), approach behavior toward an actual feared stimulus (e.g., a large dog), or performance during an analogous task (e.g., asking a child to read aloud from a magazine before a small audience).

Formal testing of intelligence, achievement, and personality may also be helpful when addressing a child with anxiety. This testing is sometimes done to check the cognitive status of a child (e.g., to see if cognitive therapy might be useful), to rule out true academic threats (e.g., learning disorder), and to assess for inflexible or maladaptive traits that could interfere with the therapy process.

Assessment: Jessica

Jessica was referred to a specialized university-based clinic that addressed youth with anxiety-related disorders and school refusal behavior. She and her parents were scheduled for an assessment, which was conducted by a clinical psychologist. Jessica was interviewed first as her parents completed various measures of child behavior, family environment, and Jessica's school refusal behavior. As with most cases of anxiety, it is important to interview the child first to convey issues regarding confidentiality and to maintain the impression that the child's input is as valuable as the parents'.

Jessica reported that she felt extremely anxious when going to school. Several reasons accounted for this. First, she was upset at leaving home because of many recent news reports that children were being abducted by strangers. In particular, she was worried that someone might inappropriately approach her or harm her in some way. She also reported vague worries that something could happen to her parents. Second, Jessica stated that she often worried about her performance before others, especially when she had to recite something at school or hand in her homework. In a related vein, she indicated that she had problems meeting new people and that her entry into middle school had been particularly difficult. Many of her current friends were in other classes, although she did see several of them at lunch.

Jessica reported several physical problems when attending school, especially stomachaches, headaches, and tightness in her shoulders. She did not appear to have the high arousal symptoms characteristic of panic attacks, however. Instead, Jessica's main anxiety symptoms appeared to be cognitive in nature—she reported almost uncontrollable worry about personal harm and embarrassment. In particular, she worried about someone hurting her before or after school, people laughing at her when she performed in front of them, teachers harshly criticizing her when she handed in an assignment, and peers rejecting her when she tried to make overtures toward developing friendships. Jessica also responded to the therapist's question about thoughts of harming herself by saying that she often felt sad but had no intention of hurting herself.

With respect to her behavioral symptoms, Jessica stated that school was the primary place that she avoided. However, she did admit that she felt alienated with peers she did not know well at social events such as parties, church gatherings of her youth group, and gymnastics. Her attendance at these events was as sporadic as her school attendance. On a hopeful note, however, Jessica was clear in stating that she wanted to go to school, but needed to feel less anxious to do so.

Jessica's parents conceded that they had little insight into Jessica's physical and cognitive symptoms of anxiety, but did say she often had trouble sleeping. They confirmed Jessica's admission about reluctance to attend social events, but said that she had no problem going out with family members or her small circle of close friends. In addition, both parents admitted to regularly acquiescing to Jessica's misbehavior, such as not going to school. Mrs. M. stated that she was worried that pushing Jessica too much would damage her psychologically, and Mr. M. simply stated that he was too confused about the situation to decide on a certain response.

An examination of the child self-report and parent/teacher questionnaires revealed high levels of social anxiety and worry and some comorbid depressive symptoms. Discussion with several of Jessica's teachers at school confirmed that she was often timid about participating in activities that involved performance before others. No direct behavioral observation was conducted of Jessica in her natural environments, but the therapist noted during Jessica's early appointments that she was shy and uneasy during her interactions with clinic personnel. Based on the total assessment data, Jessica's most salient diagnoses appeared to be social anxiety disorder, generalized anxiety disorder, and separation anxiety disorder. These were primarily related to school-oriented issues, and these were the focus of treatment.

Treatment: General Procedures

Treating children with anxiety disorders often requires a comprehensive strategy to relieve physiological, cognitive, and behavioral symptoms. For youth with high levels of arousal, such as those seen in panic attacks, treatment focuses on controlling unpleasant reactions. Examples include relaxation training and controlled breathing to ease moderate levels of arousal or exposure to strong physical symptoms of anxiety followed by relaxation. In some cases, aversive internal physical symptoms are actually induced in session to allow the client to utilize somatic control exercises, lower the severity of the symptoms, and gain mastery over them. For youth with muscle tension, as with Jessica, tension-release relaxation training is helpful.

For anxious youth with excessive worry or irrational thoughts, cognitive therapy is often helpful. This approach usually takes the form of intensely examining negative or harsh thoughts that a client may have and actively disputing them or encouraging the client to develop alternative and more realistic thoughts. To do so with anxious youth, certain questions may be posed whenever the client reports a negative or unrealistic thought. Examples of such questions include "Am I sure that this will happen?" "Do I really know what others think of me?" "How many times has this terrible thing actually happened?" and "Am I the only person who has ever had to deal with this situation?"

Cognitive therapy is often presented to children in the form of a simple model that they can remember and use. The model requires the child to recognize situations in which she feels anxious, identify thoughts that are irrational, develop alternative thoughts that are more helpful, and praise herself for doing so. For example, a youth may enter a classroom and automatically become nervous and think that everyone is staring at her. In this situation, the child may be taught to recognize the irrational thought (e.g., "everyone is staring at me") and immediately counter it with more realistic thinking (e.g., "perhaps a couple of people are staring, but not everyone"). In addition, the client is taught that the consequences of even the worst-case scenario (e.g., embarrassment) are not always that bad and that the person can cope with or handle the worst-case scenario even if it should occur. The client should also praise herself for using this coping strategy (e.g., "I'm brave for facing my fear").

However, the bulk of therapy for children with anxiety disorders, especially if severe avoidance is present, is exposure based. People with anxiety disorders are encouraged to gradually expose themselves to anxiety-provoking situations in order to (1) use their new somatic control and cognitive skills and (2) learn to habituate or become accustomed to the situation when anxiety eventually lessens. A key goal of exposure therapy is for a person to learn that avoidance of a situation is not necessary for anxiety to decline. Rather, practicing skills that help the person master physiological and cognitive symptoms of anxiety, in addition to becoming used to the situation as practice continues, helps lessen anxiety in general. Parents are encouraged to help initially with exposure-based practices between sessions, although children are later required to engage in exposure to anxiety-provoking situations on their own. In most cases, these exposures are subsequently processed with the therapist, who examines the child's patterns of anxiety.

Treatment: Jessica

Jessica's treatment focused on her muscle tension, worries, avoidance of school and social situations, and some related problems. Much of her weekly session was devoted to work between her and her therapist, but ongoing consultations with her parents, guidance counselor, and teachers were incorporated as well. Jessica's therapy began by educating her about the different response components of anxiety (i.e., physiological, cognitive, and behavioral) and identifying how these were sequenced in her case. Jessica reported that her physical symptoms and worries seemed to happen at the same time and that these usually preceded her desire to avoid or escape a situation. Therefore, the therapist began to address these problems first, but with an eye toward partially reintegrating Jessica into school.

Jessica was taught to tense and release different muscle groups, with special attention paid to areas that seemed to give her the most problems (i.e., facial and shoulder muscles). The therapist assisted with the process at first, but Jessica was later required to practice the procedures at least twice per day and during any times when she felt highly stressed. In addition, she was encouraged to tense and relax her muscles prior to bedtime to reduce tension and perhaps ease sleep.

The bulk of Jessica's therapy, however, involved cognitive therapy and gradual exposure to anxiety-provoking situations. Because of the urgency regarding her school attendance status, Jessica was initially asked to pick three classes that were not too upsetting to her. She chose history, computer, and science classes because these did not involve much performance before others and because she had some friends in those classes. The therapist also encouraged her to attend lunch, to which Jessica agreed. No problems attending these classes were reported over the next several sessions, which provided a nice foundation for later therapy.

At the beginning of Jessica's cognitive therapy, she was required to understand and identify her maladaptive thoughts. A common theme to many of her negative cognitions was catastrophization, in which Jessica would automatically assume highly aversive consequences in certain situations. For example, she was afraid of fainting during oral presentations and of being completely rejected by new potential friends. Jessica logged various thoughts she had in different social situations and identified to which category they belonged (e.g., catastrophization and overgeneralization).

In later sessions, Jessica practiced developing alternative thoughts with the therapist. For example, she came to understand that the likelihood of her fainting in class was remote given that she had never done it before and that people would rush to her aid if she did (the therapist also joked that fainting would help her avoid the situation!). In addition, Jessica explored alternative scenarios to her concerns that others would reject her. Therapy for this partly involved some social skills training so that Jessica could become a more effective converser and listener. She was also given strategies to gracefully exit a certain social situation if it was going badly.

Following several sessions of cognitive therapy and social skills practice, Jessica was given a series of difficult homework assignments. These assignments included exposures to different anxiety-provoking situations in which she would have to control her physiological and cognitive anxiety symptoms. The first exposures included additions of new classes to her daily attendance schedule. She was required to add one new class per week for 3 weeks, and consequences were established at home for nonattendance. As Jessica added classes, she was required to complete make-up work, some of which included previously difficult tasks such as oral presentations in English class and writing and solving arithmetic problems in math class. Jessica's therapist helped her practice these tasks in session beforehand, and Jessica was able to complete all of them in class with mild to moderate amounts of anxiety. Within a short period, she was attending school full time and, with established weekend homework times, caught up with her work.

The remaining therapy sessions over the next several weeks focused on Jessica's social anxiety when meeting new people. Her initial exposures involved meeting new people at the clinic with whom she had to carry out short conversations. Feedback about her performance and cognitions was regularly supplied by the therapist and Jessica's parents, who praised her for her effort and courage. Later, Jessica was required to approach different people at school to say hello, call her friends and acquaintances more often, and attend parties and church functions more independently. After each social event, Jessica and her therapist would dissect what happened and explore any problems that Jessica had. As therapy progressed, Jessica became more proficient at social situations and her daily levels of anxiety declined to only a mild level.

Long-Term Functioning

Jessica's therapy lasted almost four months, and she was functioning socially at a much more effective level than before treatment. Her secondary depressive and sleep symptoms had also dissipated, although Jessica had lingering worries about her family and her own social skills. In many anxious youth, booster sessions are sometimes needed to reinforce anxiety management skills, and this was the case for Jessica prior to the next school year. Her long-term prognosis, however, is considered good.

Case Study 1-2

Questions for Discussion

1. How does the practitioner establish rapport with the ADHD youth during the first session? Why does she delay gathering background information during the first session?
2. Why is it important for the parents to provide tight external controls for the client in this case study?
3. What is the length of the therapeutic relationship in this case study? Why? Could or should it be any different?
4. Why does the practitioner explore each parent's childhood with them? How does that contribute to the treatment?
5. What is the important factor in finding a "treatment team" to work with an ADHD child?

A Child with ADHD

Susan Bogas

Nate, age 7, could not find his favorite army men. Ellen, his mother, told him to look in his closet. Like a wild creature springing from nowhere and without a step toward the closet, Nate burst into a frenzied campaign. He stomped around the room, kicking the furniture and toys in his path and screaming as loudly as he could.

Nate's sudden escalation from calm to rage, without warning and seemingly unprovoked, was all too familiar to Ron and Ellen, Nate's parents. They did not know what made him react to an ordinary situation with such fury, and they could not predict when, and over what, an explosion would occur. They had learned, however, that there would be another incident and that during such incidents there was no reasoning with Nate. "When Nate is angry," Ellen explained. "It's as if he were possessed. His emotions come out very fast. He 'spews'. . . and has to go to his room to calm down, to regain control. He then comes down and feels remorseful."

This was a typical event in the Barclay household at the time that Nate's parents brought him to therapy. They were baffled by their third child's total inability to tolerate frustration, to be patient, and to cope with the routines and challenges of daily life. The point had come when they knew they needed help.

I had known this family, which included three boys (John, 18, Peter, 15, and Nate, 7), for more than five years. I treated their oldest son for procrastination (which turned out to be ADHD), their next son for adolescent social issues, and the couple for marital issues. Ron, a tall, thin businessman, combines a curious, incisive mind with a fierce task-oriented mentality. Ellen, a stay-at-home mom, is bright, outgoing, and energetic. She has a gift for words and great warmth and humor.

Ellen read widely about attention problems in relation to her first son and began to be concerned about Nate when he was in kindergarten. Nate was always in motion. He asked to listen to story time from under his desk. In first grade, he was in trouble a lot. At the end of first grade, the Barclays took Nate to a specially trained pediatrician who administered a "neurodevelopmental" evaluation (developed by Mel Levine, M.D., an expert in attention and learning problems). The pediatrician diagnosed Nate with attention deficit hyperactivity disorder, but found no significant learning deficits such as problems with memory, language, higher-order thinking, motor skills, or social ability.

First Session

There was no hint of negativity or defiance in Nate at the first therapy session in my office. I didn't even detect fidgetiness. Nate was tall, blond, and cute. He looked a bit wide-eyed and serious, as if he anticipated hearing a lot about how *bad* he was. As I chatted with him, asking about his friends and what they liked to do, he relaxed and told me that he loved playing with boys in his neighborhood, especially on his trampoline. Once I sensed he was comfortable, I offered Nate the option of drawing at a table in a corner of my office. It was time to hear his parents' concerns. I wanted to allow Nate to listen and to participate in the discussion, but also to have some distance from us.

He made a beeline for the table, took a chair facing the wall, and began to draw. Ron and Ellen talked about two key problems with which they struggled daily. First, Nate refused to sleep in his own room. Afraid to be alone, he slept downstairs where his parents were early in the evening and, later, beside their bed. They had no time for themselves. Second, he was extremely uncooperative. He opposed absolutely everything, refused to perform his routines and responsibilities, and defied directions and suggestions. His answer to everything was an emphatic and instant "NO!"

Ellen, who handled Nate's daily behavior, was at her "wits' end." Her stress was palpable. I decided to delay gathering background information or going over the evaluation they brought with them, steps I might have taken if the immediate situation was not so pressing. The priority was to deal in a practical way with the problems at hand. We turned to problem solving, leaving for later discussion the more theoretical questions about Nate's ADHD, its etiology and particular nature. For the first session, my goal was to develop a "map," or a structured plan, for each of the two presenting problems to be carried out by the family at home.

Nate had said earlier that he feared sleeping alone in his own room because someone could come in the window and "something bad will happen." I asked Nate, busy drawing monster and animal-like figures with big teeth, what he thought about this. He said he was embarrassed about it. His two friends slept in their own rooms, although with brothers, and he would really like to sleep in his room. I was impressed by his candor and glad to hear he was motivated to change. I suggested an interim plan. Instead of Nate falling asleep in the same room as his parents, he would fall asleep in the next room. Nate would be in the dining room, with his parents in the kitchen. Each night that he complied, he would receive a small daily reward. If this was successful, then Nate would gradually move to falling asleep in his own room. Ron proposed moving Nate's bed away from the window and closer to the door to allay his fears of someone coming in the window. He also proposed the ultimate "carrot": When Nate was able to sleep most nights in his own room, he would be given an allowance, something he wanted very much because he associated it with his older brothers.

On the second issue, Ellen gave an example of Nate's opposition to almost anything she asked him. "If I ask, 'what do you want for breakfast—pancakes?,' Nate's typical response is 'no.' I try again. 'Cereal?' 'No!' 'Waffle?' 'No!' Finally Nate will announce: 'I want pancakes! Pancakes!'" Such interactions went on all the time and left Ellen worn out and exasperated.

Explaining further, Ellen astutely observed that her own disciplinary style was that of a "negotiator." She operated with a win/win approach to situations. She knew that it did not come naturally to her to be firm, to draw the line, or to lay down the directives in black-and-white terms. Ron, by contrast, noted that he was firm and tough. However, he acknowledged that he became angry quickly and exploded when Nate did not comply.

To me, it was clear that the family's authority system needed to be organized and tightened in order for Nate to develop better internal controls. Ellen and Ron had to learn to operate from a "policy" rather than reacting to their son's behavior, either with appeasement or anger. I introduced them to the basics of setting limits and delivering consequences. My intervention, a combination of structural family therapy developed by Salvador Minuchin, Braulio Montalvo, and Jay Haley and the theories found in *1-2-3 Magic,* a book by Thomas Phelan (1996), went like this:

The child has two choices—comply with the request or take the consequence.

Lack of cooperation (refusing to make a choice) leads to a consequence.

Devise ready-to-use short- and long-term lists of consequences.

Do not engage in conversation when setting limits (actions—such as losing a play date, going to his room, or suffering an "electrical black-out"—speak louder than words).

Noncompliance with the direction or the consequences results in a time-out.

As I laid out the principles, Ellen recognized the difference between her approach to Nate's behavior and what I was advocating. Her approach amounted to appeasement, and what she needed to do was to be an authority figure. Ellen said she thought that if she negotiated so that Nate got something he wanted and she got the behavior she wanted from him, then he would be motivated to cooperate. I explained to Ellen and Ron that the reason Nate needed an authority figure was that due to ADHD with impulsivity and hyperactivity, he lacked the inner controls to contain his own behavior. He needed Ellen, as his primary caretaker, and Ron to provide tight external controls so that he could, first, learn to function responsibly and, second, gradually develop stronger inner controls himself.

The other issue I stressed was that parents must become a team. Together they must learn the skills of conflict resolution; that is, how to compromise and come to an agreement about their "policy" toward Nate. I emphasized the following:

> Expectations and consequences for Nate must be clear and precise, and the presentation of these expectations is to be in a visual mode (preferably a chart, with pictures).

From our previous work together, I knew that this couple had a strong commitment—to each other and to their children. I also knew there were some difficulties and disagreements between Ron and Ellen that would emerge and would have to be dealt with if they were to make headway. I closed our first session with a warning intended to focus them on whether they, as parents, were presenting Nate with one message or two different messages. "If you two are not absolutely clear, meaning that you deliver one 'airtight' message, and then absolutely consistent in setting expectations and carrying through on consequences, there will be no change."

Two Months Later: Ellen at the Breaking Point

The next session excluded Nate in order to allow Ellen and Ron to speak candidly and at length about their concerns. Nate had responded somewhat to the structures related to sleep. He was beginning to sleep in his own room and to earn an allowance. However, he did backslide sometimes, and the issue was by no means solved. Nevertheless, the Barclays were pleased and relieved because following the step-by-step plan showed them that Nate could make progress if they provided him with appropriate structure. Nate was proud to join his brothers in earning an allowance, and the Barclays now had some time for themselves in the evening.

Ellen, however, continued to be extremely upset over Nate's opposition to anything she asked him to do and the verbal attacks that followed. Tears overcame her as she described the ongoing obstacles that Nate presented to her every statement, request, or direction. "I hate you!" "You're mean!" "You're stupid!" "I wish you weren't my mother!" "I hate this family!" "I hate my life!" These were just some of the things he had said to her. With a mixture of desperation and sadness, Ellen said, "He doesn't like me. He doesn't want to be around me. Nothing I do works." I felt the gravity of the situation. It was time to gain some perspective by gathering background information on Nate and on Ellen.

In Nate's early history, there were extreme patterns. As an infant and even a newborn, he did not tolerate being in a car seat. He had difficulty sleeping. At about 9 months old, he started banging his head—on the crib rail, the wall, the floor—when frustrated. Ellen actually had put a helmet on him to keep him from hurting himself. As a young child, Nate developed a pattern of hitting himself when he was angry, as well as hitting, kicking, and throwing objects. In short, Nate "acted in" as well as "acted out." Hearing about those early and consistent patterns of very low frustration tolerance and of angry outbursts directed either inward or outward led me to suspect that these behaviors were "hardwired"; that is, biologically based and not the result of environmental factors such as quality of mothering or family dynamics. (It is, of course, impossible to completely sort out these "nature versus nurture" issues.)

Much to Ellen's sadness, Nate never cuddled and, unlike his brothers, did not climb into his parent's bed in the morning. He did not like to be hugged and kissed. "Sometimes Nate has a shocking lack of empathy. He is often mean to the cat, which he loves," she said. Yet each parent corroborated that Nate was an extremely social kid, choosing interaction over doing anything else. "Nate must have a play date. He's insatiable about play dates," Ellen said. Ron chuckled as he described how he would say to Nate: "C'mon, Nate, let's go take out the garbage!" and Nate would enthusiastically accompany him. Nate indeed embodied an interesting mix of traits.

I explored Ellen's history in a pointed way. I was searching for themes of conflict in her early life that related to what she was struggling with now. This is not to suggest that I doubted the reality of Nate's outrageous behavior or how incredibly difficult the behavior was for Ellen to address. I intuited, however, that something else was operating here and that its roots were in Ellen's past. I sought to identify times in Ellen's experience when she felt inadequate to a challenge and to determine whether Nate was evoking those same feelings.

Ellen

Ellen was the third of three children. Bright, kind, and cheerful, she was viewed by her parents as the "easy" one and felt loved and cherished by both. Her brother, Rob, was 8 years her senior and had learning disabilities. Her sister, Carol was 5 years older and had a difficult character—moody, angry, and demanding. Ellen, ever optimistic, constantly tried to win the affection of her big sister, but Carol was either mean to Ellen or dismissive of her. When Carol was unhappy, she often blamed Ellen. Ellen's failure to get through to her sister left her with underlying feelings of loneliness and guilt. When Ellen was 15, the sudden death of her father left her sad and aware of the precariousness of life. From this information, Ellen and I derived two key themes in her behavior. First, Ellen believed in the goodness of people. Second, she believed that she could get through to anyone if she just tried hard enough. The relationship with her sister reinforced in Ellen, as an adult, the tendency to assume the entire responsibility (and blame) for how a relationship was working and whether the other individual—her husband, son, or someone else—was pleased or displeased. She was left very vulnerable to feelings of blame, rejection, and abandonment.

Turning to the situation at hand, I asked Ellen to describe in detail how she was handling Nate and what methods she was using to get through a day with him. Her description revealed the enormous effort she was making to ensure that things worked for him. She was his coach, short-order cook, tutor, and cheerleader all wrapped in one. She prepared him for challenging situations, praised any product or sign of effort he made, structured tasks to be followed by fun activities, and, in general, made the things Nate found difficult or boring as palatable as possible. In one sense, this was excellent mothering—committed, creative, flexible, and loving. But it clearly was not effective. Nate's anger was not contained. Ellen felt hurt, rejected, and burned out. Ron was deeply concerned about Nate's continuously outrageous behavior and about Ellen's growing despair, especially because he was frequently away on business.

Due to time constraints, I cut to the chase, focusing on Ellen's immediate need for help. It was apparent that Ellen was failing to draw a line that Nate could not cross. She was allowing Nate to control the situation. I told her she needed to move in and set a limit at the moment his negativity began. I pointed out to her that, contrary to the situation with her sister, in which she had been little and could not take charge, here she was the adult and she *could* take charge. I emphasized that she must learn to hold her ground and become a strong authority figure, firm and nonnegotiating on the things Nate was required to do. As long as Nate perceived any possibility of getting his way, he would not have to muster the internal controls necessary to comply with her expectations. If he sensed that she was trying to accommodate him, he would act out of his base instincts rather than exercise control. I went over the "how to's" of setting limits and consequences, which I had laid out in the previous sessions.

A Year Later

When I next met with Nate, Ron, and Ellen, Nate was 8 years old and repeating second grade because his parents felt he would profit emotionally and academically from the extra year. We began by discussing his academic progress. Ellen praised Nate's teacher, Mrs. Turner, who combined firmness and structure with a real understanding of what Nate was struggling with. To discharge his excess energy, she allowed him to stand up during "quiet time," when singing, and to deliver messages to the office. Academically, Nate was having some difficulty with reading and could not grasp mathematical concepts such as telling time or counting money. He basically did not "get" games. As the semester progressed, Mrs. Turner suggested that Nate needed more help, so the Barclays returned to the pediatrician who had first evaluated him. Based on the earlier diagnosis of attention deficit hyperactivity disorder, Nate was placed on a trial of Ritalin, a stimulant medication commonly used for ADHD. His parents and teacher immediately saw "a different child"—one who was calm, able to sustain his focus, and able to do his work. He stopped calling out and fooling around in the classroom and was able to control himself in the library. Mrs. Turner said that for the first time, she saw Nate as able to be a "member of the team rather than captain." Nate had previously demonstrated a pattern of being bossy with children his age.

Next we addressed Nate's at-home behavior. "He's negative, mean, and utterly insatiable, and he says 'no' to everything!" Ellen reported. She went on to say that she had become more structured and firm in setting limits and was not appeasing him as she had been. She was careful to make sure that pleasurable activities and rewards followed—but did not precede—Nate's carrying through on responsibilities. Despite these efforts, the level of Nate's hostility and opposition was still so intense that things felt very out of control to Ellen. However, she found one method to stop Nate in his tracks—she called this her "drill sergeant" mode. Uncharacteristically, she would speak to him in a loud and menacing tone of voice and say something mean, such as "your brother never did that," which would upset Nate greatly. Although she said it went against her nature to be so mean, at present it was absolutely the only thing that made Nate stop being oppositional. While I did not view this method as functional for the long term, I did not intervene here because I saw Ellen as "in process" toward becoming a stronger authority figure. At this stage, she was finding, perhaps for the first time in her life, her own aggression, which she needed to access in order to stand up to her son's aggression.

Nate was quite talkative when he joined us. After he told me that school was going well, I inquired about home life. "I worry that I shout too much. I'm going to grow up like pop," Nate said, referring to Ron's father, who was not well liked. Nate also admitted to being mean to his friends. I was again impressed by Nate's candor and his ability to observe and show concern regarding his own behavior. He was maturing and developing self-awareness, and he was not identified with his angry behavior, which is to say he had not taken on the identity of an angry boy. I viewed this as a positive sign of emotional growth.

Our discussion for the remainder of the hour centered on several difficult topics and was open, honest, and nonjudgmental—although it was clear that Ron and Ellen were concerned about their son. Ellen brought up her discomfort with Nate's play, which involved "never-ending death and destruction: traps, weapons, killing, spikes, war ships, and knives." Ron, however, wondered whether Nate's aggressive drawings and play might be helping him to deal with his own aggression. Ellen added that while Nate was well liked by his peers, he had a close buddy in school with whom he got into trouble for things such as laughing at a child who gave a wrong answer, keeping children out of a game, and other mean behaviors. I ended the session by having Ron and Ellen discuss (in front of Nate) the message that they wanted to give him about his mean behavior in school. Then, I asked them to discuss the subject with Nate. They took a clear stand: "Mean behavior toward kids in school is not appropriate, and we will not tolerate it! If and when it occurs, you will be given a very stiff consequence."

Nate's explosiveness continued over the next year despite Ellen and Ron's serious efforts to tighten their at-home structures. He exploded when he was asked to do things, when he was told he must go somewhere, and, even with friends when he did not get his own way. Persistence of the problem led Ellen, Ron, and me to develop even more "airtight" strategies, which included:

- **Minimizing spontaneous requests to Nate** (anticipate what is ahead for him, and schedule all responsibilities into the routine)
- **Scheduling his afterschool obligations in detail** (viola 30 minutes, reading 30 minutes, homework 20–30 minutes; then, if everything is complete, he can play with friends)

- **No spontaneous buying** (in order to buy anything over $15, Nate must wait 2 weeks [with the request written and dated]; state "no buying" whenever leaving the house; and no spontaneous trips to McDonald's)

Structure, structure, and more structure was the operating principle.

As the year progressed (Nate was now 9 years old), Ellen was being clear, straightforward, firm, and sometimes "furious" in her approach to Nate. She had learned to allow no deviation from the plans, schedules, and routines. "I sometimes grab him and make him look me in the eye. Then I tell him what I expect him to do." She was, in short, giving Nate less "space" to act out his anger, and he was responding with somewhat better control, but there was still a long way to go.

Ron

For a long time after Nate was diagnosed with ADHD, Ron did not accept the diagnosis. Thus, his approach to the situation was ambivalent. On the one hand, he learned about ADHD, especially through attending workshops with Ellen. In therapy, he worked with Ellen on strategies and limit setting. On the other hand, when Nate attempted to negotiate every direction or had a "meltdown" over something small, Ron became impatient and angry. He often exploded. Underlying Ron's inappropriate reactions to Nate's behavior was the belief that Nate could do it (if he really wanted to). Ron judged Nate as average "compared to what a child should be able to do in our household," and he conveyed that to Ellen. He was disappointed in Nate for traits such as having to be first, refusing to share, showing limited curiosity, and making everything a struggle. What in Ron's history contributed to his resistance to accepting Nate's diagnosis and his rigid, judgmental approach to Nate?

"You are as good as your performance!" was the paradigm that Ron learned at an early age from his father. With a hint of sarcasm, he reported that he was a model son—"the best boy, the best scout, the best student." Nevertheless, he felt absolutely no support for his accomplishments, nor acknowledgment from either parent that he had done well. His face registered pain when he admitted that he did not feel his parents took pride in him. He remembered, with sadness, his father pointing out things he admired in other people.

Ron was able to link his parents' emotional coldness with certain aspects of himself. He noted, "I did not learn to give myself credit. I had no well-developed sense of self-respect and not much empathy." The lack of support he experienced left him with significant feelings of inferiority. The result of these parental messages was an interesting mix of behaviors: Ron was a very hard worker, task oriented, and focused on accomplishment. He could also be a ruthless taskmaster who was devoid of empathy and compassion. His attitude in relation to his sons, all of them, was: "If I could do it (be a hard worker, oriented to tasks and accomplishment), then so can they."

Nate as a Preadolescent

Beginning in mid-winter, when Nate was 10½ the Barclays had a series of sessions spread over a year. Tremendous growth took place that year. In general, Ron and Ellen described Nate as developing better inner controls. He accepted the structures of the household and his own routines, although he did not do his afterschool work without prompting. When angry, Nate would often comply with Ron or Ellen's direction to take the industrial-strength bat and go hit the tree in the backyard or to jump on the trampoline. Nate was beginning to participate actively in his own recovery from anger. Instead of relentless arguing, begging, and manipulating to change the rules as he used to do, Nate was also learning to negotiate in an appropriate way. For example, "Rob is available to play. Can I practice 20 minutes instead of 30? I'm negotiating, mom."

Nate continued to have serious episodes of opposition and rage, although they occurred less frequently. On one snow day, he was impossible all day. He refused to do two tasks that Ellen asked of him—read for 20 minutes and practice viola for 30 minutes. At the end of the day, Ellen broke down, sobbing. Then Nate calmed down and stopped being hostile. On another day, Ron repeatedly told Nate to get ready for church: over and over Nate refused. Ron "bellowed." Nate was shaken and complied. Ron cried.

During this period, when Nate was 11, something very significant happened. Ron stopped traveling and began to work from home. Having been away five days a week, now he was home all the time. This change in the family routine was central to what followed.

Ron was happy to be at home and delighted to have the opportunity to improve his relationship with Nate. He had a growing awareness that his older sons viewed him as critical more than supportive. He was very unhappy about this and wanted a chance to "do it right this time." Specifically, he wanted to move from "taskmaster" to a warmer, more supportive father-son relationship with Nate. However, he did not know how to reconcile this desire with his deeply internalized performance expectations.

As Ron spent time at home, his annoyance and impatience with Nate grew. He frequently exploded. Ellen and Ron argued about managing Nate. Gradually it became clear that Ron resented Nate. He was mad at Nate. For what? For being flawed. For not being as right as his brothers. In Ron's eyes, Nate was an underachiever (previously, Ron had the same belief about each of his other sons).

Being task oriented and a "doer," Ron took the initiative to have Nate tested again. Ron wanted to be satisfied that he and Ellen had done everything possible to help Nate. He was also motivated by a desire not to do "mental combat" with Nate on homework for the rest of Nate's time at home. This time Nate would be evaluated by a school psychologist for IQ ("to see what was under the hood") and to clarify his learning weaknesses. The results indicated that Nate scored in the "high average" range. He achieved a "superior" score in verbal functioning and a "high average" score in perceptual motor skills. The evaluator found that due to Nate's "attentional inefficiency" and impulsivity, he performed best in a highly structured situation. This validated the work Ron and Ellen were doing with him. Ron was pleased with the results; Ellen was not surprised. A turning point had been reached.

Ron's view of Nate began to shift. He started to perceive Nate as capable rather than incapable. He struggled not to get so mad at Nate when he worked with him. He became Nate's advocate rather than his critic. He spent time with Nate on both homework and fun activities. He was finally a true partner with Ellen in providing Nate with a solid foundation of support along with tight structures and firm limits. Ron was fully "on board" regarding the parenting of Nate.

Medication

Since Nate was 7 years old, when his second-grade teacher discretely suggested that medication might be helpful, he has been on one of the three most commonly used stimulant medications: Ritalin, Adderol, or Dexedrine. Early on, he only took medication for school. Later, Ellen learned that Nate dealt much better with his afterschool responsibilities if he had a small dose at that time as well.

One might think that with the intensity and persistence of Nate's anger and explosiveness, the family would have pressed for more treatment through medication. Actually, Ron attributes the fact that Nate was minimally medicated to Ellen's tireless work with him. I agree and add that Ellen and Ron each confronted a core personality issue and, through doing so, expanded their capabilities to deal with Nate and with each other in constructive ways. The work that each one did had a powerful and very positive effect on Nate and his ability to make progress.

Where Is Nate Today?

Perhaps the most compelling statement of where Nate is today, at age 13, was made by his father in my office in October 2001:

> I continue to be impressed, astonished, at how, with patience and structure, modeling . . . explaining . . . trying not to get mad . . . , he has been able to improve his own behaviors, which include responsibilities around the house, and his academics and music. He is at a point where he accepts his responsibilities. . . . He is able to submit himself to the applied disciplines. An example of how far he has come is reflected in something he said to me recently: "Dad, would you help me get up early tomorrow because I didn't get my reading done?" And he does it!

Does Nate take "no" for an answer these days? Ellen says he is still resistant and pushes back. She stated that they still must draw the line and be somewhat harsh at times, but "nothing like the old days." And as for "meltdowns," Ellen reported that what Nate has is an "instant flash" or "anger surge" that appears to be physical, lasts 2 or 3 seconds, and may involve "a door banging and a shoe . . . (going) across the room." Ellen feels that, even while it is going on, Nate knows that he should not be doing it. She even suspects that it's not all right with him.

The Treatment Team

Ron and Ellen "hand picked" their treatment team over the years, a "team without walls." They feel that the team was, and is, essential to their progress. The team included:

> Pediatrician (evaluation and medication)
> Family therapist (author)
> Teachers (especially Nate's second-grade teacher)
> School psychologist (evaluation)
> Tutor (organizational and study skills)

An important factor in creating a team is finding professionals who share a common understanding of the problems as well as a desire to support the child and parents through various stages and challenges. Ron and Ellen used their team as needed. The team never met as a whole, although the pediatrician and I (the family therapist) shared information from time to time. Ellen feels that Mrs. Turner, Nate's second-grade teacher, was an extremely valuable member of the team because she had a powerful effect on his self-image. Having had a first-grade teacher who viewed him as misbehaving and made him spend a lot of time "on the mat," Mrs. Turner's appreciation of Nate changed his self-image from "bad and stupid" to "charming and capable." In contrast to many other situations with a child who has behavior problems, however, I was not involved with Nate's teachers because his grades were mostly As and Bs, and his behavior problems were managed adequately by the teachers (with the cooperation of Ellen and Ron).

Conclusion

Ellen and Ron embodied an interesting and powerful combination of strengths that served them extremely well during this course of treatment with Nate. They were committed to each other and to Nate. They had high expectations of improving things within their family. Ellen had high expectations (Ron was not as sure on this one) of getting through to Nate so that he could function responsibly and on a level close to his potential. Ron and Ellen took an active role in the therapeutic process, doing their "homework," bringing in notes on incidents at home, reading about various issues, and generating their own ideas and strategies. They were able to be introspective; that is, to look at themselves individually and as a couple and to open their minds to what they were feeling or doing that was not constructive or was even destructive. They worked extremely hard, and once they began, they trusted the process and they trusted me as their guide.

The lesson for me here is that because the Barclays accomplished so much, they are an example of what it is possible to achieve. My concept of the changes that are attainable with a child who has serious behavior problems has expanded significantly. The consequence of this is that with other families, I will be stronger in communicating both a clear vision of what they can potentially accomplish and just what they have to do to achieve those ends. This is a significant contribution to my work.

There is another way that I have been impacted by the Barclays' work. They demonstrated how parental intervention, when skillfully implemented, can shape very difficult, and probably biologically based, behavior. Having worked for 20 years with children who have biologically based problems and their families, I have generally observed and come to assume that serious symptoms often require a combination of medications. (I will note that at one point in the treatment, at my suggestion, Nate had a brief trial of Catapres, an "antihypotensive" medication sometimes used with ADHD and serious behavior problems. This medication was stopped because it took away Nate's charm and ability to tell jokes.) It is to Ellen and Ron's credit that Nate has been rather minimally medicated.

Families such as the Barclays teach therapists what is possible in the realm of changing human behavior and experience. As the Barclays gained from my skills and support, I gained from their ability to sustain their efforts until they were achieving what they desired.

Reference

PHELAN, T. (1996). *1-2-3 magic: Effective discipline for children 2–12*. New York: Child Management.

Case Study 1-3

Questions for Discussion

1. The practitioner considers developmental, environmental, and sociocultural issues of the client's case even before meeting with her. Why is this important?
2. The practitioner states that she explores the depressed adolescent client "as a person rather than a problem." What is the strength of this approach?
3. How does the author's understanding of the client's developmental stage enhance the treatment process?
4. What factors may have influenced the client's family doctor to diagnose her with an anxiety disorder instead of depression?
5. How does the crisis intervention model used here differ from longer-term therapy?

Crisis Intervention with a Depressed African American Adolescent

Jewelle Taylor Gibbs

Crisis intervention is often required with adolescents who have problems of substance abuse, violent behavior, eating disorders, or suicide attempts (Meeks & Bernet, 1990; Steiner, 1996). Adolescents who are referred to crisis intervention services are often admitted after an impulsive, self-destructive act that is precipitated by a major loss, disappointment, or narcissistic injury to their self-concept. The techniques of crisis interventions can be particularly effective with these adolescents because of their developmental stage, in which they often respond more positively to short-term, highly focused, problem-solving strategies (Aguilera, 1998).

The case of Tanya, an African American female adolescent, provides an excellent example of using crisis intervention techniques to facilitate the resolution of her presenting problems, to restore her psychological equilibrium, and to strengthen her problem-solving skills. As Caplan (1964) pointed out, a crisis presents both a problem to be resolved and an opportunity for change. For adolescents who are in the process of rapid developmental changes, a crisis state may present an optimal opportunity to achieve a new personality synthesis, to develop more mature coping mechanisms, and to test out more constructive behaviors.

In analyzing this case, I applied a multidimensional conceptual framework that examines the adolescent in the context of her developmental stage, her environmental milieu, and her sociocultural background (Gibbs & Huang, 1998). This framework provides a comprehensive assessment of Tanya as a unique person, not just a typical client with a collection of symptoms and behavioral problems. Thus, Tanya's clinical symptomatology is viewed in the broader context of her adolescent developmental challenges, family background, cultural heritage and values, risk and protective factors, and support systems.

Case Description

Tanya, a 16-year-old African American adolescent, was admitted to a psychiatric emergency service late one evening for an overdose of medication. Tanya was groggy, unresponsive, and unable to report what she had ingested. Her 18-year-old boyfriend, Marlon, had rushed her to the hospital after finding her semiconscious on the floor of her family's living room.

Marlon was able to supply some information about Tanya's background and recent history to the admitting nurse. Shortly after the recent death of her mother, Tanya had moved from the rural south to an urban industrial city in the San Francisco Bay Area. She had moved in with her father, his second wife, and two younger half-sisters, aged 8 and 10.

Marlon reported that Tanya had been very unhappy with the transition from a small southern town where she had a close network of friends and relatives to a large metropolitan area where everything was strange and unfamiliar to her. She had transferred to a local high school but had been put back a grade because she was unable to do the work in 11th grade. Tanya complained that the other students made fun of her accent, her clothes, and her classroom behavior, so she hated to go to school. She also missed her church choir, her part-time job, and all of her friends. Further, Tanya had also complained that her stepmother expected her to baby-sit her younger half-sisters and made her clean and cook after school, so she couldn't work anywhere else. Her father seemed distant and preoccupied with financial problems, and she felt very isolated and lonely.

In recent weeks, Tanya had complained to her boyfriend about headaches, stomachaches, and insomnia. She had gone to the family doctor, who had prescribed some tranquilizer pills for her, but they only made her feel worse. According to the boyfriend, Tanya sometimes seemed very angry, got into screaming matches with her stepmother, was very irritable with her boyfriend, and frequently stated that her life was a mess.

Her boyfriend was worried that Tanya may have accidentally taken too many of the tranquilizers after her father had said he couldn't afford to send Tanya to visit her hometown relatives during her spring vacation. During the 48 hours following her admittance to the hospital, Tanya's condition stabilized and she confirmed much of this information in the psychiatric evaluation that was conducted before she was released from the hospital.

Issues in Assessment

The following issues are relevant to an adequate assessment of Tanya's case.

Developmental Issues

What is the impact of Tanya's developmental stage on the recent problems she has been experiencing in family disruption, school adjustment, social relationships, and community transition?

Clinical Issues

What is the significance of Tanya's somatic and affective symptomatology? What psychological state of mood do they suggest? Did the doctor who prescribed tranquilizers conduct an adequate and culturally appropriate assessment? Could there be alternative hypotheses about the underlying causes of Tanya's symptoms? After she was hospitalized, what other questions should have been addressed in assessing her behavior and affect?

Sociocultural Issues

What social and cultural factors contributed to Tanya's symptomatology? Are there specific social and cultural institutions in the African American community that provided "protective" factors for Tanya? What factors in her current social situation (and family situation) may have increased the "risk" factors for Tanya? What changes have occurred in Tanya's family and social environment in the past year that altered the balance between "protective" and "risk" factors in her psychosocial adjustment? In what ways could cultural factors potentially influence Tanya's symptoms as well as her help-seeking behaviors?

Case Discussion and Analysis

Assessment of the Therapist's Preparation and Self-Awareness

Because my first session with Tanya occurred the morning after she was admitted to a psychiatric emergency service for a suspected suicide attempt, I had only a few sketchy details about her from the notes on her medical chart. Before our initial interview, I thought it would be useful to think about three major factors that might have an important bearing on her case: developmental issues, environmental issues, and sociocultural issues. I also took a few minutes to think about my previous experience with similar cases of adolescents who had made suicide attempts of varying levels of severity, especially the few cases of African American suicide attempters I had seen or heard about. In fact, African American female adolescents, ages 15–19, have the lowest suicide rate of all race-sex groups in their age cohort, so it is a relatively rare occurrence. Although I had had direct clinical experience with only two previous cases of suicide attempters, I had conducted research on the phenomenon of African American adolescent suicide

(Gibbs, 1998; Gibbs & Hines, 1989). Moreover, it was important for me to examine my own attitudes and knowledge about adolescent suicide so that I would be able to assess Tanya's symptoms objectively but still communicate my concern and compassion for her current situation. As an African American female psychologist, I also had to be conscious of my impact on Tanya, who was young enough to be my own daughter and might easily misinterpret my interest and concern for the maternal nurturance that she had recently lost. On balance, I was also aware that the two major traits we shared—being black and female—could facilitate the development of open communication and trust in our initial session (Greene, 1993; Pinderhughes, 1989).

Assessment of Client

When I first saw Tanya in her hospital bed, I noticed that her affect was very sad, that she seemed very tired and listless, and that she avoided making eye contact with me. These symptoms were all congruent with recovery from an overdose of tranquilizers, so they were neither unexpected nor idiosyncratic. After greeting Tanya and explaining who I was and my role in the hospital, I began to ask some very general questions about how she was feeling and what had happened to her, slowly and cautiously trying to assess her current mood and her understanding of what had precipitated her visit to the emergency room (Aguilera, 1998; Ligon, 1997).

Tanya began to cry copiously as she described the feelings of loneliness, hopelessness, and despair that had led her to take the pills. I spent considerable time reassuring her, expressing empathy about her losses and the changes in her life, and offering her the opportunity to share her deepest feelings, fears, and anxieties with me. She slowly managed to gain control of her volatile emotions and seemed greatly relieved to unburden herself to a supportive adult. However, the effort exhausted her and she seemed to have little energy for a longer interview, so I promised that I would return later in the day after she had more time to rest and recover from the overdose. I had decided that it would be preferable to conduct the initial assessment interview when she was more rested, less emotionally fragile, and had had an opportunity to reflect on her feelings and her actions of the previous evening.

This decision bore fruit in our second session later in the afternoon, after Tanya's parents had visited and her condition had improved considerably. In fact, Tanya's appearance and affect had markedly improved, and she was looking much more like a typical teenager, with her hair combed and braided in an intricate style, wearing a colorful robe brought by her parents, and listening to rock music on the radio. I was struck by these rather dramatic changes in Tanya's affect and behavior, considering this a positive sign of her resiliency (Luthar, 1991; Rutter, 1987).

Tanya recognized me and greeted me with a wan, shy smile, but seemed slightly embarrassed and began playing with the tassel on the belt of her robe. Again, I decided to proceed slowly and cautiously to build up her trust and to allay her anxieties about talking further with me. At this point, I did not review our previous conversation, but focused instead on learning about Tanya as a "person" rather than as a "problem."

First, I explored *developmental* questions that would give me a better idea of her current developmental stage, how she was handling normative developmental tasks, and what concerns or issues she was currently facing. I noticed that she talked slowly and deliberately, with a distinct southern accent (in contrast to my rather rapid Northern-accented speech); she also had a good vocabulary and expressed herself clearly and with appropriate affect.

Tanya described herself as an "average" person who liked sports, music, dancing, and going to the movies. She seemed sad again when she spoke of moving away from friends, missing her church choir and other activities, and not feeling really "at home" in the Bay Area. Tanya was disappointed in her schoolwork because she had trouble keeping up with some of her classes, particularly math and science. She also complained that she was frequently teased by the African American girls in her school because of her conservative clothes and her southern accent, but there were one or two girls who had been friendly to her. Tanya's smile returned when she described her boyfriend, one of several boys who had seemed interested in her, but she was worried because he had been pressuring her for sex lately and she didn't feel ready to have that kind of relationship with any young man. As we talked about her relationship with her family, her peers, and boys and about her adjustment in school, Tanya's responses were developmentally appropriate, and her strategies to cope with the challenges of transitioning from mid-adolescence to late adolescence appeared to be flexible and relevant to her particular social context (Erikson, 1959). Tanya was in the developmental stage of mid-adolescence, a period when peer relationships take on an increasing level of importance and when youth shift a major part of their interest (or "cathexis") from family to friends (Petersen, 1988). This is also a period when belonging to a group in which you are valued and accepted is a major developmental task to be achieved because it reinforces a positive identity, promotes the development of social skills, and allows for identity experimentation. During this crucial period, Tanya had lost a loving and nurturing mother through death, a group of supportive friends through moving, and a familiar school environment through transfer. All of these abrupt transitions caused major disruptions in her family relationships, her peer relationships, and her school environment. She had to adjust to a new family with a stepmother and new siblings, to a new school with different academics standards, to a new group of peers who were extremely critical and rejecting, and to a new community with unfamiliar norms, values, and opportunities for youth. Thus, developmentally, Tanya was facing a number of major challenges without the security and stability of a cohesive family and social systems to provide her with the support and nurturance needed to achieve a positive and constructive transition to adulthood. Without such support systems, Tanya was "at risk" for the development of psychological and/or behavioral problems (Camasso & Camasso, 1986; Resnick & Burt, 1996).

While it was clear that Tanya was experiencing some doubts and confusion about her traditional values and responding to some assaults on her self-esteem, she was able to distance herself sufficiently from the responses of her peers to evaluate her own priorities and preferences. On the other hand, I needed to explore in greater depth Tanya's ambivalence about maintaining these values and behaviors in this new and different environment and to determine whether Tanya's depression was related to an internal conflict over how to maintain her self-concept and enhance her self-esteem while fulfilling her social and sexual needs (Adelson & Doehrman, 1980; Gibbs, 1986).

A second major area of assessment was Tanya's clinical symptomatology, ego strengths, coping and defense mechanisms, personality traits, level of self-awareness, and ability to manage her impulses (Meeks & Bernet, 1990; Petersen & Hamburg, 1986). Although Tanya's family doctor had prescribed tranquilizers for her, I thought her symptoms reflected an underlying mood disorder of depression, perhaps masked by some overt signs of anxiety before she ingested an overdose of pills.

The variety of somatic and affective symptoms reported by Tanya can be interpreted in several ways; for example, as signs of underlying anxiety or depression or as a mixed state of both anxiety and depression. In assessing Tanya, it is important to keep in mind that *cultural factors* do influence the expression of symptomatology. For example, an initial review of her symptoms may lead to a diagnosis of an anxiety disorder, as was determined by the doctor who prescribed tranquilizers for her. However, given the history of her recent losses and recent assaults on her self-esteem and identity, it is certainly conceivable that these symptoms reflect an underlying mood disorder of depression (Robbins & Alessi, 1985; Roberts, Roberts, & Chen, 1997).

Also helpful in evaluating Tanya's symptoms is an awareness of the tendency of low-income African Americans, particularly those who are less well-educated, to express depression through somatization. It is also not uncommon for African American adolescents to express depression through anger, irritability, and acting-out behaviors; in fact, this is characteristic of many children and adolescents in general. The clinician should explore Tanya's feelings about the death of her mother, the loss of her friends and church activities, and her demotion in school to determine whether she is masking underlying feelings of sadness, grief, and disappointment with physical symptoms and angry outbursts. The symptoms may also represent a mixture of anxiety and depression, but it is important to determine whether one affect is dominant in order to develop an appropriate treatment plan.

Tanya had reported recent feelings of depression, frequent crying spells, feelings of helplessness and hopelessness, extreme lethargy and fatigue, loss of appetite, and insomnia, and these symptoms were consistent with a diagnosis of major depression because they had lasted more than one month. She had also expressed irritability with her friends, frequent arguments with her parents, and feelings of unworthiness and guilt, all of which supported a diagnosis of major depression (Meeks & Bernet, 1990).

Despite these recent symptoms, Tanya had a history of being well adjusted in her family, at school, and in the community where she had grown up. Although she described herself as "average," she had reached the age of 16 without any major developmental or behavioral problems, according to her self-report. She appeared to have a well-integrated personality with an ability to manage her life reasonably well, to have satisfactory peer relationships, to have a set of moral values based on her strong religious beliefs, and to be engaged in a heterosexual relationship that was making her aware of the need for sexual decision making. She also had displayed signs of a subtle sense of humor and the ability to criticize her own behaviors, alternating with a sensitivity and vulnerability that was characteristic of her age. Tanya did not report any history of drug or alcohol use and stated that she had never had sexual intercourse, both of which probably reflected her religious upbringing.

Assessment of the Therapist's Knowledge of the Client's Background

In order to conduct a culturally sensitive assessment of Tanya, it is essential to have an understanding of her social and cultural background and current milieu. The clinician should evaluate the influence of Tanya's religious beliefs and her southern rural experiences on her beliefs about mental health and psychological symptomatology. The African American church has a profound influence on the values, beliefs, and norms of its members, particularly in rural southern settings. Similarly, church membership and involvement in religious activities is known to be a significant "protective" factor for African American youth and their families, insulating them from many of the social problems of low-income communities. The extended family has also traditionally been a source of support and a resource for positive development for African American youth (Boyd-Franklin, 1989; Lincoln & Mamiya, 1990; Pinderhughes, 1989).

It was important to discuss with Tanya how her recent transitions impacted these protective factors (i.e., the loss of a cohesive family unit, her church choir, and her supportive peer groups). Without these "protective factors," Tanya may have experienced a sense of isolation, loneliness, and loss of self-esteem, all of which caused her to be at risk for psychological disorders (Camasso & Camasso, 1986; Luthar, 1991; Resnick & Burt, 1996).

In assessing Tanya, I was aware of the influence of her social and cultural background on her normative behaviors and her values as well as on the expression of her clinical symptoms. As a young African American female reared in the rural South, Tanya had probably been strongly influenced by the religious beliefs and values of her fundamentalist Christian church, as well as the folkways and traditions of her African American southern community, which was a tightly knit society of extended families, cohesive social support networks, and conservative values (Lincoln & Mamiya, 1990). Moreover, when members of these communities have emotional problems, the families usually seek help initially through elders, ministers, and medical practitioners rather than from mental health professionals (Neighbors, 1985). In that cultural milieu, the tendency for people to somatize when they feel emotional distress is reinforced due to the stigma among rural African Americans of admitting to any form of psychological disorder.

Tanya had made a giant leap from the rural South to the urban West, literally changing cultural environments overnight. This factor was very important in assessing her level of stress while adapting to a major metropolitan area with a faster-paced lifestyle, far more social freedom for adolescents, and far fewer social constraints on behaviors and relationships (Myers, 1989).

While I was evaluating Tanya's clinical symptoms and her personality attributes, I was also assessing her strengths, her social supports, and the protective factors in her family and environment (Harrison et al., 1990; Jessor, 1993). In some respects, Tanya was fortunate to have a new home with a father and stepmother who were successfully functioning adults who provided her with a stable and secure family life. Although she was unhappy about her added family chores and responsibilities, she was also pleased to be reunited with her father and to get to know her younger sisters better. This was an area that I would need to explore further, but Tanya clearly expressed a mixture of positive and negative feelings about her family relationships. Similarly, she expressed some ambivalence about her relationship with her boyfriend, whom she viewed both as a major source of emotional support and as a source of potential danger in tempting her to abandon her moral standards. One of the major deficits in her life was the absence of strong female friendships, although she reported cordial relations with several of her classmates (Way, 1996).

Finally, the clinician should conduct a suicide assessment to determine the motivation behind the overdose of medication and the lethality of the intentional or unintentional behavior (Gibbs & Hines, 1989). If the clinician concludes that Tanya has, in fact, attempted suicide as a "cry for help," this assessment would dictate some very specific interventions as a part of a comprehensive treatment plan for Tanya.

My overall assessment of Tanya was of a mid-adolescent female in transition to late adolescence who was basically well adjusted and coping successfully with her environment until her mother's death precipitated a period of severe stress, which was exacerbated by an abrupt move to live with her father and his new family in a location quite geographically, socially, and culturally removed from her rural southern community. When she experienced numerous difficulties in adjusting to her new family, new community, and new school, Tanya's previous coping strategies failed her, and she experienced feelings of helplessness, hopelessness, and despair. When these feelings intensified, she experienced an episode of major depression, during which she impulsively ingested an overdose of tranquilizers, without a clear and deliberate plan to commit suicide.

Pretherapy Intervention

After I had collected sufficient information about Tanya to make the preliminary assessment that she was depressed but not psychotic or experiencing a toxic drug reaction, I suggested that it would be helpful to discuss with her some ways that she could handle her feelings better in the future and cope more effectively with her new family situation and all the changes in her environment. At that point, I was planning to engage Tanya in some immediate crisis resolution sessions before she left the hospital, and I was not certain that she would be able to return for any follow-up sessions (Ewing, 1978; Puryear, 1984).

Before I proceeded any further, I asked Tanya if she had ever had any counseling or any previous experience with mental health treatment of any kind. When she said that she had not had any previous experience in therapy, I thought it was necessary and appropriate to offer her a brief explanation about therapy, emphasizing the opportunity for her to express her feelings and talk about her problems in an atmosphere of mutual trust and confidentiality. As I suspected, Tanya had some anxieties and fears about therapy, based on her lack of knowledge and exposure to it, but we were able to discuss her fears openly, and I was able to allay her anxieties about any potential stigma, discomfort, or embarrassment she might experience if she talked with me about her concerns. I also reassured her that one of the goals of our discussion would be to help her identify her strengths and her ability to cope with similar problems in the future. Tanya seemed considerably relieved but said she needed to rest and would prefer to have me return the following day.

Hypothesis Testing

After my second session with Tanya, I was able to establish some distance from our intense interactions and to think more about testing several hypotheses to develop a psychodynamic case formulation that would lead to a recommendation for an appropriate treatment plan (Perry et al., 1987).

I had arrived at a tentative conclusion that Tanya's series of traumatic losses had resulted in a period of grief and anger that had not been recognized or addressed by her family. Tanya's abrupt move to the Bay Area to live with her father, new stepmother, and half-sisters exacerbated her feelings of helplessness and hopelessness, resulting in an episode of major depressive disorder. At the same time that her family was trying to mitigate the impact of her mother's death, Tanya may have experienced the move as a sign of rejection and double abandonment by her Southern relatives, particularly because she was being uprooted from a secure and happy environment with close friends and strong community ties (Shapiro & Freedman, 1987).

The onset of Tanya's depression was further aggravated by feelings that she was the target of scapegoating by her peers and criticism from her teachers. As she had recounted her mounting frustration with all of these stressful interactions, I noted that she had seemed particularly upset about her boyfriend's initial request for sexual intercourse. That apparently was the incident that overwhelmed her fragile ego defenses and caused her to decompensate, precipitating the abortive suicide attempt.

In fact, the overdose was probably not an intentional suicide attempt, but more probably a "cry for help," a signal to her family and her boyfriend that she felt out of control and unable to cope with these multiple demands and pressures (Gibbs & Hines, 1989; Robbins & Alessi, 1985).

Considering Tanya's religious background and conservative upbringing, she may have consciously refused to engage in sexual relations with her boyfriend, but unconsciously experienced feelings of sexual desire that made her feel immoral and guilty. These ambivalent feelings could have created a sense of panic that interfered with rational decision making and judgment, allowing her impulses to propel her into self-destructive behavior.

Although the initial information from her boyfriend, parents, and Tanya herself supported this formulation, I planned to meet with her parents again to confirm my assessment of her case. I was aware that clients in crisis are not always the most reliable informants, and I also thought I needed more developmental and family information before I made a definitive formulation of Tanya's behaviors and symptoms.

Monitoring Therapist-Client Interactions

In a crisis intervention situation, the clinician does not have the luxury of a week between sessions to analyze the case, develop the treatment plan, or consider various intervention options. Similarly, the phases of therapy are usually compressed into one to three sessions, depending on the length of the client's hospitalization. Thus, the therapy focuses on encouraging the expression of feelings about the presenting problem(s), quickly restoring the client's ego capacities, strengthening problem-solving skills, and developing a short-term treatment plan to address specific limited goals (Aguilera, 1998; Puryear, 1984).

I was aware of the time constraints in my third session with Tanya, which occurred on the morning of her second day in the hospital. Tanya seemed more relaxed, more alert, and considerably more animated after a day of rest and visits from her family and her boyfriend. I was particularly conscious of approaching Tanya with warmth, communicating my empathic understanding of her feelings, and projecting myself as a person who was genuinely concerned about her welfare. I also knew it would be important not to convey disapproval of her behavior, particularly because Tanya had a rather harsh superego and seemed to blame herself for many of the unfortunate things that had happened to her. I noticed that she responded positively to me, seemed to enjoy talking with me, and was pleased that I knew and understood some of the factors in her background and life experiences that made her a unique person. These were all positive signs of a growing rapport that I could marshal in building the mutual trust and respect needed to facilitate a rapid resolution of her current crisis.

I also recognized some of my own feelings toward Tanya, who alternately evoked maternal and "big sister" feelings in me because she sometimes reminded me of my two adolescent sons, but as a first-born daughter with three younger siblings, I could also empathize with her role as the oldest daughter in her family. I was aware of the importance of monitoring these feelings of countertransference and not allowing them to influence my relationship with Tanya (Meeks & Bernet, 1990).

Monitoring the Client's Responses and Transference

In responding to my efforts to help her, Tanya's behavior had gradually changed from an initial shyness, embarrassment, and reluctance to engage fully in the relationship to a more open, less-defensive attitude, and more reflective style of communication. She expressed discomfort about discussing her relationship with her boyfriend, probably reflecting her anxiety about their ambivalent sexual relationship. At several points in our sessions, she expressed resistance by becoming unresponsive or evasive in responding to my questions. She seemed particularly unwilling to discuss her relationship with her stepmother and half-sisters, a topic that was the source of considerable tension in her family and was one of the precipitating factors in her current crisis (Shapiro & Freedman, 1987).

In her interactions with me, Tanya seemed to reach for my maternal instincts and to search for ways to identify with me. She wanted to hold my hand throughout each session when I tried to comfort her while she was crying and in such emotional distress. As she regained some control over her emotions, she showed more curiosity about me, asked me if I had any children, and thanked me several times for helping her to "feel better about myself." Although it is not useful or appropriate to interpret transference or countertransference reactions in a crisis intervention treatment situation, it is important for the clinician to monitor these feelings and to use them to facilitate the restoration of the client's functioning and the resolution of the crisis.

Goal Setting and Problem Resolution

In the third session with Tanya, I thought it was important to discuss some short-range goals and some longer-term goals before she was discharged from the hospital. We had previously set up an appointment with her parents for a family session later that afternoon before they took her back home, but I first wanted to develop some individual goals with Tanya.

Tanya and I agreed that there were three immediate and short-term goals: getting treatment for her depression, asking her parents to participate in some family counseling sessions, and clarifying the boundaries of her relationship with her boyfriend. Since we had identified these three areas as major sources of Tanya's current stress, we selected these areas as appropriate targets of intervention.

I discussed referrals for psychiatric treatment and advised Tanya that the psychiatrist who had seen her in the emergency room had prescribed some antidepressant pills for her, so her medication would be monitored by her new therapist in consultation with the hospital psychiatrist (Aguilera, 1998).

Tanya was not sure her parents would agree to participate in family counseling, so we discussed other options, such as pastoral counseling, that might be more congruent with their cultural beliefs. She understood the importance of sharing her feelings with her parents and thought it would be helpful if she expressed her disappointment and feelings of frustration with her household responsibilities and lack of attention from her father, but she was also fearful of alienating her parents and becoming even more of a stepchild in the family. I reinforced Tanya's desire to discuss her feelings with her family and emphasized that this crisis presented an opportunity for Tanya and her whole family to discuss their mutual feelings, hopes, responsibilities, and obligations because although the family unit had really changed with her arrival, they had never really confronted the implications of those changes.

Tanya was also eager to discuss with her boyfriend, Marlon, her feelings about intimacy, her reluctance to engage in sexual relations until she felt that she was in a committed, premarital relationship, and her fears about pregnancy and sexually transmitted diseases. Although Tanya felt that Marlon was one of the most supportive people in her life, she also felt that he was causing her a great deal of emotional turmoil. Tanya realized that removing this turmoil would not only reduce her stress, but would perhaps enable her to explore other relationships.

We also explored some longer-term goals for Tanya to work toward when she was feeling stronger and in greater control of her environment. Tanya expressed a desire to become more active in her family's church in order to feel more integrated into a familiar religious community. Tanya also wanted to be more assertive about developing friendships with two or three classmates who had been friendly and supportive of her when she first arrived. Finally, Tanya realized that it was time to "stop feeling sorry for myself" and to start thinking about her plans after her high school graduation.

By the end of this third session, I was pleased to see that Tanya had made remarkable progress in less than 48 hours after being admitted to the hospital for an overdose of tranquilizers. In setting some short- and longer-term goals for herself, Tanya had exhibited an ability to identify her problems, analyze some of the causes, marshal her motivation to recover, make rational plans, and develop realistic goals to improve her overall personal, social, and family functioning (Ligon, 1997; Puryear, 1984).

Planning for Intervention

Because Tanya was a 16-year-old dependent adolescent, it was important to involve her family in the assessment and treatment plan. I met with Tanya and her parents for a final session just before she was discharged early in the evening of her second full day in the hospital. I reported my evaluation of Tanya's admitting symptoms and her current condition, emphasizing to her parents the severity of her depression but suggesting that the overdose of pills was really a "cry for help" rather than a serious suicide attempt. I then asked Tanya's parents if they had any questions or comments before I recommended my treatment plan and follow-up for Tanya.

Tanya's parents seemed very concerned about her behavior and eager to cooperate in facilitating her recovery. They both expressed relief that she had improved so swiftly and were eager to take her home, where they were planning a welcome home party with her two younger sisters. I used this as an opening to discuss Tanya's relationship with her parents and sisters and quickly realized that this topic was difficult for them to address.

After I proposed my recommendation of individual treatment for Tanya and family counseling for the entire family, Tanya's parents were enthusiastic about the individual treatment but more skeptical about family counseling. They responded that they would first like to initiate individual treatment for Tanya and asked for a recommendation for an African American therapist in the community. They said they would talk to their minister and seek his advice about family counseling, and they did acknowledge the need for the family to discuss the changes brought about by Tanya's inclusion in their household.

At the end of the session, I asked Tanya and her parents if they had any further comments or questions about Tanya's problems, her treatment in the hospital, or her follow-up treatment. Tanya spoke first and thanked me for helping her to understand all the things that had happened to her and to figure out ways to handle her problems better in the future. Her parents also were very gracious, thanking the hospital staff for "saving Tanya's life" and thanking me for my support and concern for Tanya. As the family left, I sensed that they were hopeful that Tanya would continue to improve and that their relationship with her would improve. However, I also felt that this family needed to work out their issues as a family unit and to be more supportive of Tanya's need to separate and individuate while still providing her with the nurturance and security to develop as an autonomous young adult.

Case Summary

This case of Tanya, a 16-year-old African American female who presented at a hospital emergency service with an overdose of tranquilizers, illustrates several developmental, sociocultural, and clinical issues in the assessment and treatment of a minority adolescent in a psychiatric emergency situation. Even in crisis intervention, the clinician should be mindful of cultural influences on symptomatology, behavioral norms and values, family and peer relationships, and adaptive behaviors. Most importantly, the clinician must make a very rapid assessment of the patient's clinical symptoms, their severity, and the patient's ability to cope with precipitating problems in the context of this broader conceptual framework.

In Tanya's case, I was able to develop a dynamic formulation of her symptoms and their underlying causes fairly quickly, thus enabling me to facilitate her relatively rapid reintegration after an impulsive overdose of medication in an attempt to alert her parents and her boyfriend to the fact that she was overwhelmed by her current stresses. Tanya responded positively to several sessions of crisis counseling that focused on helping her to express her feelings, to identify the sources of her emotional distress, to mobilize her problem-solving skills, and to restore her adaptive functioning. Fortunately, Tanya had a number of ego strengths, a supportive family, and a caring boyfriend, all of which suggested a positive prognosis for her recovery.

References

ADELSON, J., & DOEHRMAN, M. (1980). The psychodynamic approach to adolescence. In J. Adelson (Ed.), *Handbook of adolescent psychology* (pp. 99–116). New York: Wiley.

AGUILERA, D. C. (1998). *Case intervention: Theory and methodology* (8th ed.). St. Louis, MO: Mosby.

BOYD-FRANKLIN, N. (1989). *Black families in therapy: A multisystems approach.* New York: Guilford.

CAMASSO, M. J., & CAMASSO, A. E. (1986). Social supports, undesirable life events, and psychological distress in a disadvantaged population. *Social Service Review, 60,* 378–394.

CAPLAN, G. (1964). *Principles of preventive psychiatry.* New York: Basic Books.

ERIKSON, E. (1959). Identity and the life cycle [Monograph]. *Psychological Issues, 1.*

EWING, C. P. (1978). *Crisis intervention as psychotherapy.* New York: Oxford University Press.

GIBBS, J. T. (1986). Assessment of depression in urban adolescent females: Implications for early intervention strategies. *American Journal of Social Psychiatry, 6,* 50–56.

GIBBS, J. T. (1998). Conceptual, methodological, and sociocultural issues in black youth suicide: Implications for assessment and early intervention. *Suicide and Life-Threatening Behavior, 18,* 73–89.

GIBBS, J. T. (1999). Mental health issues of black adolescents: Implications for policy and practice. In A. R. Stiffman & L. E. Davis (Eds.), *Ethnic issues in adolescent mental health.* Thousand Oaks, CA: Sage.

GIBBS, J. T., & HINES, A. M. (1989). Factors related to sex differences in suicidal behavior among black youth: Implications for intervention and research. *Journal of Adolescent Research, 4*(2), 152–172.

GIBBS, J. T., & HUANG, L. N. (1998). *Children of color: Psychological interventions with culturally diverse youth.* San Francisco: Jossey-Bass.

GREENE, B. A. (1993). Psychotherapy with African American women: Integrating feminist and psychodynamic models. *Journal of Training and Practice in Professional Psychology, 7*(1), 49–66.

HARRISON, A. Q., et al. (1990). Family ecologies of ethnic minority children. *Child Development, 61,* 347–362.

JESSOR, R. (1993). Successful adolescent development among youth in high risk settings. *American Psychologist, 48,* 117–126.

LIGON, J. (1997). Brief crisis stabilization of an African-American woman: Integrating cultural and ecological approaches. *Journal of Multicultural Social Work, 6*(3/4), 111–122.

LINCOLN, C. E., & MAMIYA, L. (1990). *The black church in the African-American experience.* Durham, NC: Duke University Press.

LUTHAR, S. S. (1991). Vulnerability and resilience: A study of high-risk adolescents. *Child Development, 62,* 600–616.

MEEKS, J. E., & BERNET, W. (1990). *The fragile alliance: An orientation to the psychiatric treatment of the adolescent.* Malabar, FL: Krieger.

MYERS, H. F. (1989). Urban stress and the mental health of Afro-American youth: An epidemiologic and conceptual update. In R. L. Jones (Ed.), *Black adolescents.* Berkeley, CA: Cobb & Henry.

NEIGHBORS, H. W. (1985). Seeking professional help for personal problems: Black Americans' use of health and mental health services. *Community Mental Health Journal, 21,* 156–166.

PERRY, S., et al. (1987). The psychodynamic formulation. *American Journal of Psychiatry, 144*(5), 543–550.

PETERSEN, A. C. (1988). Adolescent development. *Annual Review of Psychology, 39,* 583–607.

PETERSEN, A. C., & HAMBURG, B. A. (1986). Adolescence: A developmental approach to problems and psychopathology. *Behavior Therapy, 17,* 480–499.

PINDERHUGHES, E. (1989). *Understanding race, ethnicity and power.* New York: Free Press.

PURYEAR, D. A. (1984). *Helping people in crisis.* San Francisco: Jossey-Bass.

RESNICK, G., & BURT, M. (1996). Youth at risk: Definitions and implications for service delivery. *American Journal of Orthopsychiatry, 66*(2), 172–188.

ROBBINS, D. R., & ALESSI, N. E. (1985). Depressive symptoms and suicidal behavior in adolescents. *American Journal of Psychiatry, 142,* 588–592.

ROBERTS, R., ROBERTS, C., & CHEN, Y. (1997). Ethnocultural differences in prevalence of adolescent depression. *American Journal of Community Psychology, 25*(1), 95–110.

RUTTER, M. (1987). Psychosocial resilience and protective mechanisms. *American Journal of Orthopsychiatry, 57*(3), 316–331.

SHAPIRO, E. R., & FREEDMAN, J. (1987). Family dynamics of adolescent suicide. *Adolescent Psychiatry, 14,* 191–207.

STEINER, H. (Ed.). (1996). *Treating adolescents.* San Francisco: Jossey-Bass.

WAY, N. (1996). Between experiences of betrayal and desire: Close friendships among urban adolescents. In B. J. Leadbetter & N. Way (Eds.), *Urban girls: Resisting stereotypes, creating identities.* New York: New York University Press.

Case Study 1-4

Questions for Discussion

1. How does the practitioner attempt to move the client from the precontemplation to the contemplation stage of motivation?
2. The author describes a polarization of the staff at the inpatient treatment center. How do they attempt to resolve their differences, and how does the client benefit from that effort?
3. A variety of techniques and modalities are used in this case study: individual, family, and group work and psycho-educational, cognitive behavioral, reality, art, gestalt, relaxation training, and solution-focused treatment. Finally, the author states that in later cases, she relies most on "cognitive constructivisim." Discuss the merits of the different approaches.
4. Why does the practitioner physically rearrange family members at the family therapy sessions?
5. Describe the "function" of the client's eating disorder. How is the case framed by identifying a function?

Emily: From "I'm Nothing Special" to "I Don't Need Anorexia Anymore"

M. Sean O'Halloran

Emily, age 15, was referred to the outpatient eating disorders unit at St. Anne's hospital by her parents, Jean and Carl, and their family doctor, who were all very concerned about her recent dramatic weight loss. Emily's weight had plummeted from 95 pounds to 75 pounds in less than 2 months, and her mother was particularly afraid that Emily would die if she did not get inpatient help. The family had been working with a local therapist at a community agency for a month, and although the family attended sessions regularly and Jean and Carl expressed great interest in helping Emily, the outpatient therapy was not helping. Emily had lost 8 pounds in the prior month. The family physician recommended St. Anne's because of its emphasis on treating eating disorders.

I met Emily, Jean, and Carl in the waiting room of the unit. Because they were 15 minutes late, I knew that our time would be limited today. Carl rose first and shook my hand. His brown hair was graying at the temples, he was tall and slim, his blue jeans were well worn, and his shirt sleeves were rolled up. His hand was warm and his grasp was strong; he had the sunburned and weather-beaten face of a man who had ranched and raised cattle his whole life. He introduced himself and apologized for being late, saying that it was harvest time and it was hard to get away from the work. He then introduced his wife, Jean, whose hand was cool, thin, and yet firm. She was a little over 5 feet tall and of average weight. Her dark blond hair was styled in a tight perm that made her seem older than her years, and she wore a simple housedress. Emily stayed in her chair, with her thin arms folded tightly across her chest. She wore a white, buttoned sweater, a denim jacket, and jeans. If I had not known she was 15, I might have guessed her to be about 11; she was so small and childlike in appearance. Her blond hair covered most of her face and she refused to look at me, despite her father's order to "say hello to the doctor." I wanted to convey to Emily that I was not the enemy, and I said, "I think it is really hard to feel friendly when you really don't want to be here." Emily took a quick glance up at me then. Her doe-shaped blue eyes registered a combination of fear and fierceness, and her mouth stayed in a tight line as I ushered her and her parents into my office to begin the intake interview.

In my office, I told them that today we would just talk a bit about what they saw as the concern and how I might be able to help. I explained that today's session would be brief but that I looked forward to talking to them more if they decided to make an appointment for the next week. When I asked how I might be able to help, Carl nodded his head, looked to Jean, and then looked down. Emily intently studied the loops on the carpet below her feet. Jean reported that Emily had expressed dissatisfaction with her body image for about the last year, following the rather late onset of her first period. However, relatively recent changes had alarmed Jean: Emily had lost a significant amount of weight, she was running up to 6 miles per day, her food intake was restricted, and "she's just so picky about food." Jean could not think of what in particular had precipitated the significant weight loss over the last 2 months. As he looked at Emily, Carl added, "My little girl used to smile all the time, and now she barely says hello or raises her head." I noticed Emily fidgeting with her hands, and I asked her what she thought might be going on. She said, "Everyone is making a big deal out of nothing!" When I asked her to elaborate, she argued that her parents were exaggerating her weight loss and that her community therapist and family doctor were "just really dumb." Carl raised his voice as he said, "See here, young lady, there's nobody but you being dumb now." Jean interrupted Carl, gently admonishing him, "Now she will be able to get the help she needs, that's all that matters now."

After further elaboration on the concerns of her parents and Emily's continued denial of the seriousness of the problem, I asked her if she would be willing to come again to discuss this further. Emily shrugged and said, "Why not?" We set up an appointment to meet a couple of days later.

Carl could not attend the second session, so I met with Emily and Jean. In this session, I discussed my approach to therapy, and I explained that it was important for me to talk with Emily about her concerns, her level of willingness to participate in therapy, and her desire to change. Jean seemed nervous and spoke at length about Emily's childhood and how easygoing she had been. I noticed an urgent look from Emily once or twice when she caught my eye. I asked her if she would be willing to give me some information on the history of her eating and exercise behavior. She said, "Okay, but mom . . . " and looked from her mother to me and back again. Jean seemed aware that Emily wanted to talk to me alone and quickly got up from her chair, saying, "Okay, honey, I think you will be more comfortable if I wait in the waiting room. That's okay."

In the time we had left in today's session, I wanted to encourage Emily to talk and asked what she thought this was all about. She said, "What what is all about?" I looked directly at her and slightly raised my eyebrows. She looked away and when she turned back, she had tears in her eyes. She explained that she honestly did not know why she had gotten so carried away with "getting skinny," but now that she was there it was so hard to stop it. She liked the feeling of emptiness in her stomach, and although she was hungry, she felt really good about saying "no" to eating. She knew it "drove the parents crazy," but she was not doing it to "torture them." When I probed into the impact of her weight loss on her life, she admitted that she had headaches, and that although she was tired, she felt nervous "a lot of the time" and running helped her to feel calm. As part of the intake interview, I gathered information on the history of her concerns, family history of eating disorders, weight and body image concerns, mood disorders, abuse, and other related issues. Her responses indicated a lack of a significant family history in these areas. She said that her brother, Bill, who was 2 years younger, spent most of his free time on the ranch with her dad and that her sister, Carly, who was 2 years older, was deaf and was hoping to go away to a college in Washington, DC, that specifically serves deaf students.

Toward the end of the interview, I wanted to know about Emily's motivation to change and her hopes and fears as she entered therapy. She said that she did not even want to be in therapy, that she did not have goals, and that she wished her parents would quit "pestering" her. I asked her how therapy could help with that, and she shrugged. Emily smiled slightly as she suggested that we send her parents to therapy and she could stay at home. I smiled too and asked if she would be willing to meet me in 2 weeks and to start a journal of her thoughts and feelings. "What about?" she asked. I said that anything was fine, but that maybe she could notice if her low weight, exercise, and food restriction was in any way a problem to her. She wanted to know why we could not meet sooner, and I explained I would be away at a conference.

When we next met, I was not surprised that she had not used the journal much. I was actually impressed that she had kept it for three days. She said she was just too busy to record her thoughts on the other days. Emily discussed her entries and told me that exercising was occasionally a hassle because it was too cold some mornings to run. I asked if she would be willing to give up running one day a week so that she would have more time to write in her journal or to run a little bit less each day. She easily agreed, but then mentioned that she would have to eat a little bit less or she would get fat. We explored the meaning of "fat," and Emily said one of her greatest fears in coming to therapy was that I would make her get fat. Anything over 85 pounds seemed fat to her, so I did not see the fruitfulness of arguing about numbers. I simply said that one of my goals was to help her get to a more normal weight, but that therapy would not include making her get fat.

Our next couple of therapy sessions focused on Emily's motivation to change, or lack thereof. This required examining what is good about being thin and what is not very useful about it. My hope at this point in therapy was to open the way so that Emily would be willing to move from the precontemplation to contemplation stage of motivation and move toward greater health (Prochaska, DiClemente, & Norcross, 1992). A good part of this work included psychoeducation about the implications for physical and psychological health when a person has an eating disorder, exploring social and cultural pressures on women to be thin in our society, learning to question prevailing attitudes, and decision making about how much of those values Emily wanted to continue to buy into. Her motivation to change shifted somewhat; although she was still emphatic that she did not want to gain weight, she saw the value in having her periods resume, even though she said it had been nice not having to "deal with it."

For the next month or so, our sessions had a very cognitive-behavioral focus (Garner, Vitousek, & Pike, 1997) as we began exploring Emily's preoccupation with thinness, the meaning she attached to being thin, and began challenging some of her cognitions about the value of being thin. Although the cognitive work made sense to Emily, she remained firm about not wanting to gain weight. However, she promised that she would not lose any more weight. I had a vacation planned and told Emily that I would be away for 2 weeks. She agreed to continue to monitor her thoughts, feelings, and behaviors and agreed to begin participating in an eating disorders support and education group run by the hospital. When I returned, however, events had taken a downward turn.

While I was away, Emily and her father had a big fight over food. The story I was able to piece together indicated that Emily refused to eat any dinner one night, claiming that she had eaten a big lunch. Her father grew very angry and insisted that Emily eat dinner in front of him. They sat at the table together that evening from 7 o'clock until after 10 o'clock. Emily cried, and her mother tried to cajole her into eating and pleaded with her husband to let Emily eat half of her dinner, but Carl was steadfast. Emily ate as much as she could and then complained of severe stomach pains, threw up in the kitchen, and collapsed on the floor. Her parents admitted her to the inpatient unit and that was where I found Emily when I returned. She had been at the inpatient unit for 5 days. When she saw me, her face was streaked with tears and she looked as though she had lost weight. Indeed her records reflected a weight loss of 3 pounds: she was now down to about 72 pounds. She looked devastated and pleaded with me to get her "out of this prison." The medical staff had set her discharge weight at 90 pounds, and Emily claimed it would take her "forever" to gain that much weight.

In the weeks that followed, Emily attended the inpatient groups regularly, as was required of her, but participated very little in any activities. The hospital staff, including the dietician, a nurse who facilitated a psychoeducation group, and a unit nurse, found her to be rude, uncooperative, and manipulative. The group facilitator said that she was good at trying to get the other girls to gang up on the nurse. The only staff member other than myself who seemed to have any rapport with Emily was an art therapist who facilitated a weekly group. She described Emily as quiet, but interested and productive in working on her art, especially collages. She also said that Emily seemed pleased to receive compliments on her creative expressions.

During one staff meeting in which Emily was the main focus of conversation, I marveled at the conflicts between the staff members as they reviewed Emily's behavior. A 72-pound girl had managed to split the staff into two contingents: those who saw Emily as manipulative and uncooperative and those who saw her as struggling, yet willing to engage in therapeutic work. The former group seemed to personalize Emily's behavior as an affront to them, and the latter defended Emily and did not interpret her behavior as defensive. The staff meeting lasted longer than usual as we tried to work through our own reactions and develop strategies for working together more cohesively as a team.

Emily's low point during her inpatient stay came the next week when she was weighed and was found to have gained 5 pounds. One nurse, Karen, observed how distended Emily's abdomen was and insisted that she sit in the nurses' unit for half an hour and be weighed again. Emily protested this loudly and angrily. Karen and I had not always seen eye to eye. She often grew frustrated with patients and would then demand that I or the other psychologist on the unit give direct orders to the patient, orders that were specifically her own. Lately, though, Karen and I had been trying to understand each other's perspective, and listening to each other was helping both of us to be clearer in our communication. Karen called me to see if I would be willing to meet with Emily immediately. I met with a very sad and angry Emily, who swore that Karen was out to get her and that I knew how much Karen hated her. I asked Emily what she had done to gain the weight so quickly. She said nothing but looked annoyed and turned away from me. I mentioned that sometimes people are so scared of being weighed that they do things to make it appear as though they have gained weight when they have not and asked her if she might have done that. At that, Emily ran to use the bathroom. She admitted that she had consumed nearly a gallon of water and a diet soda prior to her weigh-in. She also admitted to hiding small metal washers in her hair, which was piled high into a lovely French chignon style. Emily felt very ashamed and angry. She must have cried nearly a gallon's worth of tears after that.

I had mixed feelings about her behavior. At the moment, I felt frustrated and angry. I could understand how the hospital staff might feel manipulated by this and other behaviors Emily had displayed, such as running in the darkened stairwell at night until the startled janitor caught her or doing sit-ups in her bed at 2 a.m. Yet I also felt very sad for Emily as I thought about how desperate and driven she was to maintain a state of thinness—so much so that she was sacrificing her health, energy, and time in an inpatient eating disorders hospital. During my masters degree program, I had worked in a prison system, and I recall the relief I felt every time I left and how trapped the adolescents must have felt living in there day after day. The hospital did not feel very different to me at times, and Emily's plea's to get her out of "prison" struck me that day as puzzling. The youth in prison had to serve a sentence, but Emily seemed to be imprisoning herself.

Emily was under "house arrest" for the next few weeks. She was on the highest level of restriction, which meant that she was unable to go home on weekends or go on outings to restaurants with other patients, and she was carefully monitored 24 hours a day.

Our therapy during this time was not as productive as I would have liked. When we met, Emily complained about the hospital, the food, and the restrictions. I continued to use primarily a cognitive-behavioral approach and techniques from "Reality Therapy" (Glasser & Wubbolding, 1995) as I tried to encourage Emily to take more responsibility for herself. At some points in our work, she was so desperately unhappy that talking did not seem to do anything but add to her frustration; she sighed deeply throughout the sessions.

Recalling how helpful the art therapist found Emily's collages, I brought magazines, paper, scissors, and glue to one session and asked Emily if she would like to work on a collage with me. We worked on several projects without a clear focus; I just followed Emily's lead and encouraged her to talk about her creations and how they were related to her current concerns. Gradually, she became more open again, and I became more relaxed with her as I endeavored to follow her lead, rather than shoving her along through therapy. One day I came in and asked her if she would be willing to try something new. She seemed interested, and I gave her a thin stack of cards from which to choose a theme for the collage. I had developed the cards using some themes that are common for people with eating disorders. The themes consist of short, unfinished statements and are often useful for generating a discussion in group or individual therapy. Such themes include: "I see my body as . . . ," "In relationships with others, I feel . . . ," "What I hope most for myself is. . . ."

The card Emily selected was "My future looks like. . . ." We talked briefly about the possible components of her future, including her job, her family, her body, her interests, and where she lived. She chose to look at herself at 25, about 10 years down the road. With this in mind, Emily studied the magazines intently and began to pull out pages and stack them into piles. The time flew by quickly and Emily was disappointed when we needed to stop. I promised her that we could work on this again in 2 days and that, if she wanted to, she could begin a journal to record some of the images she had of who she could become in the next 10 years. She asked if she could take some of the magazines to work with outside our sessions. I was relieved that she had found this project worthwhile. When I returned to the hospital on Wednesday, the nurses commented on how absorbed Emily had been in writing in her journal and that, while she had not stopped completely, she was less argumentative and more cooperative in group activities.

Emily was flushed with excitement when she came into my office. "Look at all these great pictures I found!" she exclaimed as she took out the project and laid it on the floor. Emily immediately went to work, separating the images into categories, cutting out the pictures, and laying them on a larger poster board divided into the "future life" sections Emily and I had discussed previously. Emily's future self included a physical appearance consistent with today's images of thin, firm models; family images included parents and children doing fun things together, including eating meals, camping, and going to Disneyland; the future career section included images of horseback riding, horses, riding tack, Western-style riding fashions, and rodeos.

This last set of images struck me the most because Emily had never expressed an interest in horses. When I asked her to elaborate on the horse theme, she said, with much enthusiasm, that her dream was to be an equestrian and that she loved anything to do with horses and being outdoors. She said angrily that her father would not let her help him with the work on their ranch and that he only let her brother help him: "He always tells me to stay behind and help my mother with house chores." The closest she could get to ranch work was helping with the paperwork to register cattle. She cried that he was really unfair and that, more than anything, she wanted to be able to work outside. We had a family meeting planned for the following week, and I wondered aloud if Emily would share some of her images of the future with her family, especially her hopes for the nearer future so that she might be able to find a way to approach her father again. Emily expressed great skepticism that he would listen to her, let alone allow her to work on the ranch. The family sessions, which occurred almost every week, had been strained lately because Carl and Emily could scarcely speak to each other without blaming and yelling. Jean often tried to act as the peacemaker, but lately, due to interventions in therapy, she had started allowing me to facilitate their communication without feeling that she had to create peace between them. She was mostly relieved to back out of that role, saying that she found it exhausting and frustrating.

Throughout the weekend, Emily continued to work on her project, and by Monday, she had finished a 4-foot by 6-foot collage divided into life sections. Her poster was well designed, and she had made good use of the limited art materials in the hospital. Emily seemed very proud of her work, and her face glowed as she presented her future life to the other five patients in one of her therapy groups. In our individual sessions that week, we rehearsed what she would say about this project to her family, especially to her father. The day before the family session, Emily came in looking downcast and explained that her father would not take her seriously and that he would make fun of her. Although she was initially reluctant to engage in the gestalt therapy technique of empty chair work (Polster & Polster, 1973) and said she felt silly talking to empty chairs, I persisted in inviting her to try something different. She finally sighed and said in an offhand way, "Well, if it amuses you, I'll try." After a few rough starts, I was impressed at how confident Emily sounded as she made her case to her father. After finishing the empty chair work, Emily said she realized that in order to be stronger so that she could work on the ranch, she needed to have more energy. I hinted not too subtly that food was an excellent source of energy. Emily muttered "Hmmm" and rolled her eyes at me as the session ended.

The next day I felt nervous and excited for Emily as her family took their usual seats in a circular formation in my office. Carly, the eldest daughter, was away at a college workshop and could not attend. Bill, Emily's brother, wore his baseball cap over his eyes and slid into a chair beside his dad. He nodded in assent when I asked him if Emily could sit next to her dad today. Starting in about our fourth family therapy session, I had asked Jean and Carl to sit next to each other. Emily had previously sat in between them, and I had observed that she seemed to shrink down and appeared smaller sitting between her parents. She also often spoke for her parents, so I thought it would be better to create a "parental unit" seating arrangement and to have Emily sit across from them. Today Emily sat on my left, between Carl and me, and Bill sat between Carl and Jean, who sat next to me on my right. I opened the session by checking to see if there was anything the family particularly wanted to address today. Carl observed that Emily seemed happy today and patted her knee. Emily gave him a genuine smile and fidgeted in her seat. Jean commented on this too, and Bill nodded. Emily took the lead in telling her family about her project and asked them to listen to her first and ask questions later. Even Bill, who normally said little, looked interested as Emily gave her "Future Self" presentation.

At the end, Emily's parents looked very proud of her work and seemed to sit up straighter as they asked Emily questions about her future. Her dad nodded his head a bit and admitted that he had been pretty stubborn about not having the girls out on the ranch where they could get hurt. At this point, Emily looked directly at him and told him that one of her greatest hopes was to work on the ranch with him and eventually get a horse to keep on the land. She talked in a clear, firm way without the whining tone she had used in the past when making requests. Her dad looked a bit startled and scanned my eyes and Jean's to see how we were reacting. When Emily had finished, Bill simply said, "Cool." Jean said, "Well, my goodness, I had no idea," and Carl looked down. I think he could sense that all eyes were on him.

He began slowly to explain that his kids did not know that his sister, Molly, had been killed in a tractor accident when she was in her early 20s and that he was afraid to have women doing the heavy work since that time. He was quick to explain that it was a freak accident, that Molly was a smart and hard worker, and that it could have happened to anyone. He realized now that his fear had kept a gulf between him and his daughter, and he regretted it. There were tears in his eyes as he looked at Emily and said, "You can do the work when you are strong enough. You are just too darn skinny now to be of any use. You need to be strong to do this work, Emily girl." Emily began to object, seemed to think better of it, and sighed. "So does this mean I have to get fat?" she asked him. I observed aloud the plaintive tone that had entered her voice and reminded her of a promise I had once made, which was that recovery did not require her to become fat. Emily said, "I have to think about what this means."

Over the next 3 months, Emily began to metamorphose slowly into a physically and emotionally stronger young woman as she took greater charge of her health. She struggled mightily in the first month after that family session. Emily began to move toward healthier eating practices and would then withdraw from them. She gained a few pounds each week and then lost them; she took greater risks by trying different types of food, but would then get scared and start restricting herself; she was allowed to begin gentle exercise with one of her groups, but then would jog to increase her calorie expenditure and would have to remind herself constantly not to use the exercise as a way to burn calories. I sensed that Emily was frustrated with herself, so I explained to her that ambivalence and moving toward and then away from health was a more typical path out of an eating disorder than was a linear path without any bumps and detours in the road (O'Halloran, 1999). "I know, I know," she sighed. The explanation seemed to help her grasp what she was struggling with, but it did not make her journey feel easier.

At this point in treatment, I began working with solution-focused interventions to help her build on exceptions to problems and highlight her accomplishments (McFarland, 1995). Gradually, Emily was able to use these interventions to help her see her strengths and her progress. As her commitment to health grew, her relationships with the staff changed dramatically. She decided that she would write her own plan for achieving recovery and laid down clear steps regarding weight gain, calorie consumption, taking risks in groups, and confronting herself when she was slipping into unhealthy and self-defeating behaviors. She did not simply accept the recommendations of the dietician and her other therapists. She strove to take the recommendations as advice that she carefully considered. She still ate minimal amounts of full-fat cheese, but she agreed to try to eat more. She even joked that the no-fat cream cheese she used to eat tasted like she imagined spackling paste would taste.

Emily became more active in our therapy sessions and had clearly learned how to challenge her own destructive cognitions and faulty assumptions. At one point, she caught herself in a session saying, in a whiny tone, "No guy will like me if I weight 90 or 95 pounds." She stopped for a moment and then said, "If a guy does not like me because I have a little flesh on me, I suppose I don't want him anyway! He would be pretty stupid to be that shallow." As Emily allowed herself to eat more previously forbidden foods, she expressed a fear that she would do what another patient had done. Beth, a friend she had made on the unit, had shifted from anorexia nervosa to binge-eating disorder. Emily, her dietician, and I worked closely to help Emily understand what normal hunger is, distinguish between physical and emotional hungers, and rate her levels of hunger and satiety so that she could be aware of all of her hungers (Roth, 1993). Emily took to scaling very well and began to generalize this to her therapy sessions and interactions with staff and peers. She would finish a group, family, or individual session and rate it, such as "Today was a 6 on a 10-point scale; maybe if I don't whine next time, it will be an 8" or "If mom will let me and dad disagree on things without trying to sort it out, this session could be an 8."

Toward the end of our work together, Emily had moved back home, and we began to meet once every 2 weeks to help her work on relapse prevention. She was having the normal conflicts of a teen with reasonably strict parents, but the family had learned more effective and direct means of communication. Carl and Emily argued regularly, but conflicts were resolved and both heard each other out. Carl laughed during one of the final sessions, saying that Emily was actually a lot like him: "hard-headed, stubborn, and fierce about some things." They laughed together at that and the warmth between them was palpable. Jean was successful "80 percent of the time," by her own estimation, in staying out of father-daughter conflicts. She said that she needed to get away from them sometimes and had recently started a part-time job at a grocery store and attended a book club once per month. She seemed more confident, and I noticed that her clothing and hair style had been updated. Bill was happy to have Emily's help on the ranch. He marveled that although she was still pretty small, she had a lot of strength. Hearing that, Emily smiled confidently.

One of the most informative sessions for me occurred close to termination when I asked Emily to make sense of the meaning and function of her eating disorder. She told me that she had never been special in her family: "Sure I was loved and all that, but I did not feel special." Her sister was special because she was deaf and really smart. Bill was special because he was a boy. "No question about that," said Emily. Emily thought she had to create something that was special about her. She became distinguished by having anorexia nervosa. She said with some pride that she had become "an expert at anorexia" and that at one time she was even the "best" in our unit. I recalled the bout with water and small weights to fake weight gain, and I nodded; she had indeed been the best. Emily looked proud as she said, "Now I finally got a life. I am strong enough to work on the ranch, I am riding horses, I am really good at this, and I don't need anorexia anymore."

At the time of her termination, 10 months after our first session, Emily was 5 feet 1 inch tall, weighed between 93 and 95 pounds for a month, and felt "okay" at that weight. She was committed to not going below 90 or above 95. She said that 90 would be a warning sign for her that she needed to take a look at what was triggering her food restriction. As part of termination, she responded to a series of written termination summary questions about her eating disorder and her treatment. Several questions asked about what Emily learned during her treatment to control the feelings and symptoms that brought her into treatment. She responded, "It is important to do things I enjoy and to talk to someone I trust about my concerns."

To the question "If you start to feel like you are becoming overweight, what will you do?" Emily responded by saying that she would ask people she could trust what she looks like and really try to look at herself more honestly. She also talked about the value of "learning about deep relaxation, breathing, and imagery exercise to help me go to places in my imagination, like warm beaches." She practiced relaxation regularly, and she found it helpful to get plenty of sleep. Her nutritional advice to someone else was "You can eat pretty much want you want, whenever you want it, and you won't gain weight if you are really listening to your body. You can eat what you really want, not restrict, and not eat too much." She ended with the comment "hah!" After further probing, she said this meant that "you have to keep trying even if you don't believe it at first."

Two years after we stopped our work together, Emily wrote to me. I was surprised to get the letter because I had moved to another state, where I had taken a full-time job as a professor and had a small private practice. I've saved Emily's letter to this day. This is a small section of it:

> Dear Sean
>
> I am doing real well. I am horseback riding and have a boyfriend(!). He is very nice and likes horses too. I have been competing in rodeos. Boy does that take a lot of energy! School is going fine, I still don't love it, but it's okay. I just wanted to write and tell you I am doing fine. . . .
>
> Sometimes I think I am getting too fat, but then I try to think about why I am feeling that way because really I am not fat. I have been at about 95 pounds over the last year. I got rid of the clothes from when I was really thin because they were too hard to have around anymore and they reminded me of how awful it was when I was sick and in the hospital. I hope everything is okay with you. Thank you for everything,
>
> Emily

Reflections

I worked with Emily several years ago, at a time when I was less focused in my theory than I am now. Experiences like my work with Emily have made it clear to me that an explicit theoretical perspective is an essential tool in helping to guide me through some of the complexities that therapy offers me. I think I have refined my approach over the last few years. What remains absolutely the same is my steadfast belief that clients have developed an eating disorder for some reason and that it serves a useful function for them, although initially it may be a mystery to the client and the therapist what exactly that function is. My belief about this has been confirmed by the clients I have worked with over the last 15 years and most recently in my qualitative study of 13 women who developed and subsequently recovered from eating disorders. In this study, participants found the function of the eating disorder in their lives. One participant put it clearly: "I would not wish this upon anyone, but for me, it was something that, weird as it sounds, I am grateful for. I needed to go through it. I learned so much through having an eating disorder. As I say, I would not wish it on anyone, but it maybe was what I needed to do to learn how to live my life. Now I live it to the fullest. I know what matters."

The relationship I form with a client is one of the cornerstones of therapy. My primary theoretical approach is cognitive constructivism (Mahoney, 1991, 1995), which places an emphasis on the therapeutic relationship and on helping the client understand how they make meaning of their experiences. However, long before I learned about this approach, it was my natural inclination to go in that direction. I knew at some level that I would not be effective in helping clients to change unless I could form an important relationship with them. I needed to make a connection with clients so that I could see the world as they did and be able to understand their world. I am sure this sounds familiar to those who have studied Carl Rogers' person-centered therapy. Empathy is a strong part of my model. I think it is important to most theories. On the other hand, I know that being able to spot lies and manipulations is just as important as being empathic. Using immediacy and confrontation are also critical in my approach. One of the women in my qualitative study said the following; again, she put it much better than I could have:

> The advice I would give if you deal with a lot of eating disordered people is they're really good liars! They can lie very easily, and to work through the lies because I said a lot of them that they believed . . . back then. . . . I'd say the big thing is try to see through the lies, which is really hard if you've never had an eating disorder or you don't feel anything very much, because they are very good liars [laugh].

Writing this case study has made me wonder what I might have done differently with Emily if I were working with her today. I wish I had been more capable in working with the hospital staff so that there were fewer conflicts about patient care. Conflicts were not unusual in that hospital. Several participants in my qualitative study had also been inpatients in a hospital eating disorders program and made it clear that their experiences sometimes led them to develop more serious problems. I know there have been improvements in inpatient programs and that many residential treatment programs are excellent and offer services that could only have been dreamt of years ago. I do not hesitate to recommend such programs to people if they require more than the outpatient private practice work I now conduct.

One of my regrets was not meeting Carly, the sister who was deaf. Toward the end of our work, Carly had moved to Washington, DC, where she was attending Gallaudet University. If I could go back to working with Emily, I would have tried to meet her sister, who seemed "special" to Emily because of her deafness. I wonder how Emily's period of anorexia affected Carly. I think that I am more skilled than I was several years ago and that maybe those skills could have accelerated Emily's treatment, but I cannot be sure about that. I was genuinely touched to receive a letter from her more than 2 years after we had worked together. It felt very good to me that she had bothered to track me down, and I was pleased for her that things were going well in her life. Getting that letter made me realize that although I know more now, the therapist and person I was then was useful enough to play a role in her decision to move toward a healthier and more fulfilling life.

References

GARNER, D. M., VITOUSEK, K. M., & PIKE, K. M. (1997). Cognitive-behavioral therapy for anorexia nervosa. In D. M. Garner & P. E. Garfinkel (Eds.), *Handbook of treatment for eating disorders* (2nd ed., pp. 94–144). New York: Guilford.

GLASSER, W., & WUBBOLDING, R. (1995). Reality therapy. In R. Corsini & D. Wedding (Eds.), *Current psychotherapies* (5th ed., pp. 293–321). Itasca, IL: F. E. Peacock.

MAHONEY, M. (1991). *Human changes processes: The scientific foundation of psychotherapy.* New York: Basic Books.

MAHONEY, M. (1995). *Constructive psychotherapy.* New York: Guilford.

MCFARLAND, B. (1995). *Brief therapy and eating disorders.* San Francisco: Jossey-Bass.

O'HALLORAN, M. S. (1999). *Recovery from eating disorders: The insider's perspective.* Paper presented at the Annual Meeting of the Psychological Society of Ireland.

POLSTER, E., & POLSTER, M. (1973). *Gestalt therapy integrated.* New York: Vintage Books.

PROCHASKA, J. O., DICLEMENTE, C. C., & NORCROSS, J. C. (1992). In search of how people change: Applications to addictive behavior. *American Psychologist, 47,* 1102–1114.

ROTH, G. (1993). *Breaking free from compulsive eating.* New York: Plume.

II

Case Studies in Individual and Family Treatment

So many different versions of family exist today. A family is less and less likely to consist of a mother, father, and 2.2 children. Instead, a family may be blended, extended, common law, or single parent. Even a single-parent family may defy our stereotypes, being made up of a single father and his son, as in one of the case studies in this section. Families may be part of a majority culture, or they may have roots in a different culture that influences their dynamics and actions. Regardless of their structure, families consist of human beings who coexist and interact.

Just as there are a plethora of family models, there are myriad ways of approaching family treatment. Thompson and Rudolph (1992) point out the similarities within the various models of family treatment. First, they note that within most schools of family treatment, the entire family system may need to change for lasting behavioral change to occur. Second, family therapy encompasses the goal of finding a more comfortable balance of power and roles within the system. Third, in order to achieve new balance, the current dysfunctional pattern may need to be disturbed. The practitioner must ensure that this process is safe for all family members. Finally, family therapy borrows from all other approaches to mental health treatment.

Family treatment is particularly crucial in the resolution of children's and adolescents' problems, as this population is practically completely dependent on their families for physical, emotional, and social support. In fact, on reflection, almost every case study in this book contains some aspect of working with the client's family, in the many different guises that "family" takes.

There are four case studies in this chapter. In the first, Corcoran guides the family of a boy with behavioral problems through solution-focused therapy. She clearly describes and demonstrates techniques such as identifying resources through the use of exceptions, using the miracle question, and employing scaling questions. The next case study, by Bicknell-Hentges, highlights the challenges and learning opportunities inherent in working with diverse clients from families who have strong roots in a culture different from the mainstream. The exploration of the family's cultural experience is crucial to the treatment of the identified client. The practitioner relates her own struggles when the family's values conflict with her own views. Gladow and Pecora offer a moving portrait of the great strides made by a family composed of a single father and his son. The family presents with a history of conflict and is referred to the Homebuilders program, which is designed to prevent unnecessary out-of-home place-ments for children from multiproblem families. In the final case study in this section, the authors, Booth and O'Hara, are an unusual pair: the practitioner and the client's mother. It is a story of a four-year-old girl who is "acting out" and of her therapist's use of a family treatment technique called "Theraplay." We see the case from the perspec-tive of the practitioner, of the mother, and across time as they describe the experience 14 years after the intervention. These studies of family treatment, each so different, all share elements of the importance of the family bond in children's lives.

Reference

THOMPSON, C., & RUDOLPH, L. (1992). *Counseling children.* Pacific Grove, CA: Brooks/ Cole.

Case Study 2-1

Questions for Discussion

1. What are the three main types of client relationships present in solution-focused therapy treatment? Which roles do parents usually engage in? Children?
2. In reframing, the practitioner recognizes that "every problem behavior contains within it an inherent strength." How does she reframe the child's arguing behavior?
3. How and when does the practitioner engage the child in termination of treatment?
4. The practitioner acknowledges that children often use the "default" response of "I don't know" when asked a question. What are some different strategies that can help get past this response?
5. If a family cannot supply an "exception" to the problem behavior—a time when things went well—what can the practitioner do to elicit some description of a positive situation to explore?
6. What is the difference between indirect and direct complimenting? With indirect complimenting, what must the client do?
7. What techniques can be used to help children make exceptions more concrete?
8. What is externalization and how does it enable the client to approach problems less negatively?
9. How do the "miracle" question and scaling help clients clarify goals and solve problems?

Solution-Focused Therapy with Child Behavior Problems

Jacqueline Corcoran

Case Study

Rubin Cruz, age 11, was referred by the school system because of difficulty with his teacher, who reported that he often refused to follow directions and complete his schoolwork. He provoked other students into talking with him and played "class clown." He instigated arguments with the teacher and was in detention at least twice a week for these infractions. His mother, Anna Cruz, says that Rubin shows similar behaviors at home. He argues about doing chores and "everything else" and won't follow his mother's directions.

Introduction

While solution-focused therapy shares with other family therapy models a focus on the contextual nature of behavior, its unique focus is on exceptions, times when the problem is not a problem (de Shazer et al., 1986). The practitioner helps the family to identify resources used during exceptions and then shows the family how to amplify strengths and apply them to problem situations. With solution-focused interventions, people are led to imagine the future without the problem and then to develop concrete steps toward that view.

Solution-focused therapy was applied to the case example through the following techniques: assessment and engagement of the different client relationships, identification of resources through exceptions, the "miracle" question, and scaling questions.

Engagement

In solution-focused therapy, three main types of client relationships present in treatment: the customer (the voluntary client wanting to make changes), the complainant (the client who is more interested in change for another), and the visitor (the involuntary client who has been mandated to attend) (deJong & Berg, 1998). When parents bring their child to treatment for behavior problems, two types of client relationships are typically present. Parents are the complainant type; they see their child as the problem and want change to come from the child. Joining with the complainant involve aligning with the client's goals, asking coping questions, discovering previous solution-finding attempts, reframing, normalizing, eliciting details about the context, and rephrasing complaints as positive behaviors enacted in the present. These techniques will be illustrated below with Rubin's mother, Mrs. Cruz.

Children with behavior problems are usually engaged in the visitor relationship (Selekman, 1993, 1997). Generally less concerned about their behaviors than others (their parents, the school system, and the courts), children's main goal is to terminate treatment. Engagement strategies with the visitor relationship include creating goals around the referral source requirements, allowing clients to take responsibility for their own change, and asking relationship questions. Following the discussion of the engagement strategies with Mrs. Cruz, the joining techniques with Rubin are discussed.

Engagement Strategies with Parents

Parents can usually be engaged in a treatment approach that is explained as working with the child's and family's inherent strengths and that is limited in duration. The solution-focused practitioner also works to align treatment with the client's goals. She collaborates with Rubin on how they will get his parents and the school "off his back" so that he will no longer have to come for treatment. At the same time, the practitioner shares the parent's view that the focus should be on child behavior problems rather than on parenting skills.

Coping questions are another way to join with parents who complain about their child's behavior problems. If complainants' struggles are not validated, they will not readily engage in "solution talk." The main purpose of coping questions, however, is to elicit from parents the skills, abilities, and resources they have used to manage difficulties with the child and other adversity (Berg & Kelly, 2000; deJong & Berg, 1998).

For example, Mrs. Cruz was asked how she managed with the multiple stressors that afflicted her: a son that required frequent meetings with the school; full-time recep-tionist work at a state agency; and the unemployment of her husband due to injury. In answer to coping questions (How do you manage? How do you cope? How do you find the strength to keep going?), Mrs. Cruz said that she was grateful for her family and loved her two boys and her husband, no matter what the problems. The practitioner learned from this conversation that Mrs. Cruz's caring and gratitude for her family was a strength that she drew on to cope with adversity.

In the solution-focused model, clients are considered the experts on their own lives and are asked about what has and has not worked for them in the past (Bertolino & O'Hanlon, 2002). Mrs. Cruz stated that past problem-solving attempts included her husband spanking Rubin when he was younger, but she said, "He's too big for that now." Taking away privileges was another discipline method she and her husband used, but she said, "It gets to the point where Rubin'll have everything taken away from him—the TV, the phone, trips to [a local amusement park]—there's nothing left to take away, and he's arguing all the time because he's bored." She then alluded to the counseling, "That's why we have to come here, to find out other things we can do."

The practitioner said she would hold off on making suggestions and telling the family what they must do because, first of all, "they must have already heard all that." Mrs. Cruz agreed and said that Rubin's new school counselor, Mrs. Crawley, told her that Rubin should have consequences for his actions, although taking away privileges seemed to have escalated the situation. The practitioner explained that the solution-focused approach would work with the strengths and resources of family members rather than telling them what they should do.

Reframing is a solution-focused technique in which the client is given credit for positive aspects of behavior that was previously seen as negative (Berg, 1994), with the recognition that every problem behavior contains within it an inherent strength (O'Hanlon & Weiner-Davis, 1989). In Rubin's case, the practitioner laughed off Rubin's constant attempts at arguing. When she responded in this way, he laughed as well, and she reframed these behaviors as demonstrating his "sense of humor." At the same time that his attempts at arguing were being taken less seriously in session, his mother began to stop engaging in debates with him about his responsibilities. This new response pattern had the effect of reversing the negative cycle of arguing that Rubin and his mother previously shared.

The practitioner was also able to reframe Rubin's arguing in another way. She said, "Rubin can always find the angle. He would really make a good lawyer. Have you thought about that, Rubin, becoming a lawyer?" Rubin said he had, especially when he saw the lawyer shows on TV. Then the conversation turned to what he needed to accomplish in school (currently in the sixth grade) to be prepared for a potential career as a lawyer.

Normalizing can also be used with complainants to depathologize concerns and present them instead as normal life difficulties (Bertolino & O'Hanlon, 2002; O'Hanlon & Weiner-Davis, 1989). Parents sometimes have expectations of their child that are beyond the child's developmental stage, and they can become frustrated when these expectations are not met. When a parent is frustrated and places pressure on a child, some children will be even less likely to perform new behavior. Normalizing might involve educating parents on what children at certain levels can do.

For parents of preteens, normalizing can center around aspects of the child's developmental stage. For example, Mrs. Cruz complained about Rubin's choice of clothing. He would then become more defiant and insist on wearing the clothes; they would argue, and she would feel even less positively toward him. Although the practitioner could join with Mrs. Cruz by agreeing that Rubin's clothing style might seem distasteful to adults, she normalized the behavior by explaining that experimentation with nonmainstream clothing was part of a transitional phase typical of adolescence.

Solution-focused therapy concerns itself with the context of the problem, and the parent's behavior is part of this context. Inquiry about the impact of the child's behavior can be determined by asking the question, "How is this a problem for you?" (O'Hanlon & Weiner-Davis, 1989). When Mrs. Cruz was asked, "How is his wearing those clothes a problem for you?" she said that the clothing style made her son look like he belonged to a gang: "The first step, he looks the part; the next step he's playing it." She was asked if other youth in her neighborhood wore those kind of clothes but were not in gangs and performed well in school. Indeed, she had to admit, "all the kids wear that style these days, even the 'good kids.'" The question "How is this a problem for you?" sometimes changes a parent's perspective about the problem, making them focus on the specific behaviors they would like to see changed rather than on aspects of the problem that have seemingly "taken on a life of their own."

Parents who bring in their children for behavior problems usually catalog their children's negative behaviors. Similarly, Mrs. Cruz talked about Rubin's noncompliance at school, the frequent parent-teacher conferences, his lack of follow-through with rules at home, and his defiance. A key question then is, "What do you want to see instead?" with the practitioner working to identify the presence of positive behaviors. For example, rather than "not talking back," the goal becomes "following directions"; rather than "not fighting," the goal becomes "getting along with classmates."

Once his mother clarified some desired outcomes, Rubin was asked, "What do you hear your mom say she wants you to do?" Rubin's reply was, "I don't remember." In many instances, parents talk so long or in such a general manner that the gist of the message is lost, and the child is unable to reflect back their parents' expectations. In these cases, parents are asked to repeat themselves. Through this process, parents learn to be brief and specific in their requests.

Engagement Strategies with Children

The child with a behavior problem is engaged in the goal of terminating treatment as quickly as possible with these opening questions: Whose idea was it for you to come here? What do they need to see to know that you don't have to come here anymore? (Selekman, 1993, 1997). In this way, young clients see that the practitioner is not invested in a long-term relationship and will work with them to obtain results and end treatment.

Rubin answered this line of questioning in the following way:

Practitioner: Whose idea was it that you come here?

Rubin: My teacher, I guess. (*glances at his mother with a smile*) And maybe my mom, too.

Practitioner: What do they need to see to know you don't have to come here anymore?

Rubin seems a little taken aback by this question and is silent for a moment.

Rubin: I don't know.

Practitioner: Come on, I know you don't want to keep coming here. What do you need to do so that they'll be satisfied, and you don't need to come anymore?

Rubin: To be good.

Practitioner: What does being good look like?

Rubin: Not fighting.

Practitioner: What will you be doing instead of fighting?

Rubin: Being good.

Practitioner: If I were seeing you through a video camera—(*mimes this action*)— what would I see you doing?

Rubin laughs at the idea, but it gets him to think for a moment.

Rubin: Well, in school, I won't tell the teacher, "No!"

Practitioner: What will you do instead when she asks you to do something?

Rubin: I'll just do it. I'll sit there and just do my work.

In this example, the practitioner is persistent in getting the client to identify the specific behaviors that are required to end treatment as quickly as possibly, a goal in which Rubin is invested. In solution-focused therapy, in addition to the view that clients are the experts on their own lives, clients are also allowed to come up with their own answers and solutions rather than having the practitioner lecture them "on what they must do." However, Rubin, like many youngsters, used the default response of "I don't know" to reply to many of the practitioner's subsequent questions. Several different strategies may be used at this point. The first is to allow silence (Berg, 1994). The child may then become uncomfortable and talk to fill the silence. (Parents should be prevented from filling the silence themselves.) The silence should not go on too long because power struggles might result, and these inhibit rapport building. The second way to handle an "I don't know" response is to rephrase the question (Berg, 1994) so that the client understands that the practitioner will persist until the question is answered. A third way to handle an "I don't know" response is to use a relationship question.

Relationship questions ask clients to view themselves from the perspective of someone else (deJong & Berg, 1998), a process that enables clients to understand the influence of their behavior on others and to view themselves from a more objective position.

Rubin was asked, "What do you think your mom (or teacher) would say needs to happen so you don't have to come here anymore?" He still said he didn't know, so his mother was asked, "He doesn't seem to know, mom. What can you tell him about what he needs to be doing so he doesn't need to keep coming back here?" After she gave her perspective on what should happen, Rubin was asked to repeat what he heard his mother say to make sure the expectations had been clarified into specific and concrete behaviors. Relationship questions are particularly helpful with involuntary clients who, perhaps because they are not interested in changing, do not know how they can change. However, they are often aware of what others would like for them to do. This perspective is tapped with solution-focused therapy by defining what goals need to be achieved so that treatment is no longer necessary.

Exceptions

One of the main interventions for solution-focused therapy is identifying exceptions, or times when the problem is not a problem (Bertolino & O'Hanlon, 2002; de Shazer et al., 1986; Selekman, 1993). Once the parent and/or the child identifies the desired behaviors, family members are asked about times when those behaviors have already occurred. Usually, people have become so immersed in their problems and in their expectation that counseling involves discussion of the problems (O'Hanlon & Weiner-Davis, 1989), they are taken aback by questions about nonproblem times and are sometimes initially unable to answer. Practitioners must allow space (time and silence) for family members to identify exceptions, perhaps using additional probing questions if they are still unable to answer.

For example, Mrs. Cruz was asked to consider a time when Rubin washed the dishes (his nightly chore) without an argument. She said, "No, he always argues." When Rubin was asked if he could think of such an instance, he said, "I do the dishes all the time. It's Joey (his brother) who doesn't do them."

"He doesn't complain like you do," Mrs. Cruz retorted. "You complain and argue about doing anything I want you to do."

When people still struggle with finding exceptions, despite the attempts of the practitioner, questions can be asked about when the problem was less intense, frequent, or severe (O'Hanlon & Weiner-Davis, 1989). In this case, the practitioner said, "I know Rubin seems to do a lot of arguing. I wonder when he argued just a little bit or only made one comment and then did what he was supposed to do."

In answer to this prompt, Rubin produced an instance from that week in which he said he didn't want to do the dishes, he had hardly eaten anything compared to all the other people in the family, so why should he have to clean up? Despite his grumblings and attempts to get out of the chore, he went ahead and did it.

Once an exception has been identified, the practitioner probes for what was different about the contextual details of the situation: who was there, when it happened, what was happening, and how it happened (deJong & Berg, 1998). In this instance, Mrs. Cruz said she just ignored him; his argument was so "lame" that it was not worth responding to, and she went on talking to her husband, who also ignored Rubin. The practitioner paraphrased back to her, "So when you didn't pay attention to his argument, he just went ahead and did it? What does that tell you about what you can do?" Mrs. Cruz was able to see that she could ignore some of her son's attempts to engage her in debates.

If people still struggle with the request to find exceptions, examples of behavior in the session can sometimes be used. One time, Mrs. Cruz talked at length about a report from the teacher about Rubin's noncompliance. Growing bored, Rubin started playing with an alarm clock in the office until it was finally in pieces. Realizing what he had done, Mrs. Cruz shouted at him to put it back together. After a pleased look at his handiwork, Rubin began to replace the parts. The practitioner noted to Mrs. Cruz that he had followed her direction the very first time. Mrs. Cruz downplayed his compliance in this instance, saying, "It's only because you're here." The practitioner reassured Mrs. Cruz that her presence did not necessarily command obedience and pushed Mrs. Cruz and Rubin to take credit for this exception.

Another example of exception finding involved Rubin's intermittent tendency to get into fights at school. This example shows that clients often attribute their exceptions to entities other than themselves. Rather than accepting this view, the practitioner works with the client to take credit for what is different about the exception.

Practitioner: Tell me about a time when you avoided getting into a fight.
Rubin: I was in science.
Practitioner: What happened?
Rubin: This idiot threw a spitball at my head.
Practitioner: Then what did you do?
Rubin: I gave him a dirty look, told him he better watch it.
Practitioner: Then what happened?
Rubin: I turned back around and saw the teacher was watching.
Practitioner: What were you thinking?
Rubin: That I would get in trouble if I did something back. But I wanted to. Because he was still saying stuff. I don't know why Mrs. Wymann didn't hear him.
Practitioner: What did you do then?
Rubin: I just stayed turned around.
Practitioner: What were you telling yourself then?
Rubin: The teacher was still looking; I wasn't going to do nothing.

As in this example, some children and adolescents give credit to people or entities outside themselves. The practitioner must work to empower clients and help them take credit for the success: "Good, so you knew if the teacher saw you, you wouldn't let yourself fight."

Rubin said, "But if the teacher wasn't there, I would have knocked the jerk's face in." "I'm sure you would have," the practitioner said easily. "So what does that say about what you can do to avoid fights?" Rubin was eventually led to the response that he could make sure a teacher saw him when a provocative situation developed, which would prevent him from responding in a way that got him in trouble.

Another central aspect in the context of children's behavior includes the parent's role in the interaction (O'Hanlon & Weiner-Davis, 1989): "What are you doing when your child is behaving?" Parents may realize, for instance, that they have given their children special attention or remained calm. In solution-focused therapy, the context of a behavior is seen as crucial. Problems do not reside as much in the individual as in the behavior patterns, which influence others to act a certain way. With child behavior problems, parents play a large role in this context.

Complimenting

Solution-focused practitioners pay a great deal of attention to complimenting clients and being vigilant for opportunities to praise (deJong & Berg, 1998). For example, when Rubin took apart the clock in session, the practitioner praised him for his "mechanical abilities" and for following his mother's direction to put the clock back together.

As a general guideline, indirect rather than direct complimenting should be used whenever possible and can be directed toward either parent or child. A direct compliment is when the practitioner praises the client: "You did a good job." or "I liked the way you said that." An indirect compliment implies something positive about the client, but pushes the client to figure out the resources used to achieve success (deJong & Berg, 1998): "How were you able to do that?" "How did you know that was the right thing to do or say?" Compliments are more powerful when clients generate them for themselves. When clients realize their own resources, change begins to occur.

For instance, Rubin was asked about his chores, "How did you manage to do the dishes when you find it such a drag?" Rubin answered, "I just did them." He was then asked, "But how did you get yourself to do them when you didn't want to?" He answered, "There was a TV show I wanted to watch, and I knew my dad wouldn't let me go in there until I finished the dishes." The practitioner, ever vigilant for exceptions, seized on this strategy as well, bringing it to the attention of Mrs. Cruz: "How did you come up with that idea, that he doesn't get to watch TV until he's done the dishes? That's a great idea!" Mrs. Cruz admitted that her husband resorted to this tactic more than she did, but that they didn't use it as often as they could. Giving Rubin privileges when he did behave seemed to work much better than taking away privileges when he didn't behave. In an attempt to expand on the exception, the practitioner asked, "How could you do more of that?" Although withholding privileges until Rubin had completed his chores seemed an obvious solution, Mrs. Cruz had not taken advantage of this strategy until the practitioner focused her attention on it.

The practitioner also worked to evoke more compliments from the parent to the child because a solution-focused premise is "to change the viewing" as well as "the doing" (de Shazer, 1994). Rubin was asked, "What does your mom tell you when you're doing a good job or doing what she wants you to do?" When Rubin had some difficulty with this question, Mrs. Cruz saw she did not often give Rubin credit for his positive behaviors.

When parents do praise their children in session, youth are asked to repeat what they have heard their parent say. In this way, the positive message is reinforced, and parents begin to realize the powerful effect their words have on their children. When parents have a more positive view of their children and communicate this, children tend to increase their positive behaviors, and the relationship between parent and child is enhanced.

Techniques to Make Exceptions Concrete

Cognitively, young children have difficulty going into the past to retrieve exceptions (Selekman, 1997). While parents can help them with this process, other techniques are needed to bring the material into more concrete and present focus. One way to do this is through the use of drawings to make exceptions more concrete (Selekman, 1997). Rubin enjoyed drawing a picture of himself in the classroom, sitting quietly doing his work and following his teacher's directions. At the practitioner's request, he displayed, with comic-strip bubbles, what would be said aloud and what he would be telling herself. He showed the teacher saying, "Rubin, do this, do that," and himself saying, "Yes, Mrs. Wymann." In a thought bubble above his head, he wrote, "This work is boring, but I'm so smart I can finish it fast and then I can draw cartoons."

Another way to help children apply the exceptions they have identified is to role-play situations, which makes their strategies concrete. A playful atmosphere is generated in session when children are asked to assign roles to the therapist and to their parents. This sense of playfulness lightens up the negativity that surrounds problems and introduces new possibilities for behavior. Role-playing also forces members to take on new perspectives, which helps to introduce new possibilities for behavior.

Rubin role-played a situation in which a classmate had tried to provoke him into a fight by calling him "Mexican." He had previously handled the situation by hitting the classmate; a physical fight ensued, and both he and the other boy were suspended. Earlier, the practitioner had helped Rubin identify that humor was one way he could handle difficult situations. Rubin came up with a response in session (but said he would try to think of something better in the meantime): "That's right, I'm Mexican and proud of it," he said while smiling.

He enjoyed having both the practitioner and his mother play him in turn, with him acting as difficult as possible as the other boy. The practitioner complimented Rubin on making the role-play so challenging, mentioning that a lot of children just tell her that they would "walk away" from provocation without thinking through how difficult that would be and without rehearsal. Then when they are faced with a tense situation, they do not know how to enact the solutions they identified. She then had Rubin play himself, with her being the instigator. By this time, Rubin was quite amused and had no trouble laughing a lot as he said his "lines."

Externalizing

Exceptions can further be identified through a narrative intervention formulated by Michael White called "externalizing the problem" (White & Epston, 1990), which has been adopted by some solution-focused practitioners (e.g., Berg, 1994; Bertolino & O'Hanlon, 2002). Externalizing the problem involves a linguistic separation of the presenting problem from the person. Instead of the problem being one of personal dynamics and an inherent quality, it is represented as an external entity.

For young children, drawings can make externalizing explicit. For example, a child being seen for anger problems can be asked, "What do you want to call the anger?" Common responses are "the volcano" and "the tornado." Children are then asked either to draw this externalized entity or to draw themselves taking control over it. Questions are asked about times when they have control over the entity and when it has control over them to discover the strategies they enact to gain influence over their behaviors (White & Epston, 1990).

Even school-age children may enjoy playful names for the externalized objects. Rubin was asked, "What do you call all that stuff you do at school?" He answered "the crap" and thoroughly enjoyed hearing his practitioner and his mother referring to "the crap" in the ensuing conversation and in subsequent sessions. The sense of playfulness generated by the constant references to "the crap" decreased the seriousness of the problem and seemed to reduce his need to engage in these behaviors. Both the client and his mother reported that school referrals over "the crap" had decreased dramatically. Externalization enables clients to take a less serious approach to their problems, freeing them to come up with options and thus empowering them to "fight against" their external oppressors (White & Epston, 1990).

Typical externalizing questions for parents who come to treatment for their children's behavior problems involve how they can resist their children's "invitation to debate or argue" with them. This question was asked of Mrs. Cruz, who continuously said how clever Rubin was at "pushing her buttons" and engaging her and her husband in senseless arguments about chores, homework, compliance at school, and other tasks Rubin found distasteful. In response to this externalizing question, Mrs. Cruz said she would just laugh off his complaints or ignore him and make him do the task anyway.

Subsequent Sessions

In subsequent sessions, practitioners can start by asking the question, "Tell me what is better?" (Berg, 1994; O'Hanlon & Weiner-Davis, 1989). Despite the positive orientation of this question, sometimes parents still try to catalog their children's transgressions from the prior week. Rather than allowing the session to be overtaken by "problem talk," the family can be re-oriented by asking, "How could the situation have been handled instead?" This discussion could also be followed by role-play so that new behavior choices are made more concrete. This process is much more productive than spending time with a family going over in detail problems that have already occurred.

The Miracle Question

People who have experienced a negative and stressful past may easily project this past into the future and assume that their lives will always be the same. The "miracle" question is one way that clients can begin to envision a more hopeful future (Cade & O'Hanlon, 1993). In the miracle question, clients are asked to conjure up a detailed view of a future without the problem: "Let's say that while you're sleeping, a miracle occurs, and the problem you came here with is solved. What will let you know the next morning that a miracle happened?" (de Shazer, 1988). Specifics are elicited about this "no problem" experience so that clients can develop a vision of a more hopeful and satisfying future (deJong & Berg, 2001). Rubin and his mother responded in the following way to the miracle question:

Rubin: I will want to get up in the morning.

Practitioner: What will you be doing to show you want to get up?

Rubin: I will jump out of bed.

Mrs. Cruz: Instead of me telling him over and over again that he has to get up now.

Practitioner: So what will your mom notice about you, Rubin?

Rubin: She would be really surprised if I just came into the kitchen already dressed. She would turn around to yell at me, and there I would be—right behind her. It would scare her.

Practitioner: What's the next thing you would notice?

Mrs. Cruz: There wouldn't be this big hunt for his homework. He would already have it together, and we would be ready to leave on time.

Practitioner: What would you notice, Rubin?

Rubin: My mom wouldn't be all stressed out. She would be laughing and joking around with me.

The practitioner continued to elicit specific behavioral sequences for Rubin as he went to school in the morning, asking the question "What will your mom or teacher notice that you are doing or that is different about you?" to help him see the perspective of others and to demonstrate the influence of contextual factors.

Sometimes asking clients to envision a brighter future may help them to be clearer about what they want or to see a path to problem solving. By discussing the future in a positive light, hope can be generated, and change can be enacted in the present by the recognition of both strengths to cope with obstacles and signs of possibilities for change (Cade & O'Hanlon, 1993).

Scaling Questions

A more specific way to address future goals is through the scaling question intervention. Scaling questions involve ranking progress on goals on a 10-point scale (deJong & Berg, 2001). Although scaling questions are primarily used for goal setting, multiple interventions can be followed by this technique, including relationship questions, exception finding, complimenting, and task setting.

Scaling questions begin when family members are asked to identify the priority goal. In complainant-driven goals, child behaviors are the focus. The goal should be achievable (rather than perfection), limited to one setting (i.e., home or school), and involve the presence of concrete behaviors rather than the absence of negative behaviors.

Mrs. Cruz selected Rubin's school behaviors as a priority because they were the reason for the referral. Both Mrs. Cruz and Rubin were involved in developing the concrete indicators, which included "completing work without arguing," "being respectful to teacher" (which was defined even further as accepting her directions by nodding and smiling), and "leaving the other kids alone."

After the concrete indicators were formulated, Rubin was asked to rank his current functioning on a scale, with 10 defined as the behaviors listed above and 1 as "the day you called for the appointment." Rubin ranked his current functioning as a 7 and said that he did a lot of the positive behaviors already. He was complimented for having made so much progress already ("Wow, you're almost home free!") and asked how he was able to achieve this level of success.

After some discussion of exceptions, Rubin was asked a relationship question about how his mother would rank him. He said a 6 and was shocked when his mother ranked him as a 2. Rubin was asked about his stunned reaction and to account for the disparity between his and his mother's rankings. He said he couldn't account for it; his mother was his biggest supporter. Asked to elaborate, Rubin said his mother was always behind him when no one else was and always encouraged him. The practitioner asked Mrs. Cruz, "Mom, did you realize he saw you this way?"

"No, I'm really surprised." Mrs. Cruz then explained her ranking, "Rubin, you've been in detention at school twice a week practically all semester, and you've been suspended twice. I call that a 2, not a 7." This seemed to get across to Rubin, as nothing else apparently had, that he needed to make improvements in his behaviors.

At this point, he was also asked relationship questions about other people impacted by his behavior, namely his father and his teacher. He estimated his father's ranking of his behavior as a 5, which Mrs. Cruz agreed was a realistic appraisal because she was the one who handled the calls from the school and the parent-child conferences.

Chastened by his mother's ranking, Rubin ranked himself as a 2 from his teacher's perspective. Opportunities for exceptions can develop even from low rankings: "A 2!

You've already taken some steps. What have you been doing?" If clients give 1 as a ranking, then the client can be asked, "What are you doing to make sure it's not getting any worse?" In this way, clients can still be given credit for the actions they are taking to overcome their problems.

Task setting follows from the scaling by asking children, "What needs to happen so that you can move one number up on the scale before the next time we meet?" Even young children grasp the ordinal nature of the scale and often find moving up on the scale quite reinforcing in itself. Children often come into subsequent sessions and proudly announce how they have advanced on the scale. Progress is tracked over time, so the scales serve as measures of goals. Scales make goals and the steps necessary to attain these goals concrete and specific.

Summary of Subsequent Sessions and Termination

Mrs. Cruz and Rubin attended a total of five sessions. Because Rubin improved steadily on his school behaviors, according to both Mrs. Cruz and his teacher, another solution-focused scale was developed for Rubin's home behaviors. Part of his home behavior involved getting along with his 14-year-old brother, who was included in the last two sessions. Although a sixth session was scheduled, the Cruzes didn't return for their appointment. When the practitioner called Mrs. Cruz, she said that the family didn't need to come back because Rubin's behavior was so much better.

Conclusion

This case study demonstrates the solution-focused model applied to child behavior problems. The emphasis of the techniques is on identifying and elaborating the strengths of clients and families rather than focusing on their deficits. In this way, the positive aspects of children's behavior are highlighted and the strategies they use are applied to problem areas.

References

BERG, I. K. (1994). *Family-based services: A solution-focused approach.* New York: Norton.
BERG, I. K., & KELLY, S. (2000). *Building solutions in child protective services.* New York: Norton.
BERTOLINO, B., & O'HANLON, B. (2002). *Collaborative, competency-based counseling and therapy.* Boston: Allyn & Bacon.
CADE, B., & O'HANLON, W. H. (1993). *A brief guide to brief therapy.* New York: Norton.
DEJONG, P., & BERG, I. K. (1998). *Interviewing for solutions.* Pacific Grove, CA: Brooks/Cole.
DEJONG, P., & BERG, I. K. (2001). *Interviewing for solutions* (2nd ed.). Pacific Grove, CA: Brooks/Cole.
DE SHAZER, S. (1988). *Clues: Investigating solutions in brief therapy.* New York: Norton.
DE SHAZER, S. (1994). *Words were originally magic.* New York: Norton.

DE SHAZER, S., BERG, I. K., LIPCHICK, E., NUNNALLY, E., MOLNAR, A., GINGERICH, W., & WEINER-DAVIS, M. (1986). Brief therapy: Focused solution development. *Family Process, 25,* 207–221.

O'HANLON, W. H., & WEINER-DAVIS, M. (1989). *In search of solutions: A new direction in psychotherapy.* New York: Norton.

SELEKMAN, M. (1993). *Pathways to change.* New York: Guilford.

SELEKMAN, M. (1997). *Solution-focused therapy with children.* New York: Guilford.

WHITE, M., & EPSTON, D. (1990). *Narrative means to therapeutic ends.* New York: Norton.

Case Study 2-2

Questions for Discussion

1. The author openly discusses her fear of losing a client to suicide. How did she work with the client, initially, to ensure his safety?
2. How does the practitioner assess the level of the client's suicidality? Would you agree with her choice to allow him to go home, with the 24-hour watch in place?
3. Why is it crucial for the practitioner to explore the cultural experience of this family with them? How does this exploration help the identified client?
4. How does the practitioner deal with her own perceptions of a woman's role in society and how that view conflicts with the traditional cultural values of the family in this case?

Teach Me Your World: Lessons in Culture from a Family in Crisis

Lindsay Bicknell-Hentges

The First Meeting

I remember the phone call as if it happened yesterday. I was sitting in one of the small offices designated for the lowly interns when the piercing ring of the phone jolted me from the not yet completed dissertation I held in my hand.

It was my turn to answer intake calls, and the receptionist forwarded a call from a social worker at a local high school. I felt a definite surge in my pulse when the social worker asked if he could send one of his students to me immediately. The student had just confided that he was seriously considering suicide and would be accompanied by his mother to my agency. I tried to listen carefully to the limited details of the case, but a part of me was reviewing suicidal risk assessment in my head while trying to dispel an ominous sense of foreboding.

The youth was a 15-year-old male named Juan Ramirez. I must admit that I was initially more fearful of the suicide risk than the cultural issues that would come to be the greater challenge in the case. Suicidal clients always remind me of why I chose not to go into medicine. I (still) do not like to worry about my clients dying. When the receptionist called to inform me that Juan had arrived, I took a deep breath and went down to meet him.

Juan was of medium height and build. His dark hair was long on top with shorter sides. As he said his name, his voice was rather subdued and his hair fell over his eyes, giving the distinct impression that he preferred to hide from the world. Juan's mother, Maria, was a petite and attractive woman with long, dark hair. She shared the pronounced Hispanic accent of her son. Blinking away tears, she immediately began begging me to help her son. Juan responded by slumping down in his chair and hiding behind his hair.

I introduced myself and gently addressed the crisis at hand, "People seem to be very concerned about you, Juan. I know you don't know me, but can you tell me what's going on right now?"

Juan paused, his face full of pain, "I just can't take it anymore. The pressure is way too much and I don't want to deal with it anymore." Slowly he continued to talk about how he felt that he had to learn computers and make perfect grades in school. He wanted to please his father but felt that nothing that he ever did was good enough. "So I just try harder. I don't watch TV anymore. I don't see my friends. I just study and work on my computer until late in the night. I have to get a scholarship to a good college and study computers, so I can be an engineer. Then my father would be proud; then he would be happy. I could give my family money to make life easier for them. I can't stop working. I am always afraid that I will get a B on a test and not get a scholarship. Whenever I make less than an A, I get so afraid I will fail. Then I just work harder and stay up even later." Juan stopped and sighed, "I hate my life. I feel so stressed out. I never have fun. I never laugh. Lately, I find myself thinking about different ways I could die so that it would finally be over."

As Juan spoke, his mother looked stunned and cried. "Juan," she said, "This is not what your father wants for you. We want you to be happy. We love you. We want you to have friends. You don't have to work so hard. Oh my God, we don't want you to die."

As Maria talked it was clear that Juan was not buying it. His thinking was rigid and obsessive. I was looking for some crack in his thinking, some opening. I knew that I did not want this young man to be hospitalized. Outpatient therapy would be less disruptive and much less damaging to his already fragile sense of adolescent identity. However, I was unwilling to take a risk that could lead to a suicide attempt.

I knew his mother would support any protective plan, but I had to get a no-suicide contract from Juan as well. I had to broach those uncomfortable questions and assess the seriousness of Juan's plans to hurt himself. I asked Juan to describe his suicidal plans: "How would you go about killing yourself?"

Juan reported that he had thought about throwing himself on the electrified rail of the commuter train near his home. When he said this, my concern for him grew. I had hoped for a less-developed plan or one without the means so readily available, but Juan was not easing my fears. He had intent, he had a plan, and he had the means to hurt himself. I knew that I could not let him return home with his mother unless he could shift his thinking enough to agree to a no-suicide contract supported by a commitment for 24-hour supervision from his mother.

I had to reach Juan and do so fairly quickly. Despite my sense of urgency, I knew there is always only one place to start. I needed to connect with him and build a relationship. "Juan, you really are a remarkable young man. You're maturity is incredible. I have worked with many teens, and there are very few who are so seriously focused on their future. You are the kind of son that most people just dream of having." As I spoke, Juan looked up with surprise.

"I respect your goals, but I also recognize that the pressure that you are putting yourself under is too great. You have decided that the only way to ensure a successful future is through constant working and pressure on yourself. This is understandable, but people require balance. All work and all stress would make most people want to die. And if you die, Juan, you won't go to college and you won't be an engineer. You won't be able to help your family. You are trying to convince yourself that relaxing and having fun are not necessary, but they are. People work better when they are rested and take breaks from work. You are hurting your efficiency and productivity by constantly working. I know it seems crazy, but working too much starts to backfire. After a while, the reason for work becomes distant and not worth it. It seems like that is where you are."

Juan nodded and I was relieved to see that he was listening to me. "It isn't working, but I am so afraid. When I'm not working, all I do is worry," Juan said.

I could see that Juan was trapped in rigid and obsessive thinking that drove his compulsive work behavior. I knew we couldn't end this cycle in the short time that remained, but my hope for a no-suicide contract was increasing. Juan and his mother seemed more relaxed as their trust in me and in the counseling process grew.

"Juan, I know that we cannot end your worrying in the short time that we have together today, but I think that we can do some work together that will return joy to your life. The trick is that you kind of have to trust and believe me. I will not try to take suicide away as an option for you. I won't kid you. Suicide is always an option. I just want you to try some other things first. It's like you are looking into a tunnel and all you see is the darkness. But I have been down this tunnel before. I know that there is light at the end of the tunnel. You just can't see it from here because the road to the light is not straight, but curved. I can tell you that I have worked with many people who have thought of hurting themselves. They truly wanted to die, but they trusted me to try counseling first. Juan, all of those people are alive today and they all are thankful that they did not die. I believe you, too, can make it out of this pain, if you can trust me. I know that you just met me, but can you trust me on this?"

Juan did not respond immediately, and I noticed that I was holding my breath as I waited.

"Are you sure that they are glad?" Our eyes met and I felt Juan's piercing stare as he looked for any hint of deception or insincerity. I didn't flinch. "I'm sure, Juan. I wouldn't lie to you."

He looked to the floor in deep thought, "Well, maybe."

To assure him that I was not asking for too much, I quickly added, "Give me a week at a time. Today, all I'm asking is that you not hurt yourself before I see you next. We will bring in your mother and your father." I looked to his mother, "If that would be okay?" Maria quickly answered with tears flowing, "Yes, yes, of course, his father and I would do anything." Her eyes met Juan's, and I knew she was talking more to him than me.

"I have to hear you say that you can agree to that, Juan."

Juan said that he would agree, and we made an appointment for a family session the next evening. I added that Juan's mother should be sure that Juan was not alone when he returned home. With Juan listening, I outlined a protective plan of 24-hour supervision until things settled a bit. Maria told me that she was "just a housewife," so she would be with him until we met again. I wanted to comment on the "just a house-wife" part, but held the thought for later. After giving Juan and his mother the 24-hour pager number for any crisis before the next session, I said goodbye and added what a pleasure it had been to meet them.

Supervision and Beyond: Opening My Eyes to Culture

On the walk back to my office, I was accompanied by that familiar sense of uneasiness that always comes with suicidal clients. I retraced my steps. I had made a full lethality risk assessment, successfully completed crisis intervention, made a no-suicide contract, and established a protective plan. I knew that I had done everything right "in theory," but my anxiety led me to the steps of my supervisor's door.

"Got a minute?" I lied as I stuck my head through her open door.

As usual, Emma Rodriguez gave me a warm smile as she welcomed me into her office. "What's up?" she asked, and I poured out the story of my new client. Emma had great faith in my clinical abilities, having made numerous live observations of my sessions. She nodded reassuringly, interjecting approval of my session, until I finally said the client's name. "His name is Juan? Where is he from?"

I rattled off the name of his suburb, and she said, "No, I mean where did his family immigrate from? Are they from Mexico, Puerto Rico, or somewhere else?"

From her question, I knew I had blown it. I was clueless. I had no answer to her question. As I admitted this, I realized that I had missed something very crucial. I also realized that I couldn't quite answer this question about the very supervisor that I was addressing. I knew that Emma was Latina, but that was it. Despite her subtle accent and her known research interests in acculturation, I did not view Emma through a cultural lens. I admired her competence and energy and I wanted to learn from her, but I had not previously needed her help with a Latino family. Things were quickly about to change.

Emma went on to explain patiently that the immigration experiences of Mexican Americans and Puerto Rican Americans are very different. She told me of her own immigration from Mexico. She explained the ongoing tension between many Mexican Americans and Puerto Rican Americans. She also briefly explained the process of acculturation and handed me a stack of articles to read. She agreed to supervise me on the case and encouraged me to read the articles before my next session with the family.

I spent the evening reading, recognizing my ignorance on many cultural concerns and feeling grateful for my supervisor's awareness and willingness to teach me. I had to face the fact that I was not culturally competent to work with a Latino family. However, Emma's words of reassurance stayed with me. She said that part of my job was to ask the family to teach me about their culture. She added that although many Latinos share common traditions and values, each family has its own unique experiences. She encouraged me to initiate a conversation about the family's immigration very early in my work with them.

Entering the Family System

I spent a somewhat restless night hoping that the family, especially Juan, would show the next day. Thankfully, they did not disappoint. We started the session right on time. As I introduced myself, I noticed how much more aware I was of our cultural differences than I had been in my first session when I was focused entirely on the suicide issue.

Juan's father introduced himself and his daughter, "My name is Manuel, and this is Tina." His handshake was strong and solid, but his faced was taut with concern.

The father continued and I remembered from my readings the strong role that many Latino men play in their families. "I am glad to meet you," he started, "But I just wanted to say that my son cannot be suicidal. It is just not possible."

I was thrown by his statement and watched with dismay as Juan slouched down, almost melting into his chair. "Mr. Ramirez, help me understand you. I must admit that I am somewhat confused. Juan did tell me that he wanted to die, but I am sure that you have something important to add or I would not have asked you to come here." I realized that I had joined well with Juan and his mother, but had no relationship with the father at this point. Over the course of the first session, it became more clear that Juan and his mother were very close, if not enmeshed, leaving his father isolated and disengaged.

Juan's father continued with a note of irritation in his voice, "I know that my son is not suicidal. He cannot be. He has no reason to be."

He paused briefly, and I tried to be sure that my face remained neutral, despite my growing anxiety. "I know about these things. When I was his age, my father beat me and beat me. He told me that I was stupid and worthless. I tried to kill myself. I tried to hang myself, but I did not die. He cannot want to die. I never beat him. I have never called him stupid or worthless. We love him and buy him everything we can afford. I work hard to be sure my kids do not go through what I went through. Why would he ever want to die?"

The shocked looks in the room told me that this was a new revelation to us all. I felt a growing sense of admiration for this man. I knew these words could not be coming out easily.

"Mr. Ramirez," I started.

"Please call me Manuel," he interrupted.

"I would be honored, Manuel." I did not know what to say, but I spoke from the deep empathy I felt for this man, his son, and his family. It was one of those therapeutic moments when the words flow from some internal wellspring. "Clearly, your son has not shared your experience of growing up. You seem to be a very devoted father who has worked so hard not to repeat the pain of your own childhood. Juan simply seems to feel that he will let you down. I think he sees how hard you have worked and feels he must work as hard. But he can't and he lives in constant fear of disappointing you."

Manuel turned to his son, "Is this true? Juan, this cannot be. I am so proud of you. You are so smart. You will work with your mind instead of your hands like I have." As he spoke, he held out the worn hands of a laborer. "I don't want you to have these hands, the hands of my father and my grandfather and the other fathers before him. We all worked so hard, and until now, there was never enough. I hated my father when I was young, but now I see him differently. He was trying, the only way he knew."

Manuel stopped and sighed. Juan was sobbing. Tina and Maria were crying. Manuel and I fought to stop our tears before they, too, escaped down our cheeks. I waited for a moment, not sure where to go next. Then Emma's words came back to me to ground me. I asked Manuel to help me understand his personal experience of culture.

"Manuel, as you see, I am not from your culture. I appreciate your willingness to talk with me about such personal things. I see such strength and commitment in your family, and I want to help you find your own way through this crisis. Help me understand your family and culture better, if you are willing. As you teach me about your experiences, I can be of more assistance to you." I could tell from his face that he was more than willing, so I continued, "How did you come to this country?"

Manuel began to weave a story. He started with the story of his older brother with the same name. "My brother was first named Manuel. When he was 16, he left our small village in the mountains of Mexico to go to the United States. I was not born yet, but I heard that my father gave him all of the small savings the family had. He was to find work in the States and send money back to the family. People did it all the time. It was the only way to survive in our small village. There was no way to make money and not enough food."

As Manuel spoke, I noticed his family listening attentively, exhibiting a peacefulness that I had not seen before. "But they never heard from him again. The family waited and waited. No letter ever came. No money came. No one knew anything. Was he alive? Was he dead? Was he rich or poor? My mother became pregnant with me about two years after he left. She gave me my lost brother's name."

"My father never seemed to like me. When I was older, I wondered if he took out his anger for my lost brother onto me. I don't know, but I could never please him and I grew to hate him. I knew my mother loved me, but by the time I was Juan's age I wanted to die. When that didn't work, I left. I never looked back either. I never called and never wrote. I don't know if my parents are alive or dead."

As Manuel talked, I began to worry that he was saying too much, too fast. I knew I had to wind the session down, help him transition to the ride home with his family, and revisit Juan's suicidal ideation. My supervisor had been right about each family's unique cultural experience. This family did not fit the textbook profile of a Latino family. I would have never expected the father to come in and be so vulnerable in the first session, but Manuel's story was unique. His own personal pain interacted with his cultural experience in an idiosyncratic manner. There was much this family had to teach me.

After his last sentence, the room settled into an uncomfortable silence. I broke it with these words, "Manuel, you have accomplished some incredible things in your life. You are a good provider, and you have worked hard to assure that your wife and children do not suffer in the same way you did as a child. You did not carry on the abusive tradition of your father. This was not an easy task. Many a parent sets out to undo the wrongs done to him or her as a child, only to repeat the damage in another generation. You are to be commended, but we still must not ignore the pain of your son. Somehow Juan has not heard that he pleases you. Your son is desperate to hear that you are proud of him. In this, he shares some of your past pain. I have heard that you love him and are very proud of him, but it is important that Juan hears you."

Juan spoke, "Dad, I want you to be happy, but you never seem to be. I think that I am a disappointment to you."

Manuel responded slowly and deliberately, his voice cracking as he talked, "Juan, I am proud of you. It kills me to hear that you don't know that. I am not happy because I have not given you enough. I had such big dreams when I finally got to the States, even bigger dreams when I got a green card and finally became a citizen. But I am still a simple man who works with his hands. I am not smart like you. What you do with those computers amazes me, but also makes me see how little I know. It's not you, son, that I am disappointed in. It's me."

Father and son looked intently at each other across the room. I asked Juan if he had heard his father. He shook his head in affirmation. I asked if he could promise not to hurt himself before our session the next week and he nodded again. I knew it was the moment to end. I thanked the family for coming and being so honest. They looked subdued and almost stunned as they left. I was wishing that I did not have to wait until the following day to talk to my supervisor.

The Lesson Continues

I worked closely with my supervisor over the next several weeks as the Ramirez family taught me more and more. Juan was responding positively to the sessions. I quizzed him each week about his depression and suicidal thoughts, but his spirits were obviously lifting. He was spending less time studying and more time with his friends. As his spirits lifted, other issues began to take center stage in the sessions.

After spending most of the first family session working with Juan and his father, I intentionally focused on hearing from his mother and sister in the next session. Tina appeared to be a compliant child who worried about her brother and parents, but rarely made waves. Maria, Juan's mother, would only talk about her concern for Juan in the first few sessions, but hesitantly admitted some issues of her own in the third session.

"I want a job," she said, "But Manuel won't let me. We would have more money, and he would not have to work so hard. Tina is in the fourth grade, and I sit at home alone all day. I want to work."

Manuel jumped in. "A woman should stay in the home. If you are working, it means that I am not being a good husband. I am not taking care of you and being a man." As he spoke, she quickly retreated into her usual submissive position. I found myself doing mental gymnastics. I wanted to set this woman free. I knew my values as a woman with a career, and I felt like Maria was being controlled, yet I had also learned enough about the Latino culture to understand that this was probably an area of cultural difference. I struggled with wanting to support Maria and yet also to respect the role she had accepted in her family. I decided to go public with my struggle.

"This is a hard one for me. Obviously, I am a professional woman with a career. I enjoy my career and a part of me wants to support your growth. Yet, I know that up to this point, your family has let Manuel make this decision. Manuel, you and I would define a man differently. I don't think that you would be any less of a man if Maria were to work out of the home, but I respect that you feel differently. I also know that living here, you and Tina see the same images on television that I do. You are also presented with a cultural point of view in which women should have a career if they want. Maybe we should talk about these conflicting values."

That night, Maria and Manuel began a dialogue about their gender roles and culture. I directed their discussion, but tried to keep my values out of their own already confused merging of two cultures. Over time, Manuel became less rigid and Maria more assertive. I tried not to cheer, knowing they had to work out the right balance of culture for themselves. I regularly reviewed tapes of sessions with my supervisor, and she helped me see when my interpretations stepped over the line and promoted my own values.

As she focused more on herself, Maria also revisited her own immigration experience, so different from that of her spouse. She explained that she and her family had left Mexico together when she was 5 years old. They moved to Chicago and joined extended family in an urban Latino community, surrounded by other Mexican Americans. Her immersion into the culture of her new homeland was gentle and slow, starting kindergarten in an exemplary bilingual program that gradually exposed her to a new language and values. The contrast from her husband's experience was startling. I was continuing to understand the uniqueness of each person's acculturation experience.

As the parents began to openly discuss the impact of blending cultures in their lives, Juan began to move closer to his father. I held several sessions with just the two of them, discussing culture, identity, and relationships. Juan and his father started spending time together, attending soccer games and computer fairs. Juan introduced his father to computers. Manuel taught Juan how to build a window frame. At times, they had heated discussions about music and clothing, but the conflicts felt safely embedded in the now strong father-son relationship. Whereas Juan had once avoided any open expression of dissent to his father's opinions, he now knew he could be himself with his father. The love and acceptance were secure.

A few months into the family therapy, the family system had stabilized at a new point. Maria had taken a part-time job with the approval of her husband. Juan reported no signs of depression. Manuel said that he felt close to his wife and son for the first time in years. Tina was still doing well, but followed her brother's lead in becoming a little less perfect. I broached the topic of termination. The faces around the room told me that it was time. Juan smiled frequently and laughed with abandon. Maria and Manuel sat close together and exchanged the knowing looks of two connected partners.

The family was satisfied with their progress. Each of them looked happier and closer to each other, but I was feeling the heaviness of loss. These remarkable individuals had shared their lives and culture with me, an outsider. As they left the last session laughing and appreciative, I felt them walk out of my life and back into their own cultural territory. I had thanked them at the end for the willingness to share their lives and culture, but I also knew they would never understand how much I had learned and changed from our time together. Walking back to my small office, the process was completed, and I graduated to the next culture class as my office phone rang once again.

Intensive in-home services are a powerful tool for helping families. The following case study illustrates the use of goal setting and relationship building, which are critical in the Homebuilders model of home-based treatment.

Case Study 2-3

Questions for Discussion
1. What are some examples of relationship building used in this case?
2. How did the practitioner intervene to reduce conflicts between the father and son?
3. What is a "teachable moment," and how was this incorporated into the treatment?
4. What are some of the advantages and disadvantages of a home-based treatment model?

Homebuilders: Helping Families Stay Together

Nancy Wells Gladow and Peter J. Pecora

The following case involves conflict between a single-parent father and his 13-year-old son. The treatment agency is the Homebuilders Program of the Behavioral Sciences Institute (BSI), headquartered in Federal Way, Washington. Homebuilders is an intensive, home-based family preservation services program. BSI contracts with the state of Washington and city of New York to provide Homebuilders services to families who are in imminent danger of having one or more children placed outside the home in foster, group, or institutional care. Home-based family preservation programs currently exist in many states, and 28 states have at least one program attempting to replicate Homebuilders. Although theoretical approaches, clinical techniques, caseloads, and length of treatment vary from program to program, the basic goals of most programs are the same—to prevent unnecessary foster or group-home placements of children outside the home and to help multiproblem families cope with their situations more effectively.

Of these programs, Homebuilders is the most intensive in terms of its short time frame of 4 to 6 weeks per family and low caseload of two families per therapist or counselor. Therapists provide an average of 36 hours of face-to-face and phone contact to each family. The program is a skills-oriented model that is grounded in Rogerian, ecological, social learning, and cognitive behavioral theories. The intervention involves defusing the immediate crisis that led to the referral, building a relationship with the family, assessing the situation and developing treatment goals in partnership with the family, and teaching specific skills to help family members function more effectively and achieve these goals. Evaluations of Homebuilders indicate that the program is highly effective in reducing out-of-home placements and increasing the coping abilities of family members (Fraser, Pecora, & Haapala, 1988; Haapala & Kinney, 1988; Kinney, Madsen, Fleming, & Haapala, 1977).

Referrals are made to the Washington Homebuilders program through Child Protective Services (CPS) and Family Reconciliation Services (FRS), which are two subunits of the public child welfare agency. In CPS cases, the caseworker determines that one or more of the children will be placed outside the home if the family does not make certain changes to ensure the safety or well-being of the children. In FRS cases, either the parents or children have themselves requested out-of-home placement for the child due to family conflict or child behavior problems. In FRS cases, caseworkers may refer the family to Homebuilders as a way to work out the problems that are making placement a serious consideration.

Overview

The following case study highlights some of the Homebuilders treatment philosophy and techniques with an atypical, but increasingly common, type of case situation: a single-parent father and his son. However, this case was similar to most cases in that the family had a history of family problems and conflict. In this case, the child had no previous out-of-home placements; 21 percent of Homebuilders clients have already experienced previous placement. Selected client sessions are described for each of the 4 weeks of service. All the names and identifying information have been changed to protect the family's privacy.

Because of space considerations, the three contacts and work with the boy's mother have been omitted, as have the contacts with the school psychologist and other school personnel. In addition, a considerable amount of time was spent working with the father regarding his use of marijuana, which was not interfering with his job performance but was a concern to his son.

Interventions such as working with a local church and Narcotics Anonymous (NA) were attempted (with some success) but are not discussed here in order to focus on the therapist interventions regarding client relationship building, chore completion, school behavior, and anger management.

Intervention

Week 1: Gathering Information, Relationship Building, and Setting Treatment Goals

It was 7:30 p.m. when I drove up for the first time to the Barretts' small three-bedroom house in a working-class neighborhood. The referral sheet from the FRS caseworker said that Dick Barrett had been a technician for a large manufacturer in Seattle for 10 years and that his 13-year-old son, Mike, was in seventh grade. FRS became involved after Mike told his school counselor that his father had been smoking marijuana for 15 years. (This was the first time that the state had come into contact with his family.) Mike said he hated drugs, was tired of his father's constant yelling, and wanted to be placed outside the home. He also said he was afraid of his uncle, who had been living with the family for 2 months. The school counselor had already been concerned about Mike, a seventh grader for the second year who frequently neglected to turn in his homework and disrupted class by swearing at both students and teachers. Mike had already been suspended twice that semester. The referral sheet said that Dick voluntarily agreed to have the uncle move out and to quit using drugs, although he was unwilling to begin a drug treatment program. It also said the family had tried counseling several months ago through a local agency, but Mike had disliked the counselor and refused to continue.

Dick, a tall man around 50 years old, opened the door soon after I rang the bell. He invited me to sit at the kitchen table and called for Mike to join us. The family cat, Tiger, jumped on my lap. Dick and I began chatting about cats as Mike slowly walked into the kitchen, looking at the ground and making grumbling sounds. Mike smiled when he saw Tiger sitting on my lap and being scratched under the chin. Mike began to tell me stories about Tiger, and I responded with interest and a funny story about my own cat. I felt no pressure to hurry the counseling session along, as taking time for small talk and showing interest in what was important to family members was a key element of relationship building that would be the foundation of any later success in confronting clients and teaching new behaviors.

Dick began to discuss the difficulties his family had been experiencing. He said he was upset about Mike's behavior problems and lack of motivation in school. Dick said he had tried everything he knew to get Mike to improve but with no success. As Dick talked, I listened reflectively—paraphrasing parts of the content and feelings that Dick was expressing. For example, when Dick said, "Mike does not even try to improve his behavior in school," I responded, "It is frustrating for you that Mike does not seem to want to improve." After Dick spoke about Mike's abilities being much higher than his actual achievement, I said, "So it seems pretty clear that Mike has a lot more potential than he is using."

Reflective or active listening serves several purposes. First, it helps family members de-escalate their emotions. As they tell their stories and begin to feel that someone understands, they calm down and are more likely to be able to take constructive steps to improve their situation. Second, by conveying understanding, active listening helps build a positive client-therapist relationship. Third, active listening helps the therapist gain more information about the family without having to ask a lot of questions. People frequently expand on their stories when the therapist is listening reflectively. Asking many questions seems to limit what people say, and it creates the impression that the counselor is the expert who will "do something to" the family. With Homebuilders clients, it works better to recognize and treat clients as partners in the counseling process. Clients have more information about their lives than the therapist does, and their active participation in the change process is crucial. However, sometimes asking a few key questions at the right time is the most efficient way to gain behaviorally specific information. For example, in this situation, I wanted to know just what Mike's grades were. He was in three special education classes and was earning one B and two Cs in those. In his other classes, he was earning two Fs and a D.

As Dick talked, Mike remained silent, although his facial expressions and body movements frequently suggested anger toward his father. "You do not look too pleased, Mike," I said. "What do you think about all this?" Again I listened reflectively as Mike began to talk about how he hated school and his father's frequent yelling. Mike told stories about a number of arguments he and his father had that resulted in both of them swearing and saying things calculated to hurt each other. Dick agreed that this was true. I summarized, "So learning how to fight less and deal with your anger constructively is something both of you might like?" They both nodded. Dick went on to say, "Mike makes me so angry. If he would not say some of the things he does, I would not get so mad." I thought to myself that Dick could benefit from learning a basic principle about anger: No one can *make* you angry—you are responsible for your own anger. I did not mention my thought at this point, however, because pointing out errors in thinking and teaching too soon (before there has been time for sufficient information gathering and relationship building) is often ineffective.

"You have mentioned that you argue a lot more than either of you would like. Tell me what kinds of things you argue about," I requested. Dick described frustration about trying to get Mike to do chores around the house, saying that if Mike was not willing to help, he would prefer that Mike find somewhere else to live. Mike complained that his Dad was always ordering him around. Dick had been working especially hard lately to fix up the house so that it could be sold in a few months and finances between him and Mike's mother could be resolved. Dick and his ex-wife had gone through a difficult divorce 3 years ago, after 28 years of marriage and four children, the older three being over 18 years old and currently living on their own. Through mutual agreement, Dick had received custody of Mike.

"I get the picture from the caseworker that drugs have been a big issue in your family," I commented. Dick described how he had been smoking marijuana for about 15 years. He said he had also gotten into "some other things" during the time his brother-in-law, Mike's uncle, had been living there. Dick said that once the school and the caseworker became involved, he realized it was important to have his brother-in-law move out, which had been done. Dick said he had stopped using other drugs and had also voluntarily stopped using marijuana a few days ago. Dick stated that he respected Mike's right to live in a drug-free home and that he thought it would benefit himself as well to stop his drug use. "I can't afford to get fired if my work finds out about this," Dick commented.

"What do you think about this, Mike?" I asked. Mike remained silent. "If I were you, I might be a little worried that my Dad was not really going to quit using drugs," I said. "Is that anything like you're feeling, or am I way off base?" Mike opened up a little to say that his Dad had said he would quit before and had never stuck with it. Mike talked about how his siblings all use drugs and how he had been scared 3 years ago when some "bikers" had come to the house to get his oldest sister to "pay up" on some drugs. Mike said he also worried about having his father's health go downhill from drug use. I could tell from Dick's expression that this was probably the first time he had heard Mike express these concerns openly.

Soon it appeared that Mike was getting tired and it was time to end this 2½-hour initial session (about the average amount of time for a first session in the Homebuilders program). I explained more of the specifics of the Homebuilders program and gave them my home phone number as well as the backup phone numbers of my supervisor and our beeper. All of this is an effort to be available to clients 24 hours a day, 7 days a week. I then summarized the session in terms of treatment goals. "It sounds like what you two most want help on is working out a way to build more cooperation on household chores; learning how to fight less and to deal with anger more constructively; Dick, your receiving support in your efforts to be drug free; and improving your school performance, Mike. Is that how you see it?" They both nodded. Summarizing in this way checks my perception of the family's priorities for change and also gives direction for future counseling sessions. In this intake session with the Barretts, it was easier to establish goals than it is with many families. There is really no rush to determine all four treatment goals (a typical number for a 4-week intervention) at the intake session, although Homebuilders therapists generally try to have one or two goals established by the end of the first week.

The last thing I did during the first visit was to set up individual appointments with Dick and Mike. Unless family members are opposed to them, individual meetings can be helpful initially to gather additional information and continue building relationships. Later, one-to-one sessions can facilitate work on each person's goals. I gave Mike a sentence-completion sheet to fill out for our next session and checked to make sure that he understood how to do it.

When I came back 2 days later to pick up Mike for our individual session, he was listening to his stereo. I listened to a few songs with him. As we drove to McDonalds, we talked about various musical groups and our favorite TV shows. He seemed to be feeling much more comfortable with me by the time we sat down with our Cokes and French fries. I looked over the sentence completion sheet, which included sentences such as "My favorite subject in school is _____," "In my spare time I like to _____," and "I feel angry when _____." Instead of asking Mike a lot of questions, which teenagers frequently dislike, I read some of his answers in a tone of voice that encouraged him to expand on the topic. When he did, I listened reflectively to his responses, and he frequently elaborated even further. I learned that he was especially upset about his father yelling at him on a daily basis. When his father yelled, Mike found himself quickly feeling angry and sometimes yelling back. I reflected Mike's feelings of worry, embarrassment, fear, and anger about his father's use of drugs. I also checked with him on what kind of system they used at home regarding who did what household chores and if Mike earned an allowance. (I was thinking that coming up with a mutually agreed-on chore system might be the first goal we would tackle because it was so important to Dick and was a goal on which we were likely to make concrete progress.) Mike said there was no system—his dad just gave orders and Mike either complied or didn't. I suggested a system in which he would earn an allowance for doing certain agreed-on chores, and I asked what he thought a fair allowance would be, assuming his father approved this plan. He said the plan sounded agreeable and suggested $8 per week. I gave Mike an assignment to complete before the next meeting. He was to write down (1) two things he'd like to be different in his family, (2) two things he could do to help get along better with his dad, and (3) two things his dad could do to help them get along together better.

My one-to-one appointment with Dick began with his showing me the work he had done around the house to get it ready to sell. This led him to talk about his past marriage with Rita, his feelings about the marriage ending, and how Mike had gone back and forth between their homes for almost 2 years, until about a year ago. Dick thought that some of Mike's troubles were due to his going from home to home, plus the pressure of Dick and Rita's continual fighting. After an hour of actively listening to these subjects, I felt pleased that Dick was opening up, warming up to me, and appearing relieved to get some of these things off his chest. When he brought up his older children's drug involvement, I saw it as an opportunity to gently begin talking about his own drug use. (This is an example of a "teachable moment," which is a time when clients may be particularly receptive to learning because they can see the relevancy of it to their lives.) We spent some time discussing this issue and developing a plan of action.

Before ending the session, I introduced the idea of Mike's chores being based on an allowance. Dick reacted positively, saying that he thought more structure would be helpful. I noted two benefits to such a system: (1) Mike would experience the consequences of his actions, and (2) it would reduce the number of times Dick would need to tell Mike what to do. Mike had developed a tendency to blame much of his behavior on others rather than taking responsibility for his actions. In addition, like most teenagers, Mike hated to be told what to do, yet their previous system was based completely on Dick giving daily instructions. We briefly discussed what he thought a reasonable allowance would be. We agreed to negotiate this new system with Mike at the next session. I also gave Dick the same homework assignment I had given Mike.

Week 2: Active Work on Goals

As Mike, Dick, and I sat down together in the living room, I asked how things were going. Meetings often start in this way because events may have recently occurred that need to be discussed or worked out before clients are able to concentrate on the current agenda.

When I asked if they had done their homework, Dick had and Mike hadn't. Dick agreed to do something else for a few minutes while I helped Mike complete the questions. Then both told what they would like to be different in their family. Dick said he would like anger to play less of a role and for the home to be drug free. Mike said he would like less arguing and to go places together more. In discussing what each person thought he could do differently, Dick said he could try not to get angry when frustrated, and he could also be more consistent with Mike. Mike said he could help more around the house and try not to get angry so much.

On the subject of what the other person could do, Dick said Mike could be more responsible with housework and schoolwork. Mike said his dad could stay off drugs and yell less. I took this opportunity to talk about how problems in a family are almost

Behavior	Mon	Tues	Wed	Thur	Fri	Sat	Sun	Total
Straighten bedroom (by 5 p.m.)	2	2	2	2	2	2	✕	12
Bring in wood (by 5 p.m.)	2	2	2	2	2	2	2	14
Do dinner dishes (by 9 p.m.)	3	✕	3	✕	3	✕	✕	9
Take out garbage (by 9 p.m.)	2	2	2	2	2	2	2	14
Vacuum house (by 6 p.m.)	✕	✕	✕	✕	✕	9	✕	9
Change cat litter (by 6 p.m.)	✕	✕	✕	✕	✕	2	✕	2

Weekly total   60

Every 10 pts. = $1.00
58–60 pts. = $6.00 + $2.00 bonus
X = Chore not required on the day
Sunday evening is payday.

FIGURE 1   Weekly chore chart.

never one person's fault and how each family member can do things to help the other family members. I also noted the similarities in the changes they wanted and stated that I had some ideas that might help them implement some of these changes.

Next we began work on the new chore system. I explained that we would be deciding together what chores Mike would be responsible for doing, when they were to be done, how much allowance he would earn, and what he did and did not have to pay for with his allowance. We began by writing a list of all the chores possible and gave Mike a chance to pick some he would be willing to do. Dick added a few that he would like Mike to be responsible for. After a little more negotiation, we came up with a list that both felt they could live with. Mike said he really did not like doing chores. Rather than letting Dick jump in with a lecture or responding with one myself, I opted for humor. I chuckled and told Mike I certainly could understand that—Ajax and vacuum cleaners had never thrilled me either. I gave a couple of examples of how my husband and I split up chores so that neither one of us had to do all of the work. Then Dick and Mike decided how often each chore needed to be done, to what standards, and by what time of the day. We discussed which chores involved the most and the least amount of work and determined point values for each.

In deciding on allowance, Mike thought $8 per week was fair, and Dick thought $6 per week was more appropriate. After discussing it further, we agreed on a system in which Mike's basic allowance would be $6, and all he would have to pay for was his own entertainment. On the weeks when he earned at least 97 percent of the chore "points," he would get a $2 bonus and earn $8. We put this all onto a chart and filled it out as though Mike had done a perfect job (see Figure 1). The crossed-out squares on the chart indicate days when the chore need not be done.

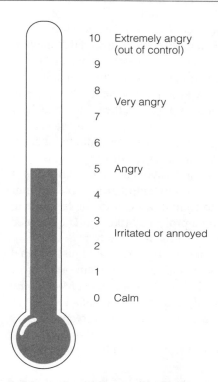

FIGURE 2   Anger thermometer.

On a blank chart, we wrote the possible points next to each chore and agreed on the time when Dick would check the jobs and fill in the points. We specified which day would be "payday" and where the chart would be placed. When Mike got a phone call, I took the opportunity to share with Dick some hints on making the chore system work most successfully. I suggested that he use the chore checking as a chance to develop goodwill with Mike by praising him for work he does well. I gave Dick a handout on "97 Ways to Say 'Very Good'." I also suggested that when Mike did not do a chore or when he did it poorly, Dick handle it matter-of-factly rather than with anger. Past experience indicated that Mike became less cooperative when Dick was angry.

The last session in Week 2 was with Mike and Dick together. Mike was upset because his father had not filled in the chore chart the last 2 days. We got the chart off the cupboard and filled it in together. Dick agreed with Mike that Mike had done all his chores so far that week. I encouraged Dick to appreciate Mike's efforts and success, and we practiced this. Mike enjoyed the encouragement.

Because anger management was one of our main goals, I introduced the topic by showing a picture of an "anger thermometer" (see Figure 2). I explained that 0 was the point where a person was calm, relaxed, and feeling no anger at all. At 2 or 3, a person often felt irritated or frustrated. At 5, a person was definitely angry; at 6 or 7, quite angry; and by 9 or 10, so enraged that he or she was out of control. At these top points, people often say and do things that they would not otherwise say or do and that they often regret later. I had both Mike and Dick identify times when they had been at various points on the thermometer. They both acknowledged that some of their most hurtful and useless fights had occurred when they were at 9 or 10 on the scale. I asked them to identify physical symptoms they experienced at various points on the scale, especially at 7 or 8 before they were out of control (for example, having a fast heartbeat, feeling hot, or having sweaty palms). I requested that they identify how they could tell that the other person was at these points. We then discussed the concept of removing oneself from the situation before losing self-control in an effort to avoid destructive fighting. I said that their symptoms at 7 or 8 should be seen as cues to temporarily leave the situation. We discussed where each person could go to calm down (for example, Mike to his bedroom, and Dick to the basement to work on a project). Mike and Dick agreed that they would try to remove themselves from the situation to avoid fights.

At one point when we were alone, Dick commented, "If Mike would just do what he is supposed to do and not talk back to me, I wouldn't have this problem of anger." I gently challenged him, saying, "I see things a little differently. I agree that Mike doing his chores and schoolwork would help. And certainly the way Mike talks to you has an influence on how you respond. But I see your response back as your responsibility and not Mike's. Each one of us is responsible for our own behavior—Mike for his and you for yours. In fact, the only behavior any of us can truly control is our own." Dick thought for a minute and agreed.

We got back together with Mike, and I talked with the two of them about using "self-talk" to decrease and control anger. To illustrate this point, I gave several examples. Then we read a short children's story together called "Maxwell's Magnificent Monster" (Waters, 1980b). This story illustrates the point that our self-talk causes us to become angry. Mike put the two concepts together and said that the monster was when a person was at 9 or 10 on the anger thermometer. Dick was quiet and seemed reflective. He said he liked the story and asked to keep it for awhile.

Week 3: Teaching, Learning, and Some Application

The first session of the week was spent initially with Dick alone. Dick talked about the meeting he had gone to at school that morning with Mike and the school psychologist. It was the first day back after vacation, and Dick had been required to go because Mike had been suspended the 2 days before the break. I listened reflectively as Dick spoke of "Mike's rude behavior" toward him and the psychologist. Dick expressed his frustration at not being able to "make" Mike improve in school. I reiterated that a person has the greatest control over his own behavior and that Dick could only do so much to influence Mike. I suggested that concentrating on staying drug free, decreasing his own angry responses, and being consistent in checking and praising Mike on chores are all areas that he could control and that could indirectly have an impact on Mike's functioning at school. We reexamined the ineffectiveness of yelling as a means to improve

Mike's school performance. I suggested he not spend too much energy on this issue now, letting Mike have more responsibility or ownership for the school problems.

Mike then joined us, and we talked about that morning's school appointment. When I brought up the issue of Mike's behavior with the school psychologist, Mike quickly mentioned some things his Dad had said to the psychologist that had embarrassed him. I said that I could understand his embarrassment, but that his actions and words toward the school counselor were still his responsibility and could not be blamed on his father. I reinforced the idea that what he says and does is his responsibility, just as what his father says and does is his father's responsibility. Because I knew this was a message Mike would not like hearing, I said it in a concise and friendly way and then moved on to the next topic. Dick said Mike had been doing extremely well on chores and had earned the full $8 for the past week. It was obvious from Mike's expression that he liked hearing his dad's praise.

The next day, I picked Mike up at school, and we went to McDonald's again for our session. Mike had a long list of complaints about his father, especially that his dad got upset and yelled about such small things. Mike said he also worried about his dad drinking more beer. I simply listened, focusing largely on reflecting the feelings Mike was expressing. At one point, I used a sheet with 20 feelings and accompanying faces showing those feelings. I had Mike pick out the feelings he felt frequently and explain when he felt them. My hope was that simply having the opportunity to vent his emotions would be helpful to Mike. However, I purposely avoided any statements blaming his father. I wanted to encourage Mike to take responsibility for his own actions rather than blaming someone else for everything. I talked with Mike about what he could and could not control. I mentioned that he could not control his father's substance abuse—that was largely his father's choice. However, I suggested a number of phrases that he could use to share his feelings about it with his father, if he would like (for example, "When I see you drinking beer, I feel scared and worried"). We discussed the support group his school counselor had told me about—a group for teens whose parents have problems with substance abuse. Mike made an agreement with me that he would go once and evaluate it. I talked about how Mike does have control over his own behavior, both at home and at school. I said I thought it was great he was doing his chores so regularly and how this had already improved things. I listened to Mike's feelings about school and then talked concretely about all the positive things his dad, counselor, and I saw in him. I encouraged him to try a little harder in school and talked about the potential of increased self-esteem and future employability. We also discussed a few career possibilities, and I told stories of some people I knew who had dropped out of school early and ended up in very low-paying jobs.

During the next session with Dick, I asked if he had read the article I had given him at our last meeting: "The Anger Trap and How to Spring It" (Waters, 1980a). Dick said yes and that it made an excellent point. He was able to summarize the main idea: Anger is a choice, and there are other choices available. I emphasized that by opting to interpret a situation in a different way (changing one's self-talk), anger can be reduced

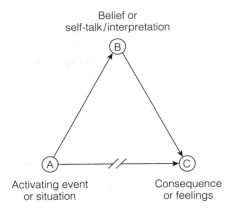

Belief or
self-talk/interpretation

Activating event
or situation

Consequence
or feelings

FIGURE 3   The rational-emotive therapy triangle.

and more helpful responses can be chosen. I talked again about the basic concept of rational-emotive therapy (RET). This time I drew the RET triangle (see Figure 3) and explained that it is not situations or events (a) that cause feelings (c), but rather our self-talk or interpretation (b) about the situation (Ellis & Harper, 1975). I gave some examples from my own life, and Dick was able to identify some situations in which using this technique could have helped him.

We discussed a handout on "The Six Steps to Anger" (Hauck, 1974), which identifies self-talk that commonly leads to problematic anger, and then I provided him with a list of calming self-talk and challenges to angry self-talk. We discussed the need to catch oneself using anger-producing self-talk and to substitute it with calming self-statements. When one of Dick's friends dropped by, we had covered so much material—Dick had been very eager for help with anger—that I saw it as a good time to end. I quickly gave Dick a book I had bought for him, one of the Hazelden Daily Meditation Series based on the 12 steps of AA (Hazelden Foundation Staff, 1988). I knew that the book fit well with the concepts Dick admired in his church group and that it could be helpful to him in his struggle with substance abuse. Dick was surprisingly touched that I bought him this. He read the meditation for that day out loud. (Dick's readiness to accept and use written materials is definitely greater than in most Homebuilders cases. A large percentage of clients will not read materials, so therapists spend considerable time discussing and role-playing concepts with families.)

The third session of the week, held with both Mike and Dick, was very encouraging. They were in good moods when I arrived, having spent a fun afternoon riding dirt bikes together. They said they had forgotten how much fun the other could be. When Dick said he planned to do more things with Mike in the future, Mike was visibly pleased. When I saw that the chore chart was filled out and that Mike had done all of his work for the second week in a row, I smiled and complimented both Dick and Mike.

Dick said that he had been working on the anger management techniques we had discussed and that they were helping. He gave an example of an incident that had occurred that morning in which Mike had approached him angrily. Rather than responding with anger as he previously would have done, Dick had been able to remain calm. Dick said it kept Mike from escalating, and they resolved the situation more quickly. Mike confirmed that his dad was calming down and that this made it more relaxing to be at home.

The remaining time was spent learning the skill of "I-messages." I explained the basic concept of I-messages as a way of communicating how another person's actions are affecting you in a manner that is most likely to be well received. The point of an I-message is to say how you feel without attacking the listener's self-esteem or saying things that are going to make the other person more defensive (Gordon, 1970). To illustrate, I spoke of a situation and then stated my feelings in an unhelpful, critical, and blaming way (a "you-message"). For example, "You were a thoughtless idiot to have left the gas tank empty when you came home last night. You never think of anyone but yourself." We discussed how they felt hearing that statement, how likely they were to want to cooperate with me, and what they felt like saying in return. Then I expressed my feelings in an "I-message." "When you left the gas tank empty, I felt irritated because I had to go to the gas station first thing and ended up being late for work." We discussed the difference. I pulled out the anger thermometer and pointed out how I-messages can be used when a person is at a low point on the scale. This increases the chances of resolution of the problem at an early stage and avoids the "gunnysacking" effect that can occur when a person lets a lot of irritations go unaddressed. Dick said he had a tendency to hold back his irritation and shared a few examples.

I diagrammed the parts of an I-message on a large pad of paper I had brought along: "When you (behavior), I feel (emotion) because (effect on me)." I gave Mike and Dick an assignment to write four I-messages for one another: two using positive emotions (proud, happy, relieved, and so on) and two using uncomfortable emotions (angry, hurt, discouraged, and so on). While Dick worked on these on his own, Mike and I moved to another room where I helped him write his messages. We then shared what each had written and discussed the experience.

Week 4: Progress Continues but Setbacks Occur

When I arrived for our one-to-one appointment, Dick said he was hungry and wanted to go to a nearby coffee shop. I drank coffee while he ate dinner. He said Mike had continued to do well on his chores. Dick thought the system was helping, and he had even noticed Mike looking for ways to improve the decorating in his bedroom. Dick said he was calming down quite a bit after realizing that he could choose responses other than anger. He also said Mike also seemed calmer and that they were warming up to one another.

Mike and I had our last individual session at the same coffee shop. Mike said he had seen his father using marijuana the previous evening. Mike expressed concerns that Dick would stop doing the chore chart, become more irritable, and use drugs more often after I was gone. We talked about some ways in which the likelihood of this could be minimized. I said that I would have a follow-up session or two with them, and

I encouraged Mike to look at the behavior he could control. I stressed that rather than giving up, he could put his main efforts into continuing to do his chores and his homework and working on the anger-management skills we had learned. Briefly, I went over the RET triangle with him, as I had with Dick, and gave him a list of possible calming self-statements. I suggested he consider using an I-message to tell his dad how he felt about seeing him use marijuana again. We wrote out a couple of possible I-messages together.

The next evening I received a phone call from Mike. I asked if he had shared the I-messages. He said no, that he had gone right to bed. He went on to say that he had been suspended from one day of school for saying "Jesus Christ" to the teacher that day. I listened reflectively to his story and feelings. Knowing that saying "Jesus Christ" at his house was part of the norm, I was not surprised that he felt puzzled about how it led to suspension. I talked about why that might have been offensive to the teacher and how different types of talk were appropriate for different settings. We went on to discuss different teachers' expectations for quiet versus talking when students are finished with work. Mike said he was shocked that his dad had not yelled at him when he learned of the suspension. Dick had simply said, "School is your responsibility." Mike said the two of them had agreed that Mike would be restricted to the house on the day of suspension. I was very pleased to see that Dick had been able to apply the concept of letting Mike take greater responsibility for school and had avoided making it another area of major friction between them. It was clear from Mike's response that Mike was more able to look at his own behavior when the problem was not complicated by an enormous argument with his father.

The termination session was with Mike and Dick together. First, we discussed school issues. Dick said he had talked to the school counselor, who said Mike had indeed improved on getting his homework in, although his classroom behavior was still a problem. We discussed some ideas Mike could try: saying his angry words to himself rather than out loud, keeping an index card of the calming self-statements in his notebook to read when getting angry, and picking a student whom he likes (but who also gets along with teachers) to model his behavior after. We also discussed the possibility of Mike being placed in a classroom for behaviorally disordered students, an idea the school counselor had suggested. Dick said he had consciously chosen not to get mad about Mike's school suspension, saying he had realized it would not help either of them. I praised Dick for this and asked Mike if he had noticed his father getting angry less often. Mike said, "No kidding. My dad's attitude has really changed." Dick and I could not help but chuckle at Mike's comment, but it obviously meant a lot to both Mike and Dick.

We looked at the chore chart. Dick said Mike had earned the full allowance for that week, too. I raised Mike's concerns that the chore chart would not be continued after I left. We agreed that Mike could remind his dad to check the chart if he forgot. We role-played how Mike could phrase his request to maximize the chances of Dick responding favorably.

We discussed the progress they had made over the last 4 weeks: Mike was doing chores, and there were fewer arguments over this subject; the frequency and intensity of fights decreased as they were able to express feelings; Mike was making small improvements in school; and there had been progress in getting Mike into a more appropriate classroom setting. Mike and Dick both said they were getting along together better, despite Dick's less frequent but continued use of drugs. Dick said he no longer wanted Mike to live elsewhere, and Mike agreed. We set up a follow-up appointment for 2½ weeks later.

Conclusions

This case illustrates some of the treatment techniques used by Homebuilders' staff to help families change their behaviors. In the Barretts' case, these included using a mutual goal-setting process, chore charts, the anger thermometer, rational-emotive therapy, I-messages, and other anger-management techniques. This case demonstrates how intensive home-based services can help families improve their functioning in a variety of areas. Part of the reason for the effectiveness of these interventions is due to a flexible treatment model that can address a wide variety of family problems, the therapist's relationship with the family, and the emphasis placed on teaching clients techniques to resolve real-life problems.

References

ELLIS, A., & HARPER, R. A. (1975). *A guide to rational living.* North Hollywood, CA: Wilshire.

FRASER, M. W., PECORA, P. J., & HAAPALA, D. A. (1988). *Families in crisis: Findings from the family-based intensive treatment project* (Final technical report). Salt Lake City: University of Utah, Graduate School of Social Work, Social Research Institute.

GORDON, T. (1970). *Parent effectiveness training.* New York: Peter H. Wyden.

HAAPALA, D. A., & KINNEY, J. M. (1988). Avoiding out-of-home placement among high-risk status offenders through the use of home-based family preservation services. *Criminal Justice and Behavior, 15,* 334–348.

HAUCK, P. A. (1974). *Overcoming frustration and anger.* Philadelphia: Westminster.

HAZELDEN FOUNDATION STAFF. (1988). *Touchstones.* New York: Harper/Hazelden.

KINNEY, J. M., MADSEN, B., FLEMING, T., & HAAPALA, D. A. (1977). Homebuilders: Keeping families together. *Journal of Consulting and Clinical Psychology, 45,* 667–678.

WATERS, V. (1980a). *The anger trap and how to spring it* (Mimeograph). New York: Institute for Rational Living.

WATERS, V. (1980b). *Maxwell's magnificent monster* (Mimeograph). New York: Institute for Rational Living.

Case Study 2-4

Questions for Discussion

1. Much of the work of Theraplay involves giving parents experience and understanding so that they can respond to children's needs. How might this parental shift change a child's view of herself?
2. Why is it important to have one practitioner working with the client (child) while another works directly with the parents?
3. This is an unusual case study in that the client's (child's) parents comment on the case 14 years after treatment. How has their perspective changed?
4. How are the parents' experiences as children germane to their current parenting styles?
5. The mother in this study describes resistance from other family members and friends about their "new form of parenting." Explain the resistance. How can a practitioner help families deal with this issue?

Using Theraplay to Interrupt a Three-Generation Pattern of Inadequate Parenting

Phyllis Booth and Deborah O'Hara

This case study describes how Theraplay was used to change an anxious, unhappy relationship between a 4-year-old girl and her mother into a happy secure one. In the process, a pattern of unhappy, distant mothering that had persisted for at least three generations was turned around. The authors of this case study are the child's therapist, Phyllis Booth, and the child's mother, Deborah O'Hara. We describe the treatment as it took place 14 years ago. Looking back on that experience, Debbie recalls her thoughts and feelings at each stage of the treatment process and gives her current view of the nature of the problem and how Theraplay treatment helped her and her family. I (P.B.) report on interviews with the child's maternal grandmother, Rosemary, about her own childhood experience; with the father, Jerry, about his experience with Theraplay; and with the child, Katie, about her memories of treatment. Each family member has given permission for this case study to be published.

Description of Theraplay

Theraplay is a treatment for enhancing attachment, self-esteem, trust in others, and joyful engagement. It is modeled on the natural patterns of healthy interaction between parents and their young children, and it is thus loving, personal, physical, and fun. If you picture a mother or a father with their 6-month-old baby, you will see the basic elements of Theraplay. Not only do parents feed, bathe, touch, stroke, rock, and cuddle their baby, they also play engaging, interactive games such as peek-a-boo, patty-cake, and "I'm gonna get you." They may toss the baby in the air, play "so big," and otherwise challenge the baby a bit. They help the child establish a routine, and they keep the child safe. They respond to the baby's needs in a sensitive, attuned manner that helps the baby regulate her emotions and activity level. When things go well, the child develops a positive picture of herself as lovable, capable and deserving of good things. She sees the world as interesting, trustworthy, and full of people who care for her. The stage is set for developing a secure attachment, which is crucial if a child is to maintain a strong sense of self and self-confidence, the ability to deal with stress, the ability to trust, and the capacity to take pleasure in relationships throughout life.

Children who are brought for treatment because their behavior causes concern to their parents and teachers often have missed out on many of these good early experiences. Sometimes their parents were not well parented themselves—a pattern that can pass from one generation to the next. Or the parents may have been ill, on drugs, overwhelmed by poverty, or lacking in support from their own parents and community. Many children are removed from such homes and placed with foster or adoptive families. Their relationship problems are then compounded by loss, and they become even less trusting. Sometimes something in the child makes it hard for the attuned, responsive interaction to develop. The child may be ill, in pain, and unable to respond to the good parenting that is offered. He may be irritable or difficult to soothe, or she may be so passive or "good" that she doesn't do her share of engaging the parents. Sometimes parent issues and child issues interact and lead to problems that require treatment, as in the case presented here.

Theraplay treatment is designed to help parents learn how to provide the kind of good parenting that their child has been missing. Often, as in this case, a great deal of the work involves changing the parents' own experience and understanding so that they can respond to their child's needs. Using the model of healthy parent-infant interaction described above, we gear the work to the emotional needs of the particular child and support the parents so that they can learn to meet their child's needs in a confident, loving way. In the process, the child's view of herself changes from negative to positive, and her parent's view of themselves changes from incompetent to competent and loving.

Presenting Problem

Katie was 4 years old when her parents, Debbie and Jerry, came to the Theraplay Institute for help. The family came for 15 treatment sessions with follow-up contacts and support over the years. Looking at Katie now, at age 18 and in her first year of college, one might assume that her early experience had been the ideal kind that outlined above, but it did not begin that way. This is how Katie's mother described what led her to seek help:

> No matter what I offer, she's not happy. Whenever she doesn't get what she wants, she throws a temper tantrum. Putting on her seat belt in the car is a major struggle. Taking her to the grocery store is a nightmare. She won't sit down in the cart and cries when I insist.

She always demands candy as we are leaving the store. When I take her to the doctor, she runs the other way. It takes both a nurse and the doctor to hold her down for her shots. It's embarrassing to have people look at her and think she is a brat and that I am an incompetent mom. I've tried everything to get her to listen to me and do what I want her to do. Time-out just doesn't work. She doesn't get along well with other children because she is so rough and demanding. I can't leave her with anyone because she cries the whole time I'm gone or they come to get me because she is so upset. I feel like a prisoner.

One day as she and I were crossing the street, Katie threw herself on the ground and refused to go one step farther. With cars whizzing by in both directions, I frantically tried everything—cajoling, bribing, begging. Finally, in despair, I grabbed Katie by the arm and pulled her to the other side of the street. Katie screamed in pain. To my horror, I realized that I had pulled Katie's elbow out of joint. After attending to the elbow, my pediatrician asked how it had happened. Upon hearing the story, he recommended that I seek psychological help for myself and for Katie.

Looking back, Debbie says:

When we came for that first interview with the two of you, I felt ashamed that I hadn't been able to figure things out. I was sure that we were going to find out something terrible: that there was something wrong with Katie or that we were terrible parents.

Ann Jernberg and I (P.B.) were the co-therapist team that worked with the family. We first asked the parents to tell us about Katie's history so that we could understand how she had become such an unhappy, demanding little girl. Because parenting is so profoundly affected by one's own experience as a child, we also asked about Debbie's and Jerry's experiences growing up.

Katie's History

This is the history as Debbie remembers telling it to us during the intake interview:

Katie is the second of our three children. Beau, who is 12, is from my earlier marriage. Hayley, who is 2 years old, was born on Katie's second birthday. Jerry and I had been married 2½ years when Katie was born. We were thrilled at the prospect of having this baby. But our happiness was short lived. At 3 months, I began bleeding profusely. The doctor told me that I was having a miscarriage. It felt as if someone had ripped my heart out. The doctor advised bed rest, and for three months I lay on my bed, scared that I would lose this baby that I wanted so much. I kept saying over and over, "Okay, just hang in there, Katie." I was determined I wasn't going to lose her. Katie was born 2 weeks late in a quick, natural childbirth. She weighed 10 pounds and seemed huge. She had a great shock of black hair, her eyes were almond shaped, and people said she looked like an Alaskan baby. One nurse, seeing my blond hair and comparing it to Katie's black hair, said, "I can't believe this is your baby." Katie was so big and solid that she filled the little crib in the nursery. I was thrilled to see her and hold her, but it was hard to hold such a big baby. I couldn't easily find a position that would allow her to nestle into my arms.

We had a lot of difficulty getting the feeding going. We just couldn't get in sync. I stopped nursing when Katie was about 3 months old, but it wasn't just the nursing that didn't go well. Katie was a challenge in every way. She would sleep all day and then be wakeful at night. Jerry and I would take turns walking the floor with her at night. Once she became upset, it would take forever to calm her down. The doctor told us to let her cry. We tried that but it didn't feel right. The doctor also advised us to wake her during the day so that she would move to a daytime schedule. It was almost impossible to wake her. It took 6 months to get her onto a schedule of any kind.

I desperately needed to get away at times, but it was almost impossible to leave her with anyone. She would become very upset and would scream for hours. I would return to a crying, upset child. It was very hard to find a sitter.

Hayley was born on Katie's second birthday. My mother came to help for a week. When she left, I remember wanting to cry; I was so overwhelmed by the needs of my two little girls and my son.

Katie was extremely quick and agile. She was always curious and on the move. I didn't know how to contain her. She could climb over the fence and get away in a flash. She got into everything. She would not listen to me. It took all my attention to watch her.

Although we had lots of difficult moments, there were some things I liked very much about Katie. When we weren't locking horns, I liked that she was full of life and carefree. She could be funny and silly and had a great sense of humor. She had a wonderful, contagious laugh.

Debbie's Reflections 14 Years Later

When I look back at my difficulties with Katie in the light of all I know now, I can see so many ways I could have handled things differently. If we had been more patient in helping her, she might have settled into a more comfortable schedule without all that interference on our part. We were trying to force her to fit our schedule. Because I was not in tune with her needs, everything was a battle. I wanted her to listen because it would be easier for me. I never imagined that she was having a hard time, too. At that point, I did not understand that it would be good for her to know that I could take charge and make things safe and fun for her. I gave up very quickly when she protested.

Although I had really longed for this baby, I began to resent her needing me so much and yet making it so difficult when I was with her. I tried to do all the things that I thought would be nice to do with a toddler, but they were not necessarily the things she wanted from me. I was unable to keep her happy, and I felt like a lousy mother.

I wanted so desperately to be a good mom. However, at that time, it meant *looking* like a good mother and having children who did not give me any trouble. I had no idea what real mothering was. Katie was such a physically active child, I should have known that asking her to sit quietly in the grocery cart was too much. I could have paid attention to her natural curiosity, let her help me choose items, let her hold things, etc. I wanted to be in charge for the wrong reasons. I had never developed the playful side of me because my life had been so serious.

Debbie's History

I grew up in a very unsettled family. I had four different "dads," moved 12 times, and went to 12 different schools from kindergarten to sixth grade. I spent weekdays with my mother and weekends with my grandmother and my alcoholic father. Nothing was ever stable. And no one was consistently available to me when I needed them.

As a child, I learned that the most important thing in life was to be independent. My mother told me that she used to prop my bottle against a pillow. I toilet trained myself by the time I was a year old. If I fell or bumped myself, my mother's immediate response was, "You're fine. Don't worry about it." When I was Katie's age, I had lots of temper tantrums. I would cry so hard that I would stop breathing and pass out. My mother tells me that she would just wait till I came to. I think my mother was afraid that she would spoil me if she comforted me at such a moment. Looking back on this now, I think that Katie's temper tantrums must have touched a very young memory in me.

Jerry's History

I grew up in a family with six sisters. I was used to lots of people around, lots of active play, lots of energy. So when Katie came along, her high energy just felt normal. She and I seldom had the kind of difficulties that she and Debbie had. Of course, I was at work all day, and it was Debbie who was home with the children. It was Debbie who felt we needed help. But I made sure that I came along.

As we were writing up this case study, I talked to Debbie's mother, Rosemary, about how her childhood experiences with her own mother might have affected the way she parented Debbie.

Rosemary's History

My father was an alcoholic. My mother was severely neurotic and suffered from nervous breakdowns. I remember coming home from school when I was five or six to find that my mother had been taken away in an ambulance. We had a nurse taking care of us, but she was very cold. After mother came home from the hospital, she would often wake in the night screaming. She would call for my oldest sister to sit up with her until she settled down. I became very quiet and observant. I shut myself off and became emotionally unavailable toward her. I never remember being touched by my mother. I thought all this was normal.

When I grew up, I needed love so much that I married the first man who chose me. And when that didn't work out, I kept looking for someone else who would choose me. I blame myself for not being more available to Debbie. Men were more important to me than she was. I thought I had to be married. I couldn't take care of myself. I was so desperate for someone to love me.

There's a big difference between how Debbie raises her children and how I raised her—or how my mother raised me. I was so afraid of touch that it took me a long time to be able to touch my children. Debbie is there for her children. She's supportive. She's affectionate with them.

Summary of Intake Information

As we listened to the story that Debbie and Jerry told us, we began to understand what might have prevented Katie and her mother from developing a happy, secure relationship. The stress of the threatened miscarriage disrupted the process of anticipation and bonding that normally takes place during pregnancy. Rather than a relaxed "getting to know you" period, Debbie spent hours "toughing it out" and telling Katie she should hang in there. Debbie now says, "I could have said, 'I'll take care of you. I won't let anything happen to you.'" Maybe even more significant is that Katie, though strong and healthy, was difficult for Debbie to relate to. Katie couldn't get onto a schedule, she was not easily calmed and soothed when upset, and there was a temperamental mismatch between the two of them.

Debbie, for her part, was not well prepared for the task of parenting an active, difficult-to-soothe baby. Her childhood experience had taught her that the world is a place where you must put up a good front, where you don't expect to be nurtured, and where you are pretty much on your own. A major part of the treatment involved helping Debbie understand how her own childhood experiences with a mother who had not been well parented herself affected her ability to mother Katie. She needed help to resolve her own issues and heal her own wounds.

We knew that Theraplay would be a good way to help this family, but before starting treatment, we used the Marschak Interaction Method (MIM) to take a close look at how Katie interacted with each of her parents so that we would know just where the difficulties arose and how we could plan to help.

The Marschak Interaction Method

The MIM is a technique for observing and evaluating the interaction between adult and child as they perform a series of simple tasks together. It allows us to assess how the child responds to the caregiver's efforts to:

- Structure the environment and set clear limits.
- Engage the child in interaction while being attuned to the child's state and reactions.
- Provide nurture, including being able to soothe and calm the child when needed.
- Provide appropriate challenge.

Katie and each of her parents were given eight tasks to do together, including playing with two squeaky animals, the parent teaching the child something she doesn't know, playing peek-a-boo, and the parent drawing a picture and asking the child to draw one just like it.

MIM Observations

Katie was a beautiful little girl with brown hair, bright brown eyes, and a shy, winning smile. Throughout the series of activities, Debbie used her most enticing voice and smile to present each activity, as if she were fearful that Katie might reject it. Katie occasionally smiled and giggled in anticipation of a new activity but was easily disappointed. Although she was cooperative at the beginning of each task, she quickly grew impatient and whined as she asked to go on to the next activity.

At one point, there was a small battle of wills between the two over who was to take charge of the teaching task. Katie showed signs of having set very high standards for herself and of lacking the confidence to meet them. For example, as she watched her mother draw, she said sadly, "I don't know how to make a mouth." Debbie then drew a simpler mouth and helped Katie complete the task. When it came to regressive, playful activities such as peek-a-boo, neither seemed very comfortable. They went through the motions of playing peek-a-boo once with no energy or pleasure. Katie then whined, "I want to play another game." Debbie looked disappointed, took a deep breath, and said, "You don't want to play? OK." A game that could have been fun left the two sad and disappointed with each other.

Debbie's Reflections on the MIM 14 Years Later

When I sat down at the table with Katie and started to read the cards, I was extremely nervous. I kept second-guessing myself. I desperately wanted to look good and to have Katie behave well. I kept thinking, "What am I supposed to be doing? How can I do it right?" As I looked at the videotape of the MIM with you the other day, I was struck by Kate's sweetness and the way she looked up at me. I can see that I was asking questions, hoping that she would be happy, turning the responsibility over to her to make decisions—anything to avoid having her throw a temper tantrum. It was almost as if I wanted her to be the mom.

When I was supposed to teach her something, she looked at me as if she was interested to see what it would be. However, I was so preoccupied with how well I was doing that I couldn't see her needs. I was frantically thinking to myself, what *can* I teach her? When I looked at her and asked, "What can I teach you?" her face sank. She then whined and pointed to something far away, trying to bail me out. It makes me realize how lost she must have felt to have a mom who didn't think she could teach anything to her 4-year-old. If only I had known about thumb wrestling or secret handshakes.

When I first brought her for treatment, I did not like Katie, probably because she was a constant reminder of my inadequacies as a mother. Now she's one of the nicest people I know. When I look back at the tape, I can see that it was not that Katie was unlikable; it was that I really didn't know how to be a good mother.

Summary of Presenting Problems

From our observations of the family during the MIM, as well as the information gathered during the intake interview, we could see that there was a striking mismatch between Katie's lively, energetic temperament and her mother's more quiet style. Katie was trying to take control and run the show, while her parents, particularly her mother, found it very difficult to set limits. It was not easy for Katie to allow herself to be nurtured and cared for. In addition, her mother was uneasy providing such care. We needed to help Katie become more confident. Our plan was to go back and recreate the good parent-child interactions that Katie needed to experience if she was to develop into a happy, confident young woman.

Our goals for Debbie were to help her set limits confidently and to feel comfortable providing the soothing, nurturing care that she had never experienced as a child. We wanted to increase her empathy for how Katie was feeling and to help her become more relaxed and playful with her. We also had the goal of helping Debbie resolve the issues with her own mother. We knew that this would be necessary before she could parent her own children in the strong, playful, nurturing, and attuned manner that they needed. Ann Jernberg, as the therapist working directly with the parents, had the primary responsibility for this part of the work. I worked directly with Katie in the playroom while her parents watched and talked with Ann. After the first few sessions, Jerry and Debbie came into the playroom to practice what they had learned as they watched me with Katie.

Description of Treatment

Because Katie had always had a great deal of difficulty separating from her mother, we predicted that she would not willingly leave her parents in the observation room and come with me into the playroom. With this in mind, I planned a particularly playful, engaging first session, one that I thought would appeal to any 4-year-old. I would give her a piggyback ride into the playroom. On the way, there I would show her where her parents would be watching through the one-way mirror. Then I would check her out, count her fingers and freckles, put lotion on her hurts, and check her strong muscles. Using her strong muscles, she would punch through a sheet of newspaper that I would stretch in front of her. Then we would crumple the newspaper into balls so that she could throw them into the hoop I would make with my arms. I thought it would be fun to play "Row, Row, Row Your Boat" and then tumble out of the boat. I planned to paint her hands with lotion to make a handprint and then show her all the nice lines and curves of her hand in the picture. Finally, I wanted to feed her some pretzels and give her a drink of juice. All of these activities were designed to engage her in playful, perhaps challenging activities and to make her feel well attended to and well cared for.

As I had predicted, Katie protested leaving her parents. Once she was in the playroom, she calmed down for a moment as I checked out her freckles, but soon she began protesting. The protests came and went, but by the time I was doing "Row, Row, Row Your Boat," she was trying so hard to get away that I had to hold her to keep her from hurting herself or me. As I held her, I quietly told her, "I know you don't like me to hold you. It's hard to leave your Mommy and Daddy. But I will make sure that you are safe. I won't hurt you and I won't let you hurt me. I want us to have some fun." In spite of my quiet reassurances, she yelled at the top of her voice, "She's killing me. Mom come save me." Had I asked her mother to come into the room at that point, I would have confirmed Katie's view that she couldn't survive without her mother there to take care of her. I wanted her to learn that I could take care of her and that we could have fun together. It was also important to model for her parents that an adult can stay with an upset child and can calm and comfort her until she feels better.

As Katie struggled and cried, I rocked her and soothed her. I cooled her forehead with a damp cloth. I blew on her cheeks and her ears. I gave her water to sip. When she began to settle down, I helped her sit up so we could play some games. Finally, I rubbed her hand with lotion and made the handprint on construction paper as I had planned. For the first time, she was really engaged. She was fascinated to see the lines in the handprint that matched those in her hand.

Although we had prepared her parents for this likelihood, it was still a great strain, especially for Debbie, to see Katie so angry and upset.

Debbie's Comments on the First Session

As I sat with Ann and watched, it felt that what Phyllis was doing with Katie threatened everything I knew. Kate's screaming made me think she was being hurt. I was ready to run in to save her from this horrible woman. I didn't know it then, but I now know that you were being kind to her, staying with her when she was upset and helping her through a difficult time. I think I *would* have tried to rescue her if Ann hadn't held me with her quiet, kind eyes. It was such a warm and caring look. Calmly she said, "She's just playing 'Row, Row, Row Your Boat.' How can that be bad? She is doing what most children would like very much." I had to agree that the game could not be bad, but I still had a nagging feeling that it might not be good for Katie. Even putting lotion on her hands seemed wrong to me, too babyish and indulgent. I just had no model for that in my head. No one had played "Row Your Boat" with me. No one had gently rubbed lotion on my hands.

Once I settled down a bit, I could see that you weren't hurting Katie and, in fact, were taking very good care of her. It made a very powerful impact on me to see you take care of her: putting cold cloths on her forehead, taking care of her scratches and bruises, comforting her when she was upset. No one had ever taken care of me like that. I think now that I might even have been jealous that she was getting what I had never had. It was painful to become aware of what I had missed, of how little I knew how to take care of her or play with her.

Later I realized that Kate's resistance and screaming were keeping her from all of the good things that Phyllis was trying to give her and that she needed so much. Because I had never had these things given to me, it was very difficult for me to give them to Katie. Because they were new to Katie, she too was probably thinking 'this can't be right.' It was so unfamiliar to both of us that it just seemed wrong. It stirred up Katie's and my problems at the same time. We both resisted.

Sessions 2 through 4

After that first session, Katie gradually calmed down and began to enjoy herself, but it took four sessions before her angry protests stopped completely. We made stacks of hands, rubbed lotion on her toes, popped bubbles, had her jump from one pillow to the next, punched newspaper, and had "snowball" fights with crumpled newspaper balls. I also found many ways to nurture and care for her—making painted footprints, combing her hair, and feeding her special treats. In order to keep our play calm and well structured, I often asked Katie to wait for a signal before jumping or punching the newspaper. To add a little fun, I would vary the signal; sometimes it was when I winked my eye, and sometimes it was when I said "watermelon" or "hippopotamus."

Behind the Mirror

While I played with Katie, Ann sat with Debbie and Jerry. As they watched, Ann helped them understand why I was paying so much attention to hurts, why I kept trying to get good eye contact, and why it was so important that I remain in charge. She also helped them resolve differences in their approach to Katie. Often she would help them see that their own early experiences were still influencing how they responded to Katie. Ann's support and availability went a long way toward filling the gap that had been left by Debbie's own early experience. She also helped Debbie understand the significance of what she was observing. In the process, Debbie began to understand what both she and Katie needed.

Debbie's Comments

Ann was the first person who had ever made herself totally available to me. She told me that I could call her any time of the day or night if I needed her. I never took advantage of it, but for the first time, I didn't feel that I was all alone. When I was a child, I couldn't contact my mother on weekends while I was staying with my grandmother. I couldn't talk to my father when I was with my mother. No one was ever just there.

Even before I came to Theraplay, I knew that I wanted to do things differently with my own children. I wanted to stay married. I wanted to stay in the same house and not move. I wanted to be at home and not work. I knew what I didn't want to do. But I didn't know that I was missing all the fun pieces. Bouncing my children on my knee. Noticing all their subtle likes and dislikes. I didn't know how to do that part. I didn't know how to create a pleasant experience for my children.

Sessions 5 through 15: Parents in Sessions

Once Katie began to relax and enjoy our play, it was time for her parents to join us in the playroom. They needed to practice the new skills they were learning so that they could carry them out at home. In order to make their entry more fun, Katie and I hid under a blanket and called for her parents to find us. Katie snuggled into my arms and giggled as her parents looked around the room saying, "I'm looking for a girl with brown hair and brown eyes. A very special girl. She has a lovely laugh. Oh, I think I heard that laugh." When they found us, I asked Mom to give Katie a great big hug.

Then we played a game of rocking Katie and "tossing" her into each other's arms on a signal. We made a tunnel of our bodies and had Katie crawl through the tunnel. We played "Mother May I" so that Debbie and Jerry could practice giving instructions and making sure that Katie followed through. We did many nurturing, soothing activities. We helped Katie become "soft and floppy" as she lay on the pillows on the floor. Then, each parent would in turn instruct her to wiggle only one finger, her tongue, and so on. We always had some food for her to eat; we rocked her and sang loving songs to her. At the end of each session, in order to extend the time in which they were really connected, I asked Debbie to hold Katie's hand all the way to the elevator.

Debbie's Experience in Sessions

When I first came into the room, you had me sit so that I could make eye contact with Kate, whether I was holding her or feeding her or just playing with her. At first, Katie refused to make eye contact, and it hit me hard to realize how disconnected we were. When I was feeding her, you helped me figure out whether she was enjoying her food, whether she was ready to stop or ready for more. All things I did not know how to do.

It came as a surprise that you made sure that I was comfortable as well as Katie. I had never thought of that. I thought that if I was doing what I was supposed to do—pleasing people—my comfort didn't matter. You taught us to notice her and anticipate her needs. We checked whether she was hot or cold, happy or sad, excited or calm. If she needed to slow down, you showed us how to calm her. Before coming to you, if I held her it was almost as a time-out so that I would not have to attend to her. Now it had a playful, loving purpose. If I held her, it was to look at her, notice her freckles, check the color of her eyes, see whether her feet were relaxed or how strong her arms were. I could tell if she needed more covers, not because I asked her to tell me, but because I felt her, and she was cold. She no longer had to scream or whine to have her needs met. I knew how to attend to them because I was so aware of her. If I rocked her, it was not to get her to be quiet because she was screaming. It was for fun, like "Row, Row Your Boat" or "Rock-a-Bye Katie." You taught us how to play.

I learned that although setting limits was hard work, it would help her feel safe and secure.

I had not been big on addressing hurts. When I was a child, I was told to be strong, don't whine, move on. Now, I could see that it is important to take care of a child's hurt. We have used a lot of Band-Aids, applying them to every real and imagined hurt. It no longer felt like spoiling or an inconvenience. It was a way of letting her know "You are important to me." I started to take joy in taking care of her.

If I made a mistake and caught myself, I could do it over again the right way instead of pretending it didn't happen. This helped my children learn that if you make a mistake, you can always fix it. A temper tantrum no longer felt like a battle of wills. I could now see that they came when Katie had become overwhelmed because I had not anticipated her need to slow down or be attended to or whatever it might be. If she had a temper tantrum, I would hold her and tell her it was OK. I would stay with her until she felt better. It was an opportunity for me to let her know that I was there for her no matter what. It was also a chance for me to learn to be better at anticipating her needs.

When I first started trying to do Theraplay with Katie, I was just going through the motions. It felt unnatural. I was stiff and awkward. When you told me to hold Katie's hand all the way to the elevator at the end of a session, I did it robotlike, as a job to be done. And Katie fought me all the way. Finally, one day I took her hand and we skipped all the way to the elevator and it was fun! I had that "ah ha" feeling—this is the way it is supposed to feel. I was no longer pretending. It was suddenly pleasurable to take care of her and to see her so happy. I liked feeling competent.

As Katie became happier, I began to delight in her happiness. She learned how to play with other children without being rough. She now smiled at the doctor as he walked into the room. The nurses, who once had to hold her down each time she got a shot, thought she was one of their most adorable clients. I took great pride in her and in the fact that I had taken an active role in putting that smile on her face. As my confidence grew, so did Katie's. I was no longer at a loss for words, solutions, help, inspiration, and fun. I finally knew what a good parent does. Thank goodness kids are always willing to give you another chance to do it over the right way.

Jerry's Comments on Treatment

The whole idea of therapy made me uncomfortable. Being in this strange situation with people looking at what kind of parent I was made me especially uncomfortable. But I felt a level of trust. You had a centeredness and kindness. You looked mature. I imagined that you had seen many children like Katie and that you knew what you were doing. I could trust you to take good care of her and to know how to help us. Ann had a patient, quiet understanding and strength that were reassuring.

Before we came to Theraplay, Katie was pretty wild. You taught me how important it was for adults to be in control. I learned how to quiet her down. We tamed her.

I remember taking time off from work. It was a big time commitment. I wanted to be there, but I also felt that this was really important to Debbie.

I was trying to be the strong, male breadwinner and to maintain a confident image. I must have appeared stiff. I didn't know how to relax. I didn't know how to be a child with my child. You taught me how to be a warm and soothing parent. I was not able to get the message until you told me and then held my hand, saying, "This is how to do it. This is what it feels like." Fathers often don't understand touch and closeness. I didn't know how to touch and hold Katie so that she could relax—the fuzzy thing. When I finally got it, she would smile and cuddle and almost purr. It was wonderful.

Katie's Memories

I remember doing a lot of fun things: jumping on pillows, playing "Row Boat," making handprints, playing hand-clapping games. I don't remember being angry and having you hold me. I just remember liking what we did. Theraplay influenced our family in a very positive way.

I really like to babysit. Kids like me. I think I learned a lot of ways of having fun with them. I also learned that you have to take charge when you are with little kids.

Debbie Describes Resistance from Family and Outsiders

Although we were enthusiastic about this new way of parenting our children, our parents were not. They told us that we were spoiling our children. Our new approach didn't fit in with how they were raised. Sometimes I think that they resented all the time we spent attending to our children's needs because that meant we had less time to attend to theirs. We were a family united.

But it wasn't just our parents who didn't understand. When Kate was about 5 years old, she had to have stitches. She was scared and hurt. The nurse asked us to move to another room. I instinctively picked her up and started to carry her. The nurse said, "She's too big to carry. Katie you're a big girl. Don't make your mom carry you." I said, "I want to carry my daughter," and kept going. I felt so strongly committed to the path we had started, no one could sway me. Finally, I knew what to do and it felt great.

Follow-Up 14 Years Later

Katie is now a lovely 18-year-old, enjoying her first year at college. Throughout her school years, she has attracted attention from teachers and parents in the neighborhood because she stands out as an unusually healthy, happy youngster. She is much in demand as a babysitter because she is so lively, playful, and loving with children. Other parents ask, "How did you raise such a wonderful girl?"

When Debbie asked Katie's third-grade teacher what she considered Katie's greatest strength, the response was "Kindness. She is the kindest child I know." Later, one of her high school teachers commented, "She is such a neat kid. She is so balanced. Some kids don't care about their work, and others care too much and become stressed out. Katie has her priorities together. She's always smiling and happy. She's comfortable in her own skin." Her swim coach adored her. He said, "She's the best kid I've ever known."

Her father says, "Katie has a very open, positive personality. She communicates to Debbie and me in a way that gives us a measure of where she is. It is important for her continued growth that she can talk with us when she has problems."

Debbie's Summary

As a mother, I have always been afraid that I might be labeled as having messed up my kids. It used to be that parents were blamed for their children's problems. Nowadays, therapists are more likely to look for the source of the problem in the children—a neurological problem, a difficult temperament—all beyond parents' control. Theraplay gave me back the power to affect my children's lives in a healthy, powerful way. Yes, my children brought their own stuff into our relationship. But, as a parent, I could decide to change their "stuff" if it was unhealthy for them and to make changes in the way they related to the world if I felt it would benefit their lives. Everything was not written in stone. It is scary to think that I have that power, but it is also wonderful to think that I can make my children's lives better. Especially since you taught me how and that it does not have to be done in the first three years. We did not start with Katie until she was 4 or Beau until he was 12.

What we learned working with Katie has been very helpful with our other two children. Although Hayley has always been an easier child, she would have times when she was unhappy or resistant, and Jerry and I would look at each other and say, "She needs a bit of Theraplay." Just 10 minutes of play would help her through a difficult moment, and she would be fine for a month. We would pick her up, swing her in a blanket, toss her in the air, and sing to her. She loved it. You could see that it really made a difference. Even Beau, who was so much older, benefited from our being able to adapt Theraplay to help him. It wasn't as easy to toss him in the air, but we knew how to talk to him, how to find good ways to make him feel good. Theraplay has become a life philosophy for me. When I would get the calls from Beau at college, I would say to myself, "*Don't panic*. You can listen and comfort him."

Katie was the one who blew the whistle on me. She would not take the little I had to offer. She was screaming for a healthy mom. She forced me to change. The other two were so good. They never protested. Thank goodness Katie did. She was saying, "This is wrong. This doesn't feel good."

While we seldom are able to follow up a case this long after treatment and to have such insightful comments from the family members, our experience with Theraplay confirms that it has a very powerful effect on all the families that come to us for treatment.

References

JERNBERG, A. M., & BOOTH, P. B. (1999). *Theraplay: Helping parents and children build better relationships through attachment-based play.* San Francisco: Jossey-Bass.

JERNBERG, A. M., BOOTH, P. B., KOLLER, T. J., & ALLERT, A. (1982). *Preschoolers and school age children in interaction with their parents: Manual for using the Marschak Interaction Method (MIM).* Chicago: Theraplay Institute.

III
Case Studies in Group Treatment

Group work seems to be a "natural" modality to use in work with children, adolescents, and their parents. The interaction and feedback that occur in a group setting are tremendously helpful for young people struggling to change behaviors or better understand their circumstances. Groups are also a wonderful means of establishing mutual support for children and for parents who need to share the common frustrations of child rearing.

Groups provide a safe setting for members to learn and practice new skills. Furthermore, compared to individual casework, more interpersonal interactions take place in group work (Toseland & Rivas, 1995), and many of the most useful interactions that occur take place between group members rather than between the members and the practitioner. Because of this, many group workers stress the concept of the group as a mutual-aid system (Gitterman & Shulman, 1986).

Group leaders who work with children and adolescents must keep several factors in mind. First, the use of active pacing can make a group more engaging and help keep the attention of children. "One of the most critical skills in active pacing is keeping the discussion on target. When one group member digresses, time is lost and other group members begin to get bored. A well-meaning group leader may allow a participant to ramble. A good group leader is able to keep the members focused on the topic at hand without offending a long-winded participant" (LeCroy & Daley, 2001, p. 103). Encouraging frequent contribution (that is, soliciting the participation of every member) is another crucial task in group work with children and adolescents. Both of these skills reflect the view of the group leader's coexisting commitment to two "clients": the individual and the group. Shulman (1992) describes this dynamic, noting that "as the group process unfolds, the worker is constantly concerned both with each individual member and with the other client, the group as a whole" (p. 284).

While much has been written on group practice, our focus is on how this modality may be best used to help children, adolescents, and their parents. The studies in this section contain several specific pointers for work with this population. In the first of the five case studies, LeCroy describes a social skills training group for preadolescent children. He delineates the planning and implementation of the techniques in the group and illustrates how this method of treatment helps young people confront stressful situations and avoid problem behaviors.

In a very different case study, Magen relates the development and evolution of a parent training program designed for families referred to a social service agency by Child Protective Services. The author describes and demonstrates the importance of group composition, structure, and pacing. We are privy to the results of a client satisfaction survey for each group meeting and observe as the author adjusts elements of the group to address client feedback.

In the next study, LeCroy and Daley outline issues facing early adolescent girls and offer a research- and theory-based approach to prevention groups with this population. They outline eight crucial developmental tasks facing girls in the transition to adulthood and describe specific techniques designed to help girls deal with body image concerns, friendships, establishing independence, and avoiding risky behaviors.

In the next study, Holleran relates the experiences of a group of young Latinas in an empowerment group. The mutual aid and support supplied in the group emerge from Holleran's approach of treating minority clients as experts in their own experience. In this way, their competence and potential are revealed during the course of the group.

In the final study in this section, Gustavsson shares her experience working with gay youth at a Gay / Lesbian / Bisexual / Transgender (GLBT) youth drop-in center. As she describes her work with this group, she sagely reminds us to question society. She describes her work with a client who is not "the problem" but whose experiences with oppression have created problems in living. Her respect and admiration for clients who deal with homophobia give her a solid base from which to help these clients. Finally, there is a study by Arbuthnot in Section VI, Using Practice Evaluation, that also relates to group practice.

References

GITTERMAN, A., & SHULMAN, L. (1986). *Mutual aid groups and the life cycle.* Itasca, IL: F. E. Peacock.

LECROY, C., & DALEY, J. (2001). *Empowering adolescent girls: Examining the present and building skills for the future with the Go Grrrls program.* New York: Norton.

SHULMAN, L. (1992). *The skills of helping individuals, families, and groups* (3rd ed.). Boston: F. E. Peacock.

TOSELAND, R., & RIVAS, R. S. (1995). *An introduction to group work practice* (2nd ed.). Boston: Allyn & Bacon.

Case Study 3-1

Questions for Discussion
1. What types of difficulties would be best suited to this model of treatment?
2. How are group members involved in the teaching of social skills?
3. How was role-playing used to teach social skills?
4. How can the group leader evaluate whether the skills are learned?

Social Skills Group for Children
Craig LeCroy

Ms. Thompson called the social services office of the school district for the third time. One of her students, Kevin, had caused so much disruption that she lost complete control of her class. It was the end of an exhausting day that was beginning to become too familiar.

I met with Ms. Thompson and other teachers about important concerns with their various students. "Kerry is so insecure and withdrawn—I'm concerned about how her brother teases her." Another teacher exclaimed, "Tom can't control his anger; when he gets mad he lets the other kids have it!" Ms. Thompson spoke mainly of Kevin: "I can't keep him in his seat and under control."

I listened to the complaints, feeling, as I had in the past, disappointed that the children could not get the individual time and attention they needed. It became clear that the children had a less-than-promising year ahead if they weren't able to gain some control or comfort in the classroom and with their peers.

Teacher concerns such as these frequently lead to the beginning of groups designed to respond to the various needs of troubled children. Groups that focus on social skills do well in addressing the various difficulties that such children face in their day-to-day lives. The purpose of social skills groups is to teach children new ways of responding to their problematic situations.

A skills-based approach has become increasingly popular as we learn more about the relationship between poor peer relationships and subsequent social difficulties. Child developmentalists stress the importance of children learning necessary peer relationship skills because without such skills, children are more easily beset with friendship difficulties, inappropriately expressed emotion, inability to resist peer pressure, and so on. Within a social skills framework, problem behaviors, such as the child behavior problems presented by these teachers, are viewed as deficits in appropriate skills. This suggests the need to teach children prosocial responses or social skills as opposed to an exclusive focus on the elimination of problem behaviors.

Teaching Social Skills

The logic behind teaching social skills is based primarily on social learning theory. Social situations are presented, and then children are taught to implement skills in responding to the various situations. The process begins with the social situation and the social skill being taught. The group discusses the use of the social skill, the rationale for the skill, and the steps used to implement the skill. Next, the stage is set for learning the skill through role-playing. The leader or group member models the skill, followed by feedback from the group members as to whether the criteria for successful demonstration of the skill were achieved. The group members take turns rehearsing the social skill in various role-play enactments. Following the acquisition of the basic skill, the group then works on more complex skill situations. Successful use of the skill requires the use and practice of the skill in the natural environment. Many variations of this basic format are used.

Starting the Group

As I reviewed the theory and rationale underlying social skills groups, the concerned teachers began to identify skills they would like to see their students learn. I try to encourage teachers to think in terms of desired outcomes they would like to see students develop rather than focusing on problems they want eliminated. Having teachers focus on outcomes brings them one step closer to specifying what objectives they believe are important for the children to acquire. I find that asking, "What would the child need to do differently to be less of a problem?" is helpful in moving the discussion to desired outcomes that are more specific and positive. When I asked this of Ms. Thompson, she began to express hope for Kevin: "Well, Kevin's a natural leader—but he needs to learn to ask for things politely and resist peer pressure to disrupt the class."

Together, we identified six children, 9 to 11 years old, who would benefit from a social skills group. The tasks of recruiting and scheduling the children, notifying and informing parents about the group, and arranging logistical details were shared by Ms. Thompson and myself. We agreed that the group would run for 10 weeks, which would give me adequate time to teach the children some specific skills, encourage application of the new skills to classroom and home situations, and teach problem-solving skills for difficult and complex situations.

An Examination of the Training Process

The skills training process proceeds in a fairly straightforward, structured way. The following sections describe the key leadership skills and procedures in a social skills group. A brief process recording from a group session follows.

Selecting Skills and Situations

When I decided to conduct the social skills group for the school, the first step was to decide what basic skills I was going to focus on. Given the identified needs of the children, I decided to focus on the skills of giving and receiving feedback, making friends, and resisting peer pressure. Other social skills programs might choose a variety of skills to teach, such as negotiating, making requests of others, being assertive, handling encounters with police, practicing pregnancy prevention skills (for example, discussing birth control and asking for information), getting a job, using independent living skills (for example, using community resources), and practicing anger control skills (LeCroy, 1986).

When broad social skills are selected, as with resisting peer pressure, then the microskills that constitute resisting peer pressure must be identified. For example, the microskills of resisting peer pressure include speaking slowly and calmly, saying no clearly and as soon as possible, continuing to refuse pressure, and suggesting another activity or leaving the situation. One of the critical and valuable aspects of social skills training is the discrete level at which the social skills are taught and learned. Breaking down the skill into small components facilitates learning and provides an increased sense of control to the group members. As the children learn small steps, they master new ways of responding to situations and gain greater self-confidence in their abilities.

Another consideration that is important in planning a social skills group is the type of problem situations that are used in the group. Providing the group members with situational problems that demand the use of the skill is important. Problematic situations need to be devised to reflect a realistic situation in which the social skills can be practiced. For example, with resisting peer pressure, situations could be constructed around pressure to steal, to cheat, to have sex, and to take drugs.

Discussing the Social Skill

To begin the process of teaching a social skill, I start with a discussion about the use of the social skills. The purpose of the discussion is to provide reasons for learning the skills and to give examples of when the skill might be used. I asked the group, "Why is it important to learn how to resist peer pressure?" If children understand the reason behind why they should use the skill, then they are more motivated to learn the skill. Furthermore, if children are given examples of how the skill can be used, then they will be motivated by understanding how to apply the skill in their day-to-day life. I also asked, "What examples can you think of where you used or could have used the skill of resisting peer pressure?"

In discussing the skill with the group, it is important to describe the skill steps needed to operationalize the skill. It is critical to break down the skill and provide the group members with a clear understanding of how the steps compose the overall application of the skill. I list the skill steps on the board, and I often tell the students that they must remember them. Together, the group works out games or acronyms to facilitate retention of the steps. When teaching the children the skill of resisting peer pressure, I listed five skill steps I wanted them to learn:

1. Look the person in the eye, and be serious.
2. Say no clearly and quickly.
3. Continue to say no if you get repeated pressure.
4. Suggest an alternative activity.
5. If pressure is continued, leave the situation.

These skill steps break down the skill of resisting peer pressure and give group members a clear idea of how to respond to peer pressure effectively. We spend some time discussing what each step means in the children's own words.

Set Up the Role-Play

Next, I set up the role-play for the group members. There are several critical decisions in composing the role-plays. For instance, I usually select a protagonist who I think can do a good job as a model for the other group members. I get the group involved in setting up a realistic role-play by asking: "What is the situation?" "Where is this taking place?" "Who would be there?"

It is important to prepare the group members to participate in and observe the role-play. I structure the group so that the group members are actively involved and listening to the role-play rather than sitting back passively, uninvolved in what is going on. I encourage the group members to define some of the characters in the role-plays. For example, I ask, "What is this person like? What kind of character should we give this person? What does this person sound or look like?" I ask the students who play the roles to pay attention to their nonverbal as well as verbal behavior in the role-play.

I also instruct the group members to be observers by giving them observer tasks. I have the observers choose a name, such as Detectives or Watchers, and I say, "Make sure the skill steps are followed" or "Someone watch the nonverbal behavior," or I ask a more general question like "Do you think this is similar to situations you know about?" By assigning the group or specific members observation tasks, they become more actively involved in the role-play and therefore acquire the skills more readily. At this time, I also discuss with group members how to give and receive feedback. I always have the children practice giving feedback prior to starting role-plays.

Modeling the Skill

For each new skill, I either model the skill or select a group member to model the skill. I model the skill so that I can carefully follow the skill steps. When a group member is used to model the skill, it is important to ensure good modeling. This can be facilitated by reviewing the skill steps with the protagonist immediately prior to the role-play. It is important to go briefly over the plan of what the role-players are going to say in the role-play enactment. I then review the skill steps for the group members who are responsible for giving the protagonist feedback on his or her performance.

Role-Play and Rehearsal of the Skill

The role-play is enacted, and the role-players do a live demonstration of the problem situation. Although the situation is contrived, the role-plays frequently become spontaneous, and each role-player must act accordingly. Following the role-play, the group members are ready to respond with their feedback. I take an active part in soliciting positive feedback, first by asking the group what the protagonist did well. I encourage and often require the protagonist to also state a self-evaluation. This is followed by a careful critique of the skill steps. "Were the skill steps followed? Which steps could have been performed better? How would you do it differently?" The leader must structure the feedback and keep the group focused on learning the discrete skill steps.

The feedback is then incorporated into another role-play. Here the protagonist must concentrate on changing his or her performance to meet the demands of the feedback. It is critical for the leader to help facilitate this by asking, "What are you going to do differently this time to use the group's feedback?" The process is continued until the protagonist has performed all the skill steps. For every skill, I provide an opportunity for each group member to be the protagonist so that each one learns the skills proficiently.

Practice Complex Situations

As the group members became proficient at the basic skills of giving and receiving feedback, making friends, and resisting peer pressure, I introduced increasingly complex situations. The use of more extended role-plays was one way that I accomplished this. I also asked the group members to bring in their own social skill situations so that the group can help them work out new responses to problematic encounters. After the group had acquired many of the basic skills, I taught the group accessory skills for dealing with problematic situations. For example, we began to focus on using problem-solving skills in addition to practicing social skills. During one of the later sessions, Kevin brought up a situation in which he had successfully resisted his friend's pressure to skip school, but his friend said he would no longer be his friend. We worked on generating different alternatives for solving Kevin's new dilemma. In addition, I encouraged the development of role taking by having the members play different roles in various social situations. In this way, I can encourage the members to experience the role. I often ask, "What does it feel like to be . . . ?" In Kevin's situation, I helped him develop some perspective taking or empathy skills by asking him to play the role of his friend. When he did this, he was able to discover some new ways to try talking with his friend.

As a leader, I try to think about what goal I am trying to achieve with the group. If the goal is skill training, then I focus the group on the acquisition of the skill: "What would you do in that situation?" If the goal is role taking or empathy, I focus on feelings by helping the children experience different feelings and roles: "How does this person feel? Why does he feel this way?" If the goal is to encourage problem solving, I focus on alternative ways of solving problematic situations and various consequences for different alternatives: "What are some other alternatives? What would happen if you choose that solution?"

Group Process Illustrated

The transcript below from the group's fourth session demonstrates the techniques and procedures used in leading a social skills group.

Leader: Today we are going to practice our social skills. One skill that we have talked about is learning to resist peer pressure. What does it mean to resist peer pressure?
[The group leader explains the purpose of the group. The leader begins by soliciting an explanation of the skill.]

Beth: It's when your friends try to force you into things.

Mark: It's when other kids get you into trouble and it's not your fault.

Leader: That's right, Beth and Mark; resisting peer pressure means other people are trying to get you to do something you don't want to do. So when you are in a situation where you don't want to do something that your friends want you to do, you need to be able to say no and do it in a way that your friends will leave you alone. What reasons can you think of for learning how to resist peer pressure? I'll start—you resist peer pressure so that you'll feel better about yourself because you didn't get talked into doing something you might feel bad about later.

[The group leader encourages and reinforces the group members to share.
    The leader summarizes the skill.
    The leader points out the influence of peers and stresses the need to learn the skill.
    The leader provides rationales for the skill. The leader begins by modeling the first response, and the group members follow in a similar fashion.]

Kevin: So you don't get into trouble with your parents.

Leader: Good, Kevin.

Wendy: So you don't get talked into using drugs.

[The leader provides reinforcement for group member participation.]

Tommy: Your friends will listen to you and know you're not just saying things.

Leader: Great, Wendy and Tommy. As a number of you have pointed out, there are a lot of good reasons to resist peer pressure. I think you have also talked about how hard it is to do. That's why we need to practice the skill. Let's go over the steps in how to resist peer pressure. Remember, practice good nonverbal skills and start by saying no as soon as possible, stick to your no, and if necessary leave the situation or suggest something different. Here's a situation we can use: two friends come up to you at recess and ask you to steal someone's homework as a joke. This is a person that gets picked on a lot, and he will probably feel picked on if you do it. Wendy, pick two people to do a role-play of this situation. OK, role-players take a minute to think of what you want to say. Everyone else can watch to see if Wendy follows the skill steps. Kevin, will you also see if she uses good nonverbal behavior? OK, let's start.

Tom: Hey, Wendy, go get Todd's homework; it's sitting right there. (points to a chair)

Kerry: Yeah, he'll never know you did it.

Wendy: Uh . . . I . . . uhmmm . . . I don't think I better.

Tom: Come on, Wendy, just do it.

Wendy: No, I can't—you do it if you want Todd's homework.

[The group leader summarizes and emphasizes the difficulty in resisting peer pressure.

The leader reviews the skill steps to identify the sequence that the members should follow in learning how to resist peer pressure. The leader puts these on the board or provides students with a handout.

The leader provides a situation for the group to ensure that the skills are understood and learned. Later, members can bring in their own situations to practice.

The leader chooses a member who can do a good job with the role-play (that is, modeling the skill) because this is the first time through.

The leader prepares the group members to listen and observe so that they can observe the model and give feedback. One member is singled out for a special task to help ensure that he pays attention. The leader must be responsible for getting everyone in the group involved in the role-play.]

Leader: OK, break. Let's give Wendy some feedback. Kevin, let's start with you; what nonverbal behavior did you observe?

Kevin: Well, she spoke up and looked Tom in the eye.

Leader: OK, good. What do you think she could have done better?

Kevin: She tripped over her words at the beginning.

[The leader begins the process of feedback by asking group members to comment on Wendy's performance. The group members have been taught to use positive feedback at first before being critical, although here they too quickly move to the critical.

The leader encourages students to share observations and then asks for specific critical feedback.]

Beth: Yeah, she could have said no better at the beginning, but the second time was better.

[The leader gets other group members to model better responses to the situation.]

Leader: Beth, what do you think would be a better response when Tom asked her to take the homework?

Beth: She could have said, "No, I don't think that is right."

Leader: Why isn't it right?

Beth: Because it would hurt his feelings.

[The group leader encourages the members to think about what it is like when someone hurts your feelings.]

Leader: Yes, I think it would. OK, any other feedback for Wendy? Well, I have some. I think Wendy did a good job of being serious. I think the second time she spoke,

she could have suggested another activity like we learned. Any ideas on what she
could have suggested?

[The leader gives his feedback, making sure that the role-play incorporates the skills
needed to resist peer pressure.]

Tom: You mean she should have said let's go play outside?

Leader: Yeah, she could have suggested they go outside and forget about taking
Todd's homework. OK, we've got a good start; let's redo the role-play, and Wendy,
try to use the suggestions for improvements the group gave you. For example, how
could you say "no" right away after Tom and Kerry put pressure on you?

Wendy: I could say, "No, I think that's mean and I don't want to do it."

Leader: Good. That's better. Let's go ahead and try it out again. Remember to say no
early on, be forceful, and suggest an alternative activity.

[The leader summarizes the suggestions and then prepares the group to redo the role-
play and incorporate the ideas suggested by the group. Here it is important to make
sure the role-players under stand how to incorporate the feedback for an improved
performance.]

The remainder of the session is devoted to continued practice and feedback. The
leader helps students to identify situations outside the group in which they can practice
skills in the upcoming week and assigns homework practice using the "buddy system."
The group closes with a brief fun game to increase social connections among the children and to keep the group interesting and fun.

Practicing Social Skills in the Natural Environment

A primary goal in teaching social skills is that the skills learned will be used in the
child's natural environment. Throughout the 10-week sequence, I encouraged the children to practice the skills outside the group. This was accomplished by giving and
monitoring homework assignments. At times, all group members were working on
the same skill—for example, after the session in which we worked on resisting peer
pressure. At other times during the 10 weeks, group members would work on different
skills; for example, Wendy would focus on starting a conversation (a discrete friendship skill), while Kevin focused on generating alternatives to peer pressure situations.
Group members were given assignments to use the skill and record the outcome in a
journal. The journals were helpful and were used by half of the group members; the
other three members typically forgot or lost their journals. For those that used them, I
reviewed the journals in the group and used them to reinforce the members' practice
outside the group. I also encouraged the use of the skills outside the group by having
the group members practice the skills with their "buddy" as a homework assignment.
"Buddies" were rotated to promote increased social interaction among all group members and to provide a variety of peer role models for each member. I consulted with
teachers as much as possible to monitor the group members' interpersonal interactions

so that examples of when and where to use the skills could be incorporated into the group procedures.

Conclusion

Promoting competence in children and adolescents is a fundamental strategy for helping young people confront stressful situations and avoid problem behaviors. It has been effectively used to help children develop new patterns of interpersonal relationships, confront new social situations, gain membership in new social groups, and learn new behavioral responses. Without adequate social skills, such experiences can become avenues to pregnancy, delinquency, drug use, and social isolation.

Social skills training is perhaps the most promising new treatment model developed for working with young people. It approaches treatment by building on the positive aspects of functioning—building needed skills for youth. Children and adolescents must adapt to and cope with an increasingly complex society. As a normal part of growing up, young people must confront the developmental task of dealing with issues such as drugs, sex, and alcohol. To be successful, we must teach our children social skills so that they can respond to difficult social circumstances and do so with self-confidence and competence.

Reference

LECROY, C. W. (1986). Social competence training. In A. R. Stiffman & R. Feldman (Eds.), *Advances in adolescent mental health* (Vol. 2, pp. 101–114). Greenwich, CT: JAI Press.

Case Study 3-2

Questions for Discussion
1. What is the purpose of the pre-group assessment interview?
2. How does the analysis of client demographics impact the formulation of the group curriculum and format?
3. What is the importance of group leaders being able to redirect and refocus the group?
4. Why do the leaders try to follow the same basic structure for all groups?
5. How did the authors define the beginning of the "performing" stage of the group?
6. How do the authors use the postsession questionnaires to guide group practice?
7. How is group composition important to the group process? What is the effect on the group of members having children of many different ages?
8. How do the leaders help prepare the group members for termination? How is the termination process somewhat thwarted?

Evidence-Based Approach to Parent Training

Randy Magen

"Another family referred by Child Protective Services." This was becoming a common refrain during staff meetings at the Family Service Agency. On one hand, the staff were proud that our agency was recognized as a valuable resource for families with multiple problems. On the other hand, we were becoming increasingly aware that as an agency, we needed specific services to offer these families. It was after one of the weekly clinical staff meetings that the agency director asked me to design a parent training program for families referred by Child Protective Services (CPS).

It had been several years since I had done any parent training. I knew from my reading of professional journals, from walking through the self-help section of my local bookstore, and from noticing flyers from other agencies that there were a plethora of approaches to parent training. How could I pick the approach or combination of approaches that would be most effective with the CPS-referred families? I had heard about Evidence-Based Practice (EBP); it seemed similar to the concept of empirically based practice that I had been taught as a graduate student. Gibbs and Gambrill (1999, p. 235) write that EBP "means integrating individual expertise (lessons learned in your work) with the best available external evidence from systematic research as well as considering the values and expectations of clients" to make practice decisions.

Who exactly were the clients and what were they expecting from our agency? I examined the last 3 months' worth of referrals from CPS to learn about the clients. Fifty-six families had been referred over the last 3 months. The agency's intake form provided information on these families (see Table 1).

TABLE 1   Demographic Characteristics of CPS Referred Families

Gender	
Female	51
Male	5
Marital status	
Single	4
Married	15
Divorced	37
Race	
Caucasian	53
African American	1
Hispanic	2
Age (average)	27.23 years
Education	
Some high school	14
High school graduate	28
Some college	10
College graduate	4
Employment status	
Unemployed	14
Part-time	34
Full-time	8
Average number of children at home	2.13
Average age of eldest child	9.02 years

Based on this data, I visualized the average client who would participate in the parent training: a divorced White woman with two children, the first of which she had as a late adolescent or young adult. For the most part, group members would be at least high school educated and employed part-time.

Three of the clients on my caseload had been referred by CPS. I was able to discuss expectations with those three clients, as well as with two clients working with other social workers in the agency. I asked each client what they wanted and needed when they came to our agency. I purposefully asked about both wants and needs, believing that each tapped into a different elements—wants are aspirational, whereas needs are basic. Several clients stated that they came to the agency to get CPS "off my back." Other expectations expressed by clients included the desire to feel less alone, to feel more in control of their children, and to be less stressed.

Design of the Group

Armed with this information, I began to make some decisions about the intervention. Because most of the potential clients were not working full-time, it might be possible to schedule the groups during the day. This would reduce the need to provide child care because the clients' children would most likely be in school. In addition, given the educational level of the clients, the clients would probably have adequate reading and writing skills for any handouts or homework assignments. Conducting parent training in a group would help target both the desire of the clients to feel more in control of their children as well as their feelings of being alone.

I asked our social work field placement student, Diane, to help me with the design of the parent training group. While each client would have individual goals, I knew that any effective group had a defined common purpose or goal. Parent training was too broad a purpose for the group. We needed something more specific. The structure of the group would follow directly from the purpose of the group. Diane was given the task of searching electronic databases for recent empirical articles on parent training. I also asked her to search the literature for an answer to the question of whether it was more effective to focus on specific parenting skills or to focus on the stress and loneliness of the parent.

Electronic searches of the literature have greatly simplified the process of finding recent and relevant articles. However, Diane's electronic search of psychological abstracts in PsychInfo resulted in 5494 "hits" on parent training. The electronic search of social work abstracts produced the somewhat more manageable number of 100. We narrowed our search by looking for articles that reviewed the literature. Three recent reviews were identified. In addition, Diane introduced me to the Cochrane Library, a database of full-text systematic reviews of the effects of health care prepared by The Cochrane Collaboration. Searching the Cochrane Library resulted in two helpful reviews, one that looked at individual and group-based parenting programs (Coren & Barlow, 2002a) and another that looked at parent training programs for improving maternal psychosocial health (Coren & Barlow, 2002b)—exactly the two issues I was interested in comparing.

The Cochrane Library review of the parent training programs stated, "These studies showed that both individual and group-based parenting programmes produced results favouring the intervention group" (Coren & Barlow, 2002a). It should be noted however that this review focused on studies of teenage parents with infants. The conclusion for the review of the studies related to improving maternal psychosocial health were more equivocal. This information and the political reality that our referral source, CPS, wanted a focus on parenting skills lead us to state that the purpose of the group was to assist parents in developing skills for managing their children's behaviors.

The Cochrane review, along with other review articles, pointed to several manuals that had been developed for parent training. Using already developed materials, especially materials that had been subjected to empirical testing, greatly simplified the design of the parent training program. Diane and I designed eight sessions to teach parents specific behavioral parenting skills. Handouts were developed on how to praise their children (i.e., reinforce behaviors), make commands, set clear rules, listen effectively, selectively ignore, and use time-outs. Diane would co-facilitate the group with me to learn more about group work practice.

Recruitment and Assessment

All potential group members would need to have an assessment interview before participating in the group. This interview would help to orient the client to the group, allow us to collect baseline assessment information, and assess the client's fit with the group. Recruitment for the group was not necessary because there were plenty of CPS referrals. However, it was important in the assessment interview to emphasize that this was a voluntary group—no one was requiring the clients to attend.

Other aspects of the orientation included differentiating between a skills-oriented group (this parent training group) and other groups such as support or self-help groups and discussing the structure of the group. We knew that if the clients had a clear understanding of the intervention, it would reduce the probability that they would drop out. Many of the clients also seemed to be comforted by meeting the group leaders one-on-one prior to the first group meeting.

The baseline assessment information included the agency's standard intake information, the specific parent-child difficulties that the client was experiencing, strengths in the parent-child relationship as well as other strengths of the client, and the results of the Eyberg Child Behavior Inventory and the Revised Behavior Problem Checklist. The latter two items are standardized scales that would help us to empirically evaluate the effect of the group intervention.

All potential group members were asked about their previous experiences in groups. We inquired about their comfort in talking with 8–10 other people about their parenting difficulties. We also evaluated whether the parents had the reading skills to comprehend the various handouts that would be used in the group. Finally, we wanted to make sure each individual client was not too different from the other clients. I knew from previous group experience that a client who is "different" from other clients because of race, intellectual capacity, or some other characteristic is more likely to be isolated and scapegoated in the group. We followed Yalom's (1985, p. 266) "Noah's ark principle," in which every group member has at least one other member who shares similar characteristics.

The first 12 clients who completed the assessment process were accepted into the group. In hindsight, perhaps we were too eager to get the group going and were not selective enough in our assessment of the group members. All 12 of the clients were Caucasian women. The group members were (to protect their confidentiality names and identifying characteristics have been disguised):

Carie, 33 years old, single, with a 7-year-old girl and 5-year-old boy
Carol, 27 years old, married, with a 7-year-old boy and a 4-year-old girl

Charlissa, 23 years old, single, with a 3-year-old girl
Chris, 30 years old, divorced, with a 14-year-old girl and a 12-year-old boy
Denise, 28 years old, married, with a 7-year-old girl
Hannah, 26 years old, married, with a 6-year-old boy and 4-months pregnant
Jessica, 32 years old, separated, with 7-year-old and 2-year-old girls
Louise, 34 years old, divorced, with 12-year-old and 10-year-old boys and a 7-year-old girl
Maurissa, 40 years old, divorced, with a 13-year-old girl
Molly, 29 years old, married, with 5-year-old twin boys
Nancy, 27 years old, married, with a 5-year-old boy
Patty, 25 years old, divorced, with an 8-year-old girl

Compared to the demographic data collected on three months of CPS referrals (see above), the group members were slightly older (29.5 years compared to 27.2 years), had fewer children at home (1.5 compared to 2.1), and had younger eldest children (7.8 years compared to 9.0 years). While these differences did not seem clinically important, they did force us to think about presenting our materials with younger examples. We also realized that we might have been mistaken in our assumption that few of these parents would need child care.

We were able to arrange for one slot to be available in our agency's crisis nursery during the 2 hours when our group was scheduled to meet. When we contacted the 12 group members to invite them to participate in the first group, we discussed the child-care issue. To our surprise, none of them expressed a need for child care.

The Group

The parenting group was scheduled to meet from 10:00 a.m. to noon every Wednesday for 8 weeks. The goals for the first meeting were to form a group. At the end of the session, we wanted each member to know the names of the other group members and to have selected one "buddy" to contact during the week. As a group leader, my goal was to ensure that every group member participated and that no one member dominated the group. The parenting content in the first session focused on identifying the A-B-C's of children's behavior. The A-B-C's refer to the *antecedents* (things that set up behaviors), *behaviors* (what the parent or child does, and *consequences* (what reinforces the behaviors). Two tasks were assigned to the group members at the end of the meeting: reading a handout on reinforcement and contacting another group member (their "buddy") during the week.

Eleven of the twelve mothers attended the first session. After the first meeting ended, we received a message from Hannah that she wasn't feeling well enough to attend. Two of the members, Charlissa and Patty, arrived about 10 minutes late. These seemed to be typical occurrences for a first group session.

Over an hour of the first session was spent on the dyad introduction exercise, in which group members break into pairs and interview each other. The interviewer then introduces the interviewee to the group. Because we had an uneven number of group members, Diane (the social work student) participated in one of the dyads. During the introductions, group members were able to make connections with each other; for example, Carie and Nancy discovered that their children attended the same school. Charlissa had the whole group laughing with a story about how her daughter had given a stuffed animal a bath in the toilet and then used some of Charlissa's expensive perfume to make the bear smell better.

Several times during the group, Jessica brought up issues about her separation from her husband. She became tearful at one point, describing how she felt both angry at her spouse and rejected by him. Both Diane and myself gently redirected her to discuss issues related to parenting. When talking about the difficulties with her two children, Jessica seemed to imply a reluctance to enforce rules and discipline her children, perhaps out of exhaustion, from feelings of guilt over the effects of the separation on her children, or for some other reason. In discussing the group with Diane after the session, we both identified Jessica as the client under the most stress.

At the end of every session, we asked clients to complete an anonymous, four-item questionnaire. The questionnaire, modeled after one designed by Rose (1984), collected simple consumer satisfaction data using two 5-point Likert-scaled questions and two open-ended questions. I knew from past experience that clients are reluctant to rate the usefulness of any session less than a 3 on the 5-point scale unless they had a very bad experience. Even though the questionnaire didn't meet criteria for a valid research instrument, it still provided clinically useful information. The average usefulness rating for the first session was 3.65, and no client had rated the group less than a 3. Open-ended comments indicated that clients enjoyed the dyad introduction exercise, and two clients expressed a desire for the social workers to be more active in the group, cutting people off who were talking off subject.

In the second session, we wanted the mothers to continue to make connections with each other—to continue the task of creating a group. The parenting content in the second session had two parts: the first was a conversation about control, and the second was an exercise on the use of reinforcement.

Molly called before the second session began to tell me that she wouldn't be able to attend because one of her sons was sick. Unexpectedly, Charlissa brought her 3-year-old daughter to the group. Diane was able to assist Charlissa in enrolling her daughter in the crisis nursery for the group meeting. Because Hannah was not at the first meeting, we spent the first 10 minutes helping her to introduce herself and learn the names of the other group members.

Only three groups of "buddies" (Carie and Nancy, Carol and Denise, and Diane and Jessica) had completed the assignment to talk with each other during the week. We had a brief discussion about their success and received a verbal commitment from the other dyads to make the buddy contacts. All the group members stated that they had completed the reading homework.

The purpose of the conversation about control was to help the parents identify which aspects of their parent-child interactions were under their control and which weren't. During this discussion, Louise received constructive feedback from the group. Louise expressed frustration with the eating habits of her 7-year-old daughter. She related that her daughter will eat only hot dogs and peanut butter and jelly sandwiches. Furthermore, the peanut butter and jelly sandwiches have to be made with the peanut butter on the top side of the sandwich and grape jelly on the bottom, otherwise her daughter will not eat the sandwich. The discussion in the group helped Louise see that she can't control her daughter's eating habits. Members of the group also suggested that in the realm of things, this was a minor problem and that Louise shouldn't spend her time getting upset about it "Let it go," Maurissa said.

The "let it go" comment seemed to ignite a spark in Jessica, who had been fairly quiet during the first part of the group session. Jessica said, "There are some things which can't just be let go of," and then went into a tearful discussion of an incident that occurred during the week between herself and her soon to be ex-husband. Group members offered sympathy to Jessica but also looked uncomfortably at the leaders during her disclosure. Empathic responses by Diane appeared to help Jessica calm down, and after several minutes we were able to redirect the discussion back to parenting issues.

The second area of discussion in the group meeting was the use of reinforcement. Rather than use technical words, we discussed the power of praise, compliments, and strokes. Maurissa made a cute connection between the use of praise and the song "A Spoonful of Sugar" from the movie *Mary Poppins*. As homework for the next week, group members agreed to monitor how often they used praise with their children and attempt to increase the amount of praise used in their homes.

The postsession questionnaires indicated that members were satisfied with the session (giving an average rating of 3.85) but were very concerned about Jessica. One member wrote on the form that the group leaders needed to do something to help her. Diane and I discussed Jessica's use of the group to discuss her marital problems. We both agreed that while this was clearly a pressing issue for her, it was not within the scope of the group's purpose nor did it fit with our contract with the other group members. As a first step, we decided that the Diane would call Jessica and attempt to engage her in individual work focusing on the separation. We also agreed to intervene quicker when Jessica brought up issues about her separation during the group meetings. Our strategy would be to redirect her to talk about how the separation was affecting her parenting.

Unfortunately, Jessica was not interested in working individually with Diane or anyone else on issues regarding her separation. She did, however, agree to meet with the group leaders 15 minutes before the next meeting to discuss how she could best use the group.

The agenda for the third session included differentiating between requests and commands and addressing guidelines for setting rules. For the first time, all 12 members were both in attendance and on time for the meeting. The leaders, modeling the use of praise discussed in Session 2, gave verbal praise to individual group members and to the group as a whole. Jessica did not arrive 15 minutes prior to the meeting to talk with the group leaders but agreed to stay after the meeting to talk.

We made a conscious attempt to follow the same basic structure in all group sessions. The purpose of this was to make the group more predictable for group members, which in turn should reduce any anxiety they might have had about the group. Furthermore, following the same structure allowed group members to take on some of the leadership tasks of the group, reducing the reliance on group leaders. An example of this latter behavior was seen in Session 3. Shortly after the opening remarks by my co-leader Diane, Carol asked the group how everyone did on their homework. While there was a bit of self-praise in Carol's question—because she had completed all of the homework tasks (making the buddy contact and monitoring and increasing the use of praise)—it was an example of a member initiating an agenda topic.

All of the pairs had made their buddy contact except Jessica and Hannah, who were now paired. The failure of this buddy contact was notable given Jessica's level of need. To give this pair an idea of how to initiate the buddy contact, we had the other pairs report on how and when they had made contact. For example, Carie and Nancy had met at their local school playground, and their children played while they discussed the week's homework on praise.

I was not feeling well during Session 3. I had a headache and found it difficult to maintain a high level of energy and listen closely to group members. This was one of those situations in which I was glad that I had a co-leader. If I missed something, I was confident that Diane would catch it. I debated whether to self-disclose my headache to the group but decided that the group needed to maintain its focus on the group members. The risk in self-disclosure was that the group would focus on me. At the break midway through the session, I quietly told Diane about my headache. Not only was I reassured by having Diane in the group, but also the postsession questionnaires showed an improvement in group members' satisfaction (3.92) and few open-ended comments. Diane joked that maybe if I had a headache every week, member satisfaction ratings would go even higher!

In meeting with Jessica after the third session, Diane and I both noted that she appeared depressed and had little to say. We made empathic and supportive comments, but the focus of the meeting was to emphasize that the purpose of the group was to help parents manage their children's behavior. We were direct in indicating that it was clear to us that her needs went beyond the group's focus. Jessica again declined our offers to assist her in dealing with issues connected to her separation. It didn't feel like we made much progress with Jessica. How she behaved in the next session would indicate whether we had made an impact.

Session 4 seemed to be a turning point in the group. Using Tuckman's (1965) model of group development, Session 4 marked the point when the group moved into the performing phase. First, for the second week in a row, all members of the group were present and on time. Second, most of the group members completed the buddy contact (Molly and Patty had not), worked on the use of praise, and finished the assigned reading. Session 4 was also the point when the group began to engage in specific problem solving around situations that each mother presented. This problem solving continued for the next four group sessions. It also might have been the discussions that ensued during this problem solving which gave me the impression that the group was performing: group members were questioning each other, providing support, offering suggestions, and using the skills that had been taught in the previous group sessions.

Diane and I spent less time giving mini-lectures, calling on group members to participate, and explaining how the group worked. Instead, we monitored the level of participation among the group members and worked at facilitating the discussion. Our interventions involved helping members to take turns participating, prompting members who were participating less, muting members who were dominating the discussion, and offering summaries at key points in the discussion.

Jessica continued to appear depressed in Session 4. She participated less than most of the other group members. When it was her turn to discuss a parenting issue, Jessica talked about the difficulties she had with her 7-year-old daughter after she returned from overnight visits at her father's house. While this could be defined and problem solved as a parent-child problem, Jessica preferred to focus on the differences in her and her separated husband's parenting practices. Obviously, our discussion with Jessica following Session 3 did not have the desired effect.

As a group leader, this was one of those times when I saw the differences between working with an individual, one-on-one, and facilitating a group. If Jessica had been an individual client, I would have had more control in helping her to focus on parenting issues or I would have had the freedom to concentrate on her conflicts with her separated husband; in the group, I had neither that power nor that freedom. Instead, the collective force of the group members kept the discussion focused on Jessica's problems with her husband. Perhaps this was helpful to Jessica, but I was uncomfortable with the discussion because it seemed to be outside the contract we had with the group members about the purpose of the group. After a lengthy discussion of Jessica's conflicts with her husband, I was able to offer a summary and move on to other group members' parenting issues.

We were then halfway through the group sessions. Postsession evaluations following Session 4 were somewhat lower than those in Session 3 (3.64), and there were three comments regarding Jessica. Two were appeals for the leaders to offer Jessica more assistance, and one comment expressed the frustration I felt as a leader: "If she wants to talk about her marriage, she should be in a different group." The frustration Diane and I had with Jessica was also being felt by some group members. We agreed to continue to redirect and cut off Jessica's comments about her husband, but we felt somewhat powerless about intervening to help her.

Session 5 of the group was designed to continue the problem solving from the previous week. In addition, the content of the session involved teaching the active listening skills of expressing feelings and empathizing. Jessica did not attend Session 5 and did not call to inform the group leaders.

One of the more satisfying aspects of conducting a skills training group occurred in Session 5. Carie offered a problem-solving suggestion to Molly that incorporated the skill of stating clear rules, one of the skills we had taught in Session 3. It was nice to see one of the group members trying hard to use the skills that were being offered in the group.

It was also during the problem solving in Session 5 that I became aware of another problem with the composition of the group, namely the differences in the ages of the children whom parents were talking about. For example, when Charlissa was discussing difficulties in getting her 3-year-old daughter to stay in bed, the entire group offered suggestions. Louise gave a good example of making a clear rule, one she had used when her children were young. However, when Chris shared her difficulties of not knowing where her 14-year-old daughter was after school, few members of the group had experiences with older children that could help her problem solve. I believe we erred by not making sure that the ages of the target children were more similar when composing the group.

Postsession questionnaire data from Session 5 were a bit higher than those from previous sessions (4.02). Interestingly, no members made negative comments to the leaders. Was this due to Jessica's absence? I must admit that I found the group easier to facilitate without Jessica present.

Diane called Jessica to find out about her absence from the group. Jessica explained that her 2-year-old daughter had been sick and this prevented her from attending the session.

Between Sessions 5 and 6, Carol called to say that she would not be attending the group any longer. Her mother had just been diagnosed with breast cancer, and Carol believed that she needed to devote her time and energy to her mother rather than to other things in her life. I offered Carol support and empathy and asked her permission to share this information with the group. I told Carol that I would miss her in group and that I had appreciated her willingness to take on a leadership role.

In addition to problem solving, the content of Session 6 was focused on the skill of ignoring. The 11 members of the group arrived on time, and most had done the homework. The exceptions were Jessica and Molly. Because Denise had been paired with Carol, Carie and Nancy agreed to take in Denise as part of their buddy contact.

The group seemed to be on autopilot at this point. As a leader, I sat back more, allowing the members to run through the problem-solving process with each client taking a turn sharing a situation. I still modeled reinforcing positive behaviors and worked to shape Jessica's issues so that they focused on parenting issues rather than conflicts with her ex-husband. The postsession questionnaire data kept with the established pattern (3.75), and there were no open-ended comments.

Session 7 was the only session in which the content focused on punishment, the use of time-outs. This session also marked the beginning of the end phase of the group. As a leader, I purposely helped the members to begin thinking about the fact that there was only one more group session. The homework for Session 7 also helped members to focus on the end; members were asked to develop a maintenance-of-change plan for the skills they had learned during the group.

Jessica did not attend Session 7. She had called her buddy, Hannah, before the group, so the group was informed of her absence. Again, I felt like the group operated more smoothly without Jessica. The postsession questionnaires also had higher scores when Jessica was not present; in this session the average was 3.95.

The plan for Session 8 was to end the group with a celebration and with every group member having a plan for maintaining the skills they learned during the group. Diane had made certificates of completion to celebrate the parents' accomplishment. Unfortunately, there was a tremendous thunderstorm the day of the last group session. Only four members showed up at the scheduled time. We all discussed the possibility of rescheduling the last session, but coordinating the schedules of 13 people proved too difficult. Diane and I attempted to provide some closure to the four members who attended, and we followed up with each of the other group members over the telephone. Rather than the group ending with a bang, it ended with a bust.

In our follow-up phone calls with the group members, we scheduled postgroup interviews. These interviews were to conduct a posttest, repeating the Eyberg Child Behavior Inventory and the Revised Behavior Problem Checklist. We also wanted to use the postgroup interview to get evaluative feedback for use in redesigning the group. Finally, the postgroup interview was a time to reinforce maintenance-of-change plans and to offer referrals for other services.

Three of the members chose not to participate in the postgroup interview. The remaining participants' scores on the Eyberg Child Behavior Inventory and the Revised Behavior Problem Checklist showed a decrease in the number and intensity of child-related difficulties. Feedback was generally positive. A couple of members gave feedback to help us improve some of the handouts. In addition, several group members made comments about group composition issues.

Was the group a success? Did we engage in evidence-based practice? Diane and I both agreed that the answer is both yes and no. What do you think?

References

COREN, E., & BARLOW, J. (2002a). Individual and group-based parenting programmes for improving psychosocial outcomes for teenage parents and their children. *Cochrane Database of Systematic Reviews, 4.*

COREN, E., & BARLOW, J. (2002b). Parent-training programmes for improving maternal psychosocial health. *Cochrane Database of Systematic Reviews, 3.*

GIBBS, L., & GAMBRILL, E. (1999). *Critical thinking for social workers: Exercises of the helping profession* (Rev. ed.). Thousand Oaks, CA: Pine Forge Press.

ROSE, S. D. (1984). Use of data in identifying and resolving group problems in goal-oriented treatment groups. *Social Work with Groups, 7*(2), 23–36.

TUCKMAN, B. W. (1965). Developmental sequence in small groups. *Psychological Bulletin, 63*(6), 384–399.

YALOM, I. (1985). *Theory and practice of group psychotherapy* (3rd ed.). New York: Basic Books.

Case Study 3-3

Questions for Discussion
1. What are the developmental issues that confront early adolescent girls?
2. What are the biopsychosocial interactions that impact early adolescent girls?
3. How was the Go Grrrls program designed to address developmental concerns?
4. How could you implement this type of program in your community?

Empowering Adolescent Girls:
The Go Grrrls Social Skills Training Program
Craig LeCroy and Janice Daley

The decibel level rises as the last bell rings. Middle school students flood the hallways, their voices loud and their laughter echoing off the walls. The participants in our new after-school program find their way to the alcove by the school entrance, where we wait to meet and greet them. They trickle in slowly, girls of a remarkable variety of shapes, sizes, skin tones, and levels of development. I think to myself that during the course of this program, I hope my co-leader and I can help each of them to appreciate their uniqueness and natural vitality.

In recent years, several popular authors have captured the attention of parents, teachers, administrators, and mental health professionals by outlining the challenges faced by adolescent girls in today's society. Through exposure to media stereotypes of women, girls feel cultural pressure to adhere to an absurd "ideal" of thinness. They watch television programs in which women are frequently assigned roles as passive, sexual beings. As they begin to mature, girls may find that their families and school environments offer less encouragement for them to participate in the classroom, sports programs, or other extracurricular activities. And all of these elements affect girls during a time of rapid and sometimes perplexing physiological change. Potential manifestations of these combined cultural and developmental factors include increasing incidences among adolescent girls of eating disorders, depression, lowered self-esteem, and decreasing levels of confidence and assertiveness.

Early adolescence appears to be a particularly harrowing time for many girls. Pipher (1995), author of the popular book *Reviving Ophelia,* has stated that "American culture has always smacked girls on the head in early adolescence" (p. 23) and that for girls, "junior high (seems) like a crucible" (p. 11). Her contention is supported by the work of Simmons and Blyth (1987), who note that at all grade levels, boys have significantly higher self-esteem than girls and that the gender difference increases by 30 percent from sixth to seventh grade.

In addition to differences in self-esteem, adolescent girls' assessment of their body image satisfaction ranks lower than boys' satisfaction at all age levels (Rauste-von

Wright, 1989). When young girls develop the belief that they are unhappy with their body and that there is little they can do about it, they can develop feelings of helplessness and hopelessness. Dissatisfaction with one's body image has been found to be associated with higher levels of depression (Fabian & Thompson, 1989; Furnham & Greaves, 1994). Furthermore, girls who feel negatively about their bodies during early adolescence appear to be more likely to develop eating disorders (Attie & Brooks-Gunn, 1989). The cultural ideal of female thinness has an even greater affect on early maturing girls, who tend to display the most dissatisfaction with their weight (Graber, Petersen, & Brooks-Gunn, 1996).

There also appear to be gender differences in the friendship networks of adolescents, with girls placing greater expectations on their friends and rating friendships as more intimate than boys rate their friendships (Claes, 1992). Close friendships offer girls an important sense of connectedness that may be critical to their development (Gilligan, Rogers, & Brown, 1990). However, as girls experience society's lack of respect for such intimacy, they begin to struggle with competing choices between independence and responsiveness or connectedness. This, according to Gilligan, leads them to silence their different voices. Helping young girls bring to their relationships a strong, assertive, and authentic self while valuing their ability for intimate relationships is critical to healthy development. Close friendships enhance a girl's sense of self-worth and help facilitate more accurate understanding of others (Sullivan, 1953).

This research suggests that there is a need for programs designed specifically for adolescent girls. The Go Grrrls program seeks to address the unique challenges that early adolescent girls encounter by providing them with practical instruction and skill-building exercises. We have chosen seventh graders as our target population in the hope that we can provide a sort of inoculation of knowledge and skill early enough so that girls may resist some of the common hazards of growing up in a culture that seems, in many respects, to be toxic to females.

An Overview of the Program

We have chosen a social skills training and psychoeducational program to be administered in a group format. Social skills training has been found to be effective in programs designed to prevent as well as remediate problems for adolescents (LeCroy, 1982). A group format is both practical for reaching large numbers of girls and developmentally appropriate because adolescents tend to strongly value social interaction with their peers.

As the girls settle into the meeting room on the first day, they are greeted by a large poster-board sign. The sign is decorated like a jigsaw puzzle, and each of the eight major topic areas of the project are written on its pieces (see Figure 1). The major topics are being a girl in today's society; establishing a positive body image, establishing a positive mindset, and establishing independence; making and keeping friends; when it all seems like too much; let's talk about sex; and planning for the future. Some of the

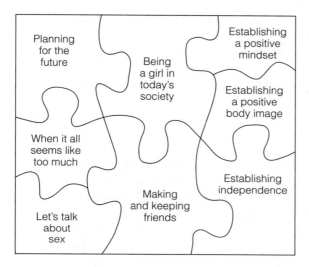

FIGURE 1 The Go Grrrls puzzle.

group sessions (such as the session on problem solving) will emphasize skill building in areas that are equally pertinent to boys and girls, but the examples and role-plays used to illustrate the skills will emphasize girls as the major actors. Other sessions (such as the session on being a girl in today's society) are designed to address areas of special concern to adolescent girls. An outline of the 13 sessions is presented below, followed by a more in-depth description of each.

The 13 Sessions

> Week 1: Being a girl in today's society
>> Session 1: Introduction/Pretest
>> Session 2: Challenging media messages
> Week 2: Establishing a positive body image and a positive mindset
>> Session 3: Body image
>> Session 4: Rethinking self-statements
> Week 3: Making and keeping friends
>> Session 5: Qualities of a friend
>> Session 6: Making and keeping friends
> Week 4: Establishing independence
>> Session 7: Problem-solving strategies
>> Session 8: Assertiveness skills
> Week 5: Let's talk about sex
>> Session 9: Sex 101 and refusal skills
>> Session 10: Risky business—alcohol, drugs, and unwanted sex

Week 1: Being a Girl in Today's Society

Session 1: Introduction/Pretest

The goals for the initial session are (1) to create a supportive atmosphere and begin building cohesiveness within the group, (2) to collect baseline data for program evaluation, (3) to introduce participants to group standards, such as confidentiality and respect for others, and (4) to introduce the program content. The girls fill out a questionnaire designed to assess their self-concept. Joan, a freckle-faced 12-year-old, looks up at me from her questionnaire and says, "Hey, this stuff is personal!" She's right, and her comment reminds me of the feminist stance that the personal is political.

We then play a "name game" to loosen everyone up and to help with introductions. Following the game, we help the girls to establish group standards by asking them to suggest their own rules for the group. If the group-generated rules do not include important areas (such as confidentiality and its limits), then the group leaders bring up these subjects. Finally, we introduce the program content by displaying a large poster with the "Go Grrrls" puzzle and encouraging each member to read one of the topics aloud. Finally, we distribute journals or Go Grrrls workbooks, which the girls are instructed to use to complete brief assignments for the group and to express themselves in any way they wish. The journals/workbooks are a tool for helping the girls incorporate what they learn into their personal lives and provide a mechanism for encouraging them to continue their self-growth and discovery after the group ends.

Session 2: Challenging Media Messages

This group is intended to promote awareness of the profusion of negative images of women and girls that abound in popular media and to equip girls with the ability and confidence to critically challenge these cultural stereotypes. Group activities for this session include creating a collage from teen magazines and evaluating lyrics from hit songs. Activities from this session are delineated in depth later in this article.

Week 2: Establishing a Positive Body Image and a Positive Mindset

Session 3: Body Image

As described in the introduction, adolescent girls are likely to develop a negative body image, and a negative body image tends to be related to low self-esteem and depression. The goals of this session are (1) to help girls accept their bodies as they are and develop a positive body image, (2) to teach them that attractiveness is based on factors other than physical traits, and (3) to encourage girls to appreciate their unique qualities, talents, and skills.

We begin by asking participants to discuss the reasons that developing a positive body image is important for girls. We then embark on a series of image-boosting activities. In one activity, girls are asked to make a list of five things they like about themselves and then to share these things aloud in the group. Group leaders construct a chart of the girls' responses as they are offered. The chart includes categories for physical aspects, social and personality traits, specials skills and abilities, and cognitive abilities. Discussion then centers around the fact that each girl has a unique set of strengths in these different categories.

Session 4: *Rethinking Self-Statements*

An important part of our program is teaching girls about the relationship between self-esteem, self-criticism, and depression. As mentioned previously, girls entering the seventh grade show a significant decline in their overall self-esteem. This session is designed to teach girls how they can avoid setting unrealistic standards for themselves and can instead give themselves positive messages to facilitate realistic goal achievement.

Participants complete fill-in-the-blank handouts, listing their unrealistic "I should" messages. We then help them to change these messages to "I want" statements that are more constructive. Finally, we describe how negative thoughts tend to generate even more negative thoughts in a sort of downward spiral, while positive self-messages tend to lead to increased confidence, in an upward spiral. An example follows:

"I should" statement: I should be liked by everyone.
"I want" statement: I want to have good friends.

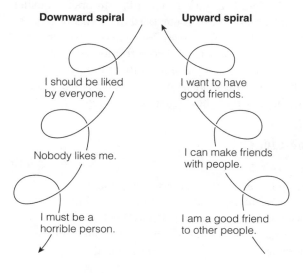

Downward spiral

I should be liked by everyone.

Nobody likes me.

I must be a horrible person.

Upward spiral

I want to have good friends.

I can make friends with people.

I am a good friend to other people.

Week 3: Making and Keeping Friends

Session 5: Qualities of a Friend

As mentioned in the introduction, adolescents are social beings. Adolescent girls, in particular, seem to value close friendships. Friendship provides a social support system that helps to bolster self-esteem, lessen depression, and ameliorate hard times. The goal of this session is to teach girls to focus less on "popularity" and more on developing intimate, satisfying friendships.

Participants are asked to brainstorm a list of qualities that a good friend might have. Each group member then fills out a "friendship want ad." A sample follows:

> Seeking a new friend: I am looking for someone to talk with and go rollerblading with. I would like someone who is friendly, outgoing, and funny. I think a friend is someone who you can tell secrets to, so I have to trust you.

Group leaders collect these ads and then randomly redistribute them. Each girl must then write a response to the friendship ad they receive. A sample response to the ad above might read:

> I am a very active person and would enjoy rollerblading. I agree with you about wanting a friend you can trust. In the past, I have had friends whom I trusted but they told my other friends things I did not want shared. I promise to be a person you can trust. I like to talk about boys! And right now I am having a lot of trouble with my Mom. Let's meet and we can see what happens.

Session 6: Making and Keeping Friends

Making and keeping friends requires a high level of social skill. This session is designed to teach friendship skills and provide group members with an arena in which they can practice these skills. Group leaders help girls to identify and practice using tools to start conversations (for example, making eye contact, asking someone a question, and saying something positive about the other person). We also discuss and practice how to communicate positive feelings and how to deal with friction when it arises in a friendship. In addition to role-plays, the girls brainstorm different ways to build, maintain, and mend friendships. They write these ideas down on strips of paper and then place them in a "friendship tool box," which they decorate and keep.

Week 4: Establishing Independence

Session 7: Problem-Solving Strategies

Adolescents often make decisions impulsively, without considering the impact of their choices. Their decisions represent "experimental" attempts to acquire skills for dealing with new situations, but unfortunately, these attempts may lead to serious consequences. Session 7 is truly a skill-building session—we teach group members a method for solving problems and then ask them to practice this method.

Group leaders encourage members to discuss some unproductive methods they have used to try to solve problems in the past (for example, ignoring problems in the hope that they will just go away or blaming someone else for the problem). Leaders then describe a five-step strategy for problem solving. Each girl receives a handout delineating these steps (see page 134). The group divides into two smaller groups, each of which is given a hypothetical problem to solve. One such example follows.

Your best, oldest friend asked you to sleep over at her house on Friday night and you told her you could. On Thursday, though, a really popular girl at school invites you (and not your friend) to her party on Friday night. What do you do?

Session 8: Assertiveness Skills
Girls are often socialized to be accommodating to others. One positive result of this socialization is that girls may acquire sensitivity to others' emotions and may develop insight into the intricacies of relationships. One potentially negative result of this socialization is that they may overlook or disregard their own thoughts and feelings in an effort to "keep the peace," or conversely, they may become frustrated when authority figures or peers do not demonstrate understanding of their needs.

Session 8 attempts to teach girls about three different options for responding to situations: assertive, passive, and aggressive. Group leaders define these terms for members, and then participants are provided with scripts depicting assertive, passive, and aggressive responses to provocative remarks or situations. They role-play these scenes for the group, and all members are asked to identify which responses are assertive, passive, or aggressive. Scripts are designed with an introduction that sets up the dialogue, and all are tailored to reflect situations that early adolescent girls are likely to face. One example follows:

Introduction to Situation 1:
One thing that really helps girls to be successful is being involved in outside activities like sports, dancing, exercise, and community work.

Sometimes when girls get to be in middle school, they feel pressure to stop doing activities that they've enjoyed for many years. Many girls stop doing these things, not because they don't enjoy them anymore, but because they are afraid that their friends will think they're not cool if they keep doing them. Let's see what happens in this situation and how being assertive can help.

Situation 1
Your ballet teacher invites you to perform at the annual dance recital. You are very excited about it, so you tell your best friend.

Person 1:   Hey, Linda, my ballet teacher just asked me to perform at the recital!
Person 2:   You aren't really going to do it, are you? Recitals are for geeks.
Person 1—response A: No, I guess not.

HANDOUT: MAKING DECISIONS AND SOLVING PROBLEMS

Here are the steps you can use for problem solving:

1. Define the problem. (What is it?)
2. Brainstorm choices. (Think of every possible solution . . . even silly ones! Don't criticize any of them yet!)
3. Evaluate the choices. (What are the pros and cons of each choice?)
4. Make your decision. (Select the best idea.)
5. If your decision doesn't work out, start over again at step 1!!!

After reviewing these steps, complete the following:

1. Define the problem.
My problem is:

_____

_____

2. Brainstorm choices. I could:	**3. Evaluate the choices.** **(Put a + or − beside each idea)**

4. Make your decision.
I decided to_____
because_____

5. If your decision doesn't work out, start back at step 1, and try another idea!

Person 1—response B: Yeah, I am, and you're just jealous because you're a complete klutz.

Person 1—response C: I've worked really hard to get this chance, and I'm excited about doing it.

Week 5: Let's Talk about Sex

Girls are usually eager to discuss sexuality by the time these sessions roll around. The Go Grrrls curriculum places an emphasis on pregnancy prevention within a broader program context that is both educational and skill based. The program includes two group meetings devoted specifically to the topic of sexuality, but it is the cumulative effect of the entire curriculum that is most likely to make a difference in a young person's behavior. The skill-building sessions included in the curriculum (assertiveness, problem solving, making and keeping friends, positive self-talk, and setting reachable goals for the future) all serve as important components in reducing teen's likelihood of engaging in early, unhealthy sexual activity. Psychoeducational components of the curriculum (confronting media messages and establishing a positive body image) boost girls' understanding of the effects of broader cultural trends on their individual lives.

Session 9: Sex 101 and Refusal Skills

During this session, we review myths and facts about sexual activity. Leaders display posters depicting male and female reproductive organs, explain the physical act of intercourse, review what goes on during the menstrual cycle, and cover other basic sexual information. Participants are then asked to place their questions about sexuality or myths they may have heard about sex into an anonymous "question can." This is the highlight of the group, and after the initial round of anonymous questions have been answered, girls usually continue to toss new questions in or to simply ask them aloud as they become more comfortable with the process. After the questions have been answered, participants discuss reasons why some teens choose to have sex and some do not. Role-play activities give girls practice in using refusal skills, and community resources for obtaining birth-control information and supplies are pointed out.

Session 10: Risky Business—Alcohol, Drugs, and Unwanted Sex

Young people are risk takers. The process of growing up consists of a series of risks as teenagers try new things. Unfortunately, some of the risks they take can have lifelong negative consequences. This session is devoted to helping girls understand some of the risks involved in using alcohol and other substances. We also establish the link between substance use and impaired judgment, including the potential for unwanted sexual activity. During this session, students brainstorm reasons why some teens choose to use substances and others choose not to use them. Each girl designs an advertising campaign that shows alcohol or other drugs as glamorous and then draws an "anti-advertisement" that responds to the first ad, debunking the glamour myth and highlighting the link between alcohol or drug use and risky sexual behaviors. Next, we play a game that demonstrates the link between substance abuse and risky behaviors and that emphasizes the real risk of exposure to STDs. After the game, leaders explain ways to reduce the risk of exposure to STDs.

Week 6: When It All Seems Like Too Much and Visions for a Strong Future

Session 11: Where to Go for Help

This topic can evoke some major issues for girls; leaders must, therefore, begin by reviewing confidentiality and limits to confidentiality with the group. Next, girls participate in an exercise designed to help them discern the difference between problems they can solve on their own and problems for which they need to seek help. The group establishes a set of general guidelines to indicate when a problem requires outside resources to solve. Next, girls are encouraged to think about the adults they trust and to consider these adults as a part of their personal resource list. Leaders then pass out the "Personal Yellow Pages" of community resources (health and social services, recreational activities, etc.) that are available to girls in their area (these must be constructed locally for obvious reasons). Girls can practice using the resource guides by reading through sample problems and suggesting appropriate agencies or individuals to contact in each situation. Finally, girls are encouraged to view "resource seeking" as a sign of intelligence and strength rather than as a sign of weakness. Leaders should be alert during and after the group for girls who are ready to disclose serious problems.

Session 12: Visions for a Strong Future

Many participants in the Go Grrrls program begin the group with a "fantasy" desire to be a model but end the group with a real plan to explore the educational requirements for becoming a physician, teacher, engineer, social worker, or physicist. In this session, we encourage girls to set long-term educational, career, and adventure goals for themselves and teach them how to create short-term objectives to help them achieve those goals. We also try to help girls establish a connection to the future by having them evaluate a list of "value" statements about world issues (e.g., environment, education, racism, etc.) and consider ways that they might truly make a difference in the future world that will be theirs. Finally, we play a "planning for the future" game, in which each girl stands in front of the group and takes a turn at drawing herself performing one of her goals while the other group members guess what goal she is drawing.

Week 7: Closure

Session 13: Closure/Review/Posttest

Our goals for the final session are (1) to review and summarize topics covered during the course of the group, (2) to collect data for program evaluation, and (3) to provide participants with a sense of closure and accomplishment at the end of the program.

Group leaders begin by conducting a brief review of all of the subjects covered during the program. Girls then complete the posttest and a satisfaction survey. Next, leaders hold a "graduation ceremony," in which they read each girl's name aloud and present her with a graduation certificate, while thanking her for some specific way that she contributed to the group. Group leaders then join in a party that usually includes pizza, music, and a raffle to distribute the incentives for attendance (e.g., a portable CD player) and journal assignment completion (e.g., a gift certificate to a local mall). Finally, just before the group is over, the leaders call everyone together and thank the group once again for all of their fine efforts.

Conducting a Session: A Closer Look

By the second session, the six girls in our group already seem to feel fairly comfortable with each other and with us. At this point, it is still important to build a sense of group cohesiveness, so we begin the session by asking if anyone can remember the "name game" we played in the opening session. "Sharp Shannon," a smart 13-year-old, declares that she can and proceeds to reel off everyone's name along with the positive adjective they chose to describe themselves. Other girls want to try their hand at this, too, and several complete the whole round of names. This serves as a good icebreaker activity, and the girls relax into the session.

It is important to note that this program has been designed for all middle school girls, not just "at-risk" students. Lily, a bright and confident track star, has already emerged as one of the group's natural leaders. We encourage her participation because the other girls are likely to follow the lead of a respected peer. After we review each other's names, Lily volunteers to read today's topic from the large puzzle. We begin each session by referring to the puzzle. This little ritual serves two purposes: it reminds the group members of topics that we've covered previously, and (2) it ties the day's topic into the larger program. She reads aloud, "being a girl in today's society," and I explain that today we will be discussing some of the messages and stereotypes about women that abound in the media and popular culture.

We divide the girls into groups by having them count off by twos. We specifically decided to split the group using this method so that group members get to know everyone better, not just one close friend whom they chose to sit beside at the start of group. Each group gets a large sheet of poster paper, with some popular magazines, scissors, glue and magic markers spread around the room. We ask each group to construct a collage depicting media images of the "ideal woman." While they work on this task, we play some popular songs—not raunchy ones, but some that contain disparaging or controversial lyrics about women's role in life. Each group engages in the same activity, then we bring the group together to share what they have learned. The smaller groups afford a greater opportunity for leaders to interface with the girls about the topic. More importantly, though, we instruct each smaller group that they will present their findings to the other group when they have finished their collage.

"I like this song!" Melissa says while dancing around. That's fine, of course. We are not trying to stop girls from listening to popular music. We are trying, instead, to teach them to listen and watch for negative media messages and learn to "talk back"(think critically) about what they hear.

"Yeah, it's got a great bass line," I agree, disarming any need for the girls to defend their music. "Let's check out what they're saying . . . " "You're supposed to be sexy," offers Eileen, a girl who has been very quiet so far. I tell her to pick a marker and write that down on the poster. Patti pastes down an image of a woman standing on a scale, frowning, with the caption "take off ugly weight in one week." They've all gotten into the spirit of the exercise, now, and they're pasting and scribbling, using all different color markers and writing upside down, sideways, and every which way. Words like *easy* and *hoochie mama* (!) appear beside images of scantily clad models, and phrases like "be a perfect mom and good cook" appear beside shots of women in traditional nurturing roles. We did, after all, lay out quite a mix of magazines and played some very different songs to reflect these messages.

Meanwhile, my co-leader is working with the other half of the group. They have also been foraging through popular magazines and listening to the songs, constructing a collage of media stereotypes of women. After about half an hour, we pull the two activity groups together to present their findings to one another. Each group can point to and be proud of a tangible product. My group volunteers to go first.

Claire, a forthright student, volunteers to speak first. She points to several images of supermodels and notes that they are all tall and skinny. Anne, a girl with East Indian ancestry, adds, "Yeah, and most of them are White, too." That's right," Claire continues, "and nobody has zits, and their teeth are all perfectly straight and real white." From these responses, I understand that they are comparing *themselves* to the airbrushed images on the page. (When women my age look at these same images, we tend to notice that no one appears old enough to drive and that certainly no one has any wrinkles.) I don't point out their self-comparison yet because I want to let both groups share their information before we begin coming to any conclusions.

The whole group giggles as another girl in the group points out an ad included in the collage. "You can even buy rubber boobs to make yourself look bigger or a rubber butt to make yours look firmer!" There is a collective shriek in the room in response to these revelations. As my group ends their presentation, they bow and the other group applauds for them. Next, my co-leader's group assembles in the front of the room. Lily begins to read from the graffiti they scribbled while listening to the songs:

> Some stuff that we thought they are saying is, like, you've gotta be sexy . . . and you're supposed to be easy, but then you're bad, like a "hoochie mama" if you do stuff. Then you're supposed to take care of your house and your husband and kids . . . but you're supposed to wear make-up while you do.

They all nod and laugh. Even though the messages that each half-group presents are roughly the same, the impact of having the girls present to each other is palpable.

We are not lecturing them or listing these stereotypes for them. They are declaring their revelations aloud, to each other. As this group ends its presentation, they bow and the other half of the group applauds their efforts.

As the nodding and laughing begin to ease, it is time to discuss the implications of the girls' findings. We challenge the girls to come up with a list of 10 stereotypes about women that they have discovered during this exercise. They eagerly grab markers and work together to list several key words and phrases. *Skinny* appears on the list, as do *big chest, ditzy, clueless,* and *buff.*

While it would be easier to simply point out the fact that no one really matches the absurd media ideal, we want the girls to come up with this idea themselves. We lead them to the point with some open-ended questions. "What do the magazines and music lyrics have in common?" my co-leader asks. They review the traits and the stereotyped behaviors and roles that they uncovered. Then we ask the million-dollar question: "What happens when we compare ourselves to these stereotypes?" Until now, no one in the room has actually stated that she does compare herself to the stereotypes. We are reaching for a deeper understanding now, and the girls become more quiet and serious.

"Well, you feel bad. And there's stuff you can't do anything about. I mean, I know I'm never gonna be tall. Everybody in my family is short," Eileen offers. Her comments open the door, and other group members begin to reveal more personal comparisons. One already slender girl admits that she is on a diet right now. The others tell her that she looks great the way she is. We have reached a true work stage for the first time in this program.

We let these revelations unfold as long as we can, but it is important that we don't close the group on this note, so we help summarize the discussion. We note that many girls and women strive to look or act like the media stereotypes, and when they cannot, they end up feeling frustrated, disappointed in themselves, and sometimes depressed. We ask them how many women they know in their real lives who look or act like the "ideal woman" from the magazines and music. No one knows any such person.

We wrap up the group with a discussion of what the girls admire about the real women in their lives . . . teachers, parents, aunts, and others. We discuss the fact that the media stereotypes of women are not only unattainable, but also undesirable in many ways. We close the group by discussing the fact that it's okay to want to look and feel good, but that it's important to learn to accept who we are and what we look like.

Conclusions

Adolescent girls face an environment that is often toxic to their healthy development. Our culture continues to portray successful and happy women as thin, long legged, and classically beautiful. Body-image problems become significant in early adolescence and can last a lifetime. Many girls begin to become obsessed with their bodies and develop serious eating disorders. Others simply become unhappy and develop feelings of depression. Adolescent girls present unique challenges, and the Go Grrrls program is designed to help them confront those challenges and prepare for a healthier and happier lifestyle.

Using empirical studies that identify the developmental issues impacting early adolescent girls the most, a psychoeducational skills training program was designed. Based on practical instruction and skill building, our program provides an inoculation of knowledge and skills to help girls cope with the pressures of growing up in today's culture. It promotes adolescent girls' positive assets and addresses relevant developmental issues. In a group format designed to build social support, the program helps girls meet the following developmental tasks:

1. Achieve a competent gender role identification.
2. Establish an acceptable body image.
3. Develop a positive self-image.
4. Develop satisfactory peer relationships.
5. Establish independence through responsible decision making.
6. Understand sexuality.
7. Learn to obtain help and find access to resources.
8. Plan for the future.

These are the critical pieces that compose the puzzle of the Go Grrrls program. We hope that all the girls will go far.

References

ATTIE, H., & BROOKS-GUNN, J. (1989). Development of eating problems in adolescent girls: A longitudinal study. *Developmental Psychology, 25,* 70–79.

CLAES, M. E. (1992). Friendship and personal adjustment during adolescence. *Journal of Adolescence, 15,* 39–55.

FABIAN, L. J., & THOMPSON, J. K. (1989). Body image and eating disturbance in young females. *International Journal of Eating Disorders, 8,* 63–74.

FURNHAM, A., & GREAVES, N. (1994). Gender and locus of control correlations of body image dissatisfaction. *European Journal of Personality, 8,* 183–200.

GILLIGAN, C., ROGERS, A., & BROWN, L. M. (1990). Soundings into development. In C. Gilligan, N. P. Lyons, & T. J. Hammer (Eds.), *Making connections: The relational worlds of adolescent girls at the Emma Willard School.* Cambridge, MA: Harvard University Press.

GRABER, J. A., PETERSEN, A. C., & BROOKS-GUNN, J. (1996). Pubertal processes: Methods, measures and models. In J. A. Graber, J. Brooks-Gunn, & A. C. Petersen (Eds.), *Transitions through adolescence: Interpersonal domains and content.* Mahwah, NJ: Erlbaum.

LECROY, C. (1982). Social skills training with adolescents: A review. *Child and Youth Services, 5,* 91–116.

LECROY, C., & DALEY, J. (2001). *Empowering adolescent girls: Examining the present and building skills for the future with the Go Grrrls program.* New York: Norton.

PIPHER, M. (1995). *Reviving Ophelia: Saving the selves of adolescent girls.* New York: Ballantine Books.

RAUSTE-VON WRIGHT, M. (1989). Body image satisfaction in adolescent girls and boys: A longitudinal study. *Journal of Youth and Adolescence, 18,* 71–83.

SIMMONS, R. E., & BLYTH, D. A. (1987). *Moving into adolescence: The impact of pubertal change and school context.* Hawthorne, NJ: Aldine.

SULLIVAN, H. S. (1953). *The interpersonal theory of psychiatry.* New York: Norton.

Case Study 3-4

Questions for Discussion

1. How are the Mexican American girls in the group treated "as experts in their own experience"?
2. What is the primary method of intervention in the Freirian model?
3. What are the major themes that emerge in the group's dialogue?
4. How does the facilitator react when group members use cultural lingo that she does not understand?

A Culturally Grounded Empowerment Group for Mexican American Girls

Lori K. Holleran

The 2000 census reports that there are now 32.8 million Latinos/as living in the United States, making up 12 percent of the country's total population (Therrien & Ramirez, 2000). Latinos/as have become a significant force of culture in the United States. It is predicted that very early in the 21st century, Latinos/as will become the largest minority group in the United States and that by the year 2050 their number will reach 100 million (Del Pinal & Singer, 1997). There are already more Latinos/as under the age of 18 than Caucasians of the same age (Therrien & Ramirez, 2000).

Two-thirds of Latinos/as in the United States are of Mexican origin, while 14.5 percent are from Central and South America and 9.0 percent are of Puerto Rican descent. Almost half of Latinos/as live in a central city within a metropolitan area, and 22.8 percent of Latinos/as were living in poverty in 1999, which was roughly three times greater than the percentage of Whites living in poverty at the same time. When Latino/a children are considered, the numbers become even more astounding: 30.3 percent of Latino/a children live in poverty. More than two out of five Latinos/as over the age of 25 have not graduated from high school, and more than a quarter have not finished the ninth grade (Therrien & Ramirez, 2000).

Clinicians need to be culturally competent when working with Latinos/as. This case study of social work practice with a small group of Mexican American Latinas provides an example of a culturally grounded group work intervention. The group is an example of a 12-week empowerment group for bicultural (Mexican and American) teen girls in a large southwestern city. The purpose of the group was to empower the young women by honoring their life experiences, choices, opinions, and values. The group also aimed to enhance self-efficacy through the mutual aid, support, and encouragement of peers.

The material in this case study is adapted from the ethnographic research of the author described in detail in her dissertation entitled "Chicano/a Youth of the Southwest: Cruising the Boundaries" and subsequent articles.

A strength perspective was the foundation of the group intervention. Based on Freire's liberation theory, relationships are marked by dialogue, questioning, and communication (Freire, 1972, 1973). The group facilitator utilized the following Freirian concepts (summarized from Blackburn, 2000):

- *Liberation:* the process by which people strive toward greater humanization, especially in the face of oppression
- *Conscientization:* the process by which people become more critically aware of their true-life situations and sources of oppression
- *Praxis:* the process by which action leads to further reflection in a dialectical path of increasing liberation

The primary method of intervention is what Freire calls *dialogue*, which requires the facilitator to be "authentic" and "creative" and can only occur with "love" in order to create a space in which the members educate themselves and each other (Freire, 1971, p. 112 as cited in Blackburn, 2000, pp. 8–9). Thus, the group transcript reads much like a conversation.

In this case study, the facilitator embraces the Freirian goal of empowering group members. One appropriate metaphor presents the facilitator as a "midwife" (Cramer, 1995, p. 194). Historically, the dominant culture has been inundated with what Enrique Trueba calls a "deficit mentality," or the belief that racial, ethnic, and linguistic minorities are, at best, culturally disadvantaged and in need of repair or, at worst, genetically or culturally inferior to the majority, which makes them beyond hope of repair (Trueba, 1999). This stance both overtly and covertly undermines client growth and perpetuates clients' sense of personal powerlessness. Cohen (1986) contends that facilitators can foster conditions in which minority clients can demonstrate and share their knowledge and expertise with their peers. When treated as experts in their own experiences, they can then experience their competence, resiliency, and potential.

These foundations for culturally grounded group work are especially crucial for minority women, for whom self-expression can itself be an act of resistance, a political gesture that challenges oppression, or a truly courageous act that can be perceived by society as threatening (Hooks, 1989). The fear of speaking out may have a negative effect on a woman's development. In general, women talk less in mixed groups and are interrupted more often (Belenky, Clinchy, Goldberger, & Tarule, 1997). This young women's group became a safe space for them to explore their challenging realities and to discover their strengths, feelings, thoughts, and dreams.

Case Study

Group Praxis Process Illustrated
The transcripts on the following pages are from the group's fifth session, and they demonstrate the Freirian techniques used to create a safe space and to empower the group members through action and reflection.

F = facilitator
V = Veronica
P = Paula
M = Monica
L = Luz
N = Nicole
S = Selina

F: Last group session, you all decided to find at least one way to "honor your voice" this week. V, you said that you wanted to start today. Do you still want to? [The facilitator opens with a reminder of the action assigned at the end of the prior group and begins the act of "praxis," or moving back and forth between action and reflection.]

V: Yeah. I found my voice, all right. I told my boyfriend that he's not my boss.

F: Wow!

(Other girls smile, some giggle, and several utter affirmative comments.)

V: Yeah. You know, I'm smarter than him. I work for my money. I bought these clothes I'm wearing. I take care of my brothers and sisters. And so where does he get off telling me what to do? Right?

(Girls nod and make various affirmative sounds and comments.)

P: Hey, I did it, too. I decided to tell my dad how frustrated I felt that he doesn't trust me. I can't go out because my dad said I was too young to go out late at night, and so I can't go out with my friends. He doesn't want me to be with them, like going out and running in the street. Because I'm younger. My best friend now spends most of her time with her boyfriend. They used to go out everywhere and like go to parties and everything. My dad won't let me be with them.

F: Bravo! Great work. Hey, I could be wrong, but it sounds like the men in your lives have super strong feelings about how you should be. Is that right? [The facilitator extracts potential oppression to explore and praises group members for asserting themselves.]

P: Totally. My dad and my boyfriend are both really protective. My brothers are, too. The funny part is that I really think that they think they are taking care of us, but we really mostly are taking care of ourselves, you know? I am really independent and that's what I respect about people. I don't really need them to take care of me.

M: I'm the same way. My boyfriend sometimes acts like I need him, but the truth is that I don't depend on anyone. Actually, I got that from my mom, who always told me, "Always be your own person. Don't ever trust a man to do it for you."

F: So she lived by that?

M: No way. She learned it because she *didn't* do it, and so she wants me to live better. It's sad she didn't get to be her own person like I do.

F: That is sad. Sounds like your mom is very wise. How about you, L? Did you find a way to honor your voice this week? [The facilitator affirms her perceptions and makes sure other members get to share their experience.]

L: Yup. I spoke up one time when I used to have stayed quiet. I told my mom how much I missed our old house. I always really liked it up there at my house when I was little. My first house was at Hart and 2nd Avenue. Ummm, it was a good house. We liked it; it was much bigger than an apartment. I lived there with my mom, my dad, and my brother.

F: Can you tell us more?

L: I have two brothers. One's 21, going on 22, and one's 18, going on 19. And the house was really big and pretty. It was two bedrooms—one was where the boys slept, and me and my mom stayed in the back. It had one bathroom in the back. It had a *big* back yard, and we had a shed. But then my aunt and cousin came to live with us, and then about 3 years ago, one of them burnt down the back. It had a lot of TVs and a lot of other valuable stuff, and then so after that, the neighbors saw what was happening, they saw that the back was burning, so we started watering it down, calling the fire engines. And finally they got it out.

(Group sits quietly listening and responds empathically with "ohhh" and comments like "that stinks.")

. . . And after that, about a month or two after, after that happened, that's when we moved out and we left a lot of stuff back there. I was sad, but my dad just lives across the street from there now. And my mom and I live separately now. Because of, like, a lot of problems. Like, my dad used to go out and my mom didn't like it much so . . . (pauses) And he still lives across the street from the house I grew up in.

F: Sounds a bit like what V, M, and P were talking about when they talked about the power their dads had in their moms' lives and their own. Hey, how did it feel to tell your mom the truth? [The facilitator draws on common grounds, reiterates potential power issues, and explores the member's perceptions about her action.]

L: A little scary, but good. I thought she'd get mad that I was complaining, but she just said, "I miss that house, too" and listened. We even started to cry about it. It hasn't been easy.

P: We haven't had it easy either. My family was always pretty poor, but we try to do the best that we can. It's, like, real hard. Still, we always tried to respect everybody.

F: Sounds like you have been through a lot. [The facilitator authentically empathizes.]

P: It was hard, with my Dad and all . . .

F: Hard?

P: My dad is, like, strict. He doesn't work. I don't know; my mom said that my dad used to get physical with her. He used to, like, hit us, but he's not that bad . . . (pause) That's about it about my dad.

F: Sounds like you both have witnessed some conflicts between your mom and dad. Anyone else have that experience?

N: My mom and dad get along now, but they didn't always. He used to drink a lot, but he stopped. He was born again and realized he needed to straighten out and be there for his family. His brother, my uncle, didn't do that, and he died because of it. I'm glad, in some ways, that my uncle was able to save my dad, in a weird way.

F: Wow. That's powerful.

V: I changed my life, too, when my friend died.

F: Really? Would you tell us about that? [The facilitator continues to empathically explores the girls' experiences and perceptions, honoring their reality.]

V: I think you should all hear the story so it can save you too. My friend, she was like my sister. But, I don't know—we were just kickin' and, like, eventually she died. She committed suicide. So that was, like, a big thing. Like, ever since she died, that's it. I changed my whole life after her because, to me, she was even closer than my brother was, 'cause we did everything together, like, anything. Whatever she needed, I tried to get it for her, and whatever I needed, she'd help me. She knew, like, that I didn't live with my mom, and her mom understood—she let me live in their house. Like, her mom, she passed away too, not too long ago, too, and that was like my second family, so, like, after they passed away, I don't know. (pause)

L: How do you understand what happened to her?

V: I don't know. Like, we were there one time, we were, like, at a party. For some reason, we were all, like, having a good time, and then she was inside the house with a bunch of friends. And, like, a lot of people nowadays, they have guns, you know, teenagers, and they have it, like, you know, for protection. But I don't know, for some reason, she just . . . I don't know; no one knows. It's like a mystery why she did it. She told me everything. We used to tell each other everything, like, even we used to talk about if we would die, who we would want at our funeral; we used to talk about stuff like that. We always used to tell each other what was on our mind, like, if anything was wrong. But she never told me nothing before she did it. That's why—it keeps me wondering every day why she did it.

F: That must be really hard for you. But it sounds like you've grown stronger from it all. [The facilitator supports, empathizes, and reframes in terms of strengths.]

V: Well, it's not as bad as a while ago. I learned to move on. There's nothing I could do but go on with my life and become a better person. I'll never forget her. It's hard sometimes. I still think about her a lot, and sometimes I get so sad and things seem all mixed up.

F: Does anyone have anything to say to V that might help her with this? [The facilitator draws on the strength, connection, and life experience of her peers.]

S: I do. (The group looks surprised because S usually says nothing in group.)

F: Go on, S.

S: I think it's really sad that V's friend did that. But, like, when my brother's best friend was killed in a fight, a bad one, that's what got my brother to turn his life around, too. He said once his friend died, they all promised they weren't going to do paint anymore just because of what happened.

F: Do paint?

N: Yeah. Some of the kids were huffin' paint and such. My brother did that for a while, too.

F: You are all being so honest in this group. I am so proud of you all. [The facilitator praises, sharing genuinely.] I have a question for all of you. A few of you have mentioned conflict, loss, and even violence. What does that mean to you?

V: I know it's because we're not White. We don't have the same things White kids have. And it's just tougher in my neighborhood. That's the way it is.

P: I think it might be about money. You say it's 'cause they're White, but I think it's 'cause they have more money.

L: Why do Whites have more money?

V: 'Cause the ones with money give the jobs to ones like them.

F: Can you say more about what you think about that? [The facilitator explores their perceptions of oppression, prejudice, and structural barriers.]

V: It's simple. I saw this show on TV once that showed when a White person and a Black or brown person goes for the same job, the White person got it even if the dark-complected person was better for the job.

L: Really?

M: I believe it. I'm Mexican; I'm kind of dark skinned.

F: Dark skinned?

M: Because my mom is real light, my grandma is real light, and all my friends are like a lighter shade of brown than I am, and I'm usually dark.

F: Do they consider you dark?

M: Yeah. But my dad is even darker than me.

P: I think it might have to do with style too.

F: Good point, P. How about you, S?

P: I wasn't finished, okay?

F: P, I'm sorry you felt interrupted, but we want to be sure that everyone gets a chance to answer. Please, go on. [The facilitator allows herself to be human, acknowledges the mistake, explains the interruption, and honors the member's need to continue.]

P: OK. I'm not the kind of person that wears the same style all the time. I'll be like one day, um, one day I'll be all dressed up like I am now, in, like, a halter top, short shorts, nice high shoes, and other times I'll dress like a tagger, all baggy and that.

N: I'm like P. I like to dress nice sometimes, like with a halter and shorts and high shoes, too.

F: How do people treat you when you're dressed like that way? [The facilitator explores the impact of the choices.]

P: Well, sometimes they'll ask me why I'm dressed like a hoochie, but I'm not; I just dress the way I want. And then, like, when I'm dressed like a tagger, they're, like, why do you wear baggy pants? And I say I like baggy pants; they feel comfortable. If I'm going out, like, I'll dress like this. My boyfriend, when I get dressed up, he gets nervous, but I don't do it to attract people; I just dress this way 'cause I like to dress and I like the way I look like this. Some people dress only one way, like either they're a tagger, or a hoochie style, or whatever.

F: Can you tell me more about "hoochies"?

P: You know, hoochies.

F: I really don't know. Can you tell me? [The facilitator humbly notes her lack of knowledge on this, making P the expert.]

P: Like, they, like, are always about getting boys. It also has to do with the friends you hang around with, like the party people. The PARTY party people—they'll dress like the way I'm dressed right now and, like, they would wear bell bottoms, their back into that and, like, hoochie girls, they wear, like, hoochie shoes and get dressed up.

F: So it's not good to be a hoochie?

N: It's okay to dress like a hoochie, but if you really are one, that's bad. It means that you put out and just don't care about yourself. Guys think you're easy. They might ask you out, but there's no way they think of you as a real girlfriend or someone that's the marrying type.

P: Yeah, mostly "hoochie" has like a bad meaning, but some like just dress or act like a hoochie and if you know her and she's not, you'd say she's not a *real* Hoochie. Just because we call you a hoochie is not necessarily because of who you are, it's just because that may be the way you dress.

F: So you don't take it as a put down if someone calls you a hoochie?

P: No, 'cause I know I'm not, like, a real Hoochie. My parents brought me up to be good. They believe that a girl shouldn't go out and should stay at home until she's ready to get married. Some parents aren't like mine and think a girl can do whatever she wants. Guys, it's like, guys, they do whatever they want anyways, 'cause, you know, their parents mostly let them do whatever. They've got more freedom than us girls. So women are more tied down, I think.

F: And you think most families are like that?

P: Yeah, I think mainly, unless they're, like, giving up and saying, like, if you're a bad girl, then you're a bad girl. (laughs) You know.

M: I hate that. I mean you either have to be, like, a perfect person or a hoochie or something. That's not right. I just want to be myself and someone who gets respect.

F: Wow, that does sound tough. It is so black and white to say you are either "good" or "bad." No wonder you hate that. Anything you could imagine you might do about it? (pause) [The facilitator is encouraging movement from reflection to action.]

M: I don't know. I could tell them about who I really am. I would only do that with the people I respect because I don't really care what other people think.

F: What qualities make you respect somebody?

M: I get respect for people when they have respect for themselves and others. Like, if they don't just mess with people, and they let others be who they are.

F: So who are you?

M: I'm a 16-year-old, big, beautiful, Mexican woman. (gesturing with her hands and puffing out her chest)

(The group laughs and says things like "Go, girl.")

F: What does it mean to you to be a Mexican woman?

M: What does it mean? Like, I'm happy that I'm Mexican and everything. I like the cultural things, like Mexican dancing. And I even took Mexican dancing lessons, like, in eighth grade. I like the food. And the Mexican holidays. And I like cruising.

F: Cruising?

M: Yeah, it's, like, even though others do it, like Blacks and Whites and all, it's mostly a Mexican thing. It's been that way for many years, that the Mexicans around here have been cruising. That's like our culture, and people have been cruising down here for so many years, for like 30–40 years. They were cruising down Central, and now that it's against the law, it's like part of the culture has been taken away. It's bad. Yeah, there was some speeding and fighting then, but it's worse now because there's no real place to go.

F: Interesting! So there's some sense of loss of identity because of the change? [The facilitator reiterates the power of this oppressive loss.]

P: Yeah. And, like, all of the teenagers have nothing to do, you know. We like to have fun and have nice cars and all, and now it's just, like, just parties, but there's more fighting because you're all crowded into one small house or small place, you know.

F: What do you think a woman's role is?

M: Let's see—getting her independence, making her own living instead of trying to deal with the husband. Because now it is different, because back then the woman would stay home and cook and everything. But now it is different, they are trying to get into the role where they can make their own life and not depend on their husband because the men are different too now. They are not like they use to be, working and stuff, but now they can come and go if they want to. Same with the women, but the women aren't that used to it or something.

F: How do you think growing up the way you did has influenced you in what you want to do with your life? [The facilitator again encourages exploration of the impact of systems.]

M: Probably makes me want to get out of here, makes me want to travel, and I, okay, I'm going to get married, but even though I'm going to get married, I'm not going to have everything revolve around him. I'm going into the army. I'm going to have my own life as well as he's going to have his own because things might not work out, and if I revolve around him, I'm not going to know what to do, and I'm not going to have a job. I want my own life.

L: Maybe you could tell your mom more about it like I did. Respect your voice.

M: Yeah. Even though it might be too late for my mom to do it different, I can tell her how I believe and what I want.

F: Does she support your dreams?

M: Yeah, that's what she wants me to do. She tells me don't just go with a guy and do nothing, make your own life. Depend on yourself. I think that if my dad wasn't around, we would do a lot better, we would be a lot better. My mom, she was starting to do exercises, she lost a lot of weight and started feeling better about herself. But he got out and so she stopped. Why do you tell me to do one thing, and you go and do the other? She was just, like, "I feel sorry for him." I go "Why, he ain't doing nothing." It's like, he's . . . God, he's done so much stuff to us, it's awful right now. Like earlier, my grandma called me and she asked me, because my dad came over yesterday, and she was, like, what was your dad doing there? I guess he was visiting the kids; I don't know. She goes, "Did your mom tell you anything?" I go, "Well, no." "Well, mija, sorry to tell you this but I told your mom if he comes back then I'm going to disown her. Your Tata not going to like it, but . . . " And maybe we won't be able to see the kids, but we told her too many times that we took too much stuff. So I don't really see my Tata anymore. I miss her. She was really a good model for me.

F: M, that's a great point. OK, we're running out of time. M's point has led to the question for you to think about before next week. Who is the biggest role model in your life and why? [The facilitator lets group activities be emergent from the input of the members.]

P: Movie stars or in real life?

F: Either way.

P: That's easy. My mom. I've learned so much from my mother. Even though she has her problems, she's very strong. I learned from her to be responsible, independent, and not to depend on anyone. I just do everything for myself. Like my boyfriend, I don't let him do nothing for me. All I need, I get for myself.

F: We'll talk more about that next session. P, will you start us off next time?

P: Sure.

References

BELENKY, M. F., CLINCHY, B. M., GOLDBERGER, N. R., & TARULE, J. M. (1997). *Women's ways of knowing*. New York: Basic Books.

BLACKBURN, J. (2000). Understanding Paulo Freire: Reflections on the origins, concepts, and possible pitfalls of his educational approach. *Community Development Journal, 35*(1), 3–15.

COHEN, E. G. (1986). *Designing groupwork: Strategies for the heterogeneous classroom*. New York: Teachers College Press.

CRAMER, E. P. (1995). Feminist pedagogy and teaching social work practice with groups: A case study. *Journal of Teaching in Social Work,* 11(1/2), 193–215.

DEL PINAL, J., & SINGER, A. (1997). Generations of diversity: Latinos/as in the United States. *Population Bulletin, 52*(3), 1–48.

FREIRE, P. (1972). *Pedagogy of the oppressed*. London: Penguin Books.

FREIRE, P. (1973). *Education for critical consciousness*. New York: Seabury Press.

HOOKS, B. (1989). *Talking back, thinking feminist, thinking black*. Boston: South End Press.

THERRIEN, M., & RAMIREZ, R. (2000). The Latino/a population in the United States: March 2000. In *Current population reports* (pp. 20–535). Washington, DC: U.S. Census Bureau.

TRUEBA, E. (1999). *Latinos unidos: From cultural diversity to the politics of solidarity*. New York: Rowman & Littlefield.

Case Study 3-5

Questions for Discussion
1. Why is group work the preferred modality for sexual minority youth?
2. Why do the authors take a more "direct approach" with Gay, Lesbian, Bisexual, and Transgendered (GLBT) youth, answering questions rather than redirecting as they would with other clients?
3. The authors describe their primary intervention with the client as "environmental manipulation and support." How does this approach lend respect to the client?

Gay Youth and Safe Spaces

Nora Gustavsson and Ann MacEachron

"Is he out there?" Tim was the first adult advisor of the drop-in center to ask the inevitable question. There are usually five advisors at each meeting, including a coordinator.

The Reverend Smear had been protesting the Gay, Lesbian, Bisexual, and Transgendered Youth (GLBTY) meetings for the last month. "Yep, he's there, and his new sign says 'God Hates Fags.' This will upset some of the youth," said Tim. We adult advisors have become accustomed or, more accurately, resigned to the protesters since the drop-in youth program at the Gay and Lesbian Center opened a few years ago. The protesters added to our workload because we had to be concerned with our participants' safety. Some of our young program participants were willing to engage the protesters in heated verbal exchanges, and we worried about escalation.

As we watched the parking lot, we noticed a new youth. He hurried past the reverend and burst through the door looking anxious. He was about 6 feet tall, 160 pounds, with sandy blond hair and blue eyes. He introduced himself as Zack. He lived in the northwest part of the city and had to take two buses to get to the center. He was a junior at one of the larger public high schools known for frequent arrests for drug use. He had learned about the center and the drop-in youth program on the Internet. We had a web page that listed activities as well as telephone numbers for community resources. The youth group meeting was about to start, so we invited Zack to join us.

Use of Group Work with Sexual Minority Youth

Zack was quiet his first night in group, but this is typical. For youth who fear they are the only GLBT young person in the world, it can be both a relief and a little overwhelming to be in a group of 30 to 70 GLBT youth. When we run educational programs (information on scholarships, health screening, job skills, etc.), we address the entire group. On other weeks, we have breakout sessions. The topics for breakouts are decided by the youth and usually include dating, family, racism, sexism, homophobia, drug use, safe sex, and religion.

Group work is our preferred modality with sexual minority youth. Many of the difficulties experienced by GLBT youth are a result of trying to live in hostile environments. Peers are especially important to GLBT youth because they often feel isolated. Finding a reference group is one of the biggest challenges that GLBT youth face.

The format for group work has evolved over the years. We divide the session into sections. The beginning always consists of introductions and greetings of all group members. The middle section is focused on a topic selected by the youth the week before. The last section is open discussion. Youth can bring up a topic or can anonymously submit ideas by writing a note and putting it in a basket that is passed around at each meeting.

The youth are assessed during each meeting. There are some young people who are not appropriate for group work. The actively psychotic youth, youth who are impaired by alcohol or other drugs, or youth who are sexually or physically aggressive are unable to participate in a group. These young people are referred to outside agencies for specialized help.

The group provides a safe space for GLBT youth. Participants learn that other young people are struggling with similar issues, and they learn new strategies for negotiating with their environments. The group encourages peers to support each other. The youth do most of the talking, and this is unusual in their lives. GLBT youth report that there are always adults willing to talk to them, but that they have rarely experienced interactions in which they felt listened to and understood.

The group is able to universalize the unique experiences and affective states of GLBT youth. Younger adolescents, ages 15 and 16, report that they like to hear the "older kids" talk about how they cope. The older kids are the 17- and 18-year-olds. Group participants are also offered the opportunity to speak privately with any of the adult advisors. This combination appears to be the most effective. Many of the adolescents have experienced individual counseling as a result of conflict in school or the home that is directly or indirectly related to their sexuality. Those counseling interactions are described as generally unhelpful by the youth.

Listening to Zack

Zack returned the next week, and the reverend was also there with his sign. We made a point of asking Zack how things were going. They were not going well. His family was not happy with his homosexuality, he felt alone at school, and he was worried about God. He asked us if we thought it was true—does God hate us? How do you answer a question like this? If this were a clinical setting and Zack was in the client role, we might have one type of answer. Depending on the casework model, we could ask Zack what he thought or why this was important or "Is this a problem?" We reject these conventional casework models for youth like Zack because they are stigmatizing and focus attention on the person, assuming a systems theory notion that if you change the person, then there will be other changes throughout the system. System theory ignores the unequal distribution of power in a system. Zack was not "the problem"; he did not need to change.

Zack was living in a noxious environment that was undermining his confidence and competence. His needs were typical of anyone his age. He did not have unresolved issues requiring extensive one-on-one counseling, but he could profit from support and environmental work. That is what we set about doing with Zack. We are aware that GLBT youth are at an elevated risk for a number of negative outcomes. We are ever vigilant for suicidal ideation. We encourage the youth to get a formal education, either in alternative schools or at community colleges. We see on a regular basis how public schools try to dissuade GLBT youth from attending. We have also seen the results of community-sanctioned physical violence. A few GLBT youth have been murdered. There have not been any arrests.

In most therapeutic models, the therapist might be reluctant to answer such a direct question directly, especially a question about religion. However, when working with vulnerable GLBT youth who receive negative messages regularly from an oppressive society, direct answers appear to be the most helpful. We answered that we did not believe in a hating God. We asked Zack about his view of God. His response indicated that he had been thinking about this topic extensively and that he was quite bright, sensitive, and thoughtful. During the discussion, Zack asked questions that were beyond our competence. We are not biblical scholars, but we do know a little. At the advisors meeting, we suggested a religion panel for the next group. Thanks to Zack, we now have a semiannual religion meeting in which religious leaders answer the youths' questions about their relationship with God and how to be a sexual yet spiritual person. The religion group is one of the best-received groups. The youth consistently report that they find it helpful, and we usually run late because of their comments and questions.

Zack continued to attend group meetings regularly and assumed a leadership role. Other youth found it easy to talk with Zack, and he was seen as a friend. He would alert us if another youth was in trouble—physically ill, homeless, or suicidal. Zack shared with the group his struggles at home and in school. In many ways, his struggles were not unique. He lived in a single-parent home with an overextended mother and a few younger siblings. The family was one paycheck away from eviction. Zack hoped to go to college, but his family needed money and encouraged him to work full-time. Because he was bright and physically strong, he was not subject to the physical assaults that many of the other youth had to deal with regularly. This is especially true for young males who are small in stature or have a developmental disability. Zack was fortunate in another way—there was a teacher that liked him and encouraged him. We have been impressed over the years with what a difference a supportive teacher or aide can make in a young person's life. The youth who seem to leave high school are those who are harassed by both students and teachers. Most of the youth have stories about the response or lack of response from school officials to reports of abuse. The youth are advised to forget about it, to not be so "obviously gay," or to go to an alternative high school.

One of the projects that Zack actively participated in was helping other youth to establish gay-straight alliances in their high schools. Allies provide much needed support for GLBT youth. Our groups are open to supporters of GLBT youth. We usually have a handful of heterosexual youth who accompany their GLBT friends. They are an asset and help to reassure GLBT youth that not everyone hates or fears them.

Zack also participated in our writing workshops. He wanted to be part of the acting group, but transportation and time were insurmountable obstacles. He wrote about God, hate, love, acceptance, dating, and hope. He submitted his material to citywide high school competitions and had pieces selected for publication. Zack seemed to be doing well, but we were still concerned. His living situation was precarious. We asked Zack to call the center if he found himself in trouble.

Unresponsive Environments

By the time Zack was in his senior year, his living situation began to deteriorate rapidly. His mother was having trouble coping with three children in adolescence. She lost her job. Her sister moved into the small family home. The youngest child was caught with drugs at school. Conflict in the home was escalating, and Zack was wondering how long he was going to be able to stay at home. We offered to refer the family for counseling. Zack thanked us for the offer but feared that his mother would only be more angry if she knew he was talking about family problems with outsiders. We had a number of family events (picnics and holiday dinners) to which GLBT youth are encouraged to invite their family. Family is defined as anyone the youth views as emotionally important. Most of the other youth bring a parent or another adult relative to these events. Zack never brought anyone. We usually had Zack sit with us at a table of supportive parents. We asked Zack if we could ask Parents and Friends of Lesbians and Gays (PFLAG) to send a couple of representatives to these family events for him. He declined the offer, adding that he appreciated the fact that we always made a place for him at meetings and events.

Zack often referred to us as Grandma Ann and Grandma Nora. We were not sure about the grandmother part. We are aware that to a 16-year-old, we do, indeed, seem ancient. We are also aware that the professional literature often describes GLBT people has having problems with boundaries and intimacy. However, we have not observed this and wonder if this view is a result of heterosexist assumptions about a normative model. This has become more perniciously virulent as politicians endeavor to define "legitimate" relationships. The only relationship that government and cultural entities are willing to accept as worthy of legitimacy and respect is monogamous, heterosexual [in light of recent political events] marriage. However, GLBT persons are denied the right to marry, thus illegitimizing and destabilizing their relationships. We understood that Zack needed a context to understand our concern for him. He had no grandparents, but he had a fantasy about how a grandmother might have treated him. At this point in his life, a grandmother fit quite nicely. We knew that in time we would lose the grandma title. That would be okay as long as it was on his timetable.

Things went downhill during the Christmas break of his senior year, and Zack found himself homeless. Friends took him in on a temporary basis. He desperately wanted to finish high school. He had applied to the local college and had been accepted with a tuition scholarship and the promise of work-study funds. He needed to survive the next six months.

Those six months were painful. He stopped coming to group meetings. We did not have a telephone number or address for him. We asked the other youth to keep an eye out for him. One youth reported seeing Zack or someone who looked like him at the infamous pick-up park where married men go to pick up young males. We were worried. We discuss HIV and other STDs extensively with the youth, and the center runs a support group for young men who are HIV positive. The size of this group has begun increasing recently.

Tim called us one night to say that he had received a call from the police. Zack had been found standing on a freeway overpass. He had climbed over the fence. The police got him down and then took him to the center. Tim was on duty. We decided to get Zack into a transitional living program. He might be the only openly gay youth in the program, but we would build in supports. We got Zack in a crisis bed for the night, began making calls the next morning, and found a program for Zack. Tim took Zack to the facility, where he received a safe place to stay, medication, and counseling. After a month in the program, Zack came to a group meeting. We had not seen him in a long time. We told Zack we had missed him and were worried about him. We developed a harm contract. We asked Zack to promise that he would call the center if he ever felt that despondent again. We told him that we had been working with the center's adult support groups and had been able to get a computer system for him as well as a gift certificate to a youth-oriented clothing store. We also solicited movie passes and promises of summer employment.

Despondent may not be an accurate description of Zack. In talking with him, we were struck by how often the themes of discouragement and defeat emerged. Describing Zack as depressed or despondent misses the environmental context of his affective state. If he was depressed or despondent, it seemed to be in reaction to how his attempts at agency were being defeated and how his striving to establish autonomy were being discouraged. These are important distinctions because they direct intervention. If Zack is defined as depressed, then he is likely to get a mix of medicines and cognitive behaviorism. If Zack is seen as discouraged by environmental forces, then efforts can be directed at minimizing these discouraging factors or developing supports to counteract the negatives of defeat.

Zack invited us to visit his placement. We set up the visit for the following week. We packed the car with the computer, printer, monitor, food (Rice Krispies with marshmallows are always well received), T-shirts, socks, sweaters, and a stuffed bear. Zack introduced us to the staff and other youth. His housemates asked if we were the grand-mothers that Zack talked about so much. While Zack appreciated the material goods we brought, he seemed much more pleased that he could say to those in his immediate living environment, "Hey, look everybody—there are people who care about me—I have not been abandoned." He walked us to the car, gave us a hug, and said, "Good-night, Ann. Goodnight, Nora. Thanks for coming." It was the first time he had not called us grandma.

We have watched Zack struggle and grow into a capable and caring young man. We continue to worry about him. He has fewer supports than do most of his peers. Our primary intervention with Zack was environmental manipulation and support. The DSM (*Diagnostic and Statistical Manual of Mental Disorders*) has little utility for a youth like Zack. There are no codes for homophobia or heterosexism. GLBT young people seem to profit from safe places to socialize with other youth where caring adults can keep an interested eye on them. It is a privilege to know these youth. They are so very brave. They battle fear and intolerance every day. They resist being labeled as "sick" and in need of therapy. They are adept at identifying their needs. Acceptance is usually number one on their list. They ask for so little.

IV
Case Studies in School-Based Treatment

School-based treatment, perhaps more than any other, depends heavily on a team of practitioners working within a structured setting. A variety of demands are placed on practitioners in this setting, including attending to students' academic, social, developmental, and emotional needs. This need to attend to "students as a whole" is illustrated in the following quote by Wolkow (1999):

> If a student is having difficulty at home, or with peers, his or her academics almost invariably will suffer. Working with a student on emotional needs when there is also an academic problem is not enough. Working on academics when a student is emotionally upset is not enough. If we are to view the child as a whole, then we must attend to all of his or her needs so that he or she may develop and function at his or her optimum. (p. 218)

Mental health practitioners who work in a school setting may find themselves using multiple modalities: individual, group, and family treatment. In the public school setting, they will inevitably encounter a diverse clientele, both culturally and socioeconomically. Their treatment goals may range from changing the systems of the school itself to better serve students and their families to working one on one with a single student struggling to hide his family's poverty from classmates. And they will almost certainly be pressed to help faculty and administration deal with aggressive or violent youth, to help these young people find more constructive ways to express themselves, and to "keep the peace" in the hallways.

The first case study in this section, presented by the team of Huxtable, Baab, Gilmartin, and Henizer, is a testament to the importance of involving all school personnel in children's progress. In addition to the theme of teamwork, the authors illustrate how they taught themselves about the cultural background of two new students at their school and used their knowledge to engage the clients and their mother in an intervention. The study also notes the importance of a good school policy to support caring staff.

In the next study, Corbin focuses on systems within the school and how practitioners can learn to use systemic interventions to address immediate issues within schools and reduce recurrences of problems. This approach to school work can lead to a better functioning school system that benefits all students.

Lochman, Salekin, and Kuhajda narrate a tale of school-based group work with aggressive children and their families. In recent years, aggressive behavior within schools has become a major concern, and communities are increasingly interested in finding methods to avoid violent outbreaks. In this case study, the authors share their method for engaging and teaching young clients methods of self-control.

Finally, Cobb and Statton deliver a case study that reveals the struggles of a Hmong youth who is the child of first-generation immigrants. The intervention is necessarily influenced by the boy's attempts to navigate the often-confusing path of cultural assimilation while dealing with the developmental demands of adolescence. All of these cases illustrate the rich experience that constitutes a school practitioner's work.

Reference

WOLKOW, H. (1999). The dynamics of working with children in schools from a systems perspective. In R. Constable, S. McDonal, & J. Flynn (Eds.), *School social work: Practice, policy, and research perspectives.* Chicago: Lyceum Books.

Case Study 4-1

Questions for Discussion
1. How do all the staff members of the school work together to help the students achieve?
2. What difficulty does the children's lack of birth certificates and other records pose?
3. How does the school/district policy contribute to the team's ability to accommodate these needy students?
4. What strengths does the family exhibit to school personnel?
5. Why does the school social worker educate staff about the Roma culture, but ask that they do not divulge the family's ethnicity to the other students?
6. How do the authors measure the success of the interaction with this family?

A Family Arrives at School

Marion Huxtable, Marcia Baab, Lynette Gilmartin, and Judy Henizer

As the school year of 2001 opened, our large urban school district embarked on a mission to raise achievement: 4 years from now, every student will be expected to exceed the state standards. All school staff, including support staff such as counselors and social workers, must show that their work promotes this goal. The staff of this elementary school geared up to focus efforts on raising achievement.

The reality that public schools accept all children regardless of circumstances complicates this mission. A variety of personal and family situations often put obstacles in the way of reaching educational goals. The mandate to "leave no child behind," therefore, requires much counseling of both children and their parents in an attempt to reduce obstacles and help children achieve. This "counseling" is done not only by the designated counselor, school social worker, and school psychologist, but by whichever staff member is with the child when a problem occurs. Helping children deal with their problems is often best done *in situ* at the moment when feelings are strong and the child wants resolution. Therefore, the principal counsels students in the lunch room, custodians console children in the hallways, special education teachers help parents understand their children, and many staff members mentor children, giving encouragement and advice. This family story illustrates how "counseling" children and families in schools is shared among many staff members who work together on children's problems, use each other's special skills, support each other, and sometimes disagree.

A Family's Story

A week after the school year began, a lively, eager mother enrolled two sons, aged 9 and 10. A week later, she brought in two of the boys' sisters, aged 12 and 13. They seemed to be a typical low-income, possibly Hispanic, family until the usual questions were asked. The office staff discovered that they had no birth certificates and no immunization records. They also had no school records because they had been living with their father and grandfather on a farm in Mexico and had not attended school there. Another puzzle was that they spoke no Spanish, in spite of having lived in Mexico for 4 years.

It was immediately obvious that none of the children could read, write, or do basic computations. The boys were placed in third and fourth grade and the girls in fifth and sixth grade. Our resource teacher worked with them from their first day at school, starting with kindergarten lessons such as learning the alphabet and numbers.

A major worry for Marcia Baab, the principal, was the lack of birth certificates. The school has a legal obligation to be on alert for any children who could have been abducted and to report such cases. The history of these children, who came to us lacking birth certificates, immunizations, and school records, raised concern. We had dealt with many issues before, but this family's combination of unusual issues and behavior that we could not explain was a worry, especially as time passed and we still could not obtain birth certificates or any school records from earlier years.

It was also very obvious that the mother was stressed. She had just gained custody of her children and had basic needs that needed to be met so that the children could attend school. Our community representative,[1] Judy Henizer, immediately visited the children's home to assess the needs and available resources. The goal was also to build a relationship with the mother because it was clear that we would need to work closely with her if we were to educate four children who were so far behind. Some parents do not understand that a school can be caring and helpful, so our community representative reaches out to parents to communicate our philosophy of family support and to demonstrate it with practical help, such as taking children to the school district's clothing bank, helping parents fill our forms for free school lunches, and helping them obtain vaccinations for children. By meeting these basic needs, we lay a foundation for a close and cooperative working relationship between home and school.

On visits to clinics to obtain immunizations, which are required by state law for children attending school, and the clothing bank to find school clothes, Mrs. Henizer had opportunities to learn about the children's background. The boys told unbelievable stories that appeared to be mythical at times and sheer bravado on other occasions. One story was about their grandfather slaying a dragon that came out of a lake and his sword remaining over the fireplace at the farm in Mexico. They told of their skill in fixing cars and bodywork, offering to repair a few of the dents in the community representative's car. They knew that people did not believe these stories and had been warned not to tell them; however, they were spending a lot of time with Mrs. Henizer and responded to her by sharing their stories.

---

[1]The community representative is an employee of the school district whose role is to bridge the gap between two communities served by a desegregated or magnet school. Because the communities served by the school may be several miles apart, the community representative assists with attendance, transportation, sharing information, troubleshooting problems, and coordinating special events, in addition to helping with basic needs and services.

Socialization

The children had been out of school for so long that they did not seem to know how to interact with other children, how to behave in a classroom, or even how to participate in a ball game. They would walk out of a classroom if they felt like it. At first, they would only play with each other. They had a closeness and concern for each other that was unusual. The principal, Mrs. Baab, found that she had to talk with the children daily, putting her arm around a shoulder or holding their hand for a close personal talk. They spent much time in the office because of their difficulty adjusting to a structured situation. Discipline had to be given in private because they were unusually self-conscious in front of their classmates. It was clear that the 4 years spent on the farm in Mexico had not prepared them for interacting with peers. They spoke no Spanish, evidently having been isolated from contact with other families. They were strong and physical, and there were concerns about safety because they would grab or hit students that bothered them. One of the boys even raised his fist to Mrs. Baab.

As we got to know the children and family, there were many surprises. They needed more food than other children and expected to be given two or three lunches. We made sandwiches for them to eat after they finished their hot lunch. Although it was very hot at the beginning of the year, the girls always wore long, heavy jeans while every other child and many adults wore the shortest and lightest clothes.

When they became very frustrated, which seemed inevitable because the children had almost no academic skills, the principal would allow them to yell and scream in her office and even curse to get their emotions out. This would sometimes go on for hours. It seemed to help when Mrs. Baab worked on her computer and pretended to be half listening. They could release their feelings without repercussions. Whenever they interacted with other students, there was conflict and they felt they had been victimized and blamed. In contrast to their inability to relate to peers, they were respectful to their teachers and knew that the teachers cared about them. At times, they wanted the principal to sit directly across from them, listen intently, and encourage them to share their feelings. They had so many needs that every member of the school team, including classroom teachers, resource teachers, community representative, nurse, school social worker, school psychologist, and even the school resource officer, were involved.

During the first few weeks of getting the children used to school, someone, often Mrs. Baab or Mrs. Henizer, had to be present every time they interacted with other children. Mrs. Baab had to be on bus duty to mentor them at the start of the bus trip, trying to prevent problems on the ride home. They lived in a low-income, primarily Hispanic area 7 miles from school, so there was time and opportunity on the bus for problems to start that would be carried on in the neighborhood and the following day as the children waited for the bus to school. Although unspoken, there was tension in the neighborhood because the family, although they could pass for Hispanic in their appearance, were clearly not Hispanic in their customs, behavior, and language, in spite of having lived in Mexico. Some of the difficulty in making sense of the family that was experienced by the adults at school must have also been felt in the neighborhood, which was almost 100 percent Hispanic.[2]

Teaching and Learning

The mission of all schools is to help children learn. We started immediately with these children to assess their skills in reading, writing, and math and found that the boys needed to start at the kindergarten level, and the girls only a little higher.

Most schools would find it almost impossible to teach children at pre-primer and primer levels in the regular third-, fourth-, fifth-, and sixth-grade classrooms where we had placed these children. Our school is different, however, because we have adopted a "Regular Education Initiative,"[3] called Project Breakthrough, in which we use existing staff, including special education staff, to serve any child who needs help. Much collaboration occurs among regular classroom teachers, special education teachers, and other staff who work with the child. We rarely place a child in special education, instead providing support to all children who need help using creative staffing and planning (Huxtable, 1997). Consequently, we were able to help these four children in small groups led by special education teachers (functioning as general resource teachers in our Project Breakthrough program) who were accustomed to adapting materials and methods for many different needs.

Our special education teacher, Lynette Gilmartin, started by finding out what the children already knew. Both of the boys knew how to write their first names. Neither of them could write the entire alphabet, and they did not know any of the sounds of the letters. Using an alphabet chart, Mrs. Gilmartin started to teach the boys the letter names, the sounds, and a word that starts with each letter. It took only a week and a half for the boys to learn this and to write the alphabet.

Mrs. Gilmartin knew right away that they were smart boys who had just lacked exposure to the basic skills. They started to work on "sight words" (recognizing words on sight), adding words every other day. If she gave them 5 words, they wanted 10: the more she gave them the better. They were excited about every new thing that they learned. Mrs. Gilmartin worked with the boys alone for an hour every day. The only thing that slowed them down was their absences—they missed days for many reasons, including illness, going to clinics to obtain immunizations, not having clothes, and fear

[2]A class action suit was brought against the school district in 1974 by the National Association of Colored People and Mexican-Americans for Equal Education. The case was settled in 1978, and the judge ordered 9 of the school district's 102 schools to be desegregated. Later, the school district went beyond compliance with the letter of the order and implemented two more phases of desegregation. In the second phase, a primary magnet school was created in a largely Hispanic and African American neighborhood, and the neighborhood children in third through sixth grade were bused to a school 7 miles away in a primarily Anglo neighborhood.

[3]The Regular Education Initiative is a model for addressing the needs of special education students in high-incidence categories, such as learning disabilities. It involves collaboration between regular and special education teachers, who teach the student in regular classes rather than in special education classes.

of leaving home after the terrorist attack on September 11, 2001. For every three days in school, they missed two days.

Mrs. Gilmartin used the children's previous experiences to engage them in books and stories. The boys told her that they worked on fixing cars and trucks and that they lived on a farm in Mexico. She took them to the school library on their first day, and they found an alphabet book that was all about cars. They said, "So this is a library!" They recited stories about their life and the things they knew. They related fantastic stories that seemed to combine reality and fantasy.

The girls received help in a small group and individually with tutors, including the school psychologist (who was team teaching with Mrs. Gilmartin) and the computer technician (who spent much time mentoring them and developed a close relationship with them). The girls' adjustment to school was even more difficult than the boys'. They were big girls who looked at least 2 years older than their age. They felt more embarrassed than the boys over their lack of skills, were too self-conscious to participate in a group, and did not fit in socially at all with fifth and sixth graders. The whole team puzzled over where they could be placed in the school district. We tried a small charter school that has many students who function below grade level, but the girls' skills were too low for them to fit into a class and their mother felt there were too many children at the school with delinquent behavior. After this short experiment, we placed them at a middle school, and two older, teenage girls in the family started at a high school.

After just 36 days at school, one of the boys could read 50 words and the other 20 words. They had little exposure to drawing or writing, and their skills with pencil and paper closely resembled those of our kindergartners. They both learned to use a computer to work on reading and math. After only 36 days, they could add and subtract 2-digit numbers. Not surprisingly, the boys' math skills developed faster than their reading. Numbers are more tangible than the letter symbols. Even so, one of the boys was much more motivated to read than to do math.

You Must Have Thought We Were from Another Planet

Every staff member found these children puzzling. Even though we have had experience with many different children and situations, these children were different, and we could not make sense of their history. Frequent efforts to obtain birth certificates and school records from schools they had attended 4 years previously failed to produce anything. There was a nagging fear that they might not be the children of the mother. There were daily frustrations for staff whose time was consumed taking care of these children. After some weeks, the mother enrolled a small cousin, who also had not attended school, but was of third-grade age. He, too, had no immunizations, birth certificate, or school records.

The children's mother was open and friendly. Her house was always open to us, and she relied on the school for support and even friendship because she had no family or friends in our city. She visited the school frequently to settle discipline problems, to ask for extra worksheets for the children, and to take books out of the library. We gave her school supplies, and she seemed eager for her children to be educated. In spite of her apparent openness, the family remained a mystery.

One day, Mrs. Henizer heard the mother speaking in a foreign language to the children and asked her what language they were speaking. The mother said it was Romanian. Mrs. Henizer had also noticed the smell of incense and candles burning in their house. The mother explained that her source of income was reading tarot cards, hence the incense and candles. As we tried to make sense of all the facts we had about the family, we wondered if they were Roma,[4] not Romanians. If they were Roma, it would explain their isolated way of life in Mexico, their lack of education, and many of the details of social behavior and history that had been hard to understand.

None of us had experience working with Roma children, so our social worker, Marion Huxtable, searched the Internet[5] for information about the Romani culture. The findings seemed to fit the pattern that we saw in this family. Because the Roma have experienced so much persecution for centuries and in every country, perhaps the mother did not want anyone to know that they were what people call Gypsies, out of fear of discrimination by the school or rejection by other children. As school personnel, there are often personal questions that we do not feel comfortable asking. Mrs. Henizer and Mrs. Huxtable wondered how much the mother wanted us to know. She was comfortable with both of us and always seemed happy to see us at her home, but we did not know if she would talk about being a Rom.

On a teacher planning day, when children stay home and teachers prepare report cards, Mrs. Huxtable did a home visit. The children were all sleeping, so the mother and Marion Huxtable sat on the front porch and talked about the children. The mother was eager for them to be educated. She had fought hard to regain custody and was struggling to keep them in school in the face of many problems. She had no income, and the father had stopped sending money. A nearby church helped her, and she was making friendly contacts with some neighbors, while trying to turn in others for drug-related activities in the tough area where she had rented this run-down house.

Mrs. Huxtable told her that she did not want to ask personal questions, but that it would help us to understand her children better if we knew more about their background and we had been wondering if they were Roma. She immediately said that they were, and when Mrs. Huxtable said that this explained so much that we had not been able to understand, she laughed and said, "You must have thought we were from another planet." Mrs. Huxtable asked about their customs and about her life as a Romani woman, and the mother explained many things about their religion and culture. As a child, she had attended school wearing long skirts. Her grandmother had made a

---

[4]The Roma are commonly called Gypsies. They have always referred to themselves, however, as Rom or Roma meaning "people." The term Gypsy is seen as offensive, and the preferred term is Rom (singular) or Roma (plural).

[5]As this case illustrates, the Internet has become a valuable source of information about many situations that school personnel have not previously encountered.

concession to modern times by reducing the number of layers of skirts she wore from seven to three. Mrs. Huxtable had read that Romani women must keep their legs covered; yet the mother was sitting here with me on this hot October day wearing shorts. She said that when her children returned to her, they hardly recognized her because she had changed her way of dressing. This was a family making a radical change in a centuries-old traditional way of life. The daughters' legs were still covered, but their mother wore shorts.

The children's mother had readily told Mrs. Huxtable that the family was Romani, which allowed us to make sense of much of the children's behavior and history. Some of the worry and frustration would be removed if the staff understood this culture that was so different from any they had worked with before. Mrs. Huxtable wrote out some information for the children's teachers, explaining that people who have experienced so much rejection tend to isolate themselves and develop a variety of self-protective behaviors, some of which we had seen in these children. At the same time, it seemed too great a risk to inadvertently let the children's peers know that their new classmates were "Gypsies." Although Mrs. Huxtable emphasized that we should use the term *Roma,* she knew that because of the boys' history of conflicts with their peers, they would quickly be called "Gypsies" and worse.

Culture and Counseling

On Halloween and the day after, the boys were absent from school. Mrs. Huxtable went to their home to encourage regular school attendance because they had missed so many days already. She discovered that all six of the enrolled children were home. Making the best of the opportunity, she stayed and talked with them. Although the mother was out, it seemed acceptable to stay because the older girls were there.

The close relationship that the family had developed with the school over the last few weeks was evident as the children all gathered round and happily talked and listened to the pep talk about school. When Mrs. Huxtable tried a few words of Romani that she had learned from websites about the Roma, the kids were delighted. She told them where she had found the Romani glossary, and they were eager to see the websites for themselves. The older girls could speak Romani well, but the boys knew only a little. Mrs. Huxtable agreed to show them the glossaries she had found on the web so that they could look up words, write them down, and make Romani/English dictionaries to show their mother. They were very excited about this plan. They taught Mrs. Huxtable to say, "Me sum gadji" (I am not Romani), and when the mother came home shortly after, the kids enjoyed the fun as Mrs. Huxtable spoke to her in Romani. The boys sent packets of Halloween candy back to school for their teachers, and one of them made a bouquet of dried flowers for Mrs. Huxtable to take to the principal. Both the mother and children always expressed appreciation of the help they received at school.

When the boys returned to school, Mrs. Huxtable showed them the Romani websites, and together they made plans to work on bilingual dictionaries and, with their limited Romani language skills, to write simple stories in their language. They were excited about their new project, anticipating how it would please their mother.

The children's mother had told Mrs. Huxtable that she had to go to court for an eviction order. She had not been able to pay the rent and was in conflict with the neighbors. However, she hoped that she would be allowed to stay because she was happy with the school. She had applied for Temporary Assistance for Needy Families (TANF) and was waiting for the Department of Economic Security to send for the children's birth certificates so that she could receive financial help and pay her rent. Mrs. Huxtable gave her information about alternative housing and shelters in case they were evicted.

Not long after, the boys were absent for several days and a home visit proved that they had been evicted. The only sign that they had been there was the children's names written on an old mattress. We heard nothing for several weeks and then received a phone call from a school in another city in our state. The children, together with two more cousins, were registering for school. Our team was gratified to hear that they would continue in school.

The Roma

There are now more than 12 million Roma in the world. They are descended from people who were displaced from India in the 11th century A.D. and migrated via the Silk Road through what is now Kashmir to Persia. The second migration occurred during the 13th century from Southwest Asia into the Balkans. From there, groups of the people who became known as Roma migrated to all parts of Europe. It was not until the 19th century that they migrated to the Americas (Patrin, 1999).

The Romani language is related to Sanskrit. Many dialects developed as the Romani people spread through Asia and Europe, adopting loan words and grammar from different languages. A Romani individual is called a Rom (the plural is Roma), pronounced with a throaty, rolling "R." The Roma are commonly and derogatively known as Gypsies in the English-speaking world.

The history of the Roma has been a continuous history of displacement and persecution since the 11th century. Persecution has taken the form of expulsion, genocide, prohibitions, and legalized discrimination in every country. During World War II, the Nazis exterminated large numbers of Roma.

The Roma's history of isolation from mainstream society has produced a unique set of customs, beliefs, and traditions, many of which affect child rearing and, therefore, the behavior of Romani children. Although the traditions may be very diluted by contact with mainstream cultures, they are likely to be sufficiently different from those of other ethnic groups to cause communication problems with formal institutions such as schools. Their culture has been passed on through an oral tradition, rich in stories, songs, and superstitions.

Until recently, Romani parents could see little value in traditional education in any country because it was impossible for them to participate in mainstream society. In addition, Romani parents were reluctant to entrust their children to schools staffed by strangers who are not Roma and who do not understand their values and customs. Historically, Romani people lived in isolated, tight-knit, protective tribes, relying on traditional crafts that require little contact with outsiders, such as metalwork, animal training, entertaining, and fortune telling. Few Roma attended more than a few years of school, attended universities, or joined mainstream professions until various Romani organizations started in recent years to advocate human and civil rights (Patrin, 1999).

The School Team

In schools everywhere, the interactions between students and staff either help or hinder how children learn to handle developmental tasks and daily problems. In the story described here, relations between the Romani children and the staff had to be built on trust, although the staff had no idea how difficult it would be for these children to trust "gadje," especially after spending the last 4 years in a Romani environment.

When the children left their father and went to live with their mother, they had to adjust to an alien culture, change their whole lifestyle, and cope with major family changes at the same time. It is not surprising that they needed so much care and attention. They did not receive formal counseling in our school, but they experienced a therapeutic environment in a regular public school that has shaped itself into a caring, though imperfect, community.

Gardner, a leading exponent of child psychotherapy, believes that "the therapist's personality, probably more than any other factor, is the ultimate determinant as to whether therapy will be successful" (Gardner, 1986). While most school personnel have not been trained in child psychotherapy, several of our staff have the personal characteristics for being a good therapist. Personal qualities such as warmth, frustration tolerance, and creativity in working with children are some of the aspects of personality that Gardner refers to as necessary to successful therapy.

Collectively, our team has a heavy concentration of the personality factors mentioned by Gardner. For example, our community representative is creative, spontaneously warm, on the children's wavelength, and enthusiastic about working with children. She immediately showed warmth and acceptance to the children and their mother. The school principal has a strong parental instinct, is always excited about the school and the work we do with children, recalls well her own childhood experiences, tolerates daily frustrations, and projects inner warmth. She used all of these qualities in her daily contact with these children. She became emotionally attached to them in a short time. The special education teacher genuinely likes children, tolerates frustration patiently, and is flexible and excited about working with low-achieving children. The children felt her enthusiasm and needed her patience. These team members not only teach the children academic skills, but also use their personal qualities therapeutically in dealing with children's developmental issues and problems. The result is that children learn ways of dealing with their problems through daily interactions with a variety of staff. In addition, they hear frequent therapeutic messages that are basically similar, but expressed in the individual ways of various adults at the school.

What the Children Learned and What the Staff Learned

Probably the hardest thing for the boys to learn was how to be part of a group in the confined space of a classroom. They often conflicted with classmates and did not understand the expectations of being in a classroom, which the other children had internalized over several years of being in school.

Given the difficulty they had in dealing with their classmates and the setting, they learned much about how to tackle the formal aspects of education, such as reading and math. They already had experience learning other tasks, such as metalwork and working with animals, but working with symbols requires a different set of skills.

They attended a total of only 36 days of school, but in that time, they learned the alphabet, a number of "sight words," how to read words in sentences, and how to add and subtract numbers. Probably the most important thing they learned was that they enjoyed these new things. One of the boys dictated the following message for his teacher to write, "This school is really great. I am going to have lots of fun this year. I hope I'll be here next year. I wake up in the morning and I can't wait to go to school."

The school staff also learned from having to adjust their skills to new situations. Our staff learned, in varying degrees, to be more tolerant of different ways of life and to be open to learning from other cultures. Our experience with this family gave us an unexpected opportunity to learn about Romani culture and its unusual history. Accepting this family and remaining open to them, especially before we knew that they were from a different culture and could not interpret their behavior, was not without conflict and clashes of opinion among the school team.

Our experience of working with a Romani family is a example of the importance of understanding some details of another culture. Once we knew that they were Roma, many of the children's behaviors became understandable. For example, it made sense that they could not be separated from each other on the playground. Their conflicts with other children could be seen as a self-protective measure to counter the rejection that they anticipated. In this account, the reader can find many examples of the relevance of culture in making sense of the family's history and behavior.

We had to learn to measure progress in different ways, other than state test scores. We could feel successful knowing that when the boys left our school, they would be better equipped to deal with the demands of school and to find their way in the American mainstream. As a Romani family, they will have to decide how much they want to assimilate into the American mainstream and how they will integrate their own culture into their lives. Progressing in school, with the commitment that it requires, carries the risk of losing some of their own history and traditions. All of the children are 4 years behind in school and will have a hard time handling the pressure for achievement that currently pervades schools. Like all Romani children, they will have to decide if it is worth it. When we heard that they were enrolling in school in another city, we knew that they wanted to continue to learn.

We also measured progress by how well we used teamwork and how flexible we were in crossing over our usual "turf" boundaries to meet the children's needs. The value of a team approach in schools is that each discipline contributes different knowledge and skills, while we all pursue the same goal of academic achievement. The team used weekly student assistance and child study meetings to communicate their successes and frustrations and to plan and share their understanding of working with students from such a different background.

For readers of this story, the lesson is that the daily contacts between children and a variety of adults in schools can be therapeutic if schools are developed as caring communities, rather than as solely academic institutions. In this environment, children experience corrective emotional experiences, acquire knowledge, and learn skills to help solve life's problems. And if you, the reader, choose to become part of the school team, you will have a share in helping young people find their place in the world.

References

GARDNER, R. (1986). *The psychotherapeutic techniques of Richard Gardner.* Northvale, NJ: Creative Therapeutics.

HUXTABLE, M. (1997). Project Breakthrough: A workable alternative to special education. *Social Work in Education, 19,* 257–265.

PATRIN. (1999). *The Patrin web journal: Romani culture and history.* Retrieved from http://www.geocities.com/Paris/5121.

Case Study 4-2

Questions for Discussion
1. What are the hallmarks of a systemic intervention? How does it act to reduce recurrences of problems?
2. Describe the important connection between adolescent developmental issues and the educational process.
3. How can a child study team use information about one student to help others in the school community?

Expanding the Practice of Clinical Work

Joanne N. Corbin

A team of educators in a middle school became aware that the local newspaper was planning a story for the following day about youth who had experienced violent deaths in the preceding year and they were concerned about their own students' reactions to the news story. The front page would feature pictures of the slain students. Because many of those killed were known to the students at their school, the educators anticipated that their students' reactions could range from sadness to anger to glorification of the victims. This team of educators decided that classroom teachers in the school would devote time at the beginning of the school day to discuss the story and the students' reactions. School staff was also on hand that morning to meet with students who were having more intense reactions. The school staff believed that by attending to the event in a proactive manner, the emotional distress and disruption that might have otherwise occurred would be reduced.

The delivery of mental health services in schools often takes the form of providing individual or group therapy, conducting psychosocial assessments, delivering case management services, and acting as a liaison between the school and community. However, the newspaper example illustrates another method of clinical practice — observing the potential effects of an action on a system and intervening. Systemic intervention is defined here as examining the relationship between the actions of an individual or subsystem and the actions of larger subsystems of which the individual or subsystem is a member. Specifically, systemic intervention involves assessing the context of an action or event, not the action or event in isolation, developing an intervention plan that considers the effect on individuals and subsystems within that context, and finally implementing this plan. A systemic intervention addresses the immediate issue and reduces recurrences.

This case study presents examples that illustrate the application of a systemic perspective in work with middle and high schools in various parts of the country. The examples are taken from my work as an outpatient therapist with adolescents, an implementation coordinator for the School Development Program (a whole-school reform program), and a creator of a social work intern program designed to increase understanding of systemic interventions within schools.

Scope of the Issue

The school setting provides ample opportunity to apply clinical practice to work with adolescents in middle and high school. The mean prevalence rate of psychopathology in adolescents aged 12 and older from 12 studies was 16 percent, with a range from 6 percent to 41 percent (Roberts, Attkisson, & Rosenblatt, 1998). Offer and colleagues (1987) found a 6-month prevalence rate of psychiatric disorders for boys ages 12–16 of approximately 19 percent and for girls ages 12–16, approximately 22 percent. Their study also found overall mental health and social service utilization rates to be approximately 9 percent and 5 percent, respectively. Roughly one-fifth of adolescents have a diagnosable mental disorder, and most of these adolescents are currently not involved with services.

In addition to psychiatric symptoms that many students experience, adolescents in general are dealing with tremendous social pressures. Violence and threats of violence, physical and sexual abuse, alcohol and substance abuse, loss of a friend or family member, homelessness, and intolerance of diversity are some common experiences among adolescents. These issues can interfere with a student's ability to attend to the classroom instruction or with the teacher's ability to deliver the instruction. Additionally, these issues affect not only the individual student, but entire classrooms or schools. The mental health services provided in schools can fill a gap by attending to the individual issues *and* attending to the overall climate created within a school.

Mental Health Services in Schools

Clinical practice has been deeply connected to education since 1906–07 when social workers provided liaison services between the school and the family (Costin, 1969). This work has continued and has broadened to address the psychoemotional needs of individual students. These needs are so great that in 2000, in addition to existing school district health and mental health personnel, there were more than 1,350 school-based health centers (Center for Health and Health Care in Schools, 2001). The school reform movement, with its focus on greater involvement from members of the school community in decision making and greater attention to academic focus, opened avenues for thinking about child and adolescent development as an essential component of the educational process. School-based decision-making teams, child study teams, student and staff support teams, and even crisis teams, commonplace in schools since school reform, have a responsibility to attend to the issues within a school that affect the developmental process for students as well as the educational process. The opening example about the educators' response to the newspaper story demonstrates how important it is for schools to be aware of and able to address the external influences on the educational program. The connection between adolescent developmental issues and the educational process is explored in the next section.

Adolescent Developmental Issues

When I provided outpatient therapy to adolescent girls, they frequently told me that they were doing poorly in or failing physical education class. They made up various excuses, such as forgetting to bring their sneakers or gym clothes, feeling ill, getting into conflicts with the teacher, or skipping the class entirely. During adolescence, girls may do poorly in physical education classes because they are uncomfortable with the changing facilities, engaging in sports or activities with boys, and the lack of sufficient time for showering and changing back into school clothes. Adolescent boys have similar concerns. Evaluating school practices for physical education classes and identifying ways to address predictable adolescent concerns would be a preventive step. This is an easily understandable example of how normal developmental experiences can make it difficult for any adolescent to meet educational expectations. How much harder might it be for adolescents experiencing socioemotional distress?

Adolescence is a time of identity reformation; all that the individual understands about herself/himself and her/his relationship to the larger community and world is changing. Physically, an adolescent is experiencing the greatest growth since the period from birth to 3 years of age. Cognitively, adolescents may be achieving formal operations. They are able to think about more ideas, issues, and possibilities than they have up until this point. Additionally, they are able to think logically about concepts and ideas as well as about things and objects; planning and organization skills also increase during this period. At the same time, it is important to remember that by 16 years of age, only 21–24 percent of adolescents have achieved formal operations in tasks that require abilities in conversation. In tasks requiring problem-solving abilities, 12–14 percent of the adolescents have achieved formal operations (Shayer & Wylam, 1978). Offer (1987) indicates that one-third of adolescents have achieved formal operations. Difficulties between adults and adolescents can arise when adults fail to realize that although they are interacting with an individual who looks physically very similar to them, an adolescent is still operating at an earlier level of cognitive development. Socially, the adolescent is finding relationships with peers and close friends to be meaningful and satisfying and often prefers friends over family. However, family relationships and influences continue to be extremely important in identity development. Psychologically, adolescents need to develop a sense of who they are in relation to others, the community, and the larger world in order to develop a coherent and stable sense of themselves. In the context of these developmental changes, schools can be difficult places to negotiate social interactions, adjust to a new sense of self, and accept a traditional school structure. This structure can be in direct opposition to the kind of growth and transformation that is needed during adolescence.

Disrespectful and oppositional behavior often lands an adolescent in trouble at school and may be manifested by the student not going to class, hanging out in the hallways, and being verbally insulting. During a workshop to support school teams in addressing problems in a systemic manner (part of my work as an implementation coordinator with the School Development Program), I asked the educators to consider the developmental needs of adolescents and how the school, classroom, or teacher can meet those needs. Once the teachers started thinking about these frustrating behaviors in light of adolescent development, they could see the potential for alternative strategies. For example, if educators think about the physical needs of adolescents, they must consider whether there is appropriately sized furniture and enough space for growing bodies. Students who begin class at 7:30 a.m. may lack sufficient sleep to be engaged in classroom activities. Because adolescents experience a growth spurt, they have increased appetites. Students may choose to be in the halls in order to stretch, stay stimulated and awake, or eat food. An administrator raised the possibility that perhaps a student was having a conflictual relationship with a teacher and being out of the class was the student's way of coping with a negative situation. While hanging out in the hall is unacceptable for the school, exploring the reasons behind the behaviors allowed the educators to think about modifications that could be made to support the learning environment. Systemic intervention implies an interconnectedness between individuals and subsystems. Everyone within the context has a responsibility in resolving a problem. Determining whether someone is right or wrong is not a part of this process.

Opportunities for Integrating Clinical Work

With the influx of school reform programs, public schools have established site-based decision-making teams, a mechanism through which major school policies and decisions are made with the input of a representative voice of the school community (Winters & Gourdine, 2000). Many schools also have teams that address the socio-emotional issues of children within the school. Not limited to the special education classified students, these teams are named something akin to a child study team. This type of team can be a part of a school's ongoing efforts to attend to the overall developmental needs of students; their focus is prevention and intervention. One example of a child study team is the Student and Staff Support Team, which is a crucial feature of the School Development Program (Comer, Haynes, Joyner, & Ben-Avie, 1996). Both the site-based decision-making teams and the child study teams offer school personnel the ability to catch potentially disruptive problems. They also provide the ability to consider parallel processes between subgroups within a school. Examples of how a school can use a team process to identify issues of concern to many students and consider parallel processes within systems are provided below.

Schools that attend to individual student concerns on their child study teams have an opportunity to take what is occurring with one student and consider how many other students may be in similar situations. An example of this type of connection was demonstrated during a meeting of one school's child study team involving school administration, support personnel, and parents about how to support the learning needs of a male student who was having attentional and organizational difficulties. The parents shared what they were doing to provide support for the attentional deficits, and the school personnel also identified areas in which they might be able to increase their support to the student. In many ways, this was quite typical of a meeting between school and family.

At the invitation of a school administrator, I was present at this meeting to provide feedback about the work of the team. After the meeting, I had an opportunity to contribute my observations. One important focus of the meeting was to help make the student as self-sufficient as possible with the support from parents and teachers. I also noted that the areas still needing support for this student were not uncommon to many students. I suggested the possibility of the school encouraging the formation of a small group of students with similar needs who could meet and support one another on organizational goals throughout the day. The administrator received this suggestion very positively. This school had a child study team that addressed individual student concerns, and they were interested in exploring alternative ways in which this team could support students. Recommending that a concern for one student could provide an opportunity to support many students helps to move a school toward thinking preventively.

Rather than thinking about individual student concerns, the systemic perspective pushes clinicians to think about who else is similarly affected and what resources are available to address this concern. Attention to the larger picture allows schools to manage situations before they become immediate concerns or even crises. A systemic perspective allows clinicians to intervene in a preventive fashion.

Working with schools that were implementing the School Development Program gave me an opportunity to structure these child study teams so that a systemic perspective was incorporated from the start. The following example shows how two school climate issues, seemingly disconnected, were viewed as two aspects of a larger systemic issue.

During a middle school's Student and Staff Support Team (a specific name for a child study team), the team members began discussing a hazard being created by students becoming increasing physically aggressive and noisy in the halls during the changes of classes. The team members expressed concern about the unsafe conditions that were being created and the possibility of a student being injured. They came up with various suggestions to lower the disruption during the class changes that satisfied everyone. The meeting proceeded, and several topics later, the team addressed overall school climate issues, particularly how the principal's medical leave was affecting the school's operations. The team described the staff as feeling at a loss and sensing a lack of structure and leadership.

As a consultant/participant on this team, my role was to provide feedback on the team's functioning in terms of process and content. As a frequent observer of this particular team, I also paid attention to the topics that arose from meeting to meeting and the possible connection between them. In this instance, I saw a connection between the topics of the decreased control of the students and the sense of a loss of structure and leadership among the staff, and I shared this with the team. Introducing a systemic perspective allowed the team to consider the parallel process between the subsystems within the school. Raising the possible connection between the two agenda items was a first and important step. The second step was for the staff to have an opportunity to process the effect of the principal's absence on them before they attended to the effect it may have on the student body. The third step was to identify ways for the existing school leadership and teaching staff to provide a sense of stability and reassurance to the students.

This example demonstrates the time that is needed to process the isolated actions that occur within schools and to see these actions as part of a larger context—nothing occurs in isolation. Sadly, there is little time for this needed reflection and planning within the school day. In this situation, the meeting was over before the members could reflect on their own thoughts and feelings. However, considering the ripple effects of the absence of leadership or even the *perception* of the absence of leadership through the subgroups within the school provided an alternative and perhaps more helpful understanding of the student body's behavior.

Summary

Intervening in a school system for the purpose of supporting students' development requires the clinician to view the identified concerns from the standpoint of many subsystems within the overall system, including the students, the staff, and the parents or community. In the case of adolescents, the clinician must also understand and include the contribution of the biopsychosocial changes that are occurring. Although this study focused primarily on adolescents, a similar process of assessment, planning, and intervention can be and is being done in elementary schools.

Clinical practice within schools is not limited to work with those students who have definable symptoms; clinical practice must be used to bring knowledge of child and adolescent development into the educational planning arena. In this way, when the overall developmental needs of students within a school are addressed and attended to, even those with more severe mental health concerns will benefit from the supportive context.

Author's Note

The School Development Program (SDP) was the vision of Dr. James Comer, a child psychiatrist, in response to his growing frustration about the widening gap in the academic and social development of minority children in relation to nonminority and upper-socioeconomic status children. As he observed this sociopolitical disruption in the

1960s and 1970s, he realized that the relationships between the school staff, parents, and students needed to be reestablished as well as basic elements of trust and shared goals. He created, with the support of many educators, a process that brings together the necessary stakeholders—parents, teachers, administrators—to provide the leadership for the school. Three major teams are created to enable this process to work: the School Planning and Management Team, the Student and Staff Support Team, and the Parent Team. The three major functions of these teams, led by the School Planning and Management Team, are to develop a comprehensive school plan, to ensure that the professional development program of the school supports the achievement of the plan, and to make sure that the school has a way of evaluating and modifying the comprehensive school plan. And finally, the SDP operates under three guiding principles: no fault, consensus decision-making, and collaboration (Comer et al., 1996).

References

CENTER FOR HEALTH AND HEALTH CARE IN SCHOOLS. (2001). *Policy and program.* Retrieved June 2003 from http://www.healthinschools.org/policy.asp.

COMER, J. P., HAYNES, N. M., JOYNER, E. T., & BEN-AVIE, M. (1996). The School Development Program. In J. P. Comer, N. M. Haynes, E. T. Joyner, & M. Ben-Avie (Eds.), *Rallying the whole village: The Comer process for reforming education* (pp. 1–26). New York: Teachers College Press.

COSTIN, L. (1969). A historical review of school social work. *Social Casework, October,* 439–453.

OFFER, D. (1987). In defense of adolescents. *Journal of the American Medical Association, 257*(24), 3407–3408.

OFFER, D. R., BOYLE, M. H., SZATMARI, P., RAE-GRANT, N. I., LINKS, P. S., CADMAN, D. T., BYLES, J. A., CRAWFORD, J. W., BLUM, H. M., BYRNE, C., THOMAS, H., & WOODWARD, C. A. (1987). Ontario child health study: Six-month prevalence of disorder and rates of service utilization. *Archives of General Psychiatry, 44,* 832–836.

ROBERTS, R. E., ATTKISSON, C. C., & ROSENBLATT, A. (1998). Prevalence of psychopathology among children and adolescents. *American Journal of Psychiatry, 155*(6), 715–725.

SHAYER, M., & WYLAM, H. (1978). The distribution of Piagetian stages of thinking in British middle and secondary school children: 14–16 year olds and sex differentials. *British Journal of Educational Psychology, 48,* 62–70.

WINTERS, W. G., & GOURDINE, R. M. (2000). School reform: A viable domain for school social work practice. In J. G. Hopps & R. Morris (Eds.), *Social work at the millennium: Critical reflections on the future of the profession* (pp. 138–159). New York: Free Press.

Case Study 4-3

Questions for Discussion

1. How does the structure of the Coping Power group help promote change? How are accommodations made for diverse individuals?

2. How do the group leaders minimize the children's sense that they are being punished by participating in the group?

3. How do the content and structure of the separate parent and child components of the Coping Power program help students achieve their goals?

4. What effort do the authors take to make the parent group accessible to their clients? How do those efforts affect attendance and group rapport?

The Implementation of the Coping Power Prevention Program for Aggressive Children and Their Families

John E. Lochman, Karen L. Salekin, and Melissa C. Kuhajda

Children's aggressive behavior has emerged as a central focus in prevention research as well as in treatment services and treatment research (Lochman, Dane, Magee, Ellis, Pardini, & Clanton, 2001; Lochman & Wells, 1996). Childhood aggression has been conceptualized as a risk marker on the developmental trajectories leading to a variety of negative adolescent outcomes, such as delinquency, substance use, and conduct problems in school and community settings (Hinshaw, Lahey, & Hart, 1993; Loeber, 1990). While the trajectories toward delinquency, substance abuse, and school problems may extend back to innate characteristics such as temperament and to broad contextual factors such as violence and drug activity within neighborhoods, the focus of prevention efforts is on malleable factors in the child's social and psychological development and in the child's immediate family context that relate to child aggression and problem behaviors. The contextual social-cognitive model of children's aggression (Lochman & Wells, in press-a) that underlies the Coping Power program evolved in large part because of research on aggressive children's social information processing (Crick & Dodge, 1994). Aggressive children have cognitive distortions at the appraisal stage of social-cognitive processing because of difficulties in encoding incoming social information and in accurately interpreting social events and others' intentions. They also have cognitive deficiencies at the problem solution stage of social-cognitive processing characterized by generating maladaptive solutions for perceived problems and having nonnormative expectations for the usefulness of aggressive and nonaggressive solutions to their social problems. Within this model, children's behavioral and social-cognitive problems arise most fundamentally out of early contextual experiences with parents who provide harsh or irritable discipline, poor problem solving, vague commands, and poor monitoring of children's behavior (Patterson, Reid, & Dishion, 1992).

Because childhood aggressive behavior is a risk predictor for later adolescent antisocial behavior and the contextual social-cognitive model addresses processes associated with children's aggressive behavior, preventive interventions can be usefully targeted at the social-cognitive and parenting processes in the model. Using the contextual social-cognitive model as a conceptual framework for identifying intervention objectives, the Coping Power program (Lochman & Wells, 1996) was developed as a multicomponent preventive intervention for aggressive children. The program is geared toward children between the ages of 9 and 13 years who have had difficulty relating to peers, teachers, and/or family members. In general, these children have a tendency to use ineffective coping styles when dealing with anger and often respond in an impulsive or aggressive manner when faced with provocation. The Coping Power program has child and parent components that can be delivered over a 9- to 18-month period of time. In addition, the program also includes active, close working relationships with children's teachers because teachers monitor children's goal completion, and they provide reinforcement for children's emerging improvements in their social skills and behavior. This study describes how the Coping Power child and parent components have been used in two cases.

Intervention research has indicated that the Coping Power program can effectively reduce children's problem behaviors. In one study, the Coping Power program was found to produce lower rates of youth-reported substance use, reductions in proactive aggression, improved social competence, and greater teacher-rated behavioral improvement at the end of intervention, in comparison to children who had not been part of the Coping Power program (Lochman & Wells, in press-b). In a second Coping Power study conducted with aggressive boys, the intervention produced lower levels of self-reported delinquent behavior, lower levels of parent-reported substance use, and higher levels of teacher-reported behavioral improvement in school at a 1-year follow-up, in comparison to a control condition (Lochman & Wells, in press-a). In addition, at the end of intervention, the Coping Power program had tended to produce improvements in the boys' angry attributions, in the boys' expectations that aggressive behavior would produce good outcomes for them, and in the consistency of parents' discipline and had produced significant improvements in the boys' internal locus of control and their abilities to accurately perceive others.

Coping Power Child Component

The Coping Power child component is a structured intervention program that uses cognitive-behavioral procedures to improve a child's ability to regulate aggressive behavior, function well in a variety of settings, and manage anger (Lochman, Lenhart, & Wells, 1996). In an attempt to address the wide range of needs of this population, the

Coping Power Program's child component has been designed to teach a variety of skills over an extended period of time (e.g., 33 sessions over the course of 18 months or 24 sessions over the course of a school year). Included in this program are sessions on goal setting, perspective taking, emotional awareness, social problem solving, and resisting peer pressure (Lochman, Wells, & Murray, in press). While the program is structured (meaning that each group member is presented the same information over the course of the program), there is a lot of flexibility with respect to the establishment of goals and the identification of individual needs. This flexibility allows the program to be applied effectively among a diverse population. The standard protocol for the Coping Power program is to have weekly sessions that are approximately 1 hour in length. Experience has shown that it is best to hold these meetings during the school day at times that the group members consider to be acceptable. The term *acceptable* means that the group members are not missing classes that they consider to be important. Perhaps the most common among these classes are physical education, music, art, and computer. Scheduling around the participants allows for a maximum level of motivation and participation—something that is considered to be central to effective implementation.

In addition to the hourly sessions, each participant engages in at least one individual meeting per month. This meeting can last anywhere from 15 minutes (a brief check-in) to an hour or more. The time frame for this meeting is not pre-established and should be directed by the needs of the individual. During these individual meetings, the group leader can, and often does, create an atmosphere that is conducive to change. While it is standard protocol to meet with each participant once per month, it is not uncommon to meet with some individuals once per week or once every 2 weeks, depending on their life context or their level of responsiveness within the group format. Participants who are not responsive during group work may need more individual meetings in order to ensure that the material is understood.

Case Example: Child Component

Anthony was excited to begin the Coping Power program. He was 11 years old and lived with his father. His brother and sister lived with their mother, and he saw them on weekends when he visited his mother. Although he knew little about the requirements of his participation, he did know that if he did well, he would get to "buy" things from the prize box. He had seen some kids coming out of group with really cool things, and all they had to do was go to a weekly meeting and have some yellow paper signed by their teacher. This seemed easy enough. "No problem!" he thought.

Anthony arrived for the group on time. His teacher knew that the group started at 9:00 a.m., and she allowed him to leave a few minutes early so that he wouldn't be late. The other kids came in shortly after he had arrived. He knew all of them and was happy to see that his best friend was included in his group. "Phew!" he thought, "I sure am glad I am not alone in this thing." As Anthony looked around at the other four members, he began to evaluate their reputations. Overall, he thought that they were okay but decided that they all were "worse" than he was. Then the group started, and immediately one of the group members asked why they were in this group, but other people weren't.

Expecting this question, the co-leaders spoke in general about factors that contributed to group selection. They talked about fighting, being disrespectful, making poor choices, and having difficulty managing anger. "Hmmm" thought Anthony. "They're telling me that I'm disobedient and disrespectful? What do they know about me? They haven't even spent any time with me. Who have they been talking to? They must be on the teacher's side!" As time passed, he thought more about his inclusion in the group and blurted out, "I ain't disrespectful to my teachers. I treat them the way they treat me. Simple. They earn their respect." After this, Anthony sat silently and began to question his participation in the program. Indeed, he was considering quitting and going back to class, but he didn't say anything to the group leaders.

Clearly, the first few sessions are very important with regard to building rapport and ensuring that the children feel comfortable and not "punished" by being involved. Knowing this, the co-leaders came prepared to address this concern. They minimized discussion about the "reasons" for inclusion in the program and focused on the fun things that they would be doing during the weeks together and on the positive aims of the program. The leaders talked about the fun they would have role-playing, how they would learn to deal with problems *without doing anything* at all (e.g., ignoring and walking away), and how they would create a video with their friends. The refocusing of attention worked. Anthony became excited and interested. The notion of "doing nothing" to deal with problems intrigued him, and he wanted to know how to do this. With the help of his co-leaders and a list of teacher-suggested goals, Anthony chose his first goal. He felt confident that he would have no difficulty meeting this goal every day. Day 1—group was over and all was well.

One week came and went. The second group began on time, and as promised, the leaders brought a box full of prizes! These prizes had to be earned, but there seemed to be many opportunities to collect points. Anthony came into the meeting with all the confidence in the world. In his mind, he had already earned the biggest prize of them all, a handheld football game that two people could play! He put down his folder, pulled out his goal sheet, and was ready to explain the reason why he did not have it signed by his teacher. He knew that he had met his goal every day and that was all that mattered, right?

Anthony was shocked and angered when he found out that no signature meant no points. It didn't matter at all that he felt that he had met his goal. He could have done nothing and been in the same predicament. He didn't understand. "This isn't fair!" he cried. "My teacher didn't sign my goal sheet. It's her fault not mine!" Anticipating that this problem would occur, the co-leaders reiterated one of the key points of the program—participants must take responsibility for their own behavior. As discussed in detail during Session 1, getting the goal sheet signed was the sole responsibility of the participant. The absence of a signature meant that no points would be allotted. This explanation did not change Anthony's attitude.

Because this problem is very common (almost a certainty), the co-leaders came prepared with an alternative way for the group members to earn points. It would be counterproductive to give points for an unsigned goal sheet because this would only reward the lack of responsibility and would set the standard for future behavior. Instead, the co-leaders created a game in which the children could earn points by participating. They could recite the group rules, talk about goal setting, talk about a problem that they are having with a peer, or create an effective plan for how to make sure that their goal sheet would be signed the following week. At the end of the second session, all was well and rapport was being established. Anthony saved his points in hopes that he would earn enough to buy the game.

Anthony progressed through the next 2 weeks and continued to have trouble remembering to get his goal sheet signed. Instead of blaming others, he took responsibility for this problem and continued to brainstorm about things that he could do to help him remember. During these weeks, Anthony focused his energy on following the rules, participating, and completing all of the homework assignments. Because of his hard work, he remained at the top of the list for points earned during each meeting. Although he did not talk about it, he appeared to enjoy being at the head of the class and he was still looking toward buying the football game. It was still in the box, and he wanted it.

Anthony arrived promptly for the fourth session and sat down beside his best friend. One of the co-leaders said, "Let's get out our goal sheets so that we can see how well each of you did this week." In general, all went well. All of them had some yes's (meaning that they had met their goal), and there were signatures on each of the yellow sheets. Today, it was easy to move on to the first topic. The children were going to learn how to identify and measure emotions. The leaders discussed how to use the idea of a thermometer in order to assess all of our emotions. If we are very angry, we are at or near the top of the thermometer. If we are only a little bit angry, the "red stuff" is just barely above the bulb. Anthony thought to himself, "This is easy. Everyone knows that we can be really mad or a little mad. What is the big deal?" Then, out of nowhere, he heard his name. One of the leaders chose to use him as an example. "How does she know about the fight that I had?" he thought to himself. "How much does she really know? I didn't even start that fight!" His thoughts kept racing through his head, and he could feel his "temperature" rising. The leader looked toward Anthony and said, "Anthony, I want you to use the thermometer to describe how mad you felt before you hit Jeremy last week. Please don't say anything. Just walk up to the point on the thermometer that equals the level of anger you felt just before you hit him." Everyone in the room went silent. They could see that Anthony was angry and they waited for him to respond. Anthony didn't say a word, but he shook his head in refusal.

One of the other leaders responded to Anthony's disengagement with a smile on his face and said simply, "It really looks like you are angry now, Anthony. Would you agree to move to the point on the thermometer where you are now? I know if I were you I would be way up at the top—the whole thing would be red. I would be very angry because I don't like talking about my personal stuff in public. It makes me feel uncomfortable and picked on." Anthony remained silent as he gradually walked to the top of the thermometer. When he stopped, the leaders smiled and congratulated him on doing something that everyone, even adults, find hard to do. He had identified his emotion as it was happening and was able to provide a measurement of how much of that emotion he was feeling. Everyone was excited for him, and two of the group members said that there was no way that they could have done that—they would have left the room. Anthony was so surprised by the change of events that he began to smile and his anger level decreased dramatically. He had received positive attention when he expected negative attention. It didn't make sense. "Hmmm," thought Anthony. "This program is harder than I thought, and I don't really get it." While it seemed like an eternity, the hour had finally ended. Points were tallied, prizes were bought, and points were saved. Next week would come quickly.

The following session began as all of the others had, and the group was able to progress much more quickly than they had before. Today's focus was on how to handle emotions and, in particular, how to handle the feeling of anger. One of the leaders went around the room and asked everyone to describe the coping strategies that they used to deal with anger. Anthony went through all of his strategies in his head. For example, he thought, "When I get mad, I make a face and glare at people. Sometimes I just walk off in a huff, and sometimes, if I get really mad, I will throw something or hit people." As he was thinking about his responses, he noted that other people reported having similar experiences, but they weren't all the same. "Interesting," he thought. "I wonder if one of these works better than another?" The leaders began the session and spoke about different strategies; they said that some worked well in some situations and not in others. They talked at length about the importance of being able to walk away from a provocative peer, to ignore people when they are just trying to make you mad, to remind yourself that it is not worth getting in trouble, and to be able to compromise in situations that aren't worth fighting over. They also discussed the importance of having hobbies or being involved in sports because these types of activities can really help people express their feelings and also help to reduce the intensity of emotions.

This session seemed to be pretty intense. Anthony wanted to begin trying to use some of these techniques because he was having some problems getting along with one of his classmates. Anthony talked about his problems in the group and together they came up with a great homework assignment. In addition to practicing using two new internal coping statements, which were things he could tell himself to manage his anger (e.g., "it's not worth it to get angry" and "it's too bad he has to act like that"), he was also going to try to ignore the person while they were teasing him. This week's homework assignment was going to be hard, and nobody was expecting him to stay calm all the time, but at least now he had some new tools to try.

Each week Anthony went home and talked to his dad about the program. Both of them were learning similar concepts, and his dad was actively trying to help him use the skills in the home environment. One of the most important aspects of the program is referred to as the PICC model (a problem-solving model), which was introduced in one session and then talked about or actively practiced for many weeks in a row. Anthony was good at using this model because he liked to have things clearly delineated for him. First, the model was easy to remember because it was called the PICC model. The PI stands for Problem Identification, the first C stands for Choices, and the last C stands for Consequences. Of course, each concept requires a lot of consideration in that a person must consider a variety of things to make good choices. For example, you must be able to take other people's perspectives and to identify individual goals in order to identify the problem. Then you have to consider all possible choices and weigh each one of those choices against the others to come up with the best plan of action.

The program made the PICC model easy to use because worksheets were provided to teachers, parents, and group members. Whenever a problem came up, Anthony could write it down and evaluate various ways to solve the problem. Also, Anthony liked the fact that his teachers were going to use this as a method of discipline in the classroom. When a student was caught using an inappropriate coping skill, that student would be required to complete a PICC worksheet. Once complete, the student would review it with the teacher and, in some cases, with the principal and/or parent. In Anthony's mind, the PICC model was a good thing.

The weeks came and went. Anthony tried his best both in and outside the group. He got a perfect score on his goal sheet for 10 weeks in a row, and he earned the Student of the Month award. Anthony was clearly pleased to state that his father had been to every one of the parent meetings and that he and his father worked hard at learning new ways of dealing with negative emotions.

Like most children, Anthony continued to experience some difficulty respecting authority and did not always do as he was told. But, to his benefit, he had learned to use a variety of coping skills (e.g., ignoring, saying coping statements in his head, and walking away) and was much more skilled in the area of perspective taking. Like most people, he had not mastered all of the techniques that were taught but he knew that he had options and he tried to use them as best he could. By the end of the year, he had earned the handheld football game.

Coping Power Parent Component

The Coping Power parent component is a 10-session group program distributed over the same 10-month period as the child component (the fifth-grade year). Our experience, described in this study, is with a briefer adaptation of the full 16-session Coping Power parent and child components (Lochman et al., in press). Parents met in groups of up to 10 parents or parent dyads and two co-leaders. Assertive attempts were made to include mothers and fathers in parent groups, although only one parent (usually the mother) attended in most cases. For some sessions, the school counselor also joined the leaders in presenting material relevant to parent involvement in the school.

The content of the Coping Power parent component (Wells, Lenhart, & Lochman, 1996) is derived from parent training programs that were based on social learning theory and developed and evaluated by prominent clinician-researchers in the field of child aggression (Patterson et al., 1992). It is designed to address caregiver and parenting risk factors for child aggression and for substance abuse (Hawkins, Catalano, & Miller, 1992). However, in addition to these "standard" parent training skills, parents in the Coping Power program also learn additional skills that support the social-cognitive and problem-solving skills that their children learn in the child component (Lochman et al., in press). These parent skills are introduced at the same time that the respective child skills are introduced so that parents and children can work together at home on what they are learning. For example, parents learn to set up homework support structures and to reinforce organizational skills around homework completion at the same time that children are learning organizational skills in the Coping Power child component. In the second and third sessions, parents are taught effective coping strategies for managing stressful events and daily hassles (e.g., taking care of themselves by routinely engaging in relaxation exercises and implementing simple time-management techniques). Similarly, their children memorize coping statements such as "I'll grow up, not blow up" and practice self-control through deep-breathing exercises. Parents also learn techniques for managing sibling conflict in the home as children address peer and sibling conflict resolution skills in the child groups. Finally, parents learn to apply the PICC model to family problem solving so that the child skills learned in the group are prompted and reinforced in the family context.

Case Example of Response to Parent Component

Initially, the leaders of the parent group found it very difficult to engage with Alice, a 35-year-old, married, working mother of three children under the age of 10. Numerous home-visit attempts were made to encourage participation in the parent component of the program. She appeared interested, stating that she planned to attend sessions, but she missed the first two. Finally, after rapport had been established between Alice and one co-leader during telephone calls and home visits, Alice admitted her fear of traveling to the university where the meetings were being held. With permission from the parents in regular attendance, arrangements were made to have the remainder of the parent meetings at the school Alice's child attended, a place that was familiar and less threatening for her and that was actually more convenient for some of the other parents as well. Before Alice's first parent meeting, a home visit was arranged to review material from previous sessions that she had missed. Now feeling more comfortable, she attended each successive session. She was also given individual attention to review ongoing homework suggestions from recent parent meetings. She readily joined in and became an active participant in the group. She expressed regret at not having attended the first two sessions and often said how helpful the parent meetings were. She was sorry to see the program come to an end.

Alice was particularly responsive at her first session, in which parents were asked to visualize how they allot their time by drawing a pie chart with a pie segment for each role they play in life. For example, Alice's pie had segments for her roles as a wife, mother, Sunday school teacher, caretaker for her father, and employee at a local factory. She exclaimed aloud, "I have no piece of pie just for me!" One of the very important lessons she learned during that session was that by neglecting herself, she was left with little to no stamina, energy, or enthusiasm to give to these other areas in her life. Throughout subsequent sessions, Alice frequently commented on how taking time for herself, no matter how brief, made her happier and more willing to implement the new parenting strategies she learned in the Coping Power program.

Alice was tearful during Session 5 as she told the group that she was seriously considering allowing her ex-husband, Jamey's father, to assume primary custody of their son because "I can't control him! He doesn't listen to anything I say!" Alice had already begun performing one parent skill that she learned in a previous session and that helps in getting children to comply with instructions—catching your child being good. That is, she noticed when Jamey, her oldest child (a fifth grader), was showing good behavior and immediately praised him with a statement such as, "I like the way you helped your little sister put on her coat, Jamey. Thank you." Before this parenting session, Alice had come directly from a meeting with Jamey's teacher and counselor, who expressed concern about Jamey's defiance and noncompliance with school rules, and it was obvious to Alice that they were not enjoying dealing with Jamey's negative behavior. Alice, in a state of desperation, thought that sending Jamey to live with his father would at least give her and their local school a break from his misbehavior. At the same time, though, she knew that this would not be a positive long-term solution for her son because she knew her ex-husband's tendency to stay very busy with his work and thus would be unable to provide much guidance for their children.

At the urging of the co-leaders and other parents in the group, Alice agreed to learn about "giving good instructions" and implement these strategies in her commands to her son throughout the next few weeks. She learned that children are most likely to obey instructions that are direct and specific, stated clearly, limited to only one or two at a time, and followed by 10 seconds of silence. At the next parent meeting, she reported Jamey's success in being more compliant with her instructions and less defiant in general, and she described an interaction she and Jamey had shared as a "turning point" in their relationship. Alice explained that a few days after the last parent meeting, she remained skeptical about her ability to effect any change in her son's willingness to comply with instructions. However, remembering her commitment to the other parents in the group, she decided to invite Jamey to dinner, just the two of them, for a special night out. She said she remembered learning about "parent-child special time" in a previous parent session—spending relaxed, non-problem-focused time with children in an effort to nourish the parent-child relationship and thereby counteract the influence of negative outside forces in the future. Jamey was receptive to his mother's invitation, and Alice reported that they had a nice dinner at one of Jamey's favorite restaurants.

Their conversation while driving home after dinner helped Alice understand the importance of giving good instructions. Jamey said something to the effect that he is a "good boy," as his mother frequently asks him to be, because "I get good grades in school." Alice immediately responded by telling her son that there was a whole lot more involved in being good besides getting good grades, although getting good grades is wonderful! Alice then described other situations that would fall under the rubric of "being good," such as being kind and respectful to his siblings and the neighbors' children at home and to his teachers and classmates at school. Alice said that she could not help but notice the shocked look on Jamey's face as he said, "Oh, so when you say 'be a good boy,' it's not enough to just get good grades?" Alice said that she smiled at him, hugged his neck, and said, "That's exactly what I mean!" As a result of this conversation, Alice said that when she wants Jamey to "be good," she makes it a point to state exactly what she wants him to do. For example, she might say "Jamey, it is homework time now. Turn off the TV and go do your homework." Alice told the co-leaders and other parents that she sometimes has to stop and plan her instructions before giving them, but her son's compliance is worth every minute of the time it takes to preplan her instructions. Best of all, as Alice learned more parenting strategies and practiced them both in role-plays during the parent sessions and in real life with her children, Jamey's behavior not only improved at home, but Alice began receiving more favorable feedback from his teachers and counselors at school.

This parenting group was very successful. Attendance was good, and group cohesiveness was evident in the parents' eagerness to share their parenting successes and difficulties with each other and the co-leaders. Outreach efforts, phone calls, and reminder notices by mail all helped to facilitate attendance. Child care was provided free of charge during the parent meetings. Refreshments were also provided for both parents and children during the meetings.

At the end of the school year, Jamey's behavior had improved to a level commensurate with the good grades that he had always earned. His mother and teachers observed that he had begun to understand what "being good" entailed and was more motivated and willing to comply with the requests of others. Both Jamey and his mother, Alice, were looking forward to a successful transition from elementary school to middle school.

Authors' Note

The completion of this case study was supported by grants from the National Institute of Drug Abuse, the Centers for Disease Control and Prevention, the Center for Substance Abuse Prevention (Substance Abuse and Mental Health Services Administration), and the United States Department of Justice. Correspondence should be directed to: John E. Lochman, Ph.D., Box 870348, Department of Psychology, The University of Alabama, Tuscaloosa, Alabama 35487.

References

CRICK, N. R., & DODGE, K. A. (1994). A review and reformulation of social information-processing mechanisms in children's social adjustment. *Psychological Bulletin, 115,* 74–101.

HAWKINS, J. D., CATALANO, R. F., & MILLER, J. Y. (1992). Risk and protective factors for alcohol and other drug problems in adolescence and early adulthood: Implications for substance abuse prevention. *Psychological Bulletin, 112,* 64–105.

HINSHAW, S. P., LAHEY, B. B., & HART, E. L. (1993). Issues of taxonomy and comorbidity in the development of conduct disorder. *Development and Psychopathology, 5,* 31–34.

LOCHMAN, J. E., DANE, H. E., MAGEE, T. N., ELLIS, M., PARDINI, D. A., & CLANTON, N. R. (2001). Disruptive behavior disorders: Assessment and intervention. In B. Vance & A. Pumareiga (Eds.), *The clinical assessment of children and youth behavior: Interfacing intervention with assessment* (pp. 231–262). New York: Wiley.

LOCHMAN, J. E., LENHART, L. A., & WELLS, K. C. (1996). *Coping Power program: Child component.* Unpublished manual. Durham, NC: Duke University Medical Center.

LOCHMAN, J. E., & WELLS, K. C. (1996). A social-cognitive intervention with aggressive children: Prevention effects and contextual implementation issues. In R. D. Peters & R. J. McMahon (Eds.), *Prevention and early intervention: Childhood disorders, substance use and delinquency* (pp. 111–143). Thousand Oaks, CA: Sage.

LOCHMAN, J. E., & WELLS, K. C. (in press-a). Contextual social-cognitive mediators and child outcome: A test of the theoretical model in the Coping Power program. *Development and Psychopathology.*

LOCHMAN, J. E., & WELLS, K. C. (in press-b). The Coping Power program at the middle school transition: Universal and indicated prevention effects. *Psychology of Addictive Behaviors.*

LOCHMAN, J. E., WELLS, K. C., & MURRAY, M. (in press). The Coping Power program: Preventive intervention at the middle school transition. In P. Tolan, J. Szapocznik, & S. Sambrano (Eds.), *Preventing substance abuse: 3 to 14.* Washington, DC: American Psychological Association.

LOEBER, R. (1990). Development and risk factors of juvenile antisocial behavior and delinquency. *Clinical Psychology Review, 10,* 1–42.

PATTERSON, G. R., REID, J. B., & DISHION, T. J. (1992). *Antisocial boys.* Eugene, OR: Castalia.

WELLS, K. C., LENHART, L. A., & LOCHMAN, J. E. (1996). *Coping Power program, Parent component.* Unpublished manual. Durham, NC: Duke University Medical Center.

Case Study 4-4

Questions for Discussion

1. Why does the practitioner delineate her cultural and other differences at the very beginning of the client-therapist relationship?
2. How do children of first-generation immigrant families often become the "spokesperson" for the family? In what ways can this be challenging to the family system?
3. How is the client affected by the process of cultural assimilation?
4. The author describes the therapeutic process in this case as "two sculptors working at a block of clay together." How does this metaphor capture the cultural and developmental facets of the case?

Zai: A Hmong Adolescent Creates His Own Way

Harriet Cobb and A. Renee Staton

Zai, a 13-year-old bilingual (Hmong and English) Hmong student, was referred to counseling by one of his teachers. She described Zai as a very bright, somewhat shy, but engaging student with a small circle of friends. He was an excellent second baseman on the school's softball team and particularly enjoyed gym class. Lately, Zai had appeared increasingly withdrawn and occasionally seemed distressed at the end of the day. His grades were still very good, but he seemed distracted and had started to turn in less comprehensive assignments. I checked Zai's file and found that his grades were indeed excellent, and his physical history was unremarkable. The records gave no indication that Zai's parents had ever been involved with the school.

Unlike most first-time students in this school-based mental health center, Zai arrived early for his first session. He was quiet and intense, avoiding significant eye contact and looking around the room rather than at me. He started the session by asking what went on in this room. I explained the purpose of counseling, saying that occasionally students needed someone to talk to who could do their best to understand and help with problems. I asked what he thought about that. He replied, "I guess that's okay." I then asked if he thought there was anything I could help him with.

Initially, Zai indicated that he was "Okay, just a little bored with school." I expressed my sympathy, saying that sometimes I got bored just looking in at the classrooms. I then tried to acknowledge the differences between us by indicating that I was not like him, though. I could only speak one language, never got the consistently high grades he got, was White, female, and adult, and could not play softball like he could; probably his experience in school was very different from mine. In fact, I wondered how he felt about talking to me in general. I knew that a little self-deprecation on the part of the therapist could facilitate communication with adolescents, and I believed I needed to explicitly address the cross-cultural nature of our relationship.

On hearing this, Zai seemed interested in me and looked at me directly for several seconds. He said he thought I might be able to help him with a few things—not everything, but a few things. Zai then told me that he had been becoming increasingly upset recently because of his relationship with his family. Zai was the second oldest of five children. His family had immigrated to the United States in 1980, so Zai and his brothers and sisters had been born here and were all U.S. citizens. Like many Hmong adolescents, however, Zai had a foot firmly planted in two cultures—Hmong and American. His parents worked to maintain their traditions and customs and spoke only Hmong at home. Zai and his siblings were therefore immersed in the Hmong culture at home; but as they attended school and spent more and more time away from home, they became increasingly Western in their thoughts and behaviors. According to Zai, all of the siblings had learned to assimilate into a more Western style at school and were "more Hmong" at home.

As the second eldest son, Zai did not have the power and prestige in the family that his older brother, Pao, had. That in itself was not problematic for Zai. Zai expected his older brother to get more attention and acclaim because that was the tradition in his family and in his culture. In Hmong tradition, males have more power and rights than females (Chan, 1994; Fadiman, 1997), and often the eldest son has the most prestige among the offspring. However, his older brother was, in Zai's view, not living up to the role of eldest son. According to Zai, Pao (a senior in high school) drank beer, did not study, and never helped with any chores around the house. Pao's behavior was an affront to Zai, not only because Zai felt it was inappropriate behavior for the eldest son, but because Zai himself was left to care for his younger siblings and to serve as a cultural interpreter for their parents, who were not fluent in English.

Although not ideal, the need for English-speaking children to translate English language and negotiate Western practices is common among Hmong families. As parents struggle to learn English and work to retain honored traditions, they may lag behind their children's ability to understand and respond to U.S. customs. Therefore, children often become spokespersons for the family when dealing with school and agency personnel. This practice, questionable in any context, is especially challenging for Hmong families. Older family members have more prestige and receive more deference than young people (Chan, 1994; Fadiman, 1997). Asking young people to talk about family concerns can be offensive to the elder family members and confusing for the young ones. Family members know that children cannot make family decisions, and they have more limited rights than their elders. The request that children share information with outsiders is often viewed as invasive and inappropriate.

In Zai's case, the fact that he was the only son willing to represent his family to physicians and social service agencies put him in a no-win situation. He understood what his family needed to do to survive in U.S. culture and was willing to help his parents work their way through the maze of social service agencies and programs. His parents relied on his ability to do this but were frustrated and at times embarrassed with

Zai's requests for information and his pleas for compliance. When I later attempted to consult with the family about Zai's progress, I found that his mother and father felt that Zai's assumption of this role was inappropriate, and it made them both feel extremely uncomfortable. If, however, Zai refused to translate for his family, he ran the risk of being embarrassed by looking "too Hmong" to school and agency personnel and perhaps allowing his family to struggle by not receiving adequate care and services. Zai's competence further complicated this situation. Physicians, counselors, and social workers seemed to forget they were talking to an adolescent. They engaged with Zai as if he were the head of the family. The pressure accompanying this role was tremendous.

In addition, Zai wanted to go to college and was becoming worried that his family responsibilities were going to interfere with his ability to study and eventually leave home. In fact, Zai implied that his parents were suspicious of his focus on academics and believed that he was using school as a way to remove himself from the Hmong way of life. Although they might support Pao if he wanted to attend college, Zai's desire to pursue higher education was threatening to them. As we continued to talk about Zai's experience, he became engaged and animated, explaining his situation to me with a rapid-fire intensity that highlighted his level of distress.

For Zai, the implications of this situation seemed overwhelming. He felt overburdened with responsibilities and insulted by the lack of appreciation he received from his parents. At the same time, though, he felt guilty for desiring that appreciation. As the younger son, he believed that he was not entitled to special recognition. Nonetheless, Zai had a nagging sense that he was being mistreated and, more importantly, that the mistreatment was never going to end. As he imagined his life in the future, he could only envision more of the same. That sense of hopelessness drove Zai to tell me that he occasionally thought about walking out in front of cars or having an "accident" that would end his sense of being forever stuck in a confining and thankless role.

As I continued to talk with Zai, I felt overwhelmed as well. I sensed his strong feeling of hopelessness and caught glimpses of unacknowledged and unexpressed anger. Thus, I took his mention of suicide very seriously. I also knew that as an adolescent Hmong boy caught in complex intergenerational struggles related to assimilation, he was particularly vulnerable to stress (Faderman, 1998). Clearly, Zai's attempts to negotiate a place for himself left him feeling trapped and at times desperate.

I also felt overwhelmed as I tried to genuinely understand Zai's situation. In American culture, children are not necessarily assumed to have distinct status or responsibility based on birth order. The closest I could get to understanding what Zai's family life must feel like was to remember how I felt when I was expected to wash the dishes while my brother was expected to mow the yard. The comparison definitely failed to capture the complexity of Zai's situation. I also felt frustrated at times with Zai's parents. I struggled to understand what I perceived as rigidity regarding the roles of their children. At one point, Zai described a little outbuilding in his family yard that would make a great study room. His parents insisted that Zai not use that room, however, so that Pao could keep his personal items there. The personal items, according to Zai, were beer and "junk" that Pao did not want his family to see. Zai said that Pao never really used the building for anything other than storage, and Zai's occasional usage of the building to study surely would not inconvenience Pao. However, the building was off-limits to Zai, and I silently agreed with Zai's implied statement that this arrangement was unfair. Trying to respond appropriately to my own countertransference added to my struggle to keep a strong therapeutic frame to our sessions.

The fact that Zai never directly expressed what I believed were underlying feelings of unfairness also made me hypersensitive about my own ignorance regarding the influence of Hmong culture on him. I became concerned that I was systematically misunderstanding Zai's world or that I would inadvertently offend him by unwittingly revealing my disapproval of his parents' actions. At this point, I realized that it was imperative that I study Hmong culture more intensely to ensure that my work with Zai was relevant and ethical.

The word *Hmong* means "free," which expresses the extraordinarily independent nature of the people from this culture (Chan, 1994; Faderman, 1998; Fadiman, 1997). Originally from China, the Hmong always lived somewhat apart from mainstream Chinese culture, which generally tolerated their autonomy. However, after being persecuted by the last dynasty during the 19th century, thousands of Hmong refused to assimilate and migrated to Laos and other Southeast Asian countries. While approximately 8 million Hmong continue to reside in China, another 4 million live in other Asian countries, Europe, the United States, and Canada. Most of the Hmong living in the United States come from Laos, where they engaged exclusively in subsistence farming, growing opium, rice, and corn. The Hmong resisted the Laotian government's attempts to force them to cease their "slash and burn" agriculture practices, which destroy lumber and, ultimately, the fertile topsoil.

The Hmong were also known as fierce warriors, and during the events leading up to the war in Vietnam, the CIA recruited the Hmong into a mercenary army. During the Vietnam War, many Hmong were sent to refugee camps in Thailand and endured the hardships of combat trauma and severe living conditions. Thousands of Hmong refugees were resettled during the middle 1970s in a number of U.S cities, primarily in the northern and eastern areas of the country. This resulted in the separation of clans, which function as extended family units, thus compounding the stress of being isolated and adjusting to an extremely alien urban culture. There was no demand for their traditional skills, and this loss of a sense of efficacy and identity was a tremendous stress for these adults.

Many participated in a secondary migration to the west, which allowed clan members to reunite and seek employment in farming. With no written language and being non-English speaking, the Hmong experienced significant psychological trauma during this transition to life in a post-industrial, information-age culture. The younger generation is English-speaking and has become more educated, serving as the cultural brokers for their parents and grandparents; this arrangement clearly disrupts the sanctity of the role of family elders (particularly older males) in the Hmong culture. Their understandable general mistrust of authority figures and outsiders means that mental health professionals must acquire cultural sensitivity and competence when working cross-generationally with individuals and their families.

Therapists working with Hmong adolescents must recognize the potential for mis-attribution and misunderstanding regarding their clients' concerns. In this particular case, I worked to integrate this information regarding Hmong culture into my under-standing of adolescents in general. As a result, I took a very pragmatic view of Zai's concerns. I saw his culture as one more dynamic affecting his perception of the world. His culture, in addition to his gender, developmental level, family context, and intel-ligence, figured into my conceptualization of Zai as a troubled adolescent. This stance enabled me to see there was no quick way to resolve Zai's struggle to exist in two cultures. Instead, I had to engage with Zai as an adolescent facing identity issues and refuse to be intimidated by the cultural differences between us.

My first goal was to ensure that my initial response to Zai's suicidality was ap-propriate for him. In our second session, we revisited our initial no-harm contract, and Zai was able to identify times during the previous week when he had felt more and less hopeless, as well as recognize the influence that his own actions had on his feelings. I tried to facilitate this awareness by specifically asking, "What were you doing or think-ing to make yourself feel better?" After our second session, I became less concerned about Zai's suicidality, but I kept this issue as a priority in my conceptualization. I had to proceed with caution when talking with Zai about his feelings of hopelessness. Many Hmong people are more willing to assume an external rather than internal locus of responsibility and to fight or flee when threatened (Fadiman, 1997). Although Zai's attribution of his stress seemed appropriately placed on external factors (his role in the family and his parents' attitudes), I wanted to try to help Zai see that there was some flexibility in how he responded to those factors. As we discussed this idea, I was afraid of offending Zai, so I checked with him frequently to ensure that I was accurately un-derstanding his experience with his parents.

Fortunately, Zai's self-awareness enabled me to assume a collaborative approach and gave me the confidence to take a "not knowing" position with him. I believed that the Western influences that Zai encountered every day were instrumental in highlighting his distress, but I did not know what an ideal resolution would be for Zai. I also knew that at times Zai felt that I could not accurately understand his situation. When trying to describe how he felt about his parents, Zai would occasionally shake his head and say, "It's okay. Never mind." I would then say, "Uh-oh. I'm not understanding something, am I?" or "I think I've missed it. Can you help me?" This request for assistance was always answered with more information and clarification. Thus, I shared with Zai my curiosity and my awareness of my own ignorance of his situation and let him clarify for me. I should add one caveat regarding this practice. As the professional in our dyad, I did not expect Zai to teach me *everything* I should know about Hmong culture. My responsibility was to be adequately informed in order to provide competent care for him. However, I was honest with him when his beliefs and experiences were difficult for me to understand, and he became skilled at providing clear descriptions and often compelling metaphors for his experience. For instance, Zai provided one especially concrete metaphor during our eighth session when he was describing what it felt like to balance both Hmong and U.S. practices. "It's like my head is a computer disk," he said. "It can only hold so much information. When I put in the 'outside' stuff [Western beliefs and behaviors], it erases some of the Hmong stuff. I don't know what to do about that." Zai, like many Hmong, somaticized his concerns (Fadiman, 1997). For Zai, the result was headache and eye pain. As I heard this, I had a clearer understanding of how Zai's problems resulted in head pain. The learning that he experienced every day when he was away from home was exciting and full of possibilities, but it hurt.

The benefit of this "not-knowing" position was the permission it gave me to wonder aloud about discrepancies that I heard in his story. I was able to share with Zai my view of possible different stories, or reframes, and discuss these views with Zai while respecting him as the authority on his own life. For instance, Zai frequently claimed that there was no way out of his situation. After one such statement, I asked Zai how his role in the family had changed over time. He described growing into more responsibility and feelings of competence and seeing his parents look to him for more assistance with the younger children. I then wondered how it could be that his role would never change again. In order to seem less confrontational, I presented this question indirectly, looking away from Zai and expressing confusion by saying "Your responsibility and place in the family have changed as you've gotten older. Your parents look to you for different things. You're able to do more. But now all that change stops. You're all going to be stuck the way you are now. I'm trying to see how that happens." Zai was accustomed to clarifying for me, so during this process he was willing to clarify not only for me but for himself. He acknowledged that the family would probably continue to change. In fact, things might possibly get worse! At this, we looped back and looked together at how his current situation was better or worse than it used to be. We also explored the ways in which he could handle more as he got older and had more resources than he had as a child. This process of indirectly facing and then exploring core beliefs occasionally led us to take a step back for every step forward. However, the process seemed interesting as well as helpful to Zai.

Unlike some Hmong clients, Zai was not looking for a quick fix to his concern (Chan, 1994; Fadiman, 1997; Sue & Sue, 2003). Perhaps because of his ability to conceptualize himself and others through both Hmong and Western lenses, Zai seemed as interested in exploration as he was in immediate resolution. Perhaps he was deferring to my authority in the session and was therefore willing to walk with me in this circuitous route around his experience. Or, equally likely, Zai felt desperate for help and was willing to be patient with my musings in the hope that our relationship would pay off in the end. Through this process, Zai allowed me to focus on and iterate his strengths, which I believe reinforced Zai's sense of self-efficacy.

As we continued to meet, I found that I increasingly trusted our relationship to take us where we needed to go because I believed that Zai saw himself as a genuine collaborator in our sessions. This belief in our process enabled me to let go of my need to evaluate his parents from my Western worldview and label their attitudes and behaviors as right or wrong. Instead, I adopted a pragmatism that mirrored Zai's approach. In doing so, I was better able to see Zai in his own context, and I developed what I believed was a more accurate and effective sense of empathy for him. This pragmatism allowed me to work with Zai to externalize the problem (Freemen, Epston, & Lobovits, 1997), which was a practice I had used with numerous adolescents. While not removing responsibility from the client, this approach avoids the tendency to label clients and requires the practitioner to keep environmental and familial influences in mind. Therefore, Zai and I spoke about "the situation," being careful not to place blame on his parents or even Pao. The process of externalization came somewhat easily to Zai for several reasons. I believe the translation from Hmong language into English language may have resulted quite naturally in Zai presenting his concerns as *it*—something other than himself. Also, externalization helped avoid self-blame, which is inconsistent with many Hmongs' beliefs. He talked about how the situation made him feel and then how he responded to it. In addition, Zai's somatization was another manifestation of *it* in his life. We used this to further our conversation of *it* and how *it* was going.

Zai and I met for 10 weeks. Zai never missed a session and never arrived late. Very quickly, Zai reported a decrease in his sense of overwhelming anxiety. In fact, by our second session, his suicidality was much less of a concern for both of us. Like many adolescents, Zai needed to re-establish trust each week. Therefore, we developed a polite ritual for the beginning of our sessions. Zai would greet me and wait quietly for me to make my initial comments. I would invite Zai to tell me what he was thinking or how things were going. Almost without fail, Zai would respond, "Everything's okay." Then I would ask, "How about at home?" He would again tell me all was well, or at least "okay." Finally, I would say, "Well, I was thinking about something that we talked about last week." I would then present whatever I was thinking about his situation, and Zai would immediately engage with me. His intensity and focus would sharpen, and we would begin our exploration. This opening ritual occurred at every session with one exception. Near the end of our time together, Zai began the session by asking if I was planning on attending a Hmong cultural celebration at a local community center. He was participating in the celebration and, I think, wanted me to see him there with his family. I did attend the ceremony, believing that my presence there would be important for several reasons. I would see Zai in the context of his family, and Zai would know that I saw him surrounded by his family and the members of his clan. I think Zai wanted me to see him as a very competent and important participant in the celebration. I also wanted to show my respect for the Hmong culture and continue to learn as much as possible about the Hmong. I hoped that my presence at the ceremony would strengthen my ties with members of the Hmong community, including powerful elders and others whom I could call on to help me navigate my relationships.

Over the course of our sessions, I expected more anger to emerge as Zai talked about his brother and parents. However, although he did tell me more about how he felt and how he perceived his situation, I did not see an increase in his willingness to blame or fault his parents. Similarly, his frustration with Pao never appeared to represent active dislike, and Zai did not overtly express what I believed was underlying anger. I eventually stopped seeking strong affect from Zai and instead focused on his sense of himself in relationship with his family members. He became able to articulate his view of himself as a good son, even though he may never be seen as the "best" son. This growing sense of himself as a worthwhile and contributing member of the family seemed to emerge from our circular explorations, in which we indirectly addressed his concerns. This process reminded me of two sculptors working at a block of clay together. We periodically stepped back to get different views of our progress. Sometimes we switched places, and Zai told me how to view the piece. I then shared my own view. Eventually, we would start working together to chip and shave until we developed a model that made sense to us. Throughout this process, Zai shared the power of creating. Also, as we externalized the problem and kept a pragmatic view, Zai seemed able to keep his core sense of self from being too threatened by the seemingly fixed nature of his family role. I believe that the active nature of our sessions helped Zai avoid the sense of hopelessness that he initially described and helped him to see his own efficacy. Thus, Zai became increasingly aware of specific things he could do to improve his situation. We then emphasized the potential for him to continue to influence and even direct his own future.

Although Zai's self-reported anxiety had decreased significantly by the fifth session, we saw each other through the end of the first semester. I viewed this time together as a chance to build a reserve of strength and confidence, and Zai seemed willing and interested in doing so. My efforts to include Zai's family were largely unsuccessful. I consulted with his parents once in person and found that, like many Hmong, they did not see a need for counseling (Sue & Sue, 2003). They believed that Zai's troubles were related to Western influences. I struggled to understand their viewpoint, but I got the definite message that their grudging consent for Zai to receive counseling was a token effort to placate school authorities. I worked hard to respect their traditions and beliefs. For example, I dressed professionally, was careful to speak in a soft voice, and directed my eye contact toward Zai's father, all with the intent to communicate my respect for this family. However, in spite of this, the family was reluctant to actively collaborate in my intervention.

Zai seemed unconcerned about his parents' lack of involvement in his counseling, and at first I wondered if he was perhaps embarrassed by them or feared they would appear too traditional. However, Zai seemed to accept his parents as they were, and I believe he sensed my efforts to at least accept them if not fully understand them. Rather than feeling embarrassment, I think he instead viewed his parents' behavior as consistent with their beliefs and therefore simply a given. I knew that a shaman, not a counselor, may be a more reasonable helper in the minds of Zai's parents, and I knew that Zai's "problem" was not necessarily one for which a shaman would be consulted. Hmong traditions have specific beliefs about the origin of suffering. Often the cause is a problem of the spirit (Faderman, 1998; Fadiman, 1997; Sue & Sue, 2003). Soul loss, in particular, means that if one's soul leaves, the individual experiences physical pain. In this case, the Hmong may look to a shaman for healing. Preventing soul loss can include the ritual of tying knots in string bracelets and calling an individual's name three times in order to, in essence, keep the soul with the body. While Zai's family had consulted a shaman in the past, I understood that I would need to maintain a respectful distance regarding spiritual concerns and allow this to be addressed in a more indigenous manner.

By our last session, Zai reported feeling more optimistic about his future and said he was experiencing fewer headaches and less eye pain. He still felt frustrated with Pao but said that Pao's life was changing, too. He saw that as Pao graduated from high school, new patterns and expectations would emerge that would affect Zai, both positively and negatively. Zai's referring teacher reported that Zai seemed less distressed and was resuming his previous high level of academic and social activity.

Zai and I agreed that he would use the winter break to see how things were going and would touch base when school resumed. Our meeting in January started slowly and awkwardly. I felt a little disappointed that we were unable to connect as genuinely as we had in the fall. Zai let me know, though, that he felt "okay" about his home life. When I tried to follow our ritual from the earlier sessions he smiled, shook his head, and said, "Really—okay."

With Zai, as with most adolescents, the passage of time and normal maturation played a part in his progress. My hope from our first meeting was that Zai would be able to see the potential for change to occur and then allow it to occur. I also think our collaborative partnership, his intelligence and kindness, and my genuine regard and curiosity helped to forge an alliance that became therapeutic. In some ways, Zai exemplified the concerns of many Hmong and other adolescents in refugee families. He was drawn toward the enticing possibilities of Western culture, but loved and respected the tradition of the Hmong culture in a poignant manner that revealed the inextricable nature of his blood ties. I did not then, nor do I now, know the ideal answer to Zai's struggle. I did believe, though, that Zai's experience was worth exploring with him, and I believed in his ability to create a new niche for himself.

References

CHAN, S. (Ed.). (1994). *Hmong means free: Life in Laos and America.* Philadelphia: Temple University Press.

FADERMAN, L. (1998). *I begin my life all over.* Boston: Beacon Press.

FADIMAN, A. (1997). *The spirit catches you and you fall down.* New York: Farrar, Straus, & Giroux.

FREEMAN, J., EPSTON, D., & LOBOVITS, D. (1997). *Playful approaches to serious problems.* New York: Norton.

SUE, D. W., & SUE, D. (2003). *Counseling the culturally different: Theory and practice* (4th ed.). New York: Wiley.

V

Case Studies in Child Welfare

Every year a major newspaper carries a story about the horrific effects of child abuse and neglect and the difficulty that the social service system has in keeping children safe and free from neglect. The child welfare "system" is a major social service entity that includes efforts by public, governmental agencies at the local, state, and federal levels as well as private efforts. The child welfare system has three fundamental purposes: the protection of children, the preservation of families, and permanency planning for children in care (Petr, 1998). Clinical work within the child welfare system includes a variety of activities, such as investigation, prevention of out-of-home placement, reunification, foster care, residential group care, adoptions, and preparation for independent living.

A lot of the challenge in effective work with children and families in the child welfare system involves the broad array of skills necessary to conduct this work. For example, workers in this field may find themselves writing investigative reports, testifying in court, coordinating treatment and follow-up care plans, and working with additional social service agencies. There are also a variety of services to be provided. Most critical is a focus on the continuity of family relationships, provision of an array of services, and attention to the continuity of professional services (Downs, Moore, McFadden, & Costin, 2000). Efforts in child welfare should reflect the basic notion that it is important to maintain the child's emotional attachments. As a result, transitions and planning for the child need to consider the best interests of the child. In a family-centered manner, an array of services should be "wrapped around" the child. Services should not occur in isolation but should be properly coordinated because families in the child welfare system often benefit from support provided by services such as parent education, supportive counseling, substance abuse treatment, financial management, and so forth. Lastly, too often services have been provided without consideration for the continuity of services. As families and children transition to different services, consideration should be made for how best to plan for the change. If a child is moving from a group home setting to a foster care setting, then a planful approach should be implemented.

Child welfare services have become more complex as these "systems" attempt to respond to the demands of society by protecting vulnerable children and providing effective services to them and their families. To meet this complexity, increased collaboration between government and agencies is needed to address "failure by fragmentation," which occurs too often in this field. Practitioners are needed to learn new skills and become highly trained to meet the challenge of families and children in the child welfare system.

This section opens with a case study by Bicknell-Hentges and Lynch, in which the practitioners confront the hard truth that a child's family will never be completely "healthy"—and yet family reunification is still the best apparent option for that child. The study is a strong reminder of the importance of "starting where the client is" and of staying with that client despite some rather grueling moments of countertransference.

Next, Hunt presents a case study about a child for whom family reunification is not an option. Indeed, this study is a chronicle of the nomadic life that a child, plagued by a history of abuse and lacking any home where she has unconditional acceptance, often lives. The piece forces the reader to confront the many problems in the foster care system.

Fitts and Phillips offer a glimpse at the chaotic lives of an African American family and their culturally competent intervention with that family. The case reveals how such an approach can be effectively used to overcome client resistance and build a therapeutic relationship with clients.

Finally, Barret and Trepper deliver a study about dealing with a family living in denial of sexual abuse and how they use a multiple systems model to effect change. The study demonstrates how a practitioner may take a neutral position about the clients' denial, but not about the abuse itself.

All of the studies in this section cause the reader to reflect on the incredible challenges facing children in the child welfare system and on the resilience of these children in the face of daunting odds. The studies also remind us of the dedication of practitioners who choose to work with these children and their families despite the barriers.

References

DOWNS, S. W., MOORE, E., MCFADDEN, E. J., & COSTIN, L. B. (2000). *Child welfare and family services: Policies and practice* (6th ed.). Boston: Allyn & Bacon.

PETR, C. G. (1998). *Social work with children and their families.* New York: Oxford University Press.

Case Study 5-1

Questions for Discussion

1. How does the practitioner maintain professionalism with a client who, at first, seems "unlikable"?
2. What are some of the problems that can result from a child's placement in residential treatment? What are some potential benefits?
3. Why must the practitioner adjust her goals to work toward "good enough" parenting skills?
4. Describe the shifting power base of the Taylor family. How does the practitioner use these shifts?
5. Why doesn't the practitioner address the verbal parenting skills with this family immediately upon commencing treatment?

Helping Families with Reunification: Returning a Child to a Less-Than-Perfect Family

Lindsay Bicknell-Hentges and John Lynch

At the time I started my work as a psychologist in a residential program for youth, I had a limited understanding of the impossible task we were attempting to undertake. "We" are all of those involved in creating systems designed to temporarily and sometimes permanently replace parents. "We" are the caseworkers, the childcare workers, the therapists, the teachers, the psychiatrists—the team that tries its best to do what can never fully be accomplished: to fill the void left when a child has been removed from the care of his or her biological parents.

My early hours as a psychologist with a youth placed in residential treatment focused on the typical, although heightened, struggle to develop a therapeutic relationship. Would I pass the test of trust with someone so scarred and bruised by other adults? I stood in line behind a long series of losses, asking this child to believe that I would somehow be different—that I would not abuse and not abandon. Somewhere in this standoff, I realized the absurdity of my request of this child. "I know your mother hurt or abused you. I know you have been abandoned by your family, foster parents, caseworkers, other therapists, friends, and teachers, but you can trust me. Really, you can trust me." Despite the difficulty of developing trust with children who have internalized a deep sense of distrust, I know that I must engage in this critical struggle to even begin forming a relationship.

Over time, I began to see how the patterns on the quilt of a child's life set the stage for the struggle of trust. I came to see the limits of what I had to offer these children. I would not offer a place to come for the holidays for the rest of their life. I would not offer the love for their future children that only a grandparent can give. I would not celebrate all their birthdays. I would not offer money and shelter when a job is lost or a relationship ends badly. I was not a parent and often had no semblance of one to offer. With all the services I had at my disposal, agencies, institutions, and therapists end up being a very poor substitute for mom and dad.

Suzie Taylor came to me after these realizations and that is probably a very good thing. In my earlier and more idealistic days, I may have written off her parents as unworkable. Her family was a White, working-class family, living in a large urban area. I met her mother first.

Linda was a tough, no-nonsense, aggressive woman. She bore the look of someone who worked hard and fought her way through much of life. She brought Suzie to me after a series of escalating altercations with the law, and she very quickly let it be known that her child had few redeeming qualities. She described her 13-year-old daughter as fat and unattractive, a pathological liar, and a thief. She added emphatically, "She's always been bad." Consistent with my training, my face and body language remained neutral, but I became aware of a growing dislike for this woman who could talk so negatively about her child. Countertransference reared its ugly head as Linda cast aside all my values of how a parent should act.

Linda reported that Suzie always wanted and craved attention. She said her husband had spoiled the girl before the birth of her younger sister. Linda found fault in anyone who showed any positive feelings for her daughter. Suzie was a year behind in school, the result of her mother placing her in a "special class" because she was not "mature enough." The mother continued, scowling as she reported that Suzie and her father were both fat. She described how the two would "throw fat jabs back and forth," beginning playfully, but often deteriorating into pain and tears as the insults just went too far. "In the end, Suzie cries and calls her father a jerk. She's just too sensitive for the family she's in. In our house, we say what we mean. If you can't take it, you shouldn't play the game." Linda went on to describe her constant conflicts with Suzie about clothing. She said that Suzie wants to wear fashions that "only look good on thin people" despite her mother's attempts to get Suzie to wear black, "which is the most slimming color in the world. I'm just trying to help her out, but she won't listen to anybody. She'd rather look like a fool."

Linda finished by saying that she just could not deal with Suzie's lying and stealing anymore. She revealed that she had told Suzie the family would send her away to a residential program if her behavior did not improve, but her behavior had continued to worsen despite these threats. "We are at the point where we don't want her in the house anymore."

Just as I was becoming aware of my feelings of anger and wondering how I would ever maintain empathy for this woman, she let me get a glimpse of her pain. In a hardened and unemotional voice, Linda revealed a family history of severe alcoholism and sexual abuse. She added that she had even tried to kill herself on two separate occasions: at the age of 14 "when I didn't think my parents loved me" and again at 19 when she and her husband had broken up prior to their marriage. Linda's language was frequently peppered with strong expletives. She wasn't kidding. Wherever she was, she spoke her mind for all to hear. She could hold her own with the best of sailors.

I was still trying to analyze what I had just observed when Linda left and returned with Suzie. Suzie was a chunky girl with the awkwardness and budding acne that signals early adolescence. After the introductions, I noticed my relief as her mother left the room.

Suzie seemed somewhat guarded and anxious when her mother brought her into my office. Clearly aware of the negative report her mother had just given me, she studied me to see if I would give her a chance. Her face began to relax as I asked her to share her own version of her pain. She spoke slowly at first, pulling her hair forward to cover her face.

Suzie reported that she began to have increasing conflict at home after entering middle school. She described how she felt more pressure in her new school and looked at the floor as she admitted that other youth teased her and called her "gay." Suzie also talked about how at times she is left with the responsibility of caring for her younger sister after school. Despite her desire and attempts to nurture this child, she was ill equipped for this responsibility. Suzie admitted her unsuccessful struggles to maintain authority, even adding that her younger sister had once slapped her in the face while chanting, "You can't make me."

I noted Suzie's sadness and questioned whether she had ever thought about hurting herself or that life was not worth living. She seemed sincere when she denied wanting to hurt herself, but she hesitated as she admitted that she sometimes had thoughts of stabbing herself when "things go wrong." Her voice cracked, and suddenly she sounded like a little girl as she said that she gets blamed for *everything* that goes wrong. Suzie looked me in the eye and paused. A single tear rolled down her cheek as she said, "After my sister was born, Mom mostly paid attention to her. I used to feel close to my father, but not anymore. I feel like I don't belong in that family. I don't feel loved anymore, but I used to. I stopped when we started talking about me leaving that family. . . . I started getting more of an attitude after going to a different school. The kids treat me bad. They make fun of me. I feel angry and hurt all of the time."

Suzie struggled to regain her composure as she talked. As I gave her the basic reflective listening responses, her hunger for validation became very apparent. She hung on every "I hear you." I felt like it had been a long time since someone had listened to this child. Our first session was nothing remarkable, but Suzie was hooked. Leaving me was difficult, and I felt a twinge of guilt sending her out to her mother. As I closed my office door, I could hear Linda yelling long after she left the building. The mother's hostile voice tone and cutting words stayed with me for much of the day.

Residential Treatment as Punishment

Residential treatment is not my favored intervention in family therapy. Removing children from their family creates new problems of its own, even opening up the possibility of the family system reorganizing without the child. However, Suzie was quickly swept into a group home right after our first session. As her mother had said, the family was fed up with Suzie's behavior, and the stage was set for failure. Linda was clearly convinced that her unruly daughter could not remain at home. I guess none of my "profound" interventions in my half hour with Linda had altered that opinion. Linda called and left the message that Suzie was no longer living at home. I don't think that I imagined the "I told you so" quality in her voice. She seemed almost vindicated that our eleventh-hour intervention had not been successful. "She may have had you snowed, but I know this girl. She's a liar and a thief." Clearly, the mother saw residential treatment as an appropriate, but long overdue punishment for Suzie.

With Suzie now out of the home, I found myself hoping for a quick reunification at best. I decided that the optimal strategy was to initially work with Suzie alone and later add the family work. I viewed her problematic behaviors as driven both by her extremely low self-esteem and rejection by her peers as well as the result of some fairly toxic family dynamics. In fact, I saw Suzie as quite resilient. Her problems had not escalated until her assaults came from both home and school. She desperately needed a place of respite to lick her wounds and discover the parts of herself that even she could like. Individual sessions with Suzie were critical because I doubted that I could provide any "safe haven" in the family sessions.

Our individual work was enjoyable, rewarding, and even fun. She came eagerly to sessions as I played the "good mother" role. I listened and supported her while she talked about her feelings as she adjusted to group home living and separation from her family. At first, she expressed the feelings of sadness and shame that she felt when "kicked out" of her family. However, over time, feelings of anger and resentment began to surface in her pain. She rather quickly adjusted to her residential setting, winning the affection of the home staff. Suzie began to realize that not everyone agreed with her family's view that she was "bad and hopeless." She expressed feelings of hope and her self-esteem lifted. She was evaluated at school, and a learning disability was identified. With appropriate support and school interventions, she started performing well academically. She now found herself in the foreign role of the perfect student and the favored resident in the home.

Each week Suzie was eager to come and tell me about her successes of the week. She became a top performer on the basketball team. Through sports and exercise, she grew less critical of her body. She quickly won more freedom and privileges, the result of her impeccable behavior in the group home. Our individual time was fulfilling as I watched Suzie succeed and prepared her for the family sessions. We worked on learning how to respond differently and less reactively to the negative triggers of family members, exploring how to avoid or cope with the "land mines" that abounded in the family territory. For example, she was learning to respond differently to remarks about her weight or clothing by breaking her family's toxic rules of engagement. She learned to ignore and not respond to the insults and became more focused on her accomplishments at school and the group home.

The family sessions were another matter. I usually feel a little guilty when I cringe at the thought of a client. Not many clients have an aversive effect on me, but Linda was adept at saying things that all psychologists know you should never say. As I explored the possible goals of my work with this family, I knew that I wanted this mother to change. I wanted her to become nurturing and validating, much less critical, and sensitive and supportive to her daughter. I also knew that this was not going to happen. My lofty goals would have set everyone up for failure, including me, so I tried to go for "What's the best you could expect in this situation?"

I set my goals for "good enough" parenting so that Suzie could be successfully returned home. I supported this goal by bolstering Suzie's resilience and helping her learn more adaptive ways of voicing her pain in the family, rather than lying and stealing. I walked a tightrope of helping her parents hear their daughter without igniting the defensiveness that was waiting to pounce on any perceived attack on their parenting. After all, Linda truly believed that the only problem in the family was Suzie.

I entered each family session delicately. Tipping the balance in such a polarized system could easily lead to the family withdrawing from treatment, leaving Suzie to languish in residential care. I practiced my positive reframes like mantras before every session, knowing that every little push on the mother would have to be balanced with many strokes.

I purposefully set up family sessions on the weekends when Suzie was on home passes with her family. I did not want these sessions to take place in the residential setting, but in my office where we would hopefully continue working after her return home. For the first session, I knew the family had entered the building when their loud arguments pierced my closed office door. I took a breath and invited the angry mob into my office.

I guess it should not have surprised me, but the first family argument I observed was about food. Suzie had been given a bag of candy by the staff of her group home. Family members went for blood when she refused to share it. I watched with a strange mixture of amazement, horror, and amusement as each person took shots in a very practiced choreography of family warfare, completely unhampered by the presence of their family therapist in the room.

My first tentative words in the family session were to encourage Suzie to share her food. To my surprise, she not only refused, but also clearly flaunted every bite by smacking her lips. Aware of my impotence in the face of the powerful family system at that point, I rather lamely suggested that no more food be brought into the sessions. I then quickly tried to regain some semblance of control by distracting everyone with introductions. Luckily for me, the family cooperated and filled me in on the daily comings and goings in the Taylor household.

Suzie's father was a large man who presented as depressed and rather disheveled. He wore a shirt that was a size too small, which failed to completely cover the belly that hung well over his belt. He introduced himself as Jimmy. I immediately felt empathy for this beaten man, who appeared to be no match for his feisty wife. He told me that his current job was stocking products in a warehouse owned by a relative. He added that he had been previously employed in a computer service company and had changed to his new job after promises of more money and prestige. Instead, he had been relegated to lifting boxes and driving forklifts while taking a significant cut in pay. Adding to his obvious shame, his wife chimed in about how much less money he was now making and how she was having to work longer hours waiting tables to try and make up for the loss.

Next, Linda introduced her youngest daughter, Mary, as her "good" daughter. Mary was a frail nine-year-old who sat through every family session looking angelic and yet connected to her older sister. Mary said that her favorite subject was reading. She appeared sad as she talked about missing her sister very much.

The voice of empathy for Suzie seemed to stimulate Linda. She sat on the edge of her seat and began cursing and complaining loudly about how Suzie was being treated in the group home. At first, I expected concern for Suzie's well-being. However, as she continued I realized that her complaints centered on the lack of a jail-like environment. Clearly, she did not think that Suzie was being punished enough. She said that she was receiving entirely too much freedom, being fed too much, and being treated too nicely.

I nodded sympathetically and began concluding the session by reviewing the time and structure of future sessions. I set the stage for ongoing discussions regarding home visits, Suzie's behavior in the group home, and lightly warned the family that we would approach the issue of how such a strong and committed family could end up in this painful situation. As I spoke, I noticed that the father appeared sad. In contrast, the mother appeared rather numb to her daughter, as if she had been distancing herself from this child for quite some time. I ended the session by stating that Suzie would be coming on home passes every weekend and that we would discuss these visits at length during our weekly sessions. Before the family had time to protest, I led them out of the room and said good-bye.

After the session, I thought about the power of the Taylor family system. Suzie stood entrenched in the "identified patient" role and triangulated in her parents' struggle for power. Historically, Suzie had been aligned with her dad, who at times defended her against her mother's attacks. However, the dad's power in the family had become depleted after his recent job change and the resulting depression that lingered afterward. As her dad's position shifted, Suzie lost her ally, and her behavior started a downward spiral. Heightened by the peer rejection she was experiencing at school, she began to escalate behaviors that assured rejection at home as well. Unfortunately, the threats to remove her from the home only escalated the problems further and Suzie was left banished and alone, the repository of all the pain and dysfunction in her family.

My goal initially was to stop the centrifugal force that was sending Suzie out into an orbit removed from her family system. I wanted to ensure continued visits in the home to block the family from stabilizing into a newly reorganized equilibrium that did not include Suzie. I also wanted to help Suzie and her family alter some of their more dysfunctional interactions and replace them with more adaptive problem-solving patterns that were less toxic. Accomplishing all this while maintaining a relationship with everyone in this extremely polarized system was quite a challenge. Although Suzie's mother was a champion at creating adversity, I kept in my mind how Suzie's words had echoed her mother's experience when she had first attempted suicide: "I thought my parents didn't love me." Despite Linda's tough and abrasive veneer, I knew I was dealing with two people who shared a desperate need for love and validation from their families. In some way, Suzie's emotional abandonment by her family replicated Linda's own family dynamics during her adolescence.

To Return or Not to Return: That Is the Question

In all of my experiences with family reunification, Suzie's parents were some of the most resistant to accepting a goal of return home. In the early stages of therapy, I could only broach the subject of returning Suzie home with the greatest care, bracing myself for the ensuing attack. The mere mention of the subject would always initiate a tirade from mother with nodding support from the father, "You don't know her. She's just faking it. She just wants to come home. She'll do the same thing when she gets home. Remember, she's a liar."

However, this subject was unavoidable. As much as it perturbed her mother, Suzie was doing very well in all aspects of her life in the group home. I noticed a particular pattern in the sessions. Whenever I said something good about Suzie, her mother jumped in quickly to discredit and attack me as if Suzie's new success represented an assault on her parenting. Fortunately, my years in working with angry, resistant adolescents have taught me how to take such attacks in the manner of a judo master. I duck under attackers and let their words roll off my back; then I interpret their need to take me down. This method works, at least most of the time, although a well-placed blow from Linda could still leave me stinging as I searched for that perfect interpretation.

In the dance of the family therapy, one of my challenges was helping the parents shift from their rigid stance that Suzie was the problem and still be able to save face. The mother in particular had invested so much energy into convincing me (and anyone else within hearing distance—a block or two) that Suzie was beyond hope. Injecting hope for Suzie was perceived as a threat and lack of validation, as well as manipulation by the "liar."

Fortunately, I was helped by something totally beyond my control. I would like to say that the therapy helped this happen, and perhaps it did, but Jimmy got a new job. Jimmy got a great job. He got the job of his life, with high status and big bucks. As Jimmy began to feel good about himself, he shifted from depression and hopelessness to a position of hope. And I obtained an ally. He began to get in touch with his feelings surrounding the loss of his daughter, even crying in one session at the thought of leaving his daughter in a group home with strangers. He was more open to exposing a vulnerable side of himself. In the sessions, he began to recall memories of fonder times with his daughter. As the mother rolled her eyes and said how he spoiled Suzie, he would reminisce about touching moments when he relished Suzie's smile and giggles. He also began to carefully review the weekend visits, attempting to highlight gains and successes, instead of problems. Over time, he became courageous in reporting how Suzie had completed her chores and other responsibilities as well as spent time with him on the computer. As his relationship with Suzie was revived, he finally was able to take the stand that he wanted his daughter back home.

Although Linda tenaciously resisted this shift, she was more receptive to another focus of the family work—the recognition that the parents had to start taking care of each other. To strengthen and improve the boundaries around the parental subsystem, the mother and father were encouraged to revisit the early years in their relationship and how they had cared for each other. They started spending time together, going out alone. With the father's lifted spirits and the rejuvenation of the marital relationship, Suzie slowly became less of a threat to her mother. Linda continued to warn everyone that Suzie was just manipulating and would return to her old tricks in no time, but her protests were becoming shorter and less intense. More session time was being spent on productive goals such as developing less toxic styles of dealing with conflict and understanding Suzie's behavior in a developmental context.

The Taylor family stands as one of the liveliest families I have had the pleasure to work with. Each week, the entire family raced into my office. Even the adults would practically push me out of the way as they jumped into their favorite chairs before anyone else could claim them. On one occasion, I had to ask the father to give up Suzie's favorite chair before war was declared and precious session time was wasted. The family most often expressed their commitment and feelings for each other through intensity and engagement in sarcastic bantering. The trouble is that the intensity too often hit the boiling point and words that started out as funny ended up causing pain. I tried to address this pattern by setting rules that outlawed name calling in sessions. I also highlighted their tendency to hurt each other by processing in-session interactions. However, at times when I was just preparing to block family interactions that were coming close to hurtful, the family would burst into laughter as everyone (but me) shared in the great humor of the moment.

Another interesting facet of working with the Taylor family was the sequencing of goals. Given the intense polarization in the family, goals that would typically be addressed first were left until relationships with all family members were firmly established. This reverse ordering of the goals meant that one of the last issues to be addressed was one of the most salient—the verbal parenting style in the family. Had I attempted to discuss how Linda spoke to her daughter in the early sessions, the family would not have been able to hear me and would probably have left therapy. The pull to immediately address such a screaming goal is strong, but families and individual clients can only start where they are. Trying to move too far, too fast only leads to frustration and failure. Thus, with the Taylors, I had to keep the focus on the next attainable goals with ongoing, carefully placed hints of coming attractions subtly added.

There's No Place Like Home (or Be Careful What You Wish For)

Over time, Suzie's goal became to return home. I must address my ambivalence regarding this goal and my fight with the staff in her group home. As so often happens, the staff that cared for Suzie became attached to her. They also carried their share of verbal bumps and bruises from sparring with Linda. As I mentioned before, Linda does not mince words. At many points along the way, she voiced her criticism of the group home and her negative descriptions of Suzie. The staff became protective of the youth and recommended that she not be returned home.

I understood this protectiveness. I shared it at times when Linda was at her fighting best. One particular session stands out in which Linda showed no mercy. The subject at hand was Suzie's cigarette smoking. Linda railed and railed about the insolence of this girl for smoking cigarettes in direct disobedience of her mother. However, Linda failed to notice the irony that while she attacked her daughter, I watched with some amusement as the pack of cigarettes rolled in the sleeve of her T-shirt moved unsteadily with each emphatic curse, not to mention the strong smell of cigarette smoke that traveled with her. I could not help but wonder what she would say if the pack fell from her sleeve as she accosted her daughter about smoking.

In these moments, I sometimes wondered if I was sane, sending this child home to a mother who was a major work in progress at best. Yet I also had watched as Linda had fought for her daughter as hard as she fought against her. Whenever she did feel that her child had been wronged, she took on that fight with the intensity of a bear protecting her cubs. In individual sessions, Linda was able to admit her identification with Suzie's pain as she remembered her own suicidal adolescence. She clearly loved her child, and the whole family had shown up week after week for an often-uncomfortable hour with me. Linda even shocked me by bringing her two adult sons to see me at points when they were in crisis. Despite her surface resistance, Linda demonstrated a deep commitment to her child and a belief in therapy that she worked to keep well hidden.

I also looked to the father and his growth and improved ability to be an advocate for his daughter. I listened to Suzie, who voiced her desire to return home with increasing intensity as time passed. What else did I have to offer her—residential care until she graduated? Or had we reached the point of "good enough" in her family? These questions were not all answered, but the time had come to at least try to return her home.

In our family sessions, I attempted to increase the odds for a successful and stable return home. We identified the rules for the home, potential problems, and developed plans for handling the most likely conflicts. Critical linkages were made with the school to ensure that appropriate academic resources were in place. In our individual sessions, I worked with Suzie on what she would say to her friends about where she had been for the past year. She felt most comfortable telling peers that her parents had sent her away to a boarding school. We also explored her feelings of loss about leaving people she now cared for and her fears about maintaining success at home. We developed strategies to help Suzie spend less time at home, such as obtaining a job and spending time with friends. As with all terminations, we reviewed the progress and gains that had been made and explored what else needed to be accomplished and monitored. I tried to empower Suzie and her parents by reviewing their accomplishments, although Linda never fully came on board with the belief that Suzie would succeed.

In our last individual session, Suzie was pensive and suggested that we draw a picture. She led the project as we drew a person walking over a covered bridge from one side of a river to another. I chose not to interpret because she appeared unaware of the symbolism, but we drew the transition together as she packed her bags and said goodbye. I reminded her that I would continue seeing her. Because our family sessions were held near their home, I was able to make this transition with them and offer support in the restabilization of the family system. Finally, we took our best shot and Suzie went home. Unlike her crisis when coming into the group home, Suzie was finally leaving because she had done well.

Because I'm putting this in writing, I would like to say that everything went perfectly after returning Suzie home. However, my years in family therapy have taught me otherwise. Suzie has remained at home and is about to graduate from high school. Her first year home was her most successful; she made the basketball team and found peer acceptance in her school. Her relationship with her parents ebbed and flowed as with most adolescents, but I discovered rather quickly after each attempt at terminating therapy that the family required periodic booster shots with me to maintain stability. One incident or another would happen and I would receive a call. In each case, a few sessions would help restabilize the family for a period of time, until the next incident occurred. Just as her father's new job was a real positive breakthrough, one of Suzie's biggest blows after returning home occurred when she did not make the basketball team. Her self-esteem plummeted, and she became more vulnerable to the ambient toxicity at home. (No, it was not totally cured!) She gravitated to a negative peer group for validation and was arrested for vandalism.

The resulting sequence of events were some of my most memorable as a clinician. Of course, Linda called me immediately after Suzie was arrested. I contacted the business involved and explained that she was in therapy and responding well to treatment. The manager then agreed to drop charges, although it was against store policy. Feeling relieved, I thought the matter was solved and scheduled a session. However, in the meantime, Linda called the manager to protest that her daughter had been questioned without a parent or attorney present. Apparently, in her usual adversarial style, she had so angered the manager in this conversation that he reinstated charges and tried to get other businesses in the complex to join him in pressing additional charges. Suzie ended up on probation. Linda can be the kind of person you do not want fighting against you *or* for you.

We reinitiated therapy and addressed the issues that pulled Suzie in this self-destructive cycle once again. In our ensuing brief work together, we revisited the pattern. Suzie remembered that when she feels insecure and threatened, she wants to behave in a way that ensures acceptance and security. However, the slightest hint that she is the family problem or is not successful overwhelms her with fear, sadness, and anger. These intense feelings can then drive her into the very behaviors that jeopardize her security and acceptance, initiating a vicious cycle in which the more she fears rejection, the more she behaves in a manner that leads to rejection. We recognized that although she has never attempted suicide like her mother, Suzie's response to rejection is clearly just as self-destructive.

After Suzie left our last (dare I say final) session, I revisited the question of her return home. I realize that her fragility in that environment requires at least periodic external support. I hope that she can graduate without another incident and I wish that the words I've said to her would echo in her head at least half as strongly as her mother's.

Case Study 5-2

Questions for Discussion
1. How does the "conditional" acceptance of the client, contingent on her behavior with a new family, set her up for failure?
2. Discuss the difficulties of finding placements for teenage girls in need of therapeutic, long-term living arrangements.
3. How are client problems potentially exacerbated by multilevel system ineffectiveness?
4. What challenges are present in comprehensive permanency planning?
5. Explore the differences and similarities in mental health versus juvenile corrections approaches.

Nothing Left to Lose: Growing Up in Foster Care

Debbie Hunt

Karen set the scene for our first meeting by hiding under a desk at the shelter where she was living. Although I saw her peering out at me mischievously, I was startled when she popped out. In spite of a broad smile and striking eyes set off by dark brown skin, she looked like a very young boy because her hair was shaved nearly to the scalp. As I looked at her, I recalled a note in the case record stating that her mother recently cut her hair as punishment.

Karen asked me if I would like to go out on the patio. Because a goal of my first contact was to establish personal rapport, I let her lead the way. For the next 45 minutes, I attempted to engage her by asking a series of casual questions, leading to more specific comments about the case. The case of maltreatment and need for out-home-care was well established, so my job was not to interview Karen, but to gauge her understanding of the situation and begin to assess her needs.

Karen occasionally perched in a chair next to me, but spent most of her time dashing back and forth. In spite of this level of activity, I sensed that she, like most children, wanted to know what her immediate future held. Especially in the early stages of case planning, caregivers are either cautious or uninformed; therefore, many children rely on their case managers to discuss future plans and time frames. While our interaction was punctuated by many interruptions such as, "I can do a cartwheel, want to see?" or "I'll go get my backpack," I thought Karen's behavior of leaving and returning signaled interest, opposed by anxiety, in our interaction.

This is my recollection of the first contact I had with Karen in the 5 years I served as her child protective services case manager. At the age of 9, Karen was assigned to the caseload of children for whom I provided care, custody, and control on behalf of the child welfare agency and the juvenile court. Karen's case was based on serious allegations of neglect and emotional abuse. Karen's teacher notified child protective services when Karen came to school with a handwritten note taped to her shirt. The note labeled her as "stupid" for ruining a brand-new shirt by spilling bleach on it. Karen's mother had instructed her to display the note all day. At the same time, Karen's older brother was observed to have healing scabs on his upper arms and back. An investigation revealed that the children's mother resorted to a number of deliberately extreme punishment measures, including withholding food, serving the same portions of uneaten food day after day, beating the male child with an electrical cord because he asked other children at school for food, forcing the children to sleep on the bathroom floor without blankets, plus other harmful and humiliating acts.

A child protective services investigator attempted to prevent removal of the children by implementing a program of family preservation services. Within days, Karen brought another note to school, authored by her mother. This note, written to the children, indicated that they needed to cooperate and "toe the line." She also wrote that she would kill herself if her children were removed. Child protective services staff removed the children and requested an emergency mental health evaluation of the mother.

Karen's mother briefly worked with our agency toward a plan of reunification, the standard starting point for all children placed out of the home. However, barriers to reunification in the form of the mother's subsequent incarceration (pursuant to this maltreatment) and unwillingness to resume a parental role led her to eventually relinquish her parental rights. While Karen is a special person, she is, perhaps more important, representative of countless children whose journey through foster care and whose quest for a permanent home is complicated, confusing, and painful for themselves and their advocates.

One problem, which emerged immediately and continued indefinitely, was the challenge of piecing together an accurate social history of these children. Karen and her older brother, then ages 9 and 12, lived with their mother, stepfather, and two younger half-siblings for only 1 year. Before that, relatives in another state had raised them. In fact, their mother reportedly did not know that her children were going to join her household until they arrived on her doorstep one evening. Karen's mother explained the extreme nature of her parenting as an attempt to instill previously lacking discipline in the children. She expressed concern that they were wild and out of control, exhibiting many bad habits that she attributed to inner-city Black culture. She, herself, cultivated a somewhat affected British accent and the mannerisms of a highly educated, professional woman. She shunned the street slang, rap music, and fashion trends her children copied and craved. She reported that her own mother was unable to handle the children any longer, in part due to behavior problems and in part due to marital problems. Her responses to the question of why her mother was cast in the role of long-term caregiver were vague. She described herself as a mother intent on the goal of pursuing an education and establishing a career to create a more stable home before she sent for her children. This perspective did not seem to be congruent with the report of her mother turning to a private detective to find her, and having done so, delivering the children without notice.

Karen's mother was haughty and defensive with me, frequently finding fault with my work and the agency's procedures. I was used to this. What I never became used to, what made even a simple conversation difficult, and what would have served as a barrier to reunification was the indifference this woman showed her older children—in sharp contrast to the perfectly scripted sugary affection she showered on her younger children. She never initiated conversation about her older children. When she answered questions about them, she was cool and aloof, reporting events and responses in a detached manner. During my early contacts with Karen and her brother, they asked about her with tears rolling down their faces. They asked me to arrange visits and even shyly suggested their own version of a reunification plan. Consistently, they sought out ways to refute and refuse to acknowledge the messages of rejection I was forced to deliver. Karen literally covered her ears and hid her face when I talked about her mother. As a result of my growing alliance with her children, I found the mother's lack of empathy and her ability to rationalize her attitude completely unnerving and often infuriating.

The children initially reported that they were subjected to physical abuse while in the care of relatives, but their mother flatly rejected this notion, saying that they were lying because their grandmother denied hurting them. The mother was unable to acknowledge the discrepancy between her own victimization and subsequently leaving her children in the same abusive environment. The children revealed little else about the details of their lives before they came to live with their mother.

The extended family was somewhat standoffish and alienated from both the mother and children. Although my agency expected me to contact and assess known relatives for placement or social support, I was unable to establish an effective liaison with Karen's maternal relatives. When reached by phone, the grandmother and great-grandmother were polite, but somewhat vague and unable to provide details of their social history. While they knew the children were in foster care, they did not ask about plans for the children. We sometimes consider the level of initiative of the family as a factor in placement decisions, and I prefer situations in which relatives ask, even demand, to be involved in decisions regarding their kin. Though I did not confront them about this, I got the distinct impression they wished to avoid the subject for fear we would pressure them to take the children back.

I had very little hope for reunification. Not only was the family history muddled, but time and separation had also hardened the mother's heart. I tried to make her children real to her by telling her about their desire to see her, reminding her of their strengths, and regaling her with their accomplishments. A few times she was able to let down her guard, but only momentarily. I tried to prod her by telling her the children needed her—to embrace them, to explain what happened, to say good-bye. I attempted to explore what emotional support she could offer them as they began to re-envision, reconfigure, and resculpt their place in the world. While she consistently refused contact during her incarceration, Karen's mother did make an attempt to provide what she could conceptualize as closure: She wrote letters, attended therapy, and prepared for good-bye sessions. Karen prepared to meet with her mother in therapeutic visitation.

Ultimately, we were unable to provide the support that Karen must have needed to face her mother. She deliberately sabotaged transportation arrangements and avoided the visits.

Given the apparent roadblocks to reunification, a practical long-term strategy for Karen was to identify a family with whom she could be placed, and once the relationship was secure, take legal steps toward permanency through guardianship or adoption. I also thought Karen's ability to accept a new family setting would depend on resolving the grief and confusion accompanying her abandonment. Karen's psychological profile was not particularly remarkable given what is typical of foster children. She was observed to be anxious and endorsed a history of abuse and abandonment. Over time and multiple disruptions in care, Karen's list of diagnoses grew to include anxiety disorder, attention deficit disorder, oppositional defiant disorder, conduct disorder, and various rule-out diagnoses such as post-traumatic stress disorder and attachment disorder. Initially, however, she was relatively young, physically healthy, engaging, and attractive. While her behavior was already demanding, she had enough going for her that it was tempting to describe her as impish or mischievous and hope that she could settle into a routine with a substitute family chosen from the foster care population.

We placed Karen with four different families. The first was chosen in a routine fashion: A family had an opening for a child matching her profile, and both the family and Karen were open to the placement. After a short honeymoon, Karen became increasingly defiant. When Karen moved to the home, an older female foster child lived there and her biological brother soon joined her. Although Karen never overtly acknowledged it, I felt that this constant reminder of her own siblings' absence tormented her. The foster sibling set of three soon disintegrated into a rivalry of two against one, with Karen as the underdog. She put a tremendous amount of energy into negative attention-getting strategies. The foster parents were average, kind-hearted people who were puzzled when Karen consistently chose the difficult course instead of equally available reasonable and pleasant options. They did not have strong behavior management skills and frequently resorted to bribes instead of discipline. A therapist visited the family home and attempted to implement a behavior management plan, but neither Karen nor the foster parents were able to benefit in the short term. When the conflicts centering on Karen threatened to disrupt a planned family vacation, the foster family began to reconsider their commitment to her care. To a kid like Karen, this type of discussion signals impending rejection, and she pulled out all the stops to bring the placement to a swift and dramatic end.

Every time a kid "disrupts," the scenario is virtually the same: The caseworker calls for an emergency placement (often shelter) and takes the client to the facility. This became a familiar routine for Karen and I. She was always cheerful, pleasant, and playful. Moving was not hard or unexpected for her. Over time, the sequence and timing of placements blur, but the pattern was the same. Every caseworker knows that important counseling opportunities occur in the car while driving from place to place. During these trips, I tried to help Karen clarify the reasons for the placement disruption. She responded as if the problems she encountered were based on idiosyncrasies of others: the staff or parents were mean, rules were too strict or unreasonable, other kids were annoying, and so on. According to her rationale, these factors were no longer relevant when she left one placement for another. I expressed the desire to find a comfortable, permanent place for her to live, and Karen endorsed that idea. She also quickly learned to verbalize a commitment to getting along with peers, treating adults with respect, and expressing her anger in acceptable ways. Arriving at the new placement, we would unload her things and go through the motions of starting all over again. After a few years and several of these trips, I told Karen that I thought of her as a nomad and suggested that she was more comfortable with the habit of moving from place to place than she was with the notion of staying put. She laughed, but her expression suggested no argument.

We chose the second, third, and fourth foster placements with greater consideration. In consultation with multidisciplinary teams in protective services and behavioral health, we narrowed down the likely candidates to single, African American women who were experienced, who would be apprised of Karen's reactions, and who were seen as generally unflappable. Some of the homes included other children, one of whom was Karen's biological brother, and at least one home included no other children. Although we always included an array of wrap-around services to support Karen in her placement, we also tried to place Karen in established therapeutic family programs— all of which had openings for troubled children, but none of which were willing to take a chance with Karen. As Karen's list of failed placements grew, so did her repertoire of oppositional behaviors, making it difficult to convince anyone to work with her.

During placement interviews and intake appointments, every staff person and foster parent clearly stated that Karen's welcome was contingent on her behavior. Although this was a common—and even reasonable—expectation, this approach was a setup for failure for a kid so skittish about commitment and accustomed to rejection. Only kids in the system who have already lost everything are asked to measure up to a standard of behavior before they can gain permanent status in a replacement family or group setting. Most kids whose home lives are not disrupted believe that their status in a family is unconditional and secure. Children raised in a single-family setting never receive the message "You can only stay with us if you behave . . . if you are good enough." Foster children never stop hearing it.

With each new campaign for placement and treatment, I became somewhat more determined to find the right balance for Karen. One of my unsuccessful crusades involved identifying and coaching potential caregivers to consider placement *only* if they could do so from a position of a genuine, up-front commitment to unconditional acceptance. I felt that if they could offer this to Karen, there was a chance she would eventually feel safe enough to reciprocate. I especially hoped to help them temper their expectations that she would (or could) meet them halfway in the early stages of the relationship. Although caregivers and their professional liaisons acknowledged this position, only a minority endorsed or embraced it.

I also looked for individuals in Karen's natural support system, such as mentors, teachers, and volunteers who had already formed the basis for a social relationship and who might be amenable to moving toward the caregiving role. While this was a promising avenue of recruitment, it also proved to be exceedingly risky and heartbreaking for Karen. Karen was an immensely appealing young girl whose overtures toward relationships were compelling for a variety of people. Unfortunately, no one was able to withstand the intensity of Karen's testing and self-sabotaging behavior once she had close contact or placement with a family. One such attempted placement started out at the insistence of a wonderfully loving woman who had an orientation to child welfare and troubled children. She had children of her own, each of whom supported their mother's decision to care for Karen. However, after a short time, Karen's acting out in school and at home became so continuous and intense that the stress of daily conflict wore on this caregiver. She soon came to view her choices as limited to helping Karen or maintaining other family, professional, and community commitments. Karen left her home the day after Christmas.

That was Karen's last family placement. Even with the tools of professional recruitment on the Internet, in the newspaper, and across county and state lines, we have not found or contacted any parental candidates. Karen is, understandably, loathe to try again. And I also found myself holding people who were eager to engage with Karen at an arm's length. Was I protecting her from further abandonment or blocking opportunities?

As her case manager, I was expected to visit Karen wherever she lived at least once a month. During these contacts, we usually started with small talk and details of daily life before I tried to steer the conversation to a dialogue regarding longer-term planning. After this last failed family placement, Karen was her usual sarcastic, playful self. She chatted amiably as long as we avoided serious discussion. When I asked her to tell me how she wanted to proceed with finding a home, she said she wanted to live with Stacey, a former foster parent. She said, "If I could, I would wave a magic wand and it would just be me and Stacey." When I suggested looking for another family, Karen became angry, rejecting any further recruiting efforts. She scoffed at the idea of being on display for strangers, even if another person like Stacey was among those strangers. She stormed off, shouting, "Why should I tell you anything; it doesn't matter what I say. You make bad choices!"

Karen's ability and desire to stay in one facility only deteriorated with time. Although she maintained a therapeutic group home placement for over a year, during peak periods of disruptiveness, it was a relief just to find a place for her to sleep. She was a member of a hard-to-place group—teenage girls in need of scarce therapeutic placement. One facility reported that Karen's roommate camped out in the living room because Karen intimidated her. More than one shelter director told me that his or her staff would resign if Karen returned. How did this child evoke such an intense response? She wasn't incredibly sullen or menacing, nor was her behavior particularly dangerous or criminal. It boiled down to this: Karen disrupted the milieu. She became adept at sensing stress or vulnerability and tweaked it to create chaos in a group setting. This was not difficult for an astute adolescent who was tuned in to the distress of her peers and aware of inexperienced staff. Karen seemed to view these situations as powder kegs and lit the fuses.

The relatively individual and personal struggle of negotiating placement and treatment for Karen was suspended when an exasperated juvenile court, probation department, mental health agency, and child welfare program agreed to place Karen in residential treatment. She was, at least superficially, accepting of this decision, and cost-containment forces in the system did not press for a quick remedy or short course of treatment. I advocated for this placement, not because I thought it was a panacea, but because it was the last opportunity for treatment for a child whose incorrigibility places her on the brink of long-term incarceration in the juvenile corrections system.

I often mull over this case, wondering what approaches would have produced a better intermediate outcome. Karen's future is still unfolding—we don't know yet if risk factors or resiliency factors will prevail. We have the resources to ensure that Karen is physically safe and grows to adulthood in the foster care system. We don't have the resources, or were not able to mobilize them, to help her feel that she *belongs*. I worry about Karen and countless others in foster care whose future relationships may be jeopardized by this void.

Case Study 5-3

Questions for Discussion

1. What are the four guiding principles of NTU? What are the five therapeutic stages?
2. What are the strengths of the B family?
3. How does the practitioner incorporate ritual into the harmony stage? What effect does this seem to have on the clients?
4. How does Mr. B react when the practitioner chooses to initiate sessions without him present? How is his resistance overcome?
5. How is NTU an Afrocentric approach to therapeutic foster care?

An NTU Afrocentric Approach to Therapeutic Foster Care

Peter Fitts and Frederick B. Phillips

Therapeutic foster care differs significantly from "regular" or "traditional" foster care due to the intense emotional and physical needs of the children placed in care. Therapeutic foster care requires providers to selectively recruit, train, and license treatment parents who are selected based on their ability to provide a safe, nurturing, and supportive environment for children's emotional and physical needs. In addition, they must have a functional understanding of emotional disorders as they become integral components of the treatment team. People selected to serve as treatment parents must complete extensive background clearances and undergo significant training in parenting emotionally disturbed or medically fragile children. Clinicians must be mindful of the importance of providing services not only to foster children, but also to foster parents, biological parents, extended family members, schools, and referring agencies.

The delivery of services to families and children can often be very challenging based on the issues inherent in any family or individual. The issues for children placed in therapeutic foster care and traditional foster care may be similar, but the dynamics for each family can vary significantly. At times, clinicians and referring agencies fall into having "common sense" expectations that the services offered to families and youth should be received willingly and without conflict. If families appear to not be gracious or thankful for services, the result can be that clinicians, referring workers, and the larger client system may eventually develop an unhealthy combative alliance or negative perception of the family. The model of therapeutic foster care that is illustrated in this case study is called NTU (pronounced "in-to") psychotherapy, which was developed at Progressive Life Center in Washington, DC. NTU is a culturally sensitive and spiritually based approach to service delivery. The model consists of four principles that serve as a framework of healing: harmony, balance, authenticity, and interconnectedness (Phillips, 1990). The NTU principles present a context in which traditional Western approaches are applied. The NTU therapeutic model has been effective in assisting families and children residing in foster care to effectively reach permanency goals (Phillips & Gregory, 1997), and the NTU therapeutic model is holistic and universal. It is holistic in the way it emphasizes the importance of and connection between the mind, body, emotions, and spirit (Phillips, 1998). It is universal in that it has applicability to all cultures, although it is grounded in an African worldview. The following case study involves members of the B family and illustrates how the NTU model of intervention was effectively utilized. The therapeutic phases of NTU unfold in five intertwined and overlapping stages: harmony, awareness, authenticity, alignment, and synthesis. Each of these stages is illuminated in the following discussion of the B family.

The Family

The B family had a long and stormy relationship with the local department of social services. The family consisted of five children, ages 14, 12, 8, 4, and 2, the biological mother, and the stepfather. The B family came to the attention of the department of social services after the stepfather had severely beaten the three older children with a plastic plumbing pipe for lying about the eldest child's blood sugar, in addition to other incidents that were assessed to be emotional abuse in the eyes of the department of social services. Workers within the local department had described the B family as being difficult to serve due to the stepfather's angry disposition, the mother's tendency to acquiesce to Mr. B's wishes and behaviors, and her failure to protect her children. In essence, the local social services staff was angry with the parents and was hesitant to interact with Mr. B due to his outspoken nature, his strong advocacy to keep his family together, and his view that the department lacked integrity. Initial assessments conducted by independent psychologists found the B children to be very articulate, intelligent, and academically on target. The program psychiatrist also assessed the children and found no need at that time to prescribe medication because they were not symptomatic.

The biological father lives in the northeast part of the United States and is disabled due to mental illness. The mother, a 40-year-old African American, is a graduate from a prestigious college and is employed at a major computer firm with a six-figure salary. In addition to her older three children, she also has a 2-year-old son and 4-year-old daughter through her union with Mr. B, a 45-year-old African American with a checkered work history. At the time of referral, he was employed as a computer sales representative. He is also an ordained minister and a certified plumber. Mr. and Mrs. B have been married approximately 4 years. The children did not support the marriage between their mother and Mr. B due to Mr. B's controlling and rigid parenting style. Mrs. B reports that she and her husband are Christians who are culturally sensitive to the needs of their family and the community. She also reported that Mr. B is the head of their family and that all final decisions are his to make, from finances to disciplining the children.

In addition to the current abuse charge, the children alleged numerous other incidents of aggression by the stepfather both emotionally and physically. The children were referred in order to address ongoing emotional and behavioral problems since being placed into therapeutic foster care. The oldest, Rena, is a 14-year-old African American female diagnosed with juvenile diabetes and major depression. Kelly is a 12-year-old African American female diagnosed with depressive disorder, and Tommy is an 8-year-old African American male diagnosed with attention deficit disorder. The children were abused after they gave incorrect information about Rena's blood sugar level to their parents. Rena has a significant history of not being insulin and diet compliant in order to keep her diabetes under control. Prior to the physical abuse, Rena required hospitalization after her blood sugar became dangerously low. The children were placed with a paternal aunt in a southern town approximately a 4-hour car drive away. The biological father was unable to care for his children due to his own struggles with major depression. Mr. and Mrs. B also have two younger children, ages 2 and 4, who are products of their union and remain in the family home.

On receiving the referral, the initial objectives were to identify the most appropriate treatment home that could accommodate three siblings, be available to facilitate and participate in supervised visits with the biological family, and would be willing to assist Rena with managing her diabetes. Part of the intake process included informing the children and the biological family of the program structure and their client rights.

A large concern for the children and the referring department was the location of the treatment home. The children did not want to be physically close to where Mr. and Mrs. B resided until therapeutic interventions had begun and the children felt safe. The permanency plan for the family was reunification. Despite the negative history of the parents, it was important to include them in the treatment process through family therapy and a parent training class.

Harmony

Harmony is the union between body, mind, emotions, and spirit that we experience when we are in synchronization. Harmony is a result of reading the internal and external cues in and around our life in a manner that confirms our purpose. In the case of the B family, it is imperative that a coherence or compatibility between the therapist and client system develops such that the therapist is experienced as a positive extension of the client system. A shared sense of belonging, nurturance, love, interdependence, the development of trust, and relaxation between the family and therapist are manifestations of the harmony phase of treatment. Techniques utilized in this phase of treatment include authenticity, self-disclosure, rituals, acceptance of where the client is, therapist composure and relaxation, and accentuation of the positive in all components of the client system.

Once the treatment parents were identified, it was important for the treatment team to contact the B family in order to plan the treatment team meeting. The program is structured so that the referred foster child(ren) and prospective treatment parent have a face-to-face match meeting and transition (weekend) visits before a placement is made; however, due to the distance involved, the match meeting and visits were not feasible. Fortunately, the children and the proposed family were able to meet and talk via telephone regularly prior to placement. This process began in March and the children were placed simultaneously in June with a two-parent family. Initially, the children appeared pleased to be back in their hometown and get reacquainted with old friends and their mother. They did verbalize and demonstrate their anxiety about seeing their stepfather again (therapeutically, a meeting of this nature with the stepfather would not occur until the children were ready, either individually or collectively). It was important to establish a meeting with the parents and program staff immediately after placement in order to begin the treatment process and establish the framework and guidelines for services. Once Mr. and Mrs. B were contacted, Mr. B verbalized his guarded desire to meet. He also verbalized his frustration and a lack of trust with the local department. A time was finally established to meet the B family. That, in itself, was felt to be a small victory because they had a history of not wanting to speak or meet with their caseworker from the local department.

Harmony Intervention

The B family was contacted by phone by the program therapist. The following dialogue occurred:

Therapist: Hello, Mr. B. My name is Kwame Taylor with Progressive Life Center. How are you?

Mr. B: I am fine.

Therapist: Great. I'm calling you because our agency will be working with your children and we want your and Mrs. B's input so that we can explore your needs as a family and those of your children. Mr. B, we know that you care deeply about your children, their best interest, and you desire to reunite your family. This is why it is important to us that we have your input and we work together toward that goal with you and your wife at your earliest opportunity.

Mr. B: Well, what is Progressive Life Center and how are you involved with our children?

Therapist: That is an excellent question! We are a part of your community committed to serving Black families. Progressive Life Center is a nonprofit mental health organization based here in Landover, Maryland. We contract with the local department of social services to provide treatment foster care services. Thanks for asking that question.

Mr. B: Well, I'll speak with my wife and call you back to schedule a time to meet. I don't know why you want to meet with us because you're going to do what you want anyway.

Therapist: Well, Mr. B I cannot speak for services that you have received in the past, and I can certainly understand your skepticism with allowing more strange people and systems into your life at this time. It sounds as if you have had some bad experiences in terms of your thoughts and feelings being heard or being understood. At this time, you are our customer. At times you may agree or disagree with the issue or topic at hand, but the overall goal is to explore the issues to move toward healing with your family and *hopefully* reunification.

Mr. B: Okay, let's meet on Tuesday at 4:00 p.m.

Surprisingly, Mr. B arrived early for the meeting, without Mrs. B. Initially, the meeting with the program director was designed to slowly begin the joining process. On arrival, Mr. B was appropriately dressed and groomed. He arrived dressed in a suit and tie and stated that he was on his lunch break. Mr. B was pleasant, provided consistent eye contact, and listened intently to the feedback and questions of the program director.

Intervention

Therapist: I'm glad to see you made it, Mr. B. How are you?

Mr. B: I'm okay.

Therapist: I see you decided to come a little early.

Mr. B: I wanted to see what you are all about. I'm not willing to be used to perpetuate the system making money with foster care. I'm currently paying child support to the state, my wife and I have paid a great deal of money in legal fees, and we've been lied on and lied to regarding our children. We are extremely tired of it. Let me ask you. Have you reviewed our files and records?

Therapist: First, Mr. B, allow me to respond to the trouble you are experiencing trying to be a good father and husband at a time when you feel little support from the community. Meeting with you gives us an opportunity to really incorporate your thoughts, feelings, and desires. I'm aware that you both feel injured and misunderstood.

Mr. B: Yes, we have.

Therapist: What will you need from us, Progressive Life Center, to help this process become productive and safe for you?

Mr. B: We need open, consistent, and genuine dialogue. We're tired of making progress and doing what we've been asked to do and then hearing something negative a week later from DSS or having what we've said turned around to mean something else.

Mr. B was informed that the relationship that he would have with the program would dictate the success and the timeline in which his children would be returned to him and his wife, if at all, based on the local department's review of the progress in therapy and their ability to comply with their case plan. Mr. B was informed of the program's design and structure and the therapeutic model utilized. Most important, Mr. B was educated about the relationship that the agency has with the local department of social services. The program director felt it was important to allay Mr. B's fears during the Harmony phase. At the end of the meeting, Mr. B stated that he would discuss the program with his wife and call back to schedule another meeting, if necessary, in order to begin the treatment process. Later in the week, the Bs phoned the program director to schedule the first family counseling session (without the children).

The first family session was successful and began with a ritual (for them the ritual was a prayer) and ended with a ritual. This was significant because it illustrated the family's willingness to be in harmony with the therapeutic relationship. After the opening ritual, the session began with basic joining techniques such as discussing personal, individual demographics such as where Mr. and Mrs. B were born and raised and how they met. Humor was interjected at various points in order to assist the family in feeling connected and comfortable. The first session closed with another ritual. The rituals paid respect to their spiritual base, which also provided them with a connection to the program. The session was successful; the harmony process was taking effect, and it appeared to reduce family anxiety and guardedness. Ultimately, a shared consciousness should exist, with the therapist being "joined" with the family system and a therapeutic bridge being established.

Awareness

Awareness is the perception or knowledge of self and of self in relation to others and the larger environment. This awareness is represented on the physical, emotional, mental, and spiritual planes of existence. Cognitive awareness of issues allows sensitivity to the facts and the definable aspects of a situation and makes available a process for defining and of knowing reality. Outcomes for this phase should illustrate the family systems ability to have an identification and expression of thoughts and feelings, a clarification of the significant factors that can be a barrier to healthier functioning, and acknowledgement of one's intentions or wants.

Several family sessions occurred with Mr. and Mrs. B over the course of the year. Simultaneously, individual and group sessions were occurring with the children. The sessions with Mr. and Mrs. B were complicated by their lack of trust with the system and their legal status with the court. It appeared that Mr. and Mrs. B were hesitant to admit being wrong in how they disciplined their children for fear that further legal retribution would come their way. In addition, the Bs expressed a great deal of anger toward their eldest daughter, Rena, who they felt distorted the truth of the abuse in order to express her dislike for Mr. B. The Bs felt that Rena influenced the views of the other children in the home and that it would take time for them to get past the anger they possessed toward Rena.

Awareness Intervention

Therapist: Mr. and Mrs. B, let's talk about your feelings. You appear angry with Rena. Could you speak to her directly?

Mrs. B: Well, there are only two parents in our home and we are them. All we ask or require is that you respect our rules and respect us. We are strong believers in traditional values.

Mr. B: For example, if a person calls our house, we expect them to identify themselves first and then ask for the person they wish to speak with. That process was hard for the kids to get used to and people may say that it is too rigid, but that is how we were raised and for us, respect is paramount.

Therapist: I hear you place a great deal of value in respect. What happens if you feel that you are not respected?

Mr. B: I guess we will be going through what we are experiencing now with DSS.

Therapist: I'm speaking more in relation to your children. It sounds as if the tables have turned somewhat for them as well. For several years, they and Mrs. B had a culture, rituals, and routines by which they lived. Mrs. B met you; you found an emotional and spiritual connection and became husband and wife. Now, the children have a different type of relationship with their mother and two new siblings who require a great deal of attention. Combine that with your efforts to create a more structured environment, and the result is the children having feelings of frustration or anger. Let's try something! Are you willing to try?

Bs: We'll see!

Therapist: I would like to do a role-play. In this role-play, I would like Mr. B to be Rena and Mrs. B to be Kelly. I will be Mr. B, okay?

Bs: All right.

The role-play allowed Mr. and Mrs. B to gain insights into how the children may have felt or thought about their interactions with the family. For the first time since the children were removed, Mr. B was able to explore why he and the children struggled in their relationship. The Bs ultimately began to understand that their children had a great amount of difficulty accepting their union and Mr. B's strict discipline style.

Awareness for the children occurred on two levels. On one level, the children had the opportunity to reside in a less restrictive household that encouraged supportive dialogue about their feelings and an opportunity to discuss feelings of rejection by their mother in favor of Mr. B. On the second level, Rena found a high level of support from Mr. West (a foster parent) who was a diabetic as well. Mr. West was able to assist Rena in getting involved with a juvenile diabetes support group and juvenile nutritionist, and the two of them were able to speak daily about their daily blood sugar levels and menus.

Rena became more aware of the complications that her condition could pose if not kept under control and of ways to change her daily behaviors. It was during this phase that Tommy (8-year-old male) expressed that he did not want to continue living apart from his parents and other siblings. He expressed frustrations with the department of social services for separating his family. Despite the discord that existed between Mr. B and the children, Tommy did not feel it was severe enough to break up their family, nor was he afraid to be with his parents.

Alignment

Alignment is the synergism of beings, both material and psychic forces, toward a central point of existence. It is the adjustment or arrangement of people and/or things in relation to each other so that a healing force becomes operative. This phase of treatment is best manifested by the catharsis, interconnectedness, restoration, and revitalization of family functioning.

As sessions with the Bs and the children progressed, Tommy frequently expressed his desire to return home. Tommy had created a timeline in which he planned to be home by the beginning of the new school year. The treatment team began family sessions between Tommy and his parents to address concerns related to the past abuse, Mr. and Mrs. B's parenting style, and Tommy's concerns about returning home. Simultaneously, Tommy's sisters were not ready to return home and were fearful about Tommy returning home. Tommy eventually began to express anger, frustration, and physical aggression toward his sisters for not wanting to return home as well.

Intervention

A family session was held with the siblings to discuss Tommy's desire to return home to his parents. They were concerned for his safety but were aware that his desire would be fulfilled. Each sibling was able to share concerns for Tommy.

Therapist: Tommy, Rena, and Kelly, I want to thank you for all of the hard work you have done so far. I know it's been hard and difficult. Okay, who will lead today's ritual?

Kelly: I want to start with a prayer for today's session.

[Kelly led the group with a prayer.]

Therapist: Thanks, Kelly. That prayer was very appropriate. A lot has happened since we last met. Let's talk about it.

[Silence for approximately 3–4 minutes]

Tommy: I'm going home. Yeah, I'm going home. I don't want to be here in foster care.

Kelly: That's stupid—why would you want to do that! You know how Mr. B is and mommy isn't going to change either!

Rena: Yeah, I don't know what's up with you.

Tommy: Daddy didn't do anything to you or me, Kelly. Rena, you're the one who got in trouble. I'm going back to Westview with mommy!

Kelly: You know it's going to be different and that Mr. B has all these rules that you don't like.

Therapist: It sounds like Tommy really wants to be home and that he needs your support as much as Kelly and Rena need your support, Tommy. What is your fear for Tommy and what do you fear may happen?

[Silence for 1–2 minutes]

Rena: I'm fearful that he will change and buy into everything that Mr. B wants him to do and that he may keep getting spanked.

Therapist: How about you? What do you think may happen to you if he returns home or yourself should you return?

Rena: I feel that I may lose my brother. I think he's afraid and is just saying he wants to return to make Mr. B happy.

Therapist: Can you state how this affects you?

Rena: I'm losing my brother, and I think it's good that he is going home if that's what he wants, but I don't think I'll be going home. Tommy, you know I care about you and I really don't want to see you go. But, in some ways, I'm a little jealous because I want to be home with mommy too.

Kelly: You need to call us and stay in touch. I'm happy here with Mr. and Mrs. West and I don't want to go back, but if that is what you want, I can't stop you.

Tommy: I want you to come home, too, but I know that won't work right now.

By helping the sisters to really communicate their fear, they were better able to communicate their love and hope for their brother in a safe constructive fashion.

Due to Tommy's continued acting-out behavior, the treatment team felt that supporting Tommy's desire to return home should be explored. The treatment team met with the local DSS.

Mr. and Mrs. B were pleased to learn of Tommy's desire to return home and were committed in treatment to addressing Tommy's concerns as well as his inappropriate behaviors. The Bs made Tommy aware that they did not want him returning home unless he was ready and comfortable. They informed Tommy that they wanted all of the children home as soon as possible. The treatment team and local department of social services collaborated to establish guidelines, goals, and conditions under which Tommy could return home, pending progress made in therapy.

Two weeks prior to the start of the new school year, Tommy returned home with 6 months of protective supervision by the department of social services. Mr. and Mrs. B were happy to have Tommy return home and were prepared to work with their daughters but still had great distrust of the local department of social services. Tommy's return home increased the communication between his sisters and the Bs.

Rena and Kelly had mixed emotions about Tommy's return home. They wanted a close relationship with their mother but did not feel that it was realistic after Mr. B entered their life. The normal mother-daughter conversation between Mrs. B, Rena, and Kelly lost the trust it once had because Mrs. B made it clear that she would share all information with Mr. B. The girls were able to verbalize to their therapist the anger toward their mother because her love for Mr. B appeared to be stronger than her love for them.

The treatment team decided that it was time to begin therapy with the girls and Mrs. B (without Mr. B). The plan was to slowly work Mr. B back into the sessions so that they could process their feelings with him as well. This plan would allow the girls to begin healing with their mother. Mr. and Mrs. B strongly objected to this approach because they were a "package and one did as the other did." Mr. B wanted the sessions to be moved from the treatment placement agency to his church, where they offered pastoral counseling. However, the local department would not support his wish due to the "counselors not being appropriately credentialed," and therapeutically, the Bs needed to begin to respect the individual emotional boundaries of their children. Mr. B returned to the agency stating that he would "attend every session with his wife and that [he] must be aware of everything that was said." At that point, the clinician informed Mr. B that he and his wife did not appear ready to move ahead with therapy based on their lack of trust in the process. Therefore, the sessions would end. At that point, the Bs left the office holding firm to their position. The therapist received a call the next day from Mr. B stating that they would go along with the recommendations, but for only three sessions. The Bs were encouraged to do five sessions, with a review of the progress after the fourth session, and they agreed.

The following week, sessions between Kelly and Ms. B began. The sessions proceeded well enough that the family began to discuss unsupervised visits and ultimately overnight visits. Mr. B was brought back into therapy after the seventh session. The sessions progressed to the point where Kelly began speaking on a regular basis again with her brother, Tommy. Kelly soon began stating that she was ready to return home. At the end of the school year, one year after Tommy returned home, Kelly returned home with six months of protective supervision by the local department of social services.

Actualization

Actualization is the materialization of potential and the utilization of new attitudes and behavior in a system's life space. This phase is manifested in the family's ability to utilize healing and practice new learning to resolve current life issues outside the formal therapeutic setting. The successful negotiation of developing issues leads to increased confidence in the family's problem-solving abilities.

The children were removed from the B family in 1997. In the spring of 1999, both Tommy and Kelly had returned home after experiencing healthy transitions and working on issues that impacted the family prior to the abuse. Only Rena remained with the same treatment family she was initially placed with. Rena had made significant progress with managing her diabetes, maintaining the honor roll in school, working part-time, and maintaining a limited relationship with her mother and stepfather.

Rena was in her last year of high school and understood through therapy and support from her treatment family that she could not feel comfortable returning to the home of her family. Family therapy occurred between Rena and Mr. and Mrs. B, and both parties respectfully came to understand what each needed to maintain a successful relationship. Rena could not see herself re-adapting to the structure of her parents' home, especially since she had become comfortable with her peers and the semi-independent lifestyle she was currently living. In a matter of a few weeks, Rena would be graduating from high school and had been accepted at a local college with a partial scholarship and with financial support from the local department of social services.

Mr. and Mrs. B were able to express their love for Rena and offer any type of support she needed, and they agreed that she needed to be emancipated. Rena's siblings have adjusted well to returning home and are performing well academically. Tommy has maintained his honor roll status at school and played in the concert band as well as being a starting linebacker in little league football. Kelly has returned to her neighborhood high school and has a part-time job as well as ongoing communication and regular visits with her treatment parents.

Synthesis

Synthesis is the integration and appropriate use of all functional resources available to the system. The client incorporates, or synthesizes, an effective problem-solving process that allows them to identify and appropriately respond to an issue as it develops, thus, minimizing the likelihood of the issue becoming a problem. The client system incorporates the healing process as its own, and healing becomes more of a natural, and thus, familiar process. The ability to problem solve is natural for the client system with flexibility, proactive involvement, and investment in systemic well-being. The ultimate outcome for this phase of treatment is the client systems' ability to be empowered, reciprocal, nurturing, authentic, supportive, resilient, and self-correcting.

The B family has initiated a healthier form of addressing family discord. Mr. and Mrs. B initially presented with a great deal of inflexibility in how their potential problems should be addressed. They often utilized an authoritarian approach that did not incorporate family dialogue. The Bs have now developed greater insights in understanding the individuality of their children and the importance of dialogue as a tool for change versus an "all or none" approach in relating. In addition, Mrs. B has become clearer about the importance of her relationship with her children.

Summary

The B family initially presented with significant emotional trauma. The outcome for the B family could have been much different had they not had the opportunity to make the commitment to therapy and utilize the appropriate supports. Mr. and Mrs. B did not initially consider the importance of their children's emotional needs early in their relationship, nor did Mr. B have the comfort or trust to allow Mrs. B the opportunity to nurture her children as she did prior to his becoming involved in the family. Mr. and Mrs. B have become more attentive to the emotional needs of her children. They have become more comfortable with utilizing alternative methods of parenting versus the "punishment" model. During the six-month period when each child was at home under protective supervision, the opportunity to return to the previous treatment home was always available if the relationship with the Bs began to worsen. Neither child expressed the desire to return to the treatment home. The Bs were supportive in encouraging the children to maintain contact with their treatment parents. They wanted the children to remain home with them not because they (the children) felt they had to, but rather, because they wanted to.

Mr. and Mrs. B attended Rena's graduation from high school and were finally able to apologize for the inappropriate discipline they had implemented in the past and for the abusive events that occurred 3 years earlier.

References

GREGORY, H. (2001). NTU psychotherapy: A pluralist approach. Unpublished manuscript.

PHILLIPS, F. B. (1990). NTU psychotherapy: An Afrocentric approach. *Journal of Black Psychology, 17*(1), 55–74.

PHILLIPS, F. B. (1998). Spirit energy and NTU psychotherapy. In R. Jones (Ed.), *African American mental health* (pp. 357–377). Hampton, VA: Cobb & Henry.

PHILLIPS, F. B., & GREGORY, S. D. P. (1996). NTU: Progressive Life Center's Afrocentric approach to therapeutic foster care. In M. C. Roberts (Ed.), *Model programs in child and family mental health.* Mahwah, NJ: Erlbaum.

PHILLIPS, F. B., & GREGORY, S. D. P. (1997). Of mind, body, and spirit: Therapeutic foster care—an innovative approach to healing from an NTU perspective. *Journal of Child Welfare League of America, 76,* 127–142.

Case Study 5-4

Questions for Discussion
1. What is the underlying purpose behind both psychological and social denial? How might treatment be facilitated when a practitioner considers denial to be an adaptive response?
2. What are the four types of denial identified by the authors, and how do they manifest?
3. What are the three interventions that the authors most often use when confronted with denial?
4. In this case study, "the therapist takes as neutral a position as possible in regard to the denial but not in regard to the abuse." Discuss the importance of this distinction, and how the practitioner walks that fine line.

Treatment of Denial Where There Is Child Sex Abuse

Mary Jo Barrett and Terry S. Trepper

One of the most frustrating elements of treating incestuous families is the tendency of their members to engage in active denial. Therapists are only human; they find incestuous abuse as abhorrent as most people do. Many therapists, who expect at least a modicum of remorse by the offending father[1] and sympathy for the child from the nonoffending mother, are incredulous when confronted with denial from both. The denial of abuse may then become the focus of a power struggle between the clinician and the family, with the result that the therapy becomes stalemated.

This case study discusses the function of denial, outlines the various types of denial that may operate within a family, and presents a case example that illustrates how denial can be effectively reduced. These interventions for denial are part of a larger program for treating child sexual abuse that we first briefly describe.

The program has been in operation for over 10 years and has treated hundreds of families, offenders, and victims. It is an intensive program based on the Multiple Systems Model (Barrett, Sykes, & Byrnes, 1986; Trepper & Barrett, 1989), which assesses and intervenes in the many "systems" that contribute to the expression of incest. Families are seen for an average of 18 months in family, marital, individual, and group therapy. Other important systems, such as the parents' families of origin or the victims' social network, are also incorporated into the treatment.

Therapy occurs in three distinct stages: Stage 1 is called "Creating a Context for Change," and its purpose is for the therapist to join with the family, network with involved legal and social agencies, create the reality that change is possible, provide a

---

[1]In this case study, the term *father* is used to refer to the offending parent, *mother* is used to refer to the nonoffending parent, and *daughter, son,* and *child* are used to refer to the child-victim. This convention makes for easier reading and should in no way be construed as suggesting that only fathers abuse children, nor that only girls are victims. Also, *father* and *mother* are used to refer to a stepfather and stepmother, again for consistency and ease of reading.

common language that will be used throughout treatment, and reduce the family's resistance to change. During Stage 1, the most vigorous effort to understand, work with, and potentially ameliorate the denial occurs. Stage 2, "Challenging Behaviors and Expanding Alternatives," is characterized by intensive therapeutic challenges to the style and structure of the individual and the family that have contributed to its vulnerability to incest. In this stage, intense individual therapy takes place. If the family or individuals are still engaging in the more subtle forms of denial, they are challenged during this stage. Stage 3, "Consolidation," is when the family is expected to incorporate the changes made during Stages 1 and 2 of therapy into their daily life with a minimum of therapist involvement. Here, denial is discussed in the past tense, and the client is asked to examine what purpose his or her previous denial served and how to prevent denial from being used as a coping mechanism in the future.

The Purpose of Denial

We have found it most helpful to consider denial as a special case of a family's natural resistance to change, to therapy, and to the intrusion into their lives by outsiders. Denial, like all resistance, is not necessarily pathological but can be an important and understandable protective device. Whether it is psychological denial, in which it is unconscious and unavailable to the client even when confronted with reality, or social denial, in which the decision to deny is conscious, the underlying purpose is protection of the individual and/or family from the overwhelming psychological and social consequences of incest. This may be considered analogous to the body's production of endorphins to mask overwhelming physical pain. Offenders deny in order to save themselves from legal repercussions and/or to defend against the psychological and emotional pain of childhood trauma that contributes to their abusive behavior. Nonoffending parents, mostly women, are often forced by society to deny because they are economically and emotionally dependent on men, the offenders, and because they wish to protect themselves from emotional and physical pain.

To the therapist, the benefits in viewing denial as a strength rather than a deficit are numerous. Instead of seeing the client's denial as hostility against the therapist, which can only lead to a defensive posture, the therapist who views denial as self-protection and a coping mechanism is free to treat the denial in the same way as any other clinical interaction. A positive view of denial allows for a more positive and respectful view of the client; this opens up the possibilities for a functional relationship. Demanding the extinction of denial as a coping mechanism is an irresponsible position for any therapist to take. By understanding denial, the therapist can expect its occurrence, build a more effective therapeutic relationship, and plan strategies to intervene.

Most therapeutic programs expect the offender to accept responsibility for the sexual abuse as part of the treatment goals. This goal must be kept in mind throughout the program. Even when accepting the protective component of denial, the therapist should be cautioned to never appear to accept the denial of the abuse itself. The therapist who appears to accept the denial may be seen as tacitly excusing the abuse and may contribute to the confusion of reality, which may lead to long-term psychopathology in the abused child. The challenge for the therapist is to accept the underlying reason for denial but not the denial of the abuse itself.

Types of Denial

In the course of our work, we have identified four types of denial commonly present in an incestuous family. Of course, not every family member denies, and any family member may manifest more than one type of denial. The four types are (1) denial of facts, (2) denial of awareness, (3) denial of responsibility, and (4) denial of impact.

Denial of Facts

Denial of facts refers to the direct and open challenge of the reality of the incestuous abuse. A family member can deny that the abuse ever occurred at all or deny certain facts associated with the abuse. Denial of facts creates the most difficult intervention and, if it persists, can have the most serious long-term consequences for the child because it assaults the very core of his or her reality. Younger children may grow up never really knowing whether what they think they experienced really occurred. When there is denial of the facts by the perpetrator and/or the nonoffending parent, it is as if the child is being victimized twice: first by the abusive act and then by the act of denial. We consider the denial of facts so potentially detrimental that we do not choose to have a child in session with a parent who is denying facts.

Not surprisingly, abusing fathers deny facts more often than other members of the family; about 30 percent of fathers in our program denied facts on entering therapy. Most often this denial is seen as a way to protect themselves from prison terms, and, in fact, attorneys advise fathers in our program to admit as little as possible in therapy because it could be used against them in court. We know our experience is not uncommon in other sexual abuse programs. Therapy becomes little more than a continual reiteration of "I didn't do it; I don't know why she said it."

About 15 percent of our nonabusing mothers deny facts at the beginning of the program. Most often, the mother's denial occurs in tandem with the father's denial, but denial can occur when just the mother denies the facts, even when both the father and the daughter admit to them. "She is lying, and maybe some of what he says is true, but she is making it worse, and he is going along with it to help his case."

Only about 4 percent of the victims in our program deny the facts. When they do so, it is usually to protect the father from being removed from the home or to keep him from going to jail. It is a reality that, in order to protect the child from further abuse, families often are separated, and unfortunately, this is not always done in a consistent or therapeutic fashion. The child is told, "Tell me about the abuse and nothing bad will happen to you," and when she does talk about the abuse, the family is split up, she may be placed in a foster home, and the father may go to jail. Consequently, it is not uncommon for an abused child to recant her story in an attempt to save the family. The child has been put in that position before—the position of sacrifice.

There is always the unsettling possibility that the members of the family are denying because the abuse actually did not occur. Based on our past experiences, we are able to say with certainty that in most cases in which a child reports sexually abuse, it likely did occur. It is now becoming somewhat less certain, especially in some savage custody cases in which children are coerced by one parent into saying that the other sexually abused them. We recommend a complete social, psychological, and medical investigation in these cases. However, it is still our experience that most cases in which the child has accused the parent of abuse are true.

Denial of Awareness

Denial of awareness is when a family member admits to the possibility of abuse but denies being cognizant of it when it happened. This form of denial is usually psychological and more conducive to therapeutic intervention. Offenders deny awareness approximately 20 percent of the time and usually say that they either were drunk, suffering from posttraumatic stress disorder, had a blackout, or perhaps thought they were with someone else because it was dark.

When mothers deny awareness, they generally say things like "I knew something was wrong in my house, but I never knew it was this" or "I can't believe it was happening right in my own household." Less common, but of more concern, is the situation in which the daughter told the mother about the abuse, but the mother states that she does not remember her daughter doing so. This form of denial is a reflection of the emotional, economical, and social disabilities that the mother suffers as a result of experiencing a spouse's or significant other's abuse. She must maintain that it did not happen in order to maintain stability in her life.

Child victims also deny awareness. This is often a very protective and functional dissociative device. Victims claim that they were asleep when the abuse occurred, they turn it into a dream or fantasy, or they don't remember much because they pretend it happened to someone else and they were just watching. This type of denial of awareness is often coupled with a mother or father who is denying the facts.

Denial of Responsibility

Denial of responsibility occurs when a family member admits to the facts about the abuse, remembers many of its occurrences, if not all of them, but suggests that someone other than the abusing father was responsible. The father and mother may blame the daughter for being seductive, not acknowledging that the daughter learned this behavior through them. Men often blame their wives for being sexually unavailable to them, again not recognizing their role in the abusive act.

Women often deny the responsibility of their husbands or boyfriends. They may ascribe responsibility to the daughter, to alcohol, or to themselves. To acknowledge that the responsibility is the offender's once again puts a woman into the dilemma of

"Am I better off with or without him?" and the choice of denial is understandably based on a set of emotional, physical, and economic circumstances.

For the children, it is most common for them to believe that they caused their own abuse. Blaming themselves stems from a combination of several possible origins. First, being a victim and living with parents who are being victims to one another and to society, the child supports what she already believes, which is "bad things happen to bad people"—in other words, learned victimization. Self-blame may also be an attempt to protect the family and themselves. Children can protect the family by creating the reality that it was their fault and no one else should be punished. If they blame themselves, then they do not have to acknowledge the psychological or emotional problems of either or both of their parents or caretakers. Finally, children of all ages feel responsible for and in the center of the world around them. Part of the normal developmental process is children's understanding, over time, of what they are responsible for and what they have control over in the world. It is often during this crucial developmental phase that children are abused sexually, physically, and emotionally. When victims become developmentally thwarted by the trauma, it strengthens their belief system that they are basically bad and that the adults whom they are taught to trust have hurt them because they deserve it. If they deserve this cruel treatment, then they must be responsible for it.

Denial of Impact

With denial of impact, the family member admits to the facts of the incestuous abuse, was consciously aware that it happened, and accepts that the abusing father is ultimately responsible for its occurrence. However, the family member does not accept the seriousness of the abuse, how the abuse may have negatively affected the victim and the entire family's functioning, or the potential for long-term psychological damage.

Abusing fathers in our program deny impact in some manner almost all of the time. Statements like "It was only fondling" or "She didn't seem to mind" are quite common. Mothers often feel that what happened to the child is not as bad as what happens to the family after the crisis of discovery. And the children, who deny impact 46 percent of the time, feel that the abuse had little effect on their life.

The denial of impact is a way for members to protect themselves and each other from acknowledging the potential for long-term emotional and psychological effects of sexual abuse. It is the mind's way of saying, "If what happened is no big deal, then what will happen to me as a result will be no big deal either."

Treatment of Denial

The ultimate goal in the treatment of denial is to have it end. However, there are no certain techniques that will end an individual's or family's denial, particularly because the denial serves very protective functions. Because we see denial as a necessary attempt by the family and its individual members to protect themselves, we do not take its appearance as a personal affront. We approach denial with a strategic focus rather than directly challenging the symptom. In other words, we have found that the most therapeutic approach that we can take with denial is to not allow ourselves to become overly controlled by the outcome. We do not have the eradication of denial as our only outcome goal. Instead, our primary goal is to eradicate abusive, oppressive, and violent interactions between family members, and the work toward this goal can begin while members are in denial. Paradoxically, the less we are focused on the denial and thus do not have a medical approach, the easier it is to establish a therapeutic relationship with clients and help them face the pain and destruction that often accompanies their admittance.

In this case study, we will illustrate, through case dialogue, three interventions that we most frequently use when confronted with denial: (1) normalization, (2) negative consequences of change (Fisch, Weakland, & Segal, 1982), and (3) pretend techniques (Madanes, 1981).

Normalization

We maintain two premises when normalizing denial. The first is that denial is a normal defense mechanism that humans use as a means of reestablishing power and control in their lives and a method of self-protection. The second premise is that we believe that people are basically good and that they aspire to attain goodness and inner peace. In the face of denial, therapists sometimes find it difficult to maintain these beliefs, but if they do, there is much more freedom therapeutically.

Normalization is a long and tedious process in which the therapeutic rhythm is crucial. The therapist is understanding and empathic with clients' need to deny and simultaneously is helping them see that it is in their own best interest to take responsibility for their feelings and behaviors in order to obtain inner peace. The dance between these two realities, protection of self and true goodness of self, continues throughout therapy.

Negative Consequences of Change

The therapist helps clients to take a close look at the negative consequences they will encounter if they give up their denial. One of the functions of the abusive behavior is an attempt on the part of the offender to gain power and control in his life. The acknowledgment of sexually abusive behavior can represent the ultimate loss of power—going to jail. By examining the negative consequences of an admittance, the therapist can help reframe this loss of control (Fisch et al., 1982; Haley, 1984). This intervention is used repeatedly in every stage of the program and with every type of denial. We want clients to recapture control over their lives in a nonabusive form. The therapist explores the problems that accompany change and potential solutions to these new problems. This exploration helps prevent future abusive situations not only in the family, but often in society (that is, courts or jail). For example, an offender can explore all of the ways he will be hurt if he admits the abuse, and he can plan with his therapist and attorney a more rehabilitative consequence. If mothers choose to believe the child, they can take a painful look at their economic situation and prepare to function independently if that becomes necessary.

Pretending

The therapist creates an "as if" scenario with clients that allows them to talk about the sexual abuse, their own victimization, and their views on family, self, and the world without admitting to anything. For example, the offender would be asked to pretend that he was a victim of sexual abuse: How does he think it would have happened to him, or how does he think it would have felt to have no one believe him? Or "if" a daughter or son had been abused by her spouse, what would a mother do in that situation? This gives people permission to explore the possibilities and still maintain their necessary control and protection.

These are only three examples of how denial can be managed in a case; however, they are the primary interventions used when helping family members master their denial. The interventions are not separated in the treatment but are interwoven with each other in many of the sessions. The case example that follows contains excerpts of actual sessions in which the therapist, through individual, family, marital, and group treatment, is helping a family weave their way through the complicated tapestry of denial.

Case Example: The Ques Case

We first met the Ques family in much the same manner that we meet the majority of our families: through the state social services department. In cases of child abuse, the systems involved are much larger than just the family; consequently, the treatment must take all of these systems into consideration. During the first call from the state worker, the therapist discovered that both the family and the worker were very angry. The worker was angry about the family's denial and resistance, and the family was angry about what they considered false and unfair allegations. Prior to the first meeting with a family, we always attempt to determine the viewpoints of all the parties involved in the case, as well as their expectations of therapy. It is crucial to understand the legal status of the case; that is, whether there is criminal court or family court involvement. The worker's perspective of the Ques family provided us with facts and some interesting opinions. First, some facts: the family consists of the father, Mark, a 38-year-old male; the mother, Doris, a 36-year-old female; Sandra, one of the alleged victims, a 14-year-old female freshman in high school; Sally, another alleged victim, a 12-year-old seventh grader; Donny, an 8-year-old male second grader; and, finally, Dotty, a 4-year-old female. The family was living together at the time of the report, and the two oldest daughters were placed in foster care because of Mark and Sally's denial of the sexual abuse. At the time of the referral, there was no criminal court involvement; all legal actions were taking place in the juvenile court proceedings.

Sandra had been at a friend's house one day looking very depressed and preoccupied. After much coaxing, it seems that she finally was convinced to tell her friend what was bothering her—she revealed that her father had been fondling her. The friend, although sworn to secrecy, was extremely upset and confused and decided to tell her own mother, who reported the abuse to the authorities. The department of social services investigated the report, and although the father and Sally, the second oldest daughter, denied the allegations, the report was considered to be substantiated, and the two oldest daughters were removed from the home for protective custody.

The opinions of the state workers provided a bit more information. The investigative worker was convinced that the girls had been abused and was extremely punitive toward both Mark and Sally for denying. He swore to the father that his time had come and that he would make sure the father would be punished for his crime. The follow-up worker, on the other hand, was not so convinced that the allegations were very severe, and she was much more concerned about some of her more serious cases. These two opinions were confusing for the family members, and all parties involved were angry about the manner in which they were treated.

We began treatment with a series of individual sessions for the father, the mother, and the two victims. The two younger children were also seen after the mother, father, and two victims had been seen. In the sessions with the youngest children, we attempted to find out what the kids thought was going on and the reasons for their sisters' absence. After some initial assessment, we also explored with them any problems they saw in the family. Excerpts from their sessions are not included here because of this case study's emphasis on denial. With the rest of the family, our only goal for the first few meetings was to establish trust and attempt to gain some foundation for mutual respect in order to ensure their return to therapy.

In the following transcribed session, the therapist had already spent some time visiting with the client (the father) and getting to know him and was beginning to work with him on normalizing the situation.

Therapist: I know you have been through a lot lately.

Mark: Damn right, and I am plenty mad that I have to be here.

Therapist: I don't blame you, but we both have to be here. You can say we both have a mandate from the state. Can you think of any way I can help?

Mark: The only way anybody can help is to get me out of this mess. Sandra is a spoiled brat. She was mad at me for punishing her, and this is how she decided to get me back. These kids get these ideas from TV, and now I am paying for it. Do you have any idea how I am being ruined because of this?

Therapist: You must feel completely out of control of your life.

Mark: I am completely out of control, but in this family I am never in control anyway.

Therapist: Can you tell me other ways that you are out of control—at work, at home, or anywhere else?

In this session, the therapist only explores and empathizes with the father's feelings of being out of control and discusses his attempted solutions for regaining control. For the first few meetings with him, there is no discussion about whether he did anything sexually abusive or not.

In the sessions with the daughters and the mother, the themes that were created are very similar. Primarily, the therapist helped them see that their ambivalence is normal—the ambivalence between wanting the abuse to stop and at the same time not wanting their father/husband to be punished severely or the family to be broken apart.

Therapist (to Sally, the daughter denying abuse):   You must be very confused by all of this. I imagine that you want to believe your sister, and of course, if your father is touching you in ways that he should not be touching his 12-year-old daughter, you must want him to stop, and yet you don't want anyone to be hurt because of this.

Sally: Sandra only cares about herself. She doesn't care that she is ruining the family. She likes it in the foster home because she can always have her way. I want to go home. If she doesn't change her story, that will never happen.

Later in the session, the therapist summarizes for Sally what she has heard.

Therapist: Sally, what you have shared with me today is very similar to what many boys and girls who have been sexually abused by their fathers tell me. I know that you have not told me that anything has happened, and right now I don't want you to tell me. [The therapist is pacing the client in an attempt to help Sally maintain control over the situation.] But you have told me that life is terrible now and would only get worse if your father did do anything to you or your sister and that you just want this to all go away. If your father sexually abused you, and I believe that he did abuse your sister [The therapist is supporting her denial but not maintaining it.], I can assure you that a part of him wants help to stop hurting the two of you. It is possible for him to be a good father and a good person and for you to love him and for him to have done a terrible thing to you and your sister. My job is to help him change that part of himself that is hurtful.

Working with a mother who is in denial about the sexual abuse of her children is one of the most difficult jobs of a therapist. Our society holds mothers almost solely responsible for the well-being of children and forgets how nearly impossible that is for a woman to do on her own. In the following session, the therapist once again normalized the ambivalence that the mother must have been experiencing in this situation.

Therapist: As a mother, you are in a terrible position, probably the most difficult position that any mother could ever be placed in. It must feel like you must choose between your husband and your daughter.

Doris: It is impossible. I cannot win no matter what I do. That is why I am doing nothing, and everyone is telling me I am such a bad mother.

Therapist: Is Mark telling you that too?

Doris: Sure. He says if I had not been so easy on the kids that Sandra would have never thought that she could have gotten away with this. I am no good no matter which way you look at it.

Therapist: Do you believe that too?

Doris: Yes. I know Mark is not lying. He would never do that, but what would make Sandra tell such a lie? I don't know what she is up to.

Therapist: Maybe neither of them is up to anything. Maybe they are both just trying to protect themselves from some pretty terrible things. Unfortunately, everyone is turning to you to be the judge, jury, and therapist.

Doris: What do you mean?

Therapist: Everyone is depending on you to figure out if it happened or not and to make everyone work together to work it out. I don't think you can or should do that, Doris. I think you have to let me work with them, and maybe you just have to believe them both right now.

Doris: How can I do that?

Therapist: I am not sure how you can do that, but I can tell you how I do it. I believe that Sandra was hurt by Mark in some sexually abusive way, and I believe that Mark must deny right now in order to take care of himself, and that is normal. I also believe that good people do some pretty terrible things. They don't want to, and they can change, but they do them. And I believe if you came out on one side or the other right now, you would be in a lot of pain and overwhelmed, and you don't have to do anything until you are ready.

The therapist also helped the victim, Sandra, make some sense of her family's denial by normalizing their denial and her own denial of impact.

Therapist: What are you thinking about what has happened since you told your friend about your father's abuse of you?

Sandra: It is not as big a deal as everyone is making it out to be. He is a jerk, but he has done a lot worse things to me than anything with sex. I don't know why everyone is making such a big deal out of this. That is what I think.

Therapist: That makes sense to me. You want your dad to stop the "bad" stuff, but you did not want all this to happen. That is the worst part of this whole thing—no matter what you do, you keep getting hurt. [Sandra begins to cry, and the therapist continues.] Right now you don't have to do anything. The rest of the people in your family have to decide what they are going to do.

Sandra: They have decided not to believe me and to turn against me.

Therapist: I am not sure they have decided not to believe you. I think they have decided to protect themselves. How could pretending that the sexual abuse didn't happen be protecting, let's say, your father, for instance?

Sandra: Well, if he never admits it, things can just stay the way they are, and he won't have to suffer at all.

Therapist: It must feel like he is still abusing you.

Sandra: Yeah, it does.

Therapist: What about your mom? How could she be protecting herself and your sister?

Sandra: My sister, that's easy. I didn't want to believe it was happening to me for the longest time. I would have said it wasn't true, too, until I had just had it and wanted it all to stop. I sometimes now wish I hadn't said anything either. It is terrible now. My mom, I don't know. I could never not believe my kid. And I'd never let my husband do anything like that to my kids.

Therapist: You have every right to be mad and feel hurt. I just want you to know I am not so sure that your mother doesn't believe you and believes him. I think it is more that if she says anything out loud, she is not sure what will happen to her and the rest of the kids. She is working on getting strong enough to have her voice. It just may take longer than you or I, or she for that matter, would like.

The therapist took as neutral position as possible in regard to the denial but not in regard to the abuse. In the following sessions, the therapist incorporated both negative consequences of change and pretend playing in order to help the family creatively find alternative solutions to the dilemma of maintaining denial.

Therapist: Mark, pretend with me for a second. Let's just say that portions of what Sandra is alleging are true. Remember I am just pretending. What do you think would happen if you admitted or agreed with what she was saying?

Mark: I know what you are getting at.

Therapist: But it is something we have to think about. There are a lot of negative consequences to finally taking control of the situation in a real way. You have always talked to me about being the man of the house. Your family needs you to be the man now and have power like you have never had it before, and that is the power to not hurt others in order to help yourself. You have told me numerous ways that you have done that. So let's just pretend now that you took control. What would happen to you?

Mark: My life would be over. I'd go to jail, and I'd kill myself before I would go to jail. There is no way I did anything or will admit to doing anything.

Therapist: Do you think more suffering is going on now or if you took responsibility for your mistake?

Mark: There would be more suffering if I said something. It would be much worse.

Therapist: Worse for you or for the family?

Mark: For me and for everyone if I said something.

Therapist: I am not so sure it would be worse for your family if you admitted to the abuse. Now they are confused, accused of lying, and separated. The kids are not with their siblings or their parents. Their mother is being ripped in two. Much could be helped if you were strong enough to talk about what happened and the problems that led up to it. And now you are choosing to have your family suffer more.

Mark: I guess for now I am. But you act as if you know everything. You don't know.

Therapist: I know what Sandra says, and I know you would have a lot of problems if you admitted anything and that you are not strong enough yet. I guess for now you have made your choice who is to suffer.

As the therapist built on these small changes, the client began to explore potential ways that both he and the family could have protection. For example, jail certainly is not the only alternative to admission, and the offender could discuss with his attorney other options, such as treatment, probation, or even work release. When jail and subsequent suicide appear to be the only alternatives, denial seems to be a much more attractive option.

In another session, the mother pretended to believe her daughter and imagined the consequences, and she became overwhelmed by the prospects.

Doris: I could never survive. [Notice that all the family members were trying to figure out how to survive in their own individual set of circumstances.] I really would be a terrible mother then. The kids and I would be on the street. Even if I could find a job that made as much money as Mark's did, how would I watch the kids or be there when they needed me? I could never protect them. My family would probably turn against me, and my friends would be disgusted.

Therapist: Is the image worse than what you are experiencing now?

Doris: I am not sure. I just wish it could be different.

Therapist: And if you had control over it being different, how would that look?

Doris: Of course, I would believe my daughter and help Mark get help, even if he was out of the home for a while. If he could still work and not abandon us, then maybe it could be better.

Therapist: Could you ever talk to Mark like you are telling me?

The therapist, after a few more sessions similar to this, helped Doris to confront Mark during a couple's session. They began to explore alternative solutions that might still protect themselves but be far less hurtful to the children.

Therapist: Mark, tell Doris some of the things that you believe she would do if her husband ever abused her kids. She is used to the same pretend stuff that you and I do in sessions.

Mark: I think you would try to kill anyone that would do that to our kids. I sure would. I know you'd divorce them, and you'd try to get everything they got and leave them ruined. I wouldn't blame you because I'd do the same thing.

Doris: I used to think that, Mark, but after therapy and the group, I am not so sure anymore. I think I would want to understand more how someone I love and lived with all these years could be both good and bad, strong and weak. I would want my family to heal. We can never heal this way. The longer it goes on, the less respect I have for you. Now I would respect you for helping to save the family before we are completely destroyed. I see things a little differently now.

After 5 months of treatment, Mark admitted to fondling both girls. Both Sandra and Sally confirmed his reports. Mark moved out of the house and was sentenced to 4 years of probation and mandatory treatment. He is still working and supporting the family, and Doris got a part-time job during school hours. The girls moved back into the house. Mark stopped denying the facts, but that was only the beginning of therapy; there were still many layers of work to do.

Mark: I realized that it could be better for the girls and me if I said what really happened. Doris really convinced me when she said that she would try to stay with me and that she believed a good man could do something terrible. I still think things could have been figured out on our own without all these people involved. But what's over is over, and we have to get on with our lives.

Summary

In this case study, we discussed the denial that is present to some degree in all child sexual abuse cases: denial of facts, denial of awareness, denial of impact, and/or denial of responsibility. Because of the social-political climate in which therapists work, we tend to become overly invested in eradicating denial before beginning treatment. However, we need to view denial as a normal and functional coping skill used by family members. In Stage 1 of our three-stage model, the three primary interventions used to focus the treatment are normalization, negative consequences of change, and pretending. The therapy progresses at the pace of the client and helps each individual and the family explore alternative solutions to their emotional and social welfare problems. As they see more alternative solutions to life's problems, they can slowly put their lives back together, piece by piece.

References

BARRETT, M. J., SYKES, C., & BYRNES, W. (1986). Systemic model for the treatment of intrafamily child sexual abuse. In T. S. Trepper & M. J. Barrett (Eds.), *Treating incest: A multiple systems perspective.* New York: Haworth.

FISCH, R., WEAKLAND, J. H., & SEGAL, L. (1982). *The tactics of change: Doing therapy briefly.* San Francisco: Jossey-Bass.

HALEY, J. (1984). *Ordeal therapy.* San Francisco: Jossey-Bass.

MADANES, C. (1981). *Strategic family therapy.* San Francisco: Jossey-Bass.

TREPPER, T., & BARRETT, M. J. (1989). *Systemic treatment of incest: A therapeutic handbook.* New York: Brunner/Mazel.

VI
Case Studies in Using Practice Evaluation

Practice evaluation is increasingly becoming part and parcel of clinical practice. The notion that any practitioner should evaluate the progress they are making or not making with their client is being promoted by the psychology, social work, and counseling professions. References to *evidence-based practice, single system designs, empirical practice,* and *data-oriented problem solvers* reflect many of the contemporary trends in practice today. For the most part, pressure concerning accountability has been a major impetus in this trend. What is the effectiveness of the treatment? Is the client getting better? Should the insurance company keep paying for treatment if there is no progress? These types of questions have kept the helping professions grounded in the demands for accountability.

For practitioners, the two skills needed for practice evaluation are how to select and use rapid assessment instruments and how to conduct ongoing monitoring and evaluation with clients. It is difficult for many practitioners to have access to the hundreds of possible assessment instruments that could be used for evaluation. As a first step, the case examples in this section guide you through that process. Also, many of the examples present information on resources that will be helpful in identifying the possible instruments or measures that could be used. Conducting ongoing monitoring is also a difficult task, primarily due to practical considerations. Overall, the key steps involved in practice evaluation include defining the problem in measurable terms, measuring the problem in an ongoing manner, assessing the results, and making data-based decisions from the information received.

What's different about the new emphasis in practice evaluation is the reliance on standardized and systematic reviews of clinical progress. Practitioners have always been interested in whether their clients are making needed changes. However, their assessments have been subjective and unreliable in the past. Using standardized measures and a systematic process in evaluating treatment outcomes increases the reliability and validity of the observations. Although not foolproof, such procedures do help us get closer to knowing the true impact of our interventions. And knowing whether or not we are truly helping the client is a critical question for any practitioner.

For example, if you were working with a teenage girl who had an eating disorder, you could measure her problem prior to any intervention. This might provide you with additional normative data and an additional perspective to add to a psychosocial assessment. For example, the Eating Disorders Inventory (Garner, 1991) is widely used and would provide information to further identify what aspects of the eating disorder are the most problematic for this client. This could in turn help you identify the priority focus for the intervention. For example, perhaps the most critical aspect is her body image disturbance. Having obtained a "baseline" or pretreatment measure you can gather ongoing assessments to assess the treatment progress of the client. Has the treatment led to a lower score on the Eating Disorders Inventory? While the client might be able to provide clear data on the number of times she purged (self-induced vomiting) since the first week of treatment, it might be harder to assess body image without an instrument like the Eating Disorders Inventory. It is important to remember that clients can experience treatment in three fundamental ways: they can get better, stay the same, or get worse. Increasingly, it is being recognized that some clients do get worse, and having a means to measure this outcome can be an important clinical tool to guide decisions.

Five case studies are included in this section on practice evaluation. The section begins with a case from Corcoran and Davis, who discuss why practitioners should consider using behavioral measures of client progress. Using examples, the authors provide a guidebook and a toolbox for evaluating one's practice.

The next case study, by Fischer, Himle, and Thyer, presents the case of an adolescent female with obsessive-compulsive disorder. They begin with some background on the use of single system designs and then provide an example of a detailed assessment and monitoring system using multiple measures of outcome. Particularly valuable is the combination of measures used to assess outcome, including a scale completed by the clinician, the client's subject rating of distress, self-recorded behavioral data, and global ratings of symptom change. This example shows the many ways that practitioners can gather and use data to assess treatment progress.

The case study by Arbuthnot and Arbuthnot demonstrates the use of evaluation applied to an entire program, in this case, a program for delinquents based on moral reasoning. They show the application of theory to practice and the process of conducting a program evaluation to provide evidence for the theory and the particular program. In today's evidence-based practice environment, the authors document the process of how to gather evidence for a program.

The case study by Franklin, Linseisen, and Soares presents an example of a psychosocial assessment integrating the use of measuring instruments into the report. The study is a pragmatic example of how to write a psychosocial report using the best available data and how to base conclusions and recommendations on the findings. Because exemplars are important in understanding one's trade, this case study is a useful model for students to follow and adapt as they learn about conducting and writing such reports.

In the final case study in this section, Blythe describes an intervention with a sexually abused boy. As the client views his own progress through the use of evaluation and feedback, he is motivated to continue with treatment. This case study is an illustration of the reciprocal effects that can be achieved with personalized evaluation methods: Treatment leads to visible and measurable results, which in turn lead to increased client motivation and belief in the change process. This case study quells the often raised student concern that evaluation is not client focused.

Reference

GARNER, D. M. (1991). *Eating disorders inventory 2. Professional manual.* Odessa, FL: Psychological Assessment Resources.

Case Study 6-1

Questions for Discussion

1. What are the advantages of using measurement of client progress as part of one's ongoing practice?
2. How was the assessment used to help the practitioner develop the treatment plan?
3. What are a SARS and a GAS, and how are they used in practice?
4. What are the advantages and disadvantages of using a measurement package like the one described in the case study?

Creating Useful Behavioral Measures of Client Progress and Outcomes

Kevin Corcoran and Mandy Davis

In current practice settings, social work and counseling students are becoming increasingly familiar with the need to systematically use process and outcome measures. Measurements serve the purpose of allowing practitioners and clients alike to monitor the process throughout treatment as well as the effectiveness at the end of the intervention. Information on process and outcome are not only valuable feedback to the client and the clinician, but are also needed by supervisors, insurance and managed care companies, and many funding agencies. This case study discusses why social workers and counselors should even bother with measurement. We also review different types of measurements that are practical and readily available, how to access measurement scales, and considerations of culture when implementing measurements. Our goal, as the title declares, is to provide you with ways of creating useful measures of a client's process and outcomes of treatment.

Why Bother? Some Benefits of Measurement

Whether you are a student or a practitioner, you are likely to ponder why you should bother using instruments in practice, especially these days when clinicians are overworked and many agencies have waiting lists. Additionally, some instruments are costly, time consuming, and incompatible with certain settings, such as brief hospitalization and single-session treatment. Many instruments are also not useful across different cultures, ethnicities and races, ages, socioeconomic status, and even regions of the country. If these impediments are not enough, once you use an instrument, you must score the darn thing, interpret that score, and explain what it means to your client.

The primary reason for using measurements in practice is that they provide *some* referent to observe possible change. Your client's scores can be compared with one another to observe change, or the scores can be compared with norms from general population and clinical samples. Measures are not, however, anything more than *some* information about the client's thoughts, feelings, or overt performances. While we believe that you should routinely and systematically measure your client's process and treatment outcomes, we do not want to overemphasize scales. We believe that measures are simply supplements to the totality of your professional judgment. That is to say, our position is that when used properly and interpreted judiciously, measurement tools may aid the assessment and diagnosis, help establish realistic treatment goals, contribute to the therapeutic activities of treatment, and provide some additional information to the clinical observations that the client is changing and that goals are being obtained.

Case Illustration

Let us consider a typical situation encountered in practice that supports the use of measurement tools. Skyler, a 15-year-old boy, and his family are referred for outpatient treatment due to several aggressive outbursts at school and his subsequent suspension. By using a rapid assessment instrument to ascertain the magnitude of anger (e.g., the State-Trait Anger Scale; Spielberger, Jacobs, Russell, & Crane, 1983), the practitioner is able to gain a "pulse-beat" on the youngster's feelings. Additionally, by comparing Skyler's scores on the instrument with those of the general population, the practitioner can actually see—observe, if you will—an indicator of Skyler's presenting problem relative to the norms of his peers. This measurement tool would provide useful information if used weekly during treatment and afterward to observe change. This feedback for the client is a powerful positive reinforcer that furthers treatment compliance.

Additionally, the use of a measure like the State-Trait Anger Scale provides persuasive evidence of the need for treatment. In this era of managed care, a critical element of authorizing treatment is whether the mental health condition is sufficiently distressing or disabling to warrant treatment. This is called "treatment necessity," derived from the notion of "medical necessity." If Skyler's score was sufficiently dissimilar from the general population or reflective of a clinical sample already receiving treatment, then most managed care utilization reviewers and clinicians alike would be persuaded that Skyler's presenting problem also warranted treatment (Corcoran & Boyer-Quick, 2002; Corcoran & Vandiver, 1996). In essence, this illustrates how measurements may assist the clinician in assessing, intervening, and even advocating for a client.

Let us consider how administering a general symptom checklist helps assess Skyler's needs. Skyler's parents feel that he has a problem with his anger and they want him referred to an anger management group. Clearly, anger management would be a useful allied service to clinical treatment. When you meet with Skyler, he presents a depressed affect and does not want to talk, simply uttering that he "doesn't have any problems." After administering the Symptom Questionnaire (Kellner, 1987), the results suggest that Skyler is clinically depressed. This information guides you to further assess for depression. The results are also used to educate the family on Skyler's symptoms so that they will support and participate in treatment decisions. As is often the case, the presenting problem is not always the focus of treatment. By using a clinical measurement tool along with information collected from all relevant people, you increase the likelihood of an accurate psychosocial assessment and diagnosis.

After the problem is identified, a plan for treatment needs to be established. The initial step in treatment planning is to determine realistic goals. This includes helping clients reframe their needs or complaints into treatment goals. The measurement tool used for diagnosis in the assessment phase now becomes a tool for establishing goals. For instance, if Skyler scored 40 on the Generalized Contentment Scale (Hudson, 1997), this score would indicate clinical depression; the treatment goal might be for him to score below 30, which indicates the absence of depression.

Once a clear goal is defined, measures help you know whether the intervention is working and whether the desired change has occurred. In most cases after a general assessment tool is administered to help determine the problem, a specific or more narrowly tailored assessment tool facilitates monitoring change. Hudson's Generalized Contentment Scale is an example of this type of instrument. Alternatively, a subscale on the general measure may be used in tracking the particular client problem. Aside from standardized instruments, individualized measures may be created for the client, such as a Self-Anchored Rating Scale.

An added benefit of using measurements is that they are likely to enhance your professional confidence, thus indirectly promote your effectiveness. Referring to Skyler's case, you may have "sensed" that he was depressed, and the score on the measurement helps validate your clinical judgment. Confidence is further enhanced when there is consistent monitoring of the intervention, allowing you to observe that you are helping the client.

A final indirect benefit of using measurement tools is the overall advantage to the professions of counseling and social work. By supporting our work and observing clinical progress through routine measurement, we contribute to the development of effective interventions and thereby strengthen our profession. This further enhances the credibility of the disciplines.

In summary, measurement tools help clinical social workers and counselors identify target problems, develop treatment goals, monitor progress and outcomes, increase professional confidence, and support the professions' growth. But if they are this powerful, why are they not used routinely by practitioners? Aside from an empirical anxiety characteristic of many master's-level practitioners, measures are *initially* difficult to locate and learn to use. We emphasize that this impediment is only when you first start using measurements. Once you have learned to use them, the difficulty and demands are minimal. We hope that the rest of this case study facilitates your finding of instruments and comfort in developing individualized measures for your clients.

The Starting Toolbox

The challenge of outfitting a clinical toolbox of measurement scales is determining which ones are appropriate for your specific population or clinical work. One of the best ways to determine if the measurement might be appropriate is to complete it yourself. This allows you to get to know the nuisances and subtleties of the measurement and provides a vicarious experience of how a client might react to it.

Clearly, if you are working with any client that is referred, you will have a much wider range of instruments to master than if you work with just a few types of clinical problems. We hope, moreover, that your practice is at least somewhat restricted to just a few problems because generalists have a much harder job mastering the depth of treatment skills available to specialists. Not only does being more specialized result in enhanced mastery of effective interventions, but it makes locating measurements more manageable and less time consuming.

To use measures in practice, it is necessary to start building a toolbox of instruments. To begin with, we recommend three types of instruments. These are one or two broadband measures such as checklists, one or two narrowband instruments that have been standardized on relevant populations and can be used over time, and one or two individualized measurements developed for the client's particular problems and treatment goals.

Broadband measures refer to instruments that ascertain the breadth of a problem or a number of dimensions in a general construct, such as "mental health." It does not necessarily ascertain a specific clinical condition in great detail. You will find it useful to routinely use a couple of broadband instruments to assess the general mental health status of clients. As illustrated with Skyler, the Symptom Questionnaire (SQ) facilitated the assessment and helped narrow the focus of treatment.

The SQ is a marvelous instrument that evaluates four major dimensions of mental health problems: depression, anxiety, somatization, and anger/hostility. It also evaluates four aspects of well-being that parallel the four clinical conditions: contentment, relaxation, somatic well-being, and friendliness, respectively. These four measures of well-being are good indirect assessments of the treatment goals. The SQ has the advantage of not only measuring the client's problem, but also indirectly measuring of the treatment goals. In Skyler's case, the goal was to increase his sense of contentment and friendliness while concurrently decreasing his feelings of depression and anger.

The SQ measures all of this with a 92-adjective checklist that takes less than 5 minutes to complete. Moreover, clients can complete the SQ with respect to different timeframes, such as how they feel right now or how they felt last month or six months ago. Similarly, clients could complete the SQ in terms of how they feel now, at their worst, and in general. This type of retrospective information provides observations of the magnitude of the general mental health conditions over a simulated time period in order to establish a trend of the client's condition.

Another highly recommended broadband measurement is the Health Survey, or HS (Ware, Kosinski, & Keller, 1994). The HS comes in two short forms, a 36-item version and a 12-item version, commonly referred to as the SF-36 and SF-12. The HS ascertains general physical health and general mental health. Each of these composite scales consists of subscales. The physical health scale consists of physical functioning, physical role, pain, and general health. The mental health composite scale consists of vitality, social functioning, emotional role, and general mental health. As with the SQ, you might find that once you have a "pulse-beat" on the physical health and mental health, one of these particular subscales is useful for monitoring client change. The composite scale can then be used again at the end of treatment as an outcome measure in comparison to the scores at the initial assessment.

This broadband measurement has been widely tested on numerous international and cultural samples. It appears, unlike so many other instruments, to be fairly sensitive to culture, gender, and age. Additionally, the HS is available free of charge and is accessible on the Internet (www.outcomes-trust.org). Like the SQ, it only takes a few minutes to complete.

Narrowband measures are instruments that focus on a particular problem and that usually do so by sampling more attributes of the domain than are found with broadband measures. Literally tens of thousands of narrowband instruments are available through commercial publishing houses, research articles, and the Internet. The ones you will want to use are relatively short, understandable to the client, quick to complete, and easily interpreted. Further, they should be sensitive to change over time and should assess a behavior state as opposed to an enduring personality trait. This type of instrument is often called a rapid assessment instrument (RAI). A RAI contrasts sharply with measures like the Minnesota Multiphasic Personality Index (MMPI) which is lengthy, time-consuming to complete, difficult and costly to score and interpret, and is completely useless for repeated administration over the course of treatment.

There are also thousands of RAIs that are relevant to clinical practice. The challenge is finding the ones you need. A number of valuable resources discuss this type of instrument (e.g., Mash & Terdal, 1997; Olin & Keatinge, 1998), as well as volumes that review lengthier instruments, such as *The Mental Measurement Yearbook* (Conoley & Kramer, 1995), *Tests in Print* (Mitchell, 1983), and *Test Critiques* (Keyser & Sweetland, 1991). There are also journals that routinely publish new instruments, such as *Behavior Assessment, Journal of Personality Assessment,* and *Psychological Assessment.*

Probably the most useful sources of RAIs are books that actually publish the instruments in their entirety. McCubbin, Thompson, and McCubbin (1996) have such a book for assessing family issues and Hudson (1997) has one for about a dozen clinical conditions. There is also Corcoran and Fischer's *Measures for Clinical Practice* (2000a, 2000b), a two-volume set of reprinted instruments for couples, families, and children and measures for adult conditions. The books include nearly 500 instruments reprinted in their entirety.

In addition to these hard-copy sources, thousands of instruments are available on the Internet. The Internet, in fact, provides access to *Mental Measurement Yearbook, Tests in Print,* and *Test Critiques,* as well as over 1,000 commercial publishing houses and several other electronic locators. Two extremely useful websites are ERIC/AE Test (www.ericae.testcol.htm) and WWW Resources for Social Workers (www.nyu

.edu/socialwork/sssrsw). Both of these websites provide access to thousands of relevant sites. While both are rather easy to navigate, you will probably find far too many instruments and be challenged to select those that are the most appropriate.

Individualized instruments, which are developed for an individual client, are another type of measurement that we recommend you routinely use. Many, if not most, of the instruments available are for clinical problems. As measures of goals, they are limited to indirectly monitoring the absence of the problems. Often, you will want to more directly ascertain the actual goal of treatment, which is where individualized instruments are useful. Two types of individualized instruments are easy to develop and use: Self-Anchored Rating Scales (SARS) and Goal Attainment Scales (GAS).

A SARS is a single item or two that reflect the goal or problem. A SARS is developed by writing polarized descriptions of the goal or problem and then arranging these two extremes on a continuum of numbers, such as 1 to 7 or 1 to 10. For children who lack the ability to make such fine recognitions, you would use a 1 to 3 or 1 to 4 continuum. To use the SARS, simply have the client simply rate his or her behavior along the continuum. For children, you can illustrate the difference creatively, such as showing a glass a little full, half full, and full. Regardless of whether the range of scores is 1 to 3 or 1 to whatever, the SARS is more accurate if you write a midlevel description of the goal or problem and place it in the middle of the continuum of scores. One specific benefit of the SARS is that it literally only takes a second or two to complete. This allows your client to measure the construct frequently and in various settings with little disruption.

The second individualized instrument that we recommend is the Goal Attainment Scale (GAS), frequently called goal attainment scaling (Kiresuk, Smith, & Cardillo, 1994). A GAS is developed by writing a description of the "expected" outcome of treatment, two descriptions of "more than expected" outcomes, and two descriptions of "less than expected" outcomes. The "expected" is the midpoint on the continuum of scores from 1 to 5 with "more than expected" and "less than expected" being scored with higher and lower numbers, respectively.

Like the SARS, it is essential that the descriptions of the outcome be clearly written, thorough, understandable, and observable to the client or some relevant other who may be making the observations. In the case of Skyler, this may be his parents, teachers, a trusted friend, or perhaps you, the clinician.

The types of instruments described here are an excellent start to supplying a toolbox with useful and practical measures of client progress and outcomes. Broadband instruments facilitate the initial assessment and problem identification, while RAIs and individualized measures are conducive to monitoring clients repeatedly over the course of treatment. All of these instruments are useful for assessing whether the client has changed by termination, and we recommend that at the end of treatment, you again administer the original broadband measures. The RAIs administered at a follow-up will help you judge whether the change is stable.

A Final Consideration of Culture

There are, of course, many more tools that you will eventually want to add to your toolbox. Moreover, this beginning approach is not without limitations. Chief among them is the fact that most instruments are not necessarily appropriate for different cultures and are not standardized with diverse groups, such as different races, genders, ages, and other pertinent characteristics of clients. An excellent discussion of these and other specific limitations is provided by Cuellar and Paniagua (2000), who not only delineate the defects but offer some solutions. Because of this type of limitation, you will find that the individualized instruments are very helpful, especially if you and your client actively work together to develop the instruments.

Measures are culturally insensitive when they reflect only the Western-European or American constructs of mental health and behavior problems. What a Western European or American considers a mental health condition or problem may very well be an appropriate and preferable behavior in a different culture, such as auditory hallucinations by some Native Americans upon the death of a parent or elder. The potential cultural bias may be decreased when you work with the client by developing individualized measures, as we have recommended.

This last concern takes use back to where we actually began: Measurements are valuable for monitoring client progress and outcomes but they must be interpreted judiciously. A measurement simply produces a number. That number serves as an indicator of the behavior and a referent point to note change. The scores, obviously, are not the problem or goal. The limitation in the number is exacerbated by culture, race, gender, age, religion, regions of the country, and . . . , well, you get the idea. Thus, we conclude by reiterating one of our initial points: Measurements are a supplement—and never a substitute—for the totality of your experience, intuition, clinical judgment, client feedback, and other credible sources of information about how your client is changing behaviors and reaching treatment goals.

References

CONOLEY, J. C., & KRAMER, J. J. (1995). *The twelfth mental measurement yearbook.* Lincoln, NE: Buros Institute of Mental Measurement.

CORCORAN, K., & BOYER-QUICK, J. (2002). How clinicians can effectively use assessment tools to evidence medical necessity and throughout the treatment process. In A. R. Roberts & G. Greene (Eds.), *The social work desk reference* (pp. 198–204). New York: Oxford University Press.

CORCORAN, K., & FISCHER, J. (2000a). *Measures for clinical practice: A sourcebook, Vol. 1, Couples, families, and children.* New York: Free Press.

CORCORAN, K., & FISCHER, J. (2000b). *Measures for clinical practice: A sourcebook, Vol. 2, Adults.* New York: Free Press.

CORCORAN, K., & VANDIVER, V. L. (1996). *Maneuvering the maze of managed care: Skills for mental health professionals.* New York: Free Press.

CUELLAR, I., & PANIAGUA, F. A. (2000). *Handbook of multicultural mental health.* San Diego: Academic Press.

HUDSON, W. W. (1997). *WALMYR assessment scales scoring manual.* Tallahassee, FL: WALMYR Publishing.

KELLNER, R. (1987). A symptom questionnaire. *Journal of Clinical Psychiatry, 48,* 268–274.

KEYSER, D. J., & SWEETLAND, R. C. (Eds.). (1991). *Test critiques* (Vol. 8). Austin, TX: Pro-Ed.

KIRESUK, T. J., SMITH, A., & CARDILLO, J. E. (Eds.). (1994). *Goal attainment scaling: Applications, theory, and measurement.* Hillsdale, NJ: Erlbaum.

MASH, E. J., & TERDAL, L. G. (1997). *Assessment of childhood disorder* (3rd ed.). New York: Guilford.

MCCUBBIN, H. I., THOMPSON, A. I., & MCCUBBIN, M. A. (1996). *Family assessment: Resilience, coping, and adaptation. Inventories for research and practice.* Madison, WI: University of Wisconsin Press.

MITCHELL, J. V. (Ed.). (1983). *Tests in print, III.* Lincoln, NE: University of Nebraska Press.

OLIN, J. T., & KEATINGE, C. (1998). *Rapid psychological assessments.* New York: Wiley.

SPIELBERGER, C. D., JACOBS, G., RUSSELL, S., & CRANE, R. S. (1983). The State-Trait anger scale. In J. N. Butcher & C. D. Spielberger (Eds.), *Advances in personality assessment* (Vol. 2, pp. 159–187). Hillsdale, NJ: Erlbaum.

WARE, J. E., KOSINSKI, M., & KELLER, S. D. (1994). *SF-36 physical and mental health summary scales: A user's manual.* Boston: Medical Outcomes Trust.

Case Study 6-2

Questions for Discussion
1. What is an SSRD and how is it used in practice?
2. What major treatment strategies were used to help the client change?
3. How did the practitioner get the client to collect data that would be useful in evaluating treatment progress in this case?
4. What skills and knowledge were evident in the application of practice evaluation to this case?

Using Multiple Evaluation Methods to Assess Client Progress: A Female Adolescent with Obsessive-Compulsive Disorder

Daniel J. Fischer, Joseph A. Himle, and Bruce A. Thyer

Clinical social workers are increasingly making use of evidenced-based approaches in their practice. An evidence-based approach to social work services is quite consistent with the Code of Ethics of the National Association of Social Workers (see www.naswdc.org), which states, in part:

- Social workers should base practice on recognized knowledge, including empirically based knowledge, relevant to social work and social work ethics. (Standard 4.01)
- Social workers should monitor and evaluate policies, the implementation of problems, and practice interventions. (5.02a)
- Social workers should critically examine and keep current with emerging knowledge relevant to social work and fully use evaluation and research evidence in their professional practice. (5.02c)

Contemporary educational standards promulgated by the Council on Social Work Education (CSWE, 2001, italics added) are also supportive of an evidence-based approach to practice, such as:

- Social work education combines *scientific inquiry* with the teaching of professional skills to provide *effective* and ethical social work services. (p. 3)
- Use theoretical frameworks *supported by empirical evidence* to understand individual development and behavior. (p. 9)
- Practice content also included identifying, analyzing, and implementing *empirically based interventions* designed to achieve client goals . . . *evaluating* program outcomes and practice effectiveness. (p. 12)
- The content prepares students to develop, use, and effectively communicate *empirically based knowledge, including evidence-based interventions.* (p. 12)

TABLE 1   Selected Sources for Information About Evidence-based Practice

Campbell Collaboration; see http://campbell.gse.upenn.edu.
Centre for Evidence-based Social Services; see www.ex.ac.uk/cebss.
Cochrane Database of Systematic Reviews; see www.cochrane.org.
Davies, H. T., Nutley, S. M., & Smith, P. (2000). *What works? Evidence-based policy and practice.* Bristol, UK: Policy Press.
Geyman, J. P., Deyo, R. A., & Ramsey, S. D. (2000). *Evidence-based clinical practice.* Boston: Butterworth Heinemann.
Gibbs, L. E. (2003). *Evidence-based practice for the helping professions.* Pacific Grove, CA: Brooks/Cole.
Gibbs, L. E., & Gambrill, E. (2002). Evidence-based practice: Counter-arguments to objections. *Research on Social Work Practice, 12,* 452–476.
Gray, J. A. M. (1997). *Evidence-based health care: How to make better policy and management decisions.* New York: Churchill Livingstone.
Sackett, D. L., Straus, S. E., Richardson, W. S., Rosenberg, W., & Haynes, R. B. (2000). *Evidenced-based medicine: How to practice and teach EBM* (2nd ed.). New York: Churchill Livingstone.
Sheldon, B., & Chilvers, R. (2000). *Evidence-based social care.* Lyme Regis, UK: Russell House.

Evidence-based practice suggests that clinicians seek out and critically evaluate available scientific evidence pertaining to potential assessment and intervention methods that address the care of individuals with selected psychosocial difficulties, determine the extent to which the available and credible evidence may have applications to the individuals for whom you are providing services, consult clients for their preferences and inform them of the scientific justification for the services you propose to provide, develop expertise in those interventive methods which seem applicable, apply these competently, and then empirically evaluate the outcomes of service. A wide array of journal articles, textbooks, and websites are now available for clinical social workers to consult for such an evidence-based approach to service (see Table 1), and the ethical social worker will make use of these and other emerging sources of scientifically reliable knowledge.

Intrinsic to conducting evidence-based practice is not only selecting valid measures of assessment and methods of intervention that have been credibly shown to be useful with similar clients and problems, but also the process of carefully appraising the outcomes of one's services with individual clients. Although this may be done using a number of research methods, among the most scientifically justifiable approaches for clinical evaluation purposes is that known as the single-system research design (SSRD).

SSRDs have been used by social workers since the mid-1960s, and examples of evaluating clinical practice outcomes with this methodology have appeared in every major social work journal (Thyer & Thyer, 1992). Most contemporary research textbooks also contain one or more chapters describing this approach, and it has been well accepted by practitioners of diverse theoretical orientations because the approach is essentially theory-neutral. Examples can be found in the social work literature that illustrate using SSRDs to evaluate psychodynamic practice, solution-focused treatment, narrative therapy, behavior analysis, cognitive-behavioral treatment, marital and family interventions, community-based practice, and social work with groups, with the variety of interventive models supporting the view that this approach is theory-neutral. The basic principles of SSRDs are deceptively simple (see Thyer, 1998, 2001a, 2001b), consisting of the following:

1. Locate one or more reliable and valid measures of client functioning that pertain to the presenting problem. These measures should be culturally appropriate, practical, easy to read or otherwise apply, and ethically sound.
2. Take several measures of client functioning, ideally before, during, and after social work intervention.
3. Graphically present the data and visually examine the results to see if the measures reflect enhanced client functioning and/or problem reduction.
4. Combine the data from step 3 with information obtained via interviews with the client, with reports from significant others in his/her life, and with other relevant indicators to draw conclusions regarding clinical outcomes.

Note that it is *not* usually possible to draw rigorous causal inferences about the presumptive effectiveness of social work intervention *per se;* instead, it is the more modest goal of trying to document simply if the client got better. If they did not, then you *can* conclude that treatment *was not* effective. If they did improve, this is best and most conservatively seen as evidence consistent with the hypothesis that social work treatment brought about these changes, while remaining aware that other factors may well have been responsible. Other influences that can result in clinical improvements include various nonspecific therapeutic factors (e.g., attention from the social worker or placebo effects), the mere passage of time, naturally occurring perturbations in functioning, other events transpiring in the client's life, and so forth. Still, simply documenting client improvements using methods that are more reliable than (and in addition to) one's client judgment, is a major step in fulfilling the mandate of evidence-based practice (EBP) and of social work in general, relating to one's professional responsibility for evaluating outcomes.

The authors of this case study are all clinical social workers who have worked for some years in providing specialized psychosocial treatment in both outpatient and inpatient mental health settings, focusing on individuals who met the criteria for what the *Diagnostic and Statistical Manual of Mental Disorders* (American Psychiatric Association, 1994) calls anxiety disorders. The third author was the field instructor for the second author when he was earning his MSW, and the second author in turn served some years later as the field instructor for the first author while he completed *his* MSW. In the following case study, the actual clinical services were provided by the first author.

Case Description

Judy (a pseudonym) was a 16-year-old Caucasian girl who presented at the Child/ Adolescent Psychiatry Outpatient Clinic with a 3-year history of severe obsessive-compulsive symptomatology and concurrent major depression. Judy and her mother reported that obsessive-compulsive symptoms first appeared at age 13. At that time, Judy developed a problem with serious facial acne and began to obsessively worry that she was contacting and spreading oily and greasy substances onto her hands and face. Greasy foods such as potato chips and snack foods, pizza, french fries, and salad dressings that left residues or sensations of residues on her hands, lips, and face were particularly anxiety producing. She began to avoid contact with these types of foods, limiting her eating to dry salads, cereals, bread, cut-up fruits, and skinless chicken. She always used utensils and typically wore rubber gloves on her hands when eating. She avoided contact with tabletops, kitchen counters, and the cafeteria at school.

Judy also developed severe, compulsive washing rituals in an effort to control the anxiety associated with her obsessions and to keep herself "clean." At the time of her evaluation with our program, Judy was spending 3–6 hours per day engaging in ritualized hand and arm washing, showering, and brushing her teeth. Individual acts of hand washing that could last 5–10 minutes each averaged approximately 15 per day. Judy's skin was noticeably red, chapped, and irritated from the tips of her fingers to just above her elbows. Her showers, which always occurred before bed, could last from 45 minutes to an hour and a half. Showers involved ritualized washing patterns, starting with her hair and working down to her feet. She completely lathered an area, turned off the water and stood with the soap on her skin until she felt "cleansed." She would repeat this 2–3 times during each shower. Toothbrushing, which took about 10 minutes each time, occurred after eating, in the morning, and at bedtime. Judy also swallowed the toothpaste because this made her feel cleaner. Judy's washing rituals consumed most of the evening hours, and she generally fell asleep between 1:00 a.m. and 3:00 a.m., after completing her rituals.

At evaluation, Judy also endorsed symptoms of major depressive disorder, including prolonged periods of sadness, diminished interest or pleasure in most activities, feelings of hopelessness and worthlessness, irritability, diminished concentration, weight loss, and occasional suicidal ideation. She had had some decline in academic performance, but remained an above-average student. Judy had virtually no meaningful friendships and reported that her obsessions and compulsions consumed her life. She met the criteria found in the *Diagnostic and Statistical Manual of Mental Disorders* (American Psychiatric Association, 1994) for a diagnosis of obsessive-compulsive disorder (OCD) and major depressive disorder (MDD) from a clinical social worker who was a trained and experienced diagnostician, and through a standardized, structured interview with another clinician who followed the protocol of the Schedule for Affective Disorder and Schizophrenia for School-Aged Children, Epidemiologic

Version (K-SADS-E; Orvaschel, 1995). At the time of her evaluation, Judy was being treated with Prozac, 50 mg daily, which seemed to have improved her depression but had minimal effect on her OCD. Judy had also had a previously unsuccessful trial of weekly outpatient cognitive-behavioral therapy, because she found it difficult to comply with the behavioral homework assignments.

Social Work Intervention

Social work intervention to address Judy's contamination obsessions and washing rituals consisted of individual cognitive-behavioral therapy (CBT) with a focus on exposure and response prevention (ERP) and complimentary cognitive techniques. The CBT program consisted of four phases: (1) behavioral assessment and treatment planning, (2) 5 days of intensive (9 hours per day) therapist-assisted ERP, (3) six weekly 1-hour sessions of individual CBT, and (4) a follow-up session at 2 months.

Behavioral assessment involved gathering information on the specific nature, frequency, duration, and severity of Judy's OCD symptoms, including anxiety-producing situational and obsessional triggers and the compulsive responses and avoidances she used to lessen or escape anxiety and discomfort. Additionally, during this phase, cognitive strategies were utilized in an effort to enhance Judy's motivation and willingness to participate in intensive ERP. Following an approach developed by March, Mulle, and Herbel (1994), Judy was encouraged to develop a cognitive framework in which OCD was externalized and viewed as a bully or enemy for her to overcome by using ERP techniques. Additionally, Judy was taught how to use self-coping statements, such as "It's just my OCD; I can win" and "My discomfort is just an OCD temper tantrum and proves I'm gaining control" to help manage initial discomfort during ERP assignments.

For the next phase of intervention, involving intensive therapist-assisted ERP, Judy and her mother checked in for 5 days at the Med Inn located within the University of Michigan Medical Center. Judy was assisted by the senior author (a clinical social worker) and a team of graduate social work students in conducting progressively more challenging ERP assignments from 9:00 a.m. until 6:00 p.m. daily. Specific ERP assignments focused directly on Judy's obsessions related to contamination from greasy, oily foods and substances and the resulting washing rituals. Four specific graduated exposure assignments were utilized. First, Judy completed hourly full body sprays with a solution of water and olive oil. She also used this solution to spray her clothes, bed, and others items (favorite teddy bears, books, and CDs) that she brought with her to the hotel. Another exposure assignment involved Judy smearing her hands with a variety of greasy foods, such as salad dressing, peanut butter, potato chips, french fries, and pizza, and spreading these "contaminants" onto her face, arms, and hair and onto objects in her environment. The third assignment included a "contaminated," greasy rag that Judy carried in her pocket. The rag was contaminated by a daily application of olive oil, various foods, and touching previously avoided surfaces in the hospital cafeteria. Judy was instructed to "recontaminate" herself with the rag every half hour throughout the day by rubbing it on her clothes, hands, and skin. Finally, all meals and snacks consisted

TABLE 2   Record of Results

	Pre-treatment	*Intensive Treatment*	*Weekly Treatment*	*Follow-up*
Obsessions	15.5	8.5	6	6
Compulsions	17	4.5	6	6.5
Total	32.5	13	12	12.5

	Spray	*Smear*	*Rag*	*Meals*
Intensive Treatment	80	95	90	90
Weekly Treatment	60	80	70	80

	Spray	*Smear*	*Rag*	*Meals*
Follow-up	80	60	40	60
	55	90	60	25
	45	40	30	10
	70	50	60	20
	40	40	30	10
	15	32	30	10
	20	30	20	10
	10	35	10	5
	10	25	10	10
	10	20	10	0

of greasy foods, such as pizza and french fries, that Judy would eat using her hands. Response prevention involved an immediate reduction in the frequency and duration of hand washing, showering, and brushing her teeth. Showering was limited to one morning shower lasting 10 minutes with limited soap available. Hand washing was allowed only after using the toilet and was limited to 30 seconds or less. She was also allowed to rinse her hands with water at the end of each treatment day. Brushing her teeth was limited to two times per day (morning and bedtime), with 1 minute allowed for each brushing. Toothpaste use was also controlled, and she was encouraged to discontinue the practice of swallowing the toothpaste. The therapeutic team consistently offered modeling, encouragement, and support throughout intervention and collaborated with Judy in developing and increasing the challenge of all exposure assignments.

The final two stages of intervention took place after Judy returned home from the 5-day intensive program. She was assigned daily ERP homework and was seen weekly for individual CBT sessions for 6 consecutive weeks. Sessions focused on a review of her progress and modification of the ERP assignments as necessary. Daily ERP homework consisted of continued use of the assignments established during the intensive treatment week. This included 10 daily applications of the solution of water and olive oil, carrying the "contaminated" rag throughout the day and rubbing it on her hands 10 times per day, applying salad dressing to her hands and leaving it on for 90 minutes per day, and eating "greasy" food for meals and snacks. All response prevention guidelines remained the same as during the intensive treatment week. After 6 weeks, Judy was asked to continue ERP assignments daily and was seen for one final follow-up session 2 months later. See Table 2.

Use of Multiple Measures

Multiple measures were used to evaluate treatment outcome, including client self-reported information, clinician observations of behavior, and parental reports. Measures were utilized to gain information on changes in symptom severity, as well as behavioral change measures aimed at assessing functional improvement. The Children's Yale-Brown Obsessive-Compulsive Scale, or CY-BOCS (Goodman et al., 1989a, 1989b), was used to rate the severity of obsessive-compulsive symptoms before and after the 5-day intensive intervention phase and at the final follow-up session (see Figure 1). The CY-BOCS is a clinician-rated scale that scores the severity of 10 items from 0 (none) to 4 (extreme). The 10 items are divided into two subscales that measure obsessions and compulsions. The CY-BOCS has been shown to have good validity and inter-rater reliability and a high degree of internal consistency (Scahill et al., 1997). CY-BOCS scores translate into symptom severity as follows: 0–7 subclinical, 8–15 mild, 16–23 moderate, 24–31 severe, and 32–40 extreme. All CY-BOCS ratings were completed by the primary therapist, a clinical social worker.

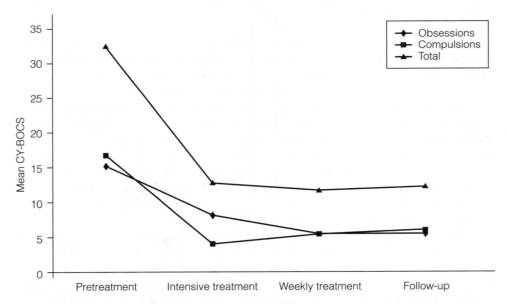

FIGURE 1 Children's Yale-Brown Obsessive-Compulsive Scale (CY-BOCS) scores before and after the 5-day intensive intervention phase and at follow-up.

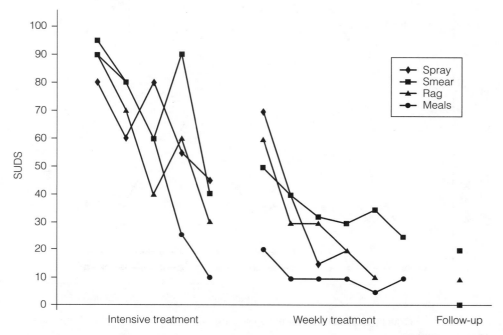

FIGURE 2   Client's subjective ratings of anxiety score (SUDS) during intensive treatment and weekly treatment sessions.

The client's subjective ratings of anxiety, as operationalized using subjective units of distress, or SUDS, were also used to monitor the effects of intentional, prolonged, and repeated daily exposure assignments, during both the intensive treatment week and subsequent weekly sessions (see Figure 2). SUDS ratings were based on a 0–100 scale with 0 representing no anxiety and 100 representing extreme or maximum anxiety. Each data point represents the average of the daily subjective anxiety ratings given by the client for each exposure task (e.g., olive oil solution, greasy foods applied to hands and skin, contamination rag, and finger-fed meals and snacks). The average daily score was obtained by summing the actual individual subjective ratings for each exposure trial and dividing this total by the number of repetitions, thereby obtaining the mean score for that specific exposure task. Increases during the intensive week treatment phase typically represent increased difficulty of the exposure tasks.

Overt behavioral data was also used in evaluating intervention outcome. Specifically, frequency and duration of hand washing, showers, and brushing teeth were monitored and recorded by Judy and her mother for 1 week prior to the start of treatment. During the intensive week intervention phase, clinical staff monitored and recorded this information, and the client and her mother collected this data during the weekly treatment phase (see Figures 3 and 4).

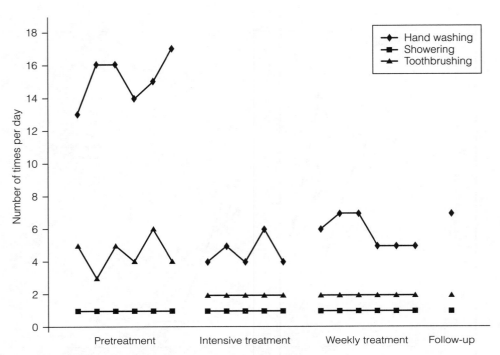

FIGURE 3 Frequency and duration of hand washing, showering, and toothbrushing one week prior to treatment.

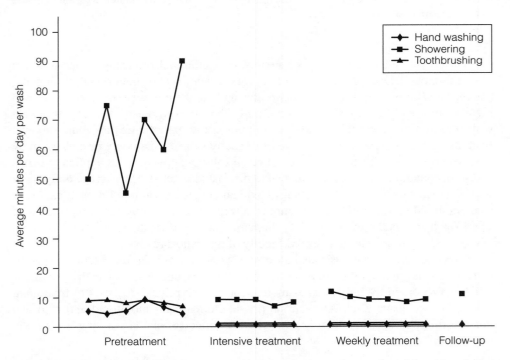

FIGURE 4 Frequency and duration of hand washing, showering, and toothbrushing during intensive treatment.

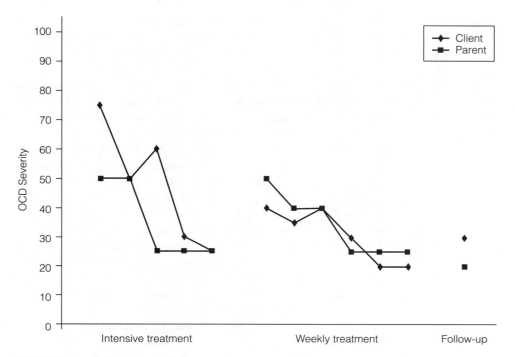

FIGURE 5   Global ratings of symptom change (daily and then weekly) obtained from client and mother.

Finally, global ratings of symptom change were obtained on a daily and then weekly basis from both Judy and her mother. They were independently asked to rate their overall impressions of symptom severity using a scale from 0 (no OCD symptoms) to 100 (worst-ever OCD symptoms). Figure 5 represents Judy's and her mother's global OCD symptom ratings.

Results and Commentary

We believe that this case study illustrates a viable approach to evidence-based practice within clinical social work. Following a careful review of the available scientific literature, we judged that the nosological system described in the DSM-IV (*Diagnostic and Statistical Manual of Mental Disorders,* 4th ed.) represented a reasonable categorization system relevant to Judy's presenting problems, namely obsessive-compulsive disorder and major depression. We supplemented the first author's clinical judgment with a more objective, structured interview protocol, the K-SADS-E, which corroborated this judgment. Multiple measures of client function were obtained before, during, and after treatment, including client-self reports (SUDS scores during exposure tasks), a structured clinician rating system (CY-BOCS scores), and direct measures of the observable behaviors that represented Judy's primary presenting problems, gathered by the client, her mother, and by clinical social work interns (frequency and duration of hand washing, showering, and toothbrushing). The SUDS scores have been shown to be a reliable and valid indicator, correlating well with psychophysiological measures of anxiety (Thyer, Papsdorf, Davis, & Vallecorsa, 1984); the CY-BOCS has strong (albeit not perfect) scientific evidence supporting its use in the assessment of individuals meeting the criteria for OCD, and the direct measures of behavior possess persuasive face validity. If resources permitted, it would have been a scientific improvement to use *two independent raters* for assessing these measures of frequency and duration and to calculate their inter-rater agreement for at least a portion of their observations, perhaps about a third of them. However, we lacked the staff to undertake this more ambitious step. Additionally, more global measures of Judy's functioning, perhaps not so narrowly focused on her OCD, would have been useful. Examples might have included pre- and post-treatment measures of life satisfaction, peer-relations, and self-image. The relationship between the comprehensiveness of assessment and knowledge gain likely follows an inverse U-spaced curve, however. Adding more and more assessment methods may have yielded more information, but at some point, Judy and her mother (and perhaps the MSW interns!) would have rebelled, finding their participation in these evaluation efforts an unacceptable burden. Thus, the clinician must perforce strive for a balance between using no scientific measures and using an overwhelming plethora of them.

The behavioral treatment was grueling but was indeed followed by considerable improvements in functioning and reduced reports of subjective distress, corroborated by the clinical judgments of the social workers involved in providing care as well as the client's mother. Treatment gains seemed to be maintained at follow-up, and the consistency of improvements in the data obtained across all four response domains (client self-reports, observers' reports, global judgments of severity, and CY-BOCS) supports the conclusion that Judy was indeed better off after her receipt of clinical social work services.

We submit that this case illustrates the application of evidence-based practice within the field of clinical social work. The chosen treatment was selected on the basis of its strong scientific support, as were the assessment measures (Fischer, Himle, & Hanna, 1998; Himle, Rassi, Haghightgou, Nesse, & Abelson, 2001; Himle & Thyer, 1989). We could not locate a "better" approach to care for Judy, in terms of its scientific credibility, and the assessment measures, while not perfect, were a considerable enhancement over otherwise unaided clinical judgment. As a scientific research design, the approach we used could be described as weak in terms of internal validity (e.g., ability to confidently claim that social work treatment *caused* Judy's improvements), but it was practical and very helpful clinically. Judy and her mother had a variety of treatment options explained to her, as well as the justification for the interventive program that was recommended. They elected to follow this approach as informed and willing consumers and, of course, could have halted their participation in the treatment program at any point. That they chose not to do so, and indeed persevered remarkably well, is a testament to the severity of the problems they experienced, their desperation, and the expertise of the clinical social worker who had the specialized knowledge necessary to design a specific, evidence-based approach to care. We believe not only that such specialized knowledge is increasingly useful to social workers, regardless of the area in which they practice, but that it is becoming an ethical mandate for responsible professional service.

References

AMERICAN PSYCHIATRIC ASSOCIATION. (1994). *Diagnostic and statistical manual of mental disorders* (4th ed.). Washington, DC: Author.

COUNCIL ON SOCIAL WORK EDUCATION. (2001). *Educational policy and accreditation standards.* Alexandria, VA: Author.

FISCHER, D. J., HIMLE, J. A., & HANNA, G. L. (1998). Group behavioral therapy for adolescents with obsessive-compulsive disorder. *Research on Social Work Practice, 8,* 629–636.

GOODMAN, W. K., PRICE, L. H., RASMUSSEN, S. A., MAZURE, C., DELGADO, P., HENINGER, G. R., & CHARNEY, D. S. (1989a). The Yale-Brown Obsessive Compulsive Scale I: Development, use, and reliability. *Archives of General Psychiatry, 46,* 1006–1011.

GOODMAN, W. K., PRICE, L. H., RASMUSSEN, S. A., MAZURE, C., FLEISCHMANN, R. L., HILL, C. L., HENINGER, G. R., & CHARNEY, D. S. (1989b). The Yale-Brown Obsessive Compulsive Scale II: Validity. *Archives of General Psychiatry, 46,* 1012–1016.

HIMLE, J. A., RASSI, S., HAGHIGHTGOU, H., NESSE, R. M., & ABELSON, J. L. (2001). Group behavioral therapy for obsessive-compulsive disorder. *Anxiety, 13,* 161–165.

HIMLE, J., & THYER, B. A. (1989). Clinical social work and obsessive compulsive disorder. *Behavior Modification, 13,* 459–470.

MARCH, J. S., MULLE, K., & HERBEL, B. (1994). Behavioral psychotherapy for children and adolescents with obsessive-compulsive disorder: An open trial of a new protocol-driven treatment package. *Journal of the American Academy of Child and Adolescent Psychiatry, 33,* 333–341.

ORVASCHEL, H. (1995). *Schedule for affective disorders and schizophrenia for school-age children: Epidemiologic Version 5*.* Fort Lauderdale, FL: Nova Southeastern University, Center for Psychological Studies.

SCAHILL, L., RIDDLE, M. A., MCSWIGGIN-HARDIN, M. T., ORT, S., KING, R. A., GOODMAN, W. K., CICCHETTI, D., & LECKMAN, J. F. (1997). The Children's Yale-Brown Obsessive-Compulsive Scale: Preliminary report of reliability and validity. *Journal of the American Academy of Child and Adolescent Psychiatry, 36,* 844–853.

THYER, B. A. (1998). Promoting research on community practice: Using single-system designs. In R. H. MacNair (Ed.), *Research strategies in community practice* (pp. 47–61). Binghamton, NY: Haworth.

THYER, B. A. (2001a). Single system designs. In R. M. Grinnell (Ed.), *Social work research and evaluation* (6th ed., pp. 148–168). Itasca, IL: F. E. Peacock.

THYER, B. A. (2001b). Single system designs. In B. A. Thyer (Ed.), *Handbook of social work research methods* (pp. 239–255). Thousand Oaks, CA: Sage.

THYER, B. A., PAPSDORF, J. D., DAVIS, R., & VALLECORSA, S. (1984). Autonomic correlates of the Subjective Anxiety Scale. *Journal of Behavior Therapy & Experimental Psychiatry, 15,* 3–7.

THYER, B. A., & THYER, K. E. (1992). Single system research designs in social work practice: A bibliography from 1965–1990). *Research on Social Work Practice, 2,* 99–116.

Case Study 6-3

Questions for Discussion

1. How did the research design used in this case study document the program's effectiveness?
2. How was the theory of moral reasoning used to develop and evaluate the program model described in this case study?
3. How can a practitioner gauge the level of reasoning of a client?
4. How is cognitive disequilibrium used to advance a client's moral reasoning stage?

The Power of Conventional Reasoning: Buffer to Antisocial Behavior in Adolescents

Jack Arbuthnot and Skylar Arbuthnot

Scene 1: A boisterous roomful of troubled and troublesome adolescents, glancing about, wondering what's going on.

Scene 2: Small groups of half of these same kids, engaged in intense, guided, Socratic discussions of how to resolve a moral dilemma.

Scene 3: Three months later, the lives of those in the discussion groups are significantly improved over those who were not.

Epilogue: A year and a half later, the improvements continue; but for those not in the groups, life continues its bleak decline.

Delinquency: Derailed on the Journey to Maturity

Pick up a newspaper and scan the headlines for a story about a teenager who has gotten himself (or, more frequently lately, herself) into some sort of trouble. In the details, one is sure to find that the adolescent involved made what we wise adults would refer to as "a really dumb decision." We shake our heads in wonder at the naiveté shown in the thought process or utter an epithet or two at the apparent total lack of concern or caring about the other people involved.

So what leads to these really dumb behavioral choices? We think a better question to ask is: What prevents them from making better choices? The former suggests that the ultimate responsibility lies somewhere in the youth's environment—peers, parents, pressures of adolescent life, etc. The latter suggests that a better choice was not made because the perpetrator lacked the skills to do so.

Clearly, behavior is multidetermined. Peer pressure, poor parental modeling, and situational variables account for appreciable amounts of variance. However, one's cognitive model of appropriate, acceptable, and desirable behavior is the primary determinant of one's action. It is one's moral reality that ultimately frames one's choices.

But what is the origin of one's morality, and why might some bring to bear higher standards for behavior than others do?

From a psychological viewpoint, morality is not simply whether a given action in a given situation is considered "right" or "wrong"; that is a philosophical question. Rather, we are interested in the reasoning behind such judgments. In fact, the specific behavioral choice is irrelevant for several reasons. The most obvious is that to look at morality from the basis of *what* is viewed as moral and immoral would involve highly subjective preferences of the decision maker. And there is the question of whether any behavior that is considered independently of the actor's reasoning and intent could be judged as moral or immoral. (By way of example, would it be moral or immoral to carry a little old lady's groceries home for her? Moral, if the intent is to help her. Less so if the intent is to collect a possible reward. Immoral if the intent is to gain her trust and "case" her house for a later break-in.)

Morality, then, is more than just a set of opinions—it is the product of reasoning. Like one's general thought processes, moral reasoning matures. At the age of 5 years, you are a considerably more sophisticated reasoner than you were at 5 months, but not nearly as sophisticated as you will be at 15, and so on (for a full discussion of this concept, see Arbuthnot & Faust, 1981; Kohlberg, 1984a, 1984b; Piaget, 1965; Wadsworth, 1989). Moral reasoning matures in much the same way as general reasoning.

This process of maturation occurs because as we learn more and are capable of synthesizing more, we often find that our ways of thinking are inadequate to resolve a dilemma. Such instances of "disequilibrium" may cause us to question our mode of thinking and may promote adaptation of our thought processes to account for new information or compelling circumstances that don't fit into our existing cognitive schemata. Eventually, we may move on to the next stage of morality—a qualitatively more advanced model of thinking, a hierarchical transformation of one's previous model of reality.

One can see how bad behavioral choices can be the result—perhaps inevitably so—of limited, immature reasoning skills. Is delinquency, then, a product of immaturity in moral reasoning? And, if so, can it be prevented by enhancing the maturity of the actors' moral reasoning? These are excellent questions, and the answer to both is "yes."

Systematic Stages of Morality

The concept of systematic developmental stages of morality was first conceived by Piaget in his work on the cognitive development of young children (Piaget, 1965). The concept was then elaborated by Kohlberg (1968, 1984b) and extended to moral maturation throughout the entire lifetime. The stages are universal, and the sequence is invariant. This order is important and cannot be circumvented; each stage builds on the thought processes of the previous one. The difference between stages is not merely in the amount of information acquired, but in the way it is dealt with, or synthesized.

That is to say, advanced thinking differs from primitive thinking not just in *quantity* of knowledge but also in *quality* of thinking (Arbuthnot & Faust, 1981).

For example, people at age 5 look much different from what they will look like when they are 50. This difference is not just in size, or *quantity,* but also in form and shape, or *quality.* So it is with morality as well. As morality develops, it does not just grow to include more information (as in specific moral knowledge, beliefs, or attitudes); it changes and redefines itself structurally (i.e., how one analyzes and synthesizes specific knowledge, beliefs, or attitudes).

Years of research in the United States and other cultures led Kohlberg to the discovery of three distinct levels of moral reasoning and within each of these, two sublevels or stages. (Kohlberg later came to believe that the third level more properly should be viewed as consisting of 5-A and 5-B, eliminating Stage 6 due both to its rarity and to lack of proof that it invariably followed Stage 5.) The three levels are called preconventional, conventional, and postconventional reasoning.

Preconventional (Stages 1 and 2) reasoning is cognitively egocentric. What is viewed as right is what is good for oneself and not prohibited by those in power. It is important to understand that it is not just that Stage 1 reasoners feel that they can do anything they want, as long as they don't get punished for it, but that they believe these actions to be moral. They uphold "right" when it is in their self-interest. Cognitively and morally, they are unable to coordinate the perspectives and rights of others with their own. This is preconventional reasoning because morality at this level is prior to consideration of what others would think is acceptable or desirable. Perhaps 10–15 percent of adults reason at this level.

In contrast, at the conventional level (Stages 3 and 4), "right" is viewed as that which conforms to the expectations of others—from family or friends to the larger society. At this level, one does "good" out of an internal desire to conform to commonly accepted external standards and to maintain a workable system. Most adults reason at this level.

Postconventional reasoning (or principled; Stages 5-A and 5-B) is more concerned with "universal ethical principles." Laws and social expectations, while useful for maintaining society, are not as important as the universal ethical principles on which laws should be based (Arbuthnot, 1992). Only 10–15 percent of adults reach this level.

Stage 1: Heteronomous Morality

Children in this stage (few, but some, adults remain at Stage 1) are concerned with deference to power, obedience, and punishment. An action that would lead to punishment is wrong—thus, actions are wrong only if one is caught and punished. Stage 1 reasoners "confuse moral rules with physical laws and . . . view rules as fixed external things, rather than as the instruments of human purposes and values" (Kohlberg, 1968, p. 488). In a rather Raskolnikovian way, they also believe that powerful people are more deserving of things than are ordinary people and that they can *morally* do whatever they want.

Stage 2: Individualism, Instrumental Purpose, and Exchange

Stage 2 reasoners are concerned with how actions and outcomes relate to themselves. This stage differs from Stage 1 in that it internalizes morality to at least some degree. Morality is no longer doing what one is told so as to not receive punishment. With Stage 2, a concrete concept of *fairness* is introduced, a kind of "marketplace" equality. Thus, "one should act to maximize one's own outcomes, while letting others do the same" (Arbuthnot & Faust, 1981, p. 56). This reasoning leads to such rationalizations as "it's okay to steal from big business because they make too much money," as well as "you scratch my back and I'll scratch yours."

Stage 3: Mutual Interpersonal Expectations, Relationships, and Interpersonal Conformity

Stage 3 thinkers are interested in conforming to the expectations of significant groups whom they value (e.g., parents, friends, teachers, policemen, etc.). Stage 3 reasoners want to be seen as "good" by others and will consider how these others will view their actions to determine whether they are right or wrong. Stage 3 thinkers are interested in maintaining their place or role in society—e.g., to be a "good" husband, a "good" wife, or a "good" child. Thus, proper in-role behavior is desirable.

Stage 4: Social System and Conscience

Stage 4 reasoners believe in rule maintenance and doing one's duty to follow the laws that hold society together. They are less interested in how those around them will view their actions, having a more objective and fixed idea of what things are "right" and what ones are "wrong." These reasoners believe that laws (as passed by legal representatives of the society) define what is right as they maintain the system and protect the general expectations of the citizenry.

Stage 5-A (previously 5): Social Contract, or Utility and Individual Rights

In Stage 5-A reasoning, it is considered most important to uphold the "basic rights, values, and mutually agreed upon contracts of a society, even when doing so might be in conflict with certain concrete rules and laws of the social group" (Arbuthnot & Faust, 1981, p. 62). Stage 5-A reasoning views the following of laws as important not because they have already been agreed on, but because every member of society has made a "social contract" to uphold such laws. If, however, a law is deemed in violation of an underlying principle of fairness or justice, it is viewed as unjust and therefore in need of change. Stage 5-A reasoners seek to change the laws to fit the greater moral principles on which a society should be based. Morality, then, is prior to law, in contrast to Stage 4 reasoning, in which law defines morality.

Stage 5-B (previously 6): Universal Ethical Principles

Stage 5-B is concerned entirely with universal ethical principles. These principles are "universal" in that they are applied consistently, both internally by the reasoner and across all reasoners of this stage. Stage 5-B reasoners are not as concerned with laws as are Stage 4 and even 5-A reasoners. Stage 5-B reasoners consider laws to be of little importance because they are created by people who do not necessarily have good morals or intentions themselves. These reasoners follow their own principles to determine moral actions and would consider following unjust laws an immoral act. Obvious examples of Stage 5B reasoners are Martin Luther King, Jr., and Mohandas Gandhi.

Psychologists determine the moral reasoning stage of individuals by presenting them with scenarios involving moral dilemmas (situations in which one or more rights are in conflict, e.g., property vs. life or trust vs. the responsibility to act). They are then asked what the character in the scenario *should* do (not what one *would* do). The behavioral choice, in and of itself, is of no importance in determining an individual's reasoning stage. Therefore, the interviewer must ask many probing questions to determine the reasoning behind an individual's answer.

The stages are universal. The progression through the stages is in an invariable order, and the sequence is the same for everyone. Everyone that is a Stage 5 moral reasoner was at one point a Stage 4 reasoner and before that a Stage 3, and so on. One cannot skip a stage; one cannot choose a stage (in the sense that one could choose a belief or attitude).

The Judgment-Behavior Consistency Problem

You've probably noticed by now that the focus has been on moral reasoning, not on moral behavior. Why? Aren't they the same? No, not at all. Some careful thought will reveal that behavior, in and of itself, lacks a moral component. Is "unauthorized use of a motor vehicle" morally wrong? It is clearly illegal. We'd probably agree that it is immoral if the user's intent was simply a selfish joyride to impress one's friends. But what if it was done by a 16-year-old whose little brother had a nasty bike accident, whose parents weren't at home, whose phone wasn't working because they couldn't pay the bill, and whose neighbor's car was parked in their driveway with the keys in the ignition. Taking that car to get the little brother to the ER seems a quite acceptable act.

Therefore, it's the reason behind an action that makes the action moral or immoral. A higher stage of reasoning does not guarantee more moral behavioral choices—but it certainly makes them more likely. Is there a relationship between reasoning stage and antisocial behaviors, such as delinquency? Yes. Numerous studies (see Arbuthnot, 1992) have shown that delinquent acts that have a victim (thereby excluding drug offenses, runaways, etc.), there is a clear relationship: Delinquent acts are committed only by Stages 1 and 2 (i.e., Level 1) children. Stage 3 and 4 (i.e., Level 2) children do not commit these acts. Why not?

Level 1 reasoners are preconventional thinkers. They lack the capacity to integrate the perspectives and needs of others into their choices of what is and is not acceptable. They are limited to weighing only the impact or consequences for themselves. They do not value the good opinion of others—they cannot put themselves in the role of their "victims" in order to look back at their own behavior and condemn it.

Thus, the transition from Stage 2 to Stage 3 (or, Level 1 to Level 2) is critical because it provides a cognitive buffer against antisocial behavior in young people. This raises an intriguing question: If we could design an intervention that would facilitate the movement of teenagers from Stages 1 and 2 to Stage 3, would we see an attendant decrease in antisocial behaviors and an increase in desirable behaviors? It is just this question that motivated this case study.

Why Are We Not All Moral Philosopher Kings?

Not everyone reaches the highest stages of reasoning. In fact, few people ever reason at what Kohlberg originally called Stage 6 (now Stage 5-B). Because of (a) limitations in general cognitive skills or (b) lack of proper stimulation from one's social environment, moral development stops at a particular stage. This cessation of development may not be irreversible, however. People who have stopped at a particular stage may, at any point in their life, start to advance once again if conditions allow for such development.

Let's look at these two enabling factors a bit more closely. Space limitations prohibit a detailed treatment of cognitive development, but perhaps the reader has a general notion of the stage theory of Jean Piaget. From infancy through adulthood, individuals pass through universal and invariant stages of general reasoning abilities: sensorimotor (S-I) in the first 2 years or so, then preoperations (P-O) through early childhood, then concrete operations (C-O) in later childhood, and, finally formal operations (F-O) in the teenage or early adult years. Cognitively, the progression is from (S-I) coordinating sensorimotor actions; to (P-O) elementary and literal use of symbols, with trial-and-error problem solving using physical objects; to (C-O) the acquisition of reversible and coordinated thought and the conservation of various qualities, such as quantity, number, space, time, etc.; and, finally, to (F-O) systematic and hypothetical thought, with problem solving at a purely symbolic level.

As you might expect, there is a necessary but not sufficient relationship between Piaget's and Kohlberg's stages. Can you picture a Stage 5 moral reasoner who is at Piaget's sensorimotor, preoperational, or concrete operational stage? No. Research has shown (Arbuthnot, Faust, Sparling, & Key, 1983) that Stage 1 reasoning requires pre-operational thought, Stage 2 requires concrete operational thought, Stage 3 requires beginning formal operational thought, and Stage 4 requires full formal operational thought.

Therefore, one reason why someone might not advance to higher stages of moral reasoning is that they simply lack the general cognitive capacity to do so. Nonetheless, some may have the required cognitive capacity, yet still lag behind their potential in moral reasoning stage. Why? Because they lack the facilitating social environment that would stimulate moral reasoning development.

Assuming that one has the cognitive capacity to advance in moral reasoning—i.e., one's Piagetian stage is ahead of one's Kohlbergian stage—what is required for moral reasoning development is the creation of a state of disequilibrium between one's current mode of resolving moral dilemmas and the next higher stage. In other words, one needs to puzzle over, or wrestle with, the fact that how one resolves conflicting moral rights is inadequate, that "something is missing." For example, Kelly, a 13-year-old in Stage 2, believes that it is morally acceptable to shoplift from stores because "they have a lot of stuff, they make a lot of money, so they can afford it; besides, it's like Robin Hood, y'know, 'cause you're just taking from the rich (them) and giving to the poor (me)." This self-serving perspective is morally inadequate because it does not coordinate the rights of the storeowner with Kelly's views. To advance, Kelly needs to become aware of the conflict (which, of course, can only happen once Kelly has the more general cognitive capacity to take the store owner's perspective) and to be sufficiently engaged in the conflict (i.e., to empathically "feel" the store owner's problem) to want to resolve it.

Creating this disequilibrium requires getting our Stage 2 reasoner "into the head" of the other party. This could be done through some Socratic dialogue or through role-playing. Kelly could be asked, "Let's assume that your parents own a small store. It's tough running a business—lots of bills to pay, not much profit. A bunch of kids have been coming in after school, and some of them have been shoplifting stuff. It's beginning to add up. Your parents are losing money and find that they can't make all their payments for rent and new merchandise, so they have to cut back at home—no new clothes for you, and maybe you lose your allowance. Does this seem fair?" "Well, no!" "Why not?" Once the inconsistency of the Stage 2 perspective is clear, Kelly needs to be presented with a "+1" stage perspective—in this case, a Stage 3 argument. "How do you think the shoplifters would be seen by others when it becomes apparent what damage and suffering they have caused to your family?" Or a role-play could be set up in which Kelly plays the storeowner and others play the shoplifting kids, while yet others serve as an evaluating audience.

Children who grow up in families in which there are few or no discussions of moral issues or dilemmas or who have low-stage parents who cannot provide the "+1" stage perspectives necessary to create cognitive disequilibrium are at a real disadvantage. Similarly, children who do not experience the logical consequences of their decisions or who receive arbitrary (usually physical) punishments for transgressions, do not learn to take the perspectives of the ones transgressed against. Children who are not allowed to assume responsibilities and to take on new roles do not have the opportunity to see situations from a variety of perspectives. Children whose role models are intolerant of differences in lifestyles, values, and cultures remain cognitively and morally stunted.

The Moral Reasoning Development Intervention

At the urging of a concerned juvenile court judge, we designed an in-school intervention for behavior-disordered adolescents (for details, see Arbuthnot & Gordon, 1986). The students were nominated by teachers as those who were most disruptive and most frequently in trouble, both in and out of school. They were called together, given an overview of the project, and invited to join. Based on teacher ratings, the volunteering students (with parental permission) were rank ordered, counted off into pairs, and assigned to a treatment or control group based on a coin toss. (The volunteers did not differ significantly in teacher ratings from the nonvolunteers.) All participants were evaluated for moral reasoning stage. All were at various combinations of Stage 1 and/or Stage 2 reasoning.

The students in the treatment group were divided into small groups, with more or less equal distribution of moral reasoning stages and gender.[1] These groups met in school for one class period per week for about 3 months. The group meetings were carefully constructed to provide Socratic discussions and role-plays of moral reasoning dilemmas. The initial dilemmas were chosen by the researchers on the basis of intrinsic interest to this age group and to present compelling conflicts of moral issues that could be addressed at Stages 1, 2, and 3. During the first third of the intervention, the group leader (the senior author) played a dominant role in guiding the discussions to ensure "+1" reasoning for all students. During the second third, responsibility for the discussions shifted to the students, with modest guidance from the leader. For the final third, the students supplied dilemmas from their own lives and led the discussions.

Upon completion of the intervention, moral reasoning stages were again assessed, teacher ratings were repeated, and archival data were gathered from school and court records. Approximately a year and a half later, we repeated all of these assessments (having had no further contact with the students). Figure 1 summarizes the results.

First, it is apparent that the moral reasoning development intervention was effective. With stage scores converted to a more sensitive scale (Moral Maturity Score, in which pure Stage 1 reasoning equals 100, pure Stage 2 equals 200, etc.), we were able to increase reasoning by a third of a stage on average—no mean feat, given that a comparable change in an enriched social environment might require several years. (These data were not examined separately for those with and without the enabling Piagetian-Kohlbergian gap.) Even more remarkably, without further intervention, the treatment group's reasoning scores continued to improve over the next 18 months, while those of the control group showed a gradual (nonsignificant) decline.

Did behaviors follow suit? Yes. Disciplinary referrals (in school) declined and stayed low for the treatment group. For the control group, they remained initially unchanged but then increased dramatically over time. Contacts with the police and courts showed a steep decline for the treatment group versus a slight increase for the controls (though both had declined to zero at the follow-up). Improvements in school absenteeism and tardiness also favored the treatment group. Grades in courses requiring use of logical reasoning skills diverged over time. And, by the follow-up assessment, teacher ratings finally reflected the treatment groups' changed behaviors.

---

[1]The control group received no intervention whatsoever during the period of this study. A later study employed an attention control group that met for discussions of interesting but nonmoral issues. Its pre-, post-, and follow-up scores did not differ from the original control group.

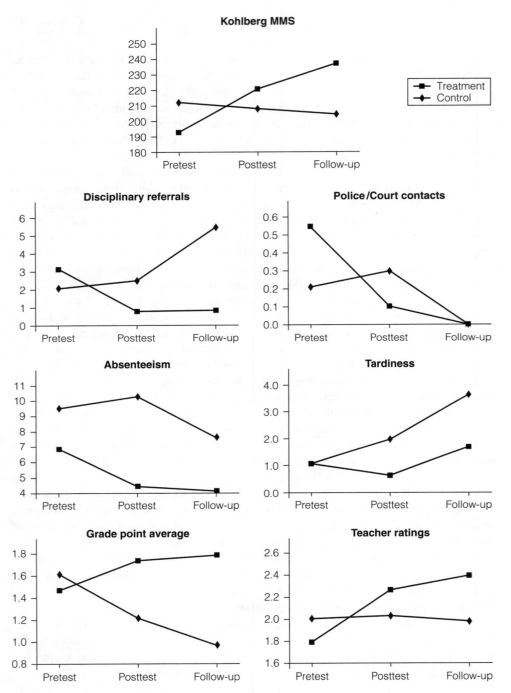

FIGURE 1 Results of the assessments approximately a year and a half later.

Were these behavioral changes caused by improvements in moral reasoning? Such cause-and-effect relationships are very difficult to prove. Intuitively, it makes sense. Furthermore, there was a strong correlation between improvements in moral reasoning scores and all behavioral improvements—i.e., the students whose reasoning improved the most also had the most improvement in behavior, and students whose reasoning showed declines also tended to be the ones whose behavior worsened (reverse stepwise multiple regression final adjusted squared multiple correlation at the initial follow-up was 0.90).

What Does It All Mean?

Most young people are confronted by situations in which antisocial behavior is tempting. Some yield, some don't. Why the difference? These situations are often accompanied by considerable peer pressure, excitement, shortened time perspectives, and substance abuse. They may be very difficult to resist. If one's peers are preconventional reasoners, there will also be a self-serving logic that makes the proposed action seem justified. The fear of punishment may deter those preconventional reasoners who see a high enough probability of detection and capture.

For the conventional reasoner, however, resistance is far more likely. For these youth, the primary motivation in moral reasoning is gaining the approval of significant others. Thus, this external standard for evaluation of a tempting action is always present, and, unlike their cognitively egocentric peers, they will have a standard to refer to when evaluating the wisdom of a given act.

For the preconventional reasoner, what is right is that which gets you what you want or that which protects you from harm. There is a lack of mutualistic thinking, or a consideration of the perspectives of others. There is a lack of empathic role taking (caring about the consequences for others). There is a lack of guilt or adverse self-judgment. In the words of Steven Duguid (1981), the judgment of the preconventional offender is that "Goodness, justice, humility, honesty and similar qualities are mere hypocrisy or the attributes of a fool." In sharp contrast, the opposite is the case for the conventional reasoner.

Unfortunately, one cannot simply *instruct* a child to be fair, to be moral, or to be a conventional level reasoner. The preaching approach to morality is ineffective because it teaches only specific beliefs and does not facilitate the development of more sophisticated reasoning about moral issues. (If mere preaching was effective, religious leaders could simply gather the flock, read the Ten Commandments once, close up shop, and go play golf.) Moral reasoning is *cognitively constructed* in an active fashion; it is not passively received, ready made. A sense of fair play can become part of one's worldview only through a series of experiences that compel the individual to examine and reconcile his or her views with those of others and with the hypothetical consequences of universal adoption of the individual's point of view. There is no substitute for examined experience.

To paraphrase the comments of Keith Whetstone, a reformed career criminal, if antisocial behavior is only a question of the probability of getting caught, people will continue to engage in antisocial behavior. They will stop only when whether or not to do so becomes a moral question. This is the power of acquiring conventional reasoning.

References

ARBUTHNOT, J. (1992). Sociomoral reasoning in behavior-disordered adolescents: Cognitive and behavioral change. In J. McCord & R. Tremblay (Eds.), *Preventing antisocial behavior: Interventions from birth through adolescence* (pp. 283–310). New York: Guilford Press.

ARBUTHNOT, J., & FAUST, D. (1981). *Teaching moral reasoning: Theory and practice.* New York: Harper & Row.

ARBUTHNOT, J., FAUST, D., SPARLING, Y., & KEE, W. (1983). Logical and moral reasoning in preadolescent children. *Psychological Reports, 73,* 644–670.

ARBUTHNOT, J., & GORDON, D. A. (1986). Behavioral and cognitive effects of a moral reasoning development intervention for high-risk behavior-disordered adolescents. *Journal of Consulting and Clinical Psychology, 54,* 208–216.

DUGUID, S. (1981). Rehabilitation through education: A Canadian model. In L. Morin (Ed.), *On prison education* (pp. 43–54). Ottawa: Canadian Government Publishing Centre.

KOHLBERG, L. (1968). *International encyclopedia of the social sciences.* New York: Crowell, Collier and Macmillan.

KOHLBERG, L. (1984a). *Essays on moral development: Vol. 1. The philosophy of moral development.* San Francisco: Harper & Row.

KOHLBERG, L. (1984b). *Essays on moral development: Vol. 2. The psychology of moral development.* San Francisco: Harper & Row.

PIAGET, J. (1965). *The moral judgment of the child.* New York: Free Press.

WADSWORTH, B. (1989). *Piaget's theory of cognitive and affective development* (4th ed.). New York: Longman.

Case Study 6-4

Questions for Discussion
1. What psychosocial factors do you believe were important to include in the assessment?
2. How were the standardized measures incorporated into the psychosocial assessment?
3. How were family strengths incorporated into the assessment?
4. What considerations are important when using standardized measures in a psychosocial assessment?

Using Standardized Measures to Enhance Psychosocial Reports: A Case Example

Cynthia Franklin, Tammy Linseisen, and Liliane Cambraia Windsor

Assessment in social work practice is:

> A process of problem selection and specification that is guided in social work by a person-in environment, systems orientation. Assessment is used to identify and measure specific problem behaviors as well as protective and resilience factors, and to determine if treatment is necessary. Information is usually gathered from a variety of sources (e.g. individual, family members, case records, observation, rapid assessment tools and genograms). (Jordan & Franklin, 2003, p. 1)

Psychosocial assessments are perhaps one of the most common types of assessments performed by social workers that work with children and families.

Social workers are asked to perform psychosocial assessments on children and their families for the purpose of studying the child and their social situation. As a part of the psychosocial report, social workers provide information on the developmental, family, social, and environmental issues confronting the child and their family. Family, social, and environmental information provides a context for the child's problem and makes sure that a person-in-environment viewpoint is considered.

The psychosocial assessment helps social workers determine what a family's needs, their strengths, and what interventions are best suited to help the child and family. Social workers in fields like school social work and child welfare use psychosocial reports to communicate with other professionals about the current status of the child and of family problems and to assist other professionals in intervention planning.

In recent years, social workers have started using scales and standardized measures to enhance their evaluations of children and families (Corcoran, 2000; Corcoran & Fisher, 2000; Jordan & Franklin, 1995, 2003). Even though the psychosocial report remains important to social work practice, few examples have been given for including the findings from measurement instruments in these reports. This case study illustrates how to write up a psychosocial assessment, including the findings from measurement instruments, in the body of the report. The case study report is from a real case, but the names and some of the facts and identifying information have been changed to protect the confidentiality of the clients.

Case Example of Psychosocial Assessment Report

Data Sources for the Psychosocial Evaluation

- Interviews and observations of family and children on two different occasions, December 1, 2001, and December 5, 2001
- Reports from the police and child protective services
- Telephone interview with school social worker
- Two standardized measures of family functioning:
  - The Family Assessment Device
  - The Parenting Scale

Identifying Information

Tony and Lisa were referred for an assessment following their involvement in the local child protective services (CPS). Tony is a 43-year-old African American and Hispanic male. Lisa is a 36-year-old Anglo female. The couple has four children: Brandy, age 5; Mary, age 3; Jason, age 2; and Johnny, 18 months. They own their own home at 600 Longhorn Drive in Austin, Texas. The family has lived in this residence for the last 5 years. Tony works at Brubaker Trucking Company, and Lisa is a stay-at-home mother. The family income is $75,000 per year.

Presenting Problem

CPS, following a report by one of Lisa's family members that Tony had hit Lisa with a belt while he was physically disciplining two of the children, investigated the family. The police were called to the home, and Tony was arrested for assaulting his wife. According to the police report, the altercation had left marks on Lisa's face and arms, although the arresting officers saw no physical marks on the children. Lisa called her family member to come and stay with her and the children, and the family member, in turn, contacted CPS officials.

Lisa initially pursued a protective order from her husband, but she informed CPS workers that it was only in effect "if she enforced" it. She indicated that her mother told her that she should not "call the law" on any man that is providing for her and her children. Lisa provided the money for Tony's bail, and he returned to the home only days after the incident.

CPS workers investigated the allegations of physical abuse of the children, and although risk factors were identified, the allegations were ruled out. Tony and Lisa, however, expressed a willingness to participate in community services at Family Serve, a local agency, and this resulted in a psychosocial assessment prior to receiving further help with their family problems.

Other circumstances included the fact that Tony and Lisa had suffered through a miscarriage only 3 months prior to their involvement with CPS. Their fifth child, John, died during pregnancy due to constricted blood flow in the umbilical cord. The loss of their child was a significant stressor for the couple, and Lisa in particular expressed an interest in receiving help to cope with her feelings of "severe depression."

Family History

In addition to their four children, Tony also has another son, Jeremy, from a previous relationship in high school, but the son has never lived with the couple. From Tony's report, he and his son Jeremy are somewhat estranged, and Tony regrets having had a child when he was so young. He has offered to take care of Jeremy, have him live with Lisa and himself, etc., but "Jeremy appears to be doing things the hard way at this time." He is now supposedly incarcerated for unknown reasons and his exact where-abouts are unknown.

The 5-year-old child, Brandy, is currently attending kindergarten at Pokey Oaks Elementary in Austin, Texas. From observations of the school social worker and the current social worker during a meeting with the mother, father, and children on December 1, 2001, Brandy is very well behaved and developmentally on task. Brandy is also bright and is doing well in school. Lisa, the mother, says that Brandy loves to get attention. She is easy going and helps her mom a lot.

Mary, the 3-year-old girl, also appears to be developmentally on task for a child her age. Developmental history indicates that all milestones are within normal limits. Mary does escalate and can get very agitated, at times throwing temper tantrums, and her mother has a difficult time controlling her. Lisa describes this child as being the most difficult of her children to parent. According to Lisa, Mary will do anything to get her mom's attention, and she is constantly competing with her younger brothers. No significant eating or sleeping problems were reported. Mary appeared to be an active 3-year-old toddler who wanted to explore, but the worker did not observe any abnormal behaviors.

The 2-year-old boy, Jason, appears to be developmentally appropriate. Developmental history indicates that all milestones are within normal limits. Jason is walking and talking and appears to be a normal, active boy. According to Lisa and Tony, he does not have any significant eating, sleeping, or behavioral problems. Jason "loves to say no to everything and everyone." That drives his mom crazy sometimes, but they have been able to manage it. According to Lisa, the main problem with Jason is that he is still not potty trained and requires a lot of attention.

Johnny is the baby. He is a healthy 18-month-old who is passing through all developmental milestones in an appropriate manner. He crawled at 6 months and walked at 12 months. He currently sleeps through the night, and Lisa describes him as very calm and easy going. Due to his age, Lisa spends most of her time taking care of him.

Marital History

Tony and Lisa have been married for 7 years. Before they married, the couple dated for 1 year and lived together for 2 years. The couple has never separated. At the present time, however, they are not spending any time together apart from the children, and their marital relationship appears to be distressed. Lisa took care of the four children by herself without a break for the past year, and Lisa and Tony have not had a date in over a year and a half. They currently have minimal support for child care. Lisa's sister, Lilly, sometimes helps with the children, but she works and has a family of her own and cannot help out that much. Lisa and Lilly have had difficulties getting along in the past and this has hindered any type of mutual support, as well. The couple have attended a local Baptist church, and Lisa has sought some counseling sessions from the pastor in the past and help from the "Mother's Day Out" program, but she has not used the program in the last year. The couple has not attended a church service in the last 4 months. Lisa said she was pretty sick with her last pregnancy, and they were saving money for the baby and maybe a bigger home. Tony said he told Lisa that they could not get a bigger home unless they saved more money and that they could not afford the "Mother's Day Out" program. "That's just the reality of life and money," he said.

When Lisa was asked what she liked best about Tony, she said she admired his strength. "Nothing gets to him. He is a strong person and a hard worker." Tony answered the question by saying that Lisa had always been there for him and is a caring, family-oriented person. He especially liked her because she wanted to have a lot of kids, as he did. Tony said, "I always wanted to be a Dad," and he stated that he wanted a "big family."

When asked about the stress of losing their fifth child, Lisa was open about the pain that she has endured, and she cried while sharing the story. Tony, however, sat stoically and offered no further information regarding the miscarriage. Lisa reported that she could never go through pregnancy again after what she has experienced. Tony turned away from her on hearing this and folded his arms, appearing somewhat angered by this disclosure. When asked to share his feelings, he rolled his eyes and refused to elaborate other than saying, "She is overreacting. Bad things happen sometimes. You can't just give up."

Lisa and Tony gave different reports about their marital adjustment and satisfaction. Tony said that he thought things were going pretty well until the "big blow-up" and CPS got involved. Lisa disagreed, however, stating that she feels that they are growing apart and have been getting into more arguments over the last year. Lisa stated that Tony seems angrier. "He is yelling more and does not come home or leaves and stays gone for hours when he is angry." Tony denied any problems with managing his anger. He stated that the time when CPS was called was the only time that he had hit his wife. He blamed Lisa's sister, saying, "She should have stayed out of our lives. She has got a lot more problems than we do." Lisa agreed that he had not hit her in the past, but he had hit the wall a few times and knocked things off the table. This had only occurred a few times over the last 3 years. "He usually just leaves," she said.

Tony also reported that he believed that he and Lisa use "too much" physical discipline with the children. Tony indicated that his wife is "inept" with taking care of the kids, so the kids are "out of control" and have to be spanked in order to behave. Lisa rolled her eyes and said that he "just wants the kids to be perfect." She agreed that they did get spanked 3–4 times a week, especially Mary because she is hardest to control.

Lisa and Tony reported coping with the stresses of life in very different ways, and both agreed that their differences in style contributed to "fights." Lisa talks and cries, while Tony likes to do physical things and gets very quiet. According to the reports given during the interview with the couple, Tony works out in the weight room, enjoys the sport of boxing, and coaches boxing several days a week. Lisa sometimes becomes frustrated with Tony's coping style because she does not know what he is thinking. Lisa also complained that Tony does not listen to her or help her with the children at all. She then told Tony that he is the reason that she has been diagnosed with depression and has begun to take the medication Zoloft to improve her mood. When asked what her depressive symptoms have been, Lisa stated that she cries a lot, gets angry and frustrated very easily, and feels very "chaotic," meaning that she cannot think right or finish what she starts. Tony echoed these symptoms and added that she "needs to get it together." Lisa admitted to occasional thoughts of suicide and self-harm but denied having these thoughts presently.

Tony responded to the question "What trait would you change about your wife if you could?" by saying, "Lisa is too emotional and unable to cope with the demands of life." When asked how long Lisa had been unable to cope, he thought hard and said that she has always been kind of emotional, but that it has gotten worse over the past year. "I think since she found out she was pregnant again." Lisa agreed that she was not sure about this last pregnancy. They already had four children under 5 years old, and she wanted to stop at four children. Tony said that he was happy about the other child. He considered children a "blessing from the Lord." Tony said that he just wanted Lisa "to get things together" for the sake of their family life. Tony shook his head and shared that his mother had raised a big family all by herself while his father was working and that he did not understand why his wife could not "just do the same thing" because he has enough to worry about at work besides her always crying and not being able to do her job with the children. At this point, Lisa started to cry again and held her head in her hands. Tony did not make any attempt to comfort her. Lisa said that she sometimes feels "all alone" and overwhelmed taking care of so many children under the age of 5. "It is just hard," she sobbed.

Lisa described her husband as "stubborn," unwilling to change or compromise at times, and unwilling to talk. He does not help her with the children, does not understand how badly she feels, and expects too much from her as a partner and a mother. She would have him "listen and help more" if she could change one trait about him.

Despite their difficulties both Tony and Lisa said that they wanted to try and work things out and stay together "for the sake of their kids." Both said they still loved each other, but Lisa said she doubted sometimes if they "could ever be happy" because they were so different than one another. She cried when making this statement, and Tony shook his head, scowled, and looked down.

Tony's Family Background

Tony is the only male of six children born to his parents, and the second oldest child in the family home. He currently does not have much contact with his family of origin with the exception of family reunions and holidays because the family lives in different states and cities. Tony's family was working class. His father was a construction worker and his mother a homemaker. His mother was Catholic but converted to the Pentecostal religion. She raised the children in a strict Pentecostal church, but his father did not often attend the services. Tony says he still considers himself to be a Christian, although sometimes a "backsliding one."

Tony's father, who died of a stroke in 1991, was African American. He and Tony's mother were together for 22 years before he died. His father, Tony Sr., was approximately 32 years older than his mother and was 72 years old when he died. It is evident when talking to Tony that he loved his father very much. His happiest memory is having played in a father-son baseball game with his father one summer, and his saddest memory is his father's death.

Tony's mother, Maria, was reportedly 17 years old when Tony was born. She is Hispanic and apparently does not speak English well. She currently lives with his oldest sister in Georgia and helps with her children and household. Tony reports that his mother was the disciplinarian of the family and that she still tries to discipline him now. When she calls and visits, she gives him a tongue-lashing if she hears anything negative about him. Tony described his mother as "funny, blunt, and sensitive." She cries easily, especially if she is sad. She did not work outside the home while he was growing up. Tony stated that his father "did not take any shit from anybody" and that he was very protective of their family. Tony did not realize until after his father's death how much his father had protected him and rescued him from his mistakes. He clearly still grieves over this loss today. Tony related that he was "spoiled by his family," which meant that he generally got what he wanted. He stated that this has hurt him in the long run because he had to learn much later in life how to be responsible for himself. Tony related that his parents used physical discipline, including spankings with a belt and sometimes with switches.

Tony did not do very well in school and was not committed to learning. He stated that he went to school because his parents made him go and because he liked to play sports. He remembers being very popular in school and enjoying that aspect of being there. He went away to college but completed only one semester. He quickly learned that he was not ready to be away from home and returned to his parents' home for a safety net.

Tony indicated that he wrote a $100 check on his father's closed bank account and was charged with misdemeanor forgery by passing. He was then late for his court appearance, and the judge moved his charge to a third-degree felony level and sentenced him to 4 days in jail. He was sentenced to 3 years' probation and ordered to pay a $250 fine. This occurred 11 years ago. He reported no other criminal involvement until his recent arrest for domestic assault.

Tony denied any alcohol or drug use or abuse. Although Tony said he drank a lot in his younger years, he had put all his "partying" behind him to raise his family. Lisa said that Tony does not drink a lot anymore and that she did not drink at all because she sees "what it does to people through [her] family."

Tony indicated that he has moved from job to job for many years but apparently has settled down now as a delivery driver. He has been in this job for 5 years and is now in a supervisory role. Tony also volunteers at a local gym, coaching boxing, and he seems to enjoy this very much.

Lisa's Family Background

Lisa is the second of three children born in a lower-middle-class family. Lisa's father worked for the telephone company, and her mother worked part-time as a teacher's aide when extra money was needed. Lisa's older sister is less than 2 years older than her, and Lisa described this as difficult for her. Apparently, Lisa felt very competitive with Lily, never feeling that she "got enough" from her family. Although Lisa denied any problems with alcohol herself, both of her siblings as well as her father have struggled with alcohol use and abuse. Lisa said that she is very different than her siblings and does not feel particularly close to them.

She said she got a lot of support from a local Protestant church and the Girls Club while growing up. She belonged to a youth group and went on camping trips with the Girls Club. Lisa said she still enjoys attending church and likes it when Tony takes the family.

When asked, Lisa could not recall a specific "happiest" childhood memory, but she reported her freshman year of high school as the saddest time in her life. Apparently, her coach died of a heart attack that year, and she also lost two friends to accidents. Lisa related that other than these losses, she had never experienced a family loss until her miscarriage. She considers herself to have been the responsible child in her family, but she did not feel appreciated or loved by them. She apparently "fell from [her] parents' grace" further when they learned that she was dating an older African American man.

Both of Lisa's parents disciplined the kids, but Lisa found it much easier to be disciplined by her father because her mother would sit in silence with her. She was sent to her room, talked to, and spanked by her father. Lisa's family was not very "touchy-feely," and the siblings demonstrated their anger through words and fist fights. Her parents would apparently fume at each other and would often "fight physically."

The one thing Lisa would change about her childhood, if she could, would be that she fell in love too young with the wrong person. She did not elaborate but did say that the person was not her current husband. Lisa graduated from high school and was the senior class historian. She was not involved in many team sports, although she did enjoy running track for fun. She did not attend college but worked in sales and enjoyed her job. She quit work 7 years ago to marry Tony and have children. Lisa has never been arrested.

Lisa is starting to exercise more because she considers herself to be overweight. She has talked with some friends about this problem and is reading magazines about diets. Tony reminds her on a daily basis that she has not yet lost her pregnancy pounds. She does not use drugs or alcohol, and she does not regularly take any medications except for Zoloft, which was prescribed for her depression by her family physician, Dr. Leonard McCoy, within the last month.

Results from Family Measurement Instruments

The Family Assessment Device

The Family Assessment Device (FAD) is a 66-item questionnaire designed to evaluate family functioning (Epstein, Baldwin, & Bishop, 1983). This measure assesses six dimensions of family functioning: *problem solving,* which measures how families solve both financial and affective problems (social support and abilities to nurture); *communication,* which measures how directly families talk to one another versus using indirect, ineffective communication; *roles,* which measures how appropriately families distribute roles and monitor and give account for those role responsibilities; *affective responsiveness,* which measures how families respond to crisis and whether they can use their emotions in a congruent way; *affective involvement,* which measures how much empathy family members have for one another and whether they can maintain appropriate boundaries for their emotional involvement; *behavior control,* which measures the family's style for keeping one another safe, meeting each other's needs, and monitoring outside relations in the family; and *overall family functioning* (or *general functioning*), which provides an overall measure of how well the family functions (Jordan & Franklin, 2003).

Psychometric Properties of the FAD

The FAD demonstrates fairly good internal consistency with alphas for the subscales ranging from .72 to .92. Test-retest data is not available. The scale demonstrates some degree of concurrent and predictive validity and has been shown to discriminate between clinical and nonclinical samples (Corcoran & Fisher, 2000).

Scoring of the Family Assessment Device

Scores on the FAD range from 1 (healthy) to 4 (unhealthy).

Results from the Family Assessment Device

As far as it is known, these scores appear to represent valid assessments of the couple with this instrument. The results of the FAD are as follows. See Figure 1.

As the bar graph indicates, results of the assessment with the FAD support the finding from the interviews with the couple. Overall, Lisa views the problems in her

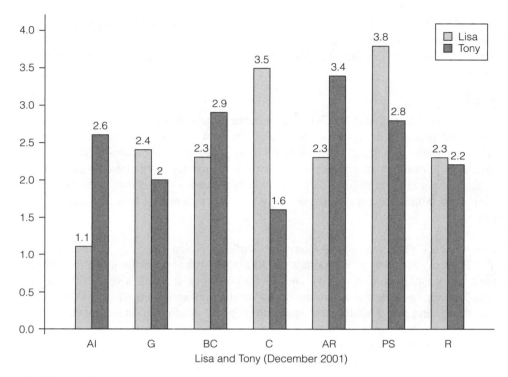

FIGURE 1   The Family Assessment Device scores at psychosocial assessment.

family to be worse than Tony views these problems, and this is especially true in the areas of affective involvement, communication, affective responses, and problem solving. Tony's scores, though, also indicate that there is room for improvement in the problem-solving and behavioral-control dimensions of family life. The couple shows the strongest agreement on the roles dimension and overall (general) family functioning subscales.

What these findings suggest is that Lisa does not feel very understood by her husband and is asking for more empathy and responsiveness than Tony is giving at this time. Observations during the interview indicate that Tony is an extremely "tough-minded" individual who expects total independence and self-sufficiency from his wife. He did not display affectionate or empathetic verbal responses or behavior; neither did he directly communicate his feelings about the recent loss of the child or show congruent emotions that might be associated with this loss. Instead, he expressed his belief that you have to be "tough and cope with whatever life brings you." These types of nonemotional, "stoic" responses may account for the differences as seen on the FAD.

At the same time, however, Tony believes that his family is having difficulties solving problems and also views his family as not meeting the needs of one another or being in a safe place right now. Perhaps the recent involvement of CPS has helped

Tony to see these issues more fully. Tony's responses on the FAD suggest that he has some awareness that his family is failing to meet emotional and safety needs and does not have capacity to resolve family problems, especially in the area of family emotional support.

The Parenting Scale

The Parenting Scale (PS) is a 30-item instrument designed to measure dysfunctional discipline practices in response to young children who are preschoolers (Arnold, O'Leary, Wolff, & Acker, 1993). The PS consists of three subscales: *laxness*, which measures permissive discipline; *overreactivity*, which measures parenting behaviors such as anger and irritability; *verbosity*, which measures verbal responses that reflect prolonged talking; and a *general score*, which is a measure of overall parental functioning.

Psychometric Properties of the Parenting Scale

The PS has good internal consistency with alphas with .84 for the general score, .83 for laxness, .82 for overreactivity, and .63 for verbosity. It also has very good stability with 2-week, test-retest correlations of .84 for the total score. Finally, the PS has good concurrent and discriminant validity. Factor analysis confirmed its structure.

Scoring of the Parenting Scale

Scoring is based on a 7-point rating scale anchored by 1 (effective) and 7 (ineffective) forms of parenting behavior.

Results from the Parenting Scale (PS)

As far as it is known, these scores appear to represent valid assessments of the couple with this instrument. The results of the PS are as follows. See Figure 2.

The results from the assessment of the PS are consistent with the results from the FAD. Overall, Lisa views her parenting skills with their young children much more negatively than Tony views his skills. At the same time, however, Tony does see some problems in the areas of laxness and verbosity.

These scores mean that Lisa is acknowledging parenting difficulties, in general, across all areas and is indicating that these problem are quite severe. Lisa's scores indicate that there is especially too much laxness (permissiveness) and anger used with the children. Tony, on the other hand, acknowledges difficulties in permissiveness, but not to the degree that Lisa acknowledges these problems. This is an interesting finding because it was Tony who complained the most in the interview about the laxness with the children, but mostly in relation to Lisa's behavior. Tony also acknowledges too much long verbal communication used to parent children and he sees this as being the worst problem. It is interesting that Tony's score on overreactivity was so low because during the interview, he acknowledged that both he and his wife used discipline that is too harsh such as too-frequent spankings of their children. Tony's low score may

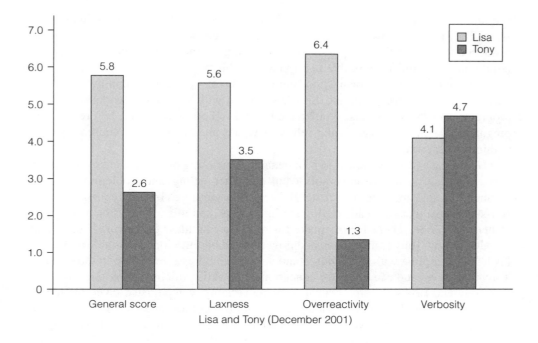

Lisa and Tony (December 2001)

reflect, however, a defensive posture toward the anger items on the scale and his unwillingness to acknowledge the use of anger in general. This would be consistent with his responses during the interviews that suggested he did not want to discuss himself as being an angry person or having an "anger problem."

Family Strengths

Lisa and Tony both possess a number of strengths to build on. Both are verbal and intelligent. They both appear willing to seek help from outside sources to improve their family relationships. Both Tony and Lisa said they would like to learn more about parenting their children without having to punish them so harshly. When asked if they would be willing to attend therapy sessions for their individual and couple problems, for example, Tony said he would come with his wife and Lisa said that she would like both sessions for herself and her husband.

Lisa and Tony have similar values and agree on their life goals, roles, and functions. They appear to have formed complimentary roles, although they obviously need some help in negotiating these functions at this time. Tony shows a deep devotion to his family and is a good financial supporter. He has established himself in his job and is doing very well. Lisa likes this attitude in Tony and wants to be a full-time homemaker.

Overall, the couple appears to be stable when it comes to their financial and living situation. They own their own home and car, for example, and they have lived in the same residence for the last 5 years. Lisa appears to be a good money manager and keeps the family on track, and Tony is able to provide a livable wage.

Tony and Lisa have shown a good amount of involvement in the community. Tony coaches boxing at the gym, and Lisa has friends with whom she works on weight programs and diets. She also volunteered at the school and church before her last pregnancy. The couple has similar religious values and has attended church together within the past year.

Both Lisa and Tony appear to be amenable to working on needed changes. Lisa is very emotionally sensitive and is able to talk about her feelings and problems in an open manner. She appears to be very critical of herself, as observed by the frequent negative self-statements that she made during the interviews, and this may also be a symptom of her depression. These factors make Lisa a good candidate for both individual and couple therapy. Tony is more stoic and private about his emotions but is able to discuss his harsh discipline with his children and says he could use some help in those areas. Tony may be a good candidate for educational and skills training approaches.

Tony and Lisa's children appear to be remarkably well adjusted given the recent stressors (loss of child, family violence, marital difficulties, and CPS investigation). Tony and Lisa appear to love each other and their children and are committed to staying in their marriage. Their stability appears to be a positive factor in favor of their being able to reduce risk factors and resolve current problems.

Current Issues and Clinical Summary

Clearly, Tony and Lisa have serious marital difficulties, and both need help with their parenting skills and harsh discipline practices. Positive communication and mutual support seem to be significantly impaired at present, and the children seem to be at risk for overdiscipline, if not abuse, because of the chaotic household and distressed marital relationship of the parents. Further domestic violence is also possible as long as the marital relationship is challenged to this degree.

Individual Issues

Lisa is also psychologically impaired and emotionally vulnerable and needs further assessment for her mood disorder. Because of her recent pregnancy and loss of a child, attention should also be given to ruling out postpartum depression and assessing her capabilities to nurture and care for her own children in her current state of mind. This is especially warranted given her negative self-appraisals on the Parenting Scale and her viewpoints concerning the lack of emotional support she feels from her husband. These needs were most apparent and expressed with strong emotions by Lisa both in the interviews and on the Family Assessment Device. In addition, Lisa is admittedly grieving over the recent loss of her child while attempting to manage her children and salvage her marriage. She is likely struggling with guilt about the loss of her child because of her own ambivalence about conceiving and bearing the child.

Couple Issues

It appears that Lisa and Tony presently have very different expectations of each other's roles in both marriage and child rearing. Tony seems to expect Lisa to perform as his own mother did with regard to homemaking and raising the family, but Lisa is currently unable and possibly unwilling to perform these duties alone. Tony does not understand his wife's diagnosis and what he might do to help her regain the control that he is asking from her.

Tony expressed that he loved his wife and family and was committed to working to keep the family together. In the practitioner's assessment, however, Tony is having difficulty offering emotional support to his wife through her loss and behaves in ways that minimize his own difficulties with both anger and loss. Lisa, on the other hand, feels compelled to emphasize issues of emotional neglect and to criticize her husband for his lack of responsiveness.

Due to her own needs and their evident marital distress, Lisa is also not able to acknowledge Tony's positive intentions and support in other ways (i.e., financial support and attempts at helping her with discipline of the children). This appears to be taken by Tony as very disrespectful and perhaps even an assault on Tony's masculinity and fatherhood role. Lisa appears to exaggerate his negative characteristics in an attempt to get his attention. Overall, Tony's reactions to Lisa's concerns are met with a total minimization of problems.

Lisa's emotional sensitivity appears to be difficult for Tony to comprehend and cope with, and he either distances himself even further or openly criticizes his wife about her emotional needs and issues. This pattern is causing a great deal of anger between the couple, and the constant displays of mutual criticism put the couple at risk for further marital distress and crisis.

Some of the issues between Lisa and Tony may arise from cultural differences, in that Tony is assuming the strong male role that is expected in his Latino culture and was taught to him by his mother. At the same time, he is acting out the African American cultural view of his father toward suffering and coping with hardships without complaining. Lisa, on the other hand, is from the Anglo culture and has different values and expectations for him. In fact, in Lisa's life history, she indicated that she experienced her father as a more nurturing and fair person than her mother. Helping the couple to accept and accommodate basic differences in their values, expectations, and cultural differences might help this couple reduce their negative interactional patterns.

Parenting Issues

Both Lisa and Tony agree that they need help with parenting their children and need to learn new parenting skills. At this time, Tony appears to blame Lisa more for these parenting problems than he takes responsibility himself. Lisa has expressed concerns about her ability to parent so many children under the age of 5. She has asked for help with structure and scheduling for the children, and it is unclear how the children have coped with the family's turmoil, the marital violence they have witnessed, and the physical punishment they have received. The 3-year-old, Mary, appears to be at most risk for abuse due to the fact that she is perceived by the parents as more difficult than the other children. However, all of the children are clearly at risk as long as the current marital and family stressors continue. It might be worthwhile to individually assess the children and their behaviors in order to assess their needs more clearly.

Clinical Recommendation

Lisa appears to have some early developmental history that would predispose her for sensitivities to loss and rejection (i.e., nonacceptance of her mother, the death of a coach, and bad experiences with her first love relationship). These experiences may make her especially vulnerable to major depressive disorder. It is recommended that Lisa be seen in individual cognitive-behavioral therapy to assess and treat her mood disorder and symptoms of grief and loss. Cognitive-behavioral therapy has been found in clinical trials to be an especially efficacious treatment for depression and appears to be the best-suited therapy for Lisa's symptoms. Because Lisa is currently taking the Selective Serotonin Reuptake Inhibitor (SSRI) medication, Zoloft, for her mood disorder, it is recommended that Lisa be referred to a psychiatrist for a medication consultation to ensure that she is getting the best possible pharmacological treatment for her diagnosis. Tony should be provided with some psychoeducational sessions to help him understand and respond appropriately to his wife's mood disorder.

Lisa and Tony should both be seen in behavioral couple's therapy to address their marital problems and role dysfunctions. Behavioral couple's therapy has been found in clinical trials to be an efficacious treatment for marital distress. It has also been shown to be an effective treatment for women with depression, which suggests that the couple's therapy may help Lisa's mood disorder as well. This intervention may also address deficits in the couple's communication, problem-solving, and parenting skills.

In addition, Lisa and Tony should attend a parenting workshop and a group for improving parenting skills that is offered by the Parents Anonymous organization. This group will address their harsh discipline practices in more detail. At least for the short term, until the current crisis has been resolved, the couple should resume using the "Mothers Day Out" program and work with their therapist to obtain additional parenting and caretaking services so that the stress of parenting their four children can be reduced for Lisa.

Finally, it is recommended that the children be brought to a play therapy group at Family Serve for observations and that the family participate in a few sessions of family therapy so that the children may be observed and assessed further.

Guidelines to Follow When Writing a Psychosocial Assessment Report

Creating a good psychosocial assessment report requires analytical skills, writing skills, and creativity. A practitioner must be able to weave information into a coherent narrative that is rich in detail and tells the client's story. In order to develop this type of narrative report, the practitioner must obtain detailed information in the areas covered in this example report. Multiple sources of information are used to obtain this information, and these sources might include face-to-face interviews, reports from collateral sources such as a school, background information questionnaires, checklists, and standardized measures. In the example report on Tony and Lisa, the practitioner obtained reports from two collateral sources: child protective services and the school social worker. The practitioner also interviewed the couple on two different occasions and had them complete two standardized measures of family functioning. The children were included in one of those interviews for observation purposes. The standardized measures were chosen because they related to the family's presenting problems and provided a separate and objective source of evaluation information.

Notice that in each part of the psychosocial report, the practitioner carefully documented and illustrated the different points about the client's history and current functioning with the words of the client and examples from the interview. It is important to use words that are very behavioral and descriptive so that someone reading the report can gain a clear picture of the way the client is functioning. The use of vague words or descriptions takes away from the purpose of the report, which is to communicate to other professionals the presenting problems, social/developmental history, social context, current functioning, and strengths of the client. It is also important for the practitioner to offer integrations and summaries of what is learned about the client so that others reading the report can focus on the most cogent issues.

Integrating the Measures as Part of the Psychosocial Assessment Report

As in this case example report, it is equally important to describe the measurement instruments used, what they measure, their psychometric features, and what the scores on each of these measures mean. For others reading the assessment, it is also important to display the scores and to write a narrative that explains the scores and their interpretations as they relate to the client's current functioning. In order for standardized measures to complement the psychosocial assessment report, the measures must be integrated with the other information in the report so that the scores and interpretations become just another piece of information to be considered in a matrix of information.

The practitioner should ask the following questions when electing to use standardized measures in a psychosocial assessment:

1. What measures could complement the information I am gathering? (Practitioners may also want to consider whether the measures will have value to monitor the progress of the client in therapy or to be used to assess outcomes as well.)
2. Are these measures valid, reliable, and clinically useful?
3. Are these measures appropriate for the client group I am serving?
4. Do I know how to use this measure and have competence to score and interpret the measure?
5. Once I have selected an appropriate measure for use, is it a valid assessment? Did the client have the reading level and understanding to complete the measure? Is there any reason to believe that the scores are unreliable or faked?
6. How should I present the measures and scores to the readers? (As is illustrated in the example report, graphs of the scores and a narrative summary are needed.)
7. What do the scores mean in relationship to the other information I have gathered? How do the scores complement the information, add to the information, and offer inconsistent information, for example?
8. Finally, how can the findings from the standardized measures be used to support the clinical recommendations for intervention in the psychosocial assessment?

References

ARNOLD, D. S., O'LEARY, S. G., WOLFF, L. S., & ACKER, M. M. (1993). The Parenting Scale: A measure of dysfunctional parenting in discipline situations. *Psychological Assessment, 5,* 137–144.

CORCORAN, J. (2000). *Evidence-based social work practice with families: A lifespan approach.* New York: Springer.

CORCORAN, K., & FISHER, J. (2000). *Measures for clinical practice: A sourcebook* (3rd ed.). New York: Free Press.

EPSTEIN, N., BALDWIN, L., & BISHOP, D. (1983). The McMaster Family Assessment Device. *Journal of Marital and Family Therapy, 9,* 171–180.

FRANKLIN, C., & JORDAN, C. (1999). *Family practice: Brief systems methods for social work.* Pacific Grove, CA: Brooks/Cole.

JORDAN, C., & FRANKLIN, C. (1995). *Clinical assessment for social workers.* Chicago: Lyceum Books.

JORDAN, C., & FRANKLIN, C. (2003). *Clinical assessment for social workers* (2nd ed.). Chicago: Lyceum Books.

Case Study 6-5

Questions for Discussion

1. What problems developed as a result of the sexual assault?
2. How did the practitioner get the client to collect data that would be useful in evaluating treatment progress in this case?
3. How was the plan for treatment influenced by the results of the data collected about the client's problem?
4. How did the worker reduce the self-blame that is common among victims of sexual assault?

Evaluating the Treatment of a Sexually Assaulted Child

Betty J. Blythe

This case study describes the treatment of a young boy who was sexually assaulted. Services were delivered by a social worker in a sexual assault treatment program. As with all of her cases, the worker used measurement and research tools to define the target problems, specify indicators of these problems, and routinely monitor the client's progress throughout and following treatment. This paper describes the treatment and evaluation of this case.

The client, a 12-year-old boy named Gary, was sexually molested by an adult man. The boy was returning from softball practice when the man, who was dressed as a utility meter reader, enticed him into a wooded area. The man performed oral sodomy on Gary and forced the boy to fellate him. Before allowing him to leave, the man threatened to harm Gary and his family if he told anyone about the episode.

On returning home, Gary immediately told his older brother about the attack, and his brother called their parents. Gary's parents took him to the local hospital emergency room, where he was examined. The hospital social worker referred Gary to the sexual abuse treatment program at the local community mental health center.

As is typical at this agency, the intake interview was conducted over the telephone by the social worker who would continue to see the client. At the time of the intake, Gary was still extremely upset by the incident. He was afraid to leave home and walk anywhere by himself. He refused to attend softball practice, even if his parents drove him there. Most upsetting to Gary were frequent flashbacks in which he recalled the attack. Like many victims of sexual assault, he felt both depressed and guilty. Gary indicated that he feared that his assailant might carry out his threats to hurt Gary or his family.

The social worker told Gary that his feelings and the flashbacks were common responses by people who have been sexually assaulted. She also said that, working together, they could try to reduce the frequency of the flashbacks and improve his mood so that he was less depressed. Gary said he was willing to come for counseling and that he wanted to work on these areas.

The worker next began to further specify the two target problems, flashbacks and depression. She asked Gary to describe the flashbacks in detail. He said that a flashback was like seeing and feeling the experience again, as if he were back in it. The worker also learned that reliving the attack through the flashback was accompanied by a strong sense of fear, increased heartbeat, sweating, fear for his life, and feelings of helplessness and rage. There did not seem to be any pattern that might predict when the flashbacks would occur. They happened throughout the day and evening, regardless of whether he was alone or with someone, and in any setting. Gary reported that a flashback lasted 4 or 5 minutes and that they all were of equal severity. After a flashback episode, Gary typically anguished about how he might have avoided the attack. He experienced strong feelings of sadness and guilt. This information helped the worker better understand the nature of the flashbacks and determine what interventions would likely be helpful or not helpful.

The worker told Gary that she wanted him to begin keeping a record of how often he had flashbacks each day. She explained that this information would help her determine if she was helping him reduce the frequency of the flashbacks. If they did not occur less frequently after a few sessions, she said she would change what she was doing in some way. In addition, information collected about what Gary was doing at the time of a flashback would confirm or refute their conclusion that there was no pattern associated with the flashbacks. The worker asked him to get some 3 × 5 index cards and make two columns, one labeled "day" and the other labeled "flashbacks." She also told him to fill in the days and dates in the first column. In the second column, Gary was to record what he was doing when the flashback occurred and any other information he wanted to provide about the flashback itself. At the end of the telephone intake, the worker went over the request to collect information about flashbacks with Gary's mother, explaining how the cards should be completed and the purpose for doing so. She asked his mother to help him prepare the cards immediately and to remind him to carry a card with him and to fill it out.

To establish the level of the problem before Gary talked to her (the baseline), the worker questioned Gary carefully to determine how many flashbacks he had experienced over the past several days. She did this by having Gary describe his routine on the previous day and then indicate if he had had any flashbacks. In this manner, the worker was able to get Gary to go back over the day of the intake and the 2 days since the attack. If the worker had felt at any point that Gary was not able to provide accurate information about the frequency of the episodes, she would have abandoned the questioning. This type of baseline is called a reconstructed baseline.

The worker then explained to Gary that she wanted him to complete a questionnaire when he came to the office. She said that the questions did not have right or wrong answers and that they would help her better understand his feelings of sadness and depression. She also told him that she would go over the questionnaire with him and that he would complete it occasionally to help them determine if he was getting less depressed. Gary agreed to fill out the questionnaire. The questionnaire actually was a standardized measure, the Generalized Contentment Scale (Hudson, 1982). It is relatively short (25 items) and uses simple, understandable language to assess the level of depression. As with the self-report measure of flashbacks, the worker also described this measure and its application in the treatment to Gary's mother and gave her an opportunity to ask any questions.

Gary came in for his first session 4 days later. Before he saw the worker, the receptionist gave him the standardized measure to complete in the waiting room. When the worker saw Gary, she asked how he was doing. Gary soon volunteered the information that he had collected about flashbacks. The social worker added these data to a graph she had started with the reconstructed baseline. She told Gary that they would add his information to the graph each time he came to a session, and she repeated that the information would help them determine if she was helping him. The information about what Gary was doing at the time a flashback occurred validated their suspicions that there was no discernible pattern associated with the flashbacks. The flashbacks apparently occurred in numerous settings and when Gary was alone and with others. The worker and Gary agreed that there was no need to continue collecting additional information about the antecedents of each flashback. The worker asked if Gary had any difficulty in collecting the information, and he said that he was embarrassed to get the card out when he was around other people. The worker asked Gary if it would be easier to carry some small beads in his pocket and move a bead from one pocket to another each time he had a flashback. At the end of each day, Gary could count the beads and put this information on the index card. Gary responded that he would prefer to use that method, and the worker gave him 10 beads.

At this point, she also scored the Generalized Contentment Scale. Gary's score of 54 indicated that he indeed was depressed. The scale has a clinical cutting score of 30, which means that clients scoring above this level have a "clinically significant problem." The worker relayed this information to Gary in a matter-of-fact fashion and tried not to alarm him or otherwise lead him to worry unnecessarily about being depressed.

Intervention

Having achieved some understanding of the baseline level of the problem, the worker was ready to begin intervention. The intervention was actually a combination of several different techniques.

Psychoeducation

The worker gave Gary information about sexual assault and how people typically respond after being assaulted or experiencing other crisis situations. She emphasized that these feelings would not last forever. She also stressed that Gary was not to blame for the attack, but rather that the assailant had committed a crime against Gary. The actual attack was always portrayed as a violent act rather than as a sexual act.

Environmental Manipulation

With the approval of Gary and his mother, the worker contacted Gary's school and arranged for Gary to ride a bus to and from school (previously he had walked). She also involved Gary's family in the intervention by having a family member stand at the bus stop with Gary in the morning and meet his returning bus in the afternoon. Gary's mother was responsible for organizing this schedule to ensure that a family member was available to help him.

Empathic Listening and Normalizing Feelings

Gary was encouraged to express his feelings about being attacked. As noted in the intake interview, these feelings included fear, anger, sadness, and guilt. Later, Gary began to express a desire to gain revenge. The worker helped Gary "name" and recognize these feelings because he did not always have words to describe them. She also attempted to normalize the feelings so that Gary realized that these feelings were not unusual or inappropriate.

Relaxation and Calming Self-Talk

Gary was taught deep-breathing exercises to help him calm himself when he felt a flashback starting or when he began to feel uncomfortable or fearful. The worker and Gary developed a set of self-statements that Gary could also use at these times. The worker stressed the importance of making accurate statements to help Gary regain a realistic sense of security. Examples of calming self-statements were "Nobody will attack me here in the classroom" and "Try to stay calm. I am in a safe place now." By recording the flashbacks, Gary had become aware of his early feelings when a flashback was developing. Thus, he was often able to use relaxation and calming self-talk to interrupt a flashback before it developed fully. Over time, as Gary ventured out alone, these statements were revised to include messages reminding Gary that he knew how to respond if he saw a suspicious person or if someone approached him.

Reframing Gary's Role During the Attack

The worker repeatedly pointed out that Gary had demonstrated courage, intelligence, and fast thinking when he was attacked. He had managed to get and remember a clear description of the assailant. When the assailant asked his name, Gary gave a phony name. Moreover, he had managed to tell his brother about the attack and to talk about it with the hospital staff, the police, and the social worker, all of which were stressful and difficult interactions. The worker also emphasized that Gary was a survivor rather than a victim.

These interventions were delivered over the course of five weekly sessions in the worker's office. The environmental manipulations were instituted immediately, followed by the educational intervention. The relaxation and calming self-talk were introduced during the third week. The other interventions were used as needed in each session. Because it was so difficult to track exactly when some of these interventions were used or whether they were used at "full strength" during each week of the intervention, no attempt was made to specify the intervention beyond calling it a combination of the five components listed previously.

Results

Each week, Gary brought in his information on the flashbacks. He completed the Generalized Contentment Scale before two additional office visits and when it was mailed to him 3 months after treatment was terminated.

As depicted in Figure 1, the baseline data indicate that Gary was having an average of 8.42 flashbacks per day. Although the actual daily number varied from 7 to 10 flashbacks, the range was not too great and the worker felt that she had a good idea of the general level of the problem. Also, the number of flashbacks was increasing somewhat before intervention, so it does not appear that the problem was being resolved without intervention. Over the course of intervention, the frequency of the flashbacks generally decreased, with a striking exception on day 16. When Gary brought in these data, the worker asked about that day in particular. Gary told her that he had had to give the police additional information about the attack and examine some photographs of suspects. Talking about the incident in this way made him quite uneasy and

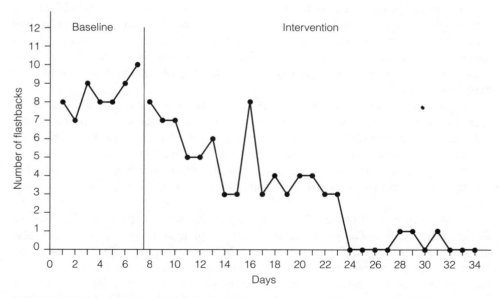

FIGURE 1   Number of flashbacks per day during baseline and intervention phases.

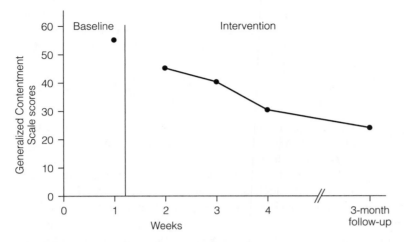

FIGURE 2   Generalized contentment scores during baseline and intervention phases.

brought the whole incident back. Note that the trend did not continue to go downward for a few days after day 16, as it had before that time. By the last week of treatment, however, the flashbacks had sufficiently reduced such that the worker felt she could terminate treatment.

At this last session, the social worker explained to Gary that she would contact him by telephone at a later date to see how he was doing. Accordingly, she called him 3 months after termination. The worker asked Gary if he would collect data on flashbacks for 1 week. He said he would do so but that he was no longer having any flashbacks. When the worker contacted Gary a week later, he indicated that he had not experienced any flashbacks.

Figure 2 depicts Gary's scores on the Generalized Contentment Scale. As can be seen, his scores dropped to just under 30, the clinical cutting score. Hudson (1982) indicates that such borderline scores must be interpreted cautiously. The worker observed, however, that Gary's mood seemed to have improved. He was involved in more activities again and generally showed more enthusiasm for whatever he was doing. His mother confirmed these observations. Thus, the worker decided it was safe to close the case.

At the 3-month follow-up, the social worker also sent a copy of the Generalized Contentment Scale to Gary and asked him to complete and return it. His score, also depicted in Figure 2, was 23, suggesting that he was continuing to be less depressed. During the telephone call to set up the follow-up data collection, the worker also asked Gary some general questions about how he was doing. This anecdotal information served to confirm the quantitative information, all of which suggested that Gary was continuing to improve.

Discussion

The data Gary and the worker gathered portray continued improvement in terms of the frequency of the flashbacks that Gary experienced and the severity of his depression. Although they in no way "prove" that the interventive package led to Gary's improvement, the data provided ongoing, routine information about the two problems being dealt with in treatment, flashbacks, and depression. Had the trends not been in the direction of improvement, the worker could have quickly revised the treatment plan.

Defining the exact nature of a flashback so that it could be measured through self-report by the client yielded information for practice, as well as evaluation, purposes. The worker learned that there were no apparent precipitants of the flashbacks, so the intervention package did not need to focus on particular events that might be leading Gary to experience the flashbacks. Information about the intensity and nature of the flashbacks suggested that certain components of the treatment package might be helpful, particularly using relaxation and coping self-statements, normalizing feelings, and reframing his role in the assault. Because the baseline could be reconstructed in part and then continued after the telephone intake, the worker was able to get an idea of the level of the target problems without withholding intervention. If the baseline had not been stable (that is, if it had fluctuated so widely that it was difficult to know what the "average" level of the problem was), the worker probably would have initiated intervention anyway because her goal in collecting the data was to measure client progress rather than to determine whether her intervention was responsible for the progress.

The treatment plan itself was allowed to unfold in the manner that the worker thought was best for Gary, without being modified in any way because the case was being evaluated. The intake process could have had certain interventive qualities, thereby affecting the baseline levels recorded by Gary, but the worker did not worry about this. In fact, the data suggest that the client experienced flashbacks with approximately the same frequency both before and after the telephone intake. Further, the intervention did not have to be artificially carved up with certain components being delivered in certain sessions because the worker was not interested in determining which were the more or less effective ingredients of the intervention.

At the close of treatment, the termination date was set when the social worker thought that Gary had made sufficient progress, based on both the data and her clinical impressions, including interviews with Gary and his mother. Termination was not artificially delayed to allow more data to be collected. Moreover, the follow-up point provided an opportunity for the worker to determine whether the client was maintaining his gains.

In short, the evaluation of this case did not needlessly consume the client's or worker's time. The information gathered through data collection was helpful to the client and to the worker. As the data began to suggest improvement, Gary felt both relief and increased motivation to continue practicing the relaxation exercises and calming self-talk. The data informed the worker as she made certain clinical decisions. Although it did not lead to tremendous clinical revelations, the monitoring helped the worker and client stay focused on the treatment goals, to readily see that the client was making some improvement, and to eventually realize that the case could be closed. Obviously, adjunct information collected in the sessions and through interactions with Gary's mother was also helpful in the clinical decision-making process.

Reference

HUDSON, W. W. (1982). *The clinical measurement package: A field manual.* Homewood, IL: Dorsey Press.

TO THE OWNER OF THIS BOOK:

I hope that you have found *Case Studies in Child, Adolescent, and Family Treatment* useful. So that this book can be improved in a future edition, would you take the time to complete this sheet and return it? Thank you.

School and address:_____

Department:_____

Instructor's name:_____

1. What I like most about this book is:_____

   _____

   _____

2. What I like least about this book is:

   _____

   _____

3. My general reaction to this book is:

   _____

   _____

4. The name of the course in which I used this book is:

   _____

5. Were all of the chapters of the book assigned for you to read?

   If not, which ones weren't?_____

6. In the space below, or on a separate sheet of paper, please write specific suggestions for improving this book and anything else you'd care to share about your experience in using this book.

   _____

   _____

   _____

BUSINESS REPLY MAIL
FIRST-CLASS MAIL   PERMIT NO. 102   MONTEREY CA

POSTAGE WILL BE PAID BY ADDRESSEE

Attn: Helping Profession, Lisa Gebo

BrooksCole/Thomson Learning
60 Garden Ct Ste 205
Monterey CA 93940-9967

OPTIONAL:

Your name: _____ Date: _____

FOLD HERE

May we quote you, either in promotion for *Case Studies in Child, Adolescent, and Family Treatment* or in future publishing ventures?

Yes: _____   No: _____

Sincerely yours,

Craig Winston LeCroy

Janice M. Daley